the
Vampire Film

Also by James Ursini

The Noir Style (1998)
Roger Corman: Metaphysics on a Shoestring (1998)
What Ever Happened to Robert Aldrich? (1995)
More Things Than Are Dreamt Of (1994)
David Lean and His Films (1992)
The Life and Time of Preston Sturges, An American Dreamer (1976)
Film Noir Reader (Editor) (1996)
Film Noir: An Encyclopedic Reference to the American Style (Co-Editor, 3rd Edition) (1992)

Also by Alain Silver

The Noir Style (1998)
Roger Corman: Metaphysics on a Shoestring (1998)
What Ever Happened to Robert Aldrich? (1995)
More Things Than Are Dreamt Of (1994)
The Film Director's Team (1992)
David Lean and His Films (1992)
Raymond Chandler's Los Angeles (1987)
The Samurai Film (1983)
Robert Aldrich: A Guide to References and Resources (1979)
Film Noir Reader (Editor) (1996)
Film Budgeting (Editor) (1996)
Film Noir: An Encyclopedic Reference to the American Style (Editor) (1992)

Alain Silver and James Ursini

the
Vampire Film

From Nosferatu to Interview with the Vampire

Limelight Editions

NEW YORK

The Vampire Film, Third Edition, November 1997

Copyright © 1975 by A.S. Barnes and Co., Inc.
Copyright © 1993, 1997 by James Ursini and Alain Silver

Manufactured in the United States of America.

Library of Congress Cataloging-in-Publication Data

Silver, Alain, 1947-
        The vampire film : from Nosferatu to Interview with a vampire / by
Alain Silver and James Ursini. -- 3rd Limelight ed.
               p.   cm.
        Includes bibliographical references and index.
        ISBN 0-87910-266-7
        1. Vampire films--History and criticism.   I. Ursini, James.
II. Title.
PN1995.9.V3U77   1997
791.43'675--dc21   97-34919
                                                                    CIP

This edition is affectionately dedicated
to the memories of our fathers,

Vincenzo Ursini

and

Elmer Silver.

Contents

Edvard Munch, *Vampire*

She was a phantom of delight
When first she gleamed upon my sight;
A lovely apparition, sent
To be a moment's ornament.

William Wordsworth

Preface to the
Third Edition

In the Preface to the First Edition of this book, we called it a "critical survey," a term which was intended to reveal its underlying methodology. Because the movies to be considered are those which treat the vampire phenomenon, they are easily identified as a genre or, at least, a sub-genre of the horror film. They are also regarded by many filmgoers, as well as producers, as part of the broader context of exploitation films. Consequently the actual productions vary widely in the motives which created them and, as one might expect of any group of films, in quality. All the films discussed in this study, regardless of their cost or the makers' intent, reflect this generic fact. As a result, in exploring how films are expressions of the genre as a whole and not merely their popularity or critical reputation, we have sometimes chosen to allocate space to little-known titles which evidence a novel approach over lengthier discussions of accepted "classics." Hopefully this method will present an overall conception of the vampire film that is truly representative of the richness and variety of all the motion pictures which fall into this category.

When it was initially published in 1975, this book was the first full-length study of the vampire film in English. After eighteen years and many other writing projects, it was not without trepidation that we returned to it in 1993. Once we had reaffirmed to ourselves, as did several reviewers at the time, that our basic approach to the genre was a sound one, the primary challenge in planning a completely updated Second Edition was how to incorporate the new material, i.e. the substantial number of vampire films which had been released in the intervening years. The decision for both the Second and this Third Edition, as the Vampire approaches the millennium, was the same.

Since our original outline had a thematic rather than chronological basis, we ultimately decided to mirror that structure with four added chapters examining again the male and female figures in their newest incarnations and the vampire in fact and other media. While each new chapter can stand alone, a reader who so desires can move directly from the original "Dracula" sub-section of Chapter Two to the "New Age Dracula" in Chapter Five or follow any other thematic line. For the Third Edition we have included an Additional Filmography of the most recent titles. We have also added an Appendix which surveys other books on the genre and an updated Bibliography.

Unlike the American *film noir*, a movement that cuts across generic lines, or the work of an *auteur*, subjects on which we have also recently collaborated, the vampire film is defined neither by a unity of vision nor by a cultural context. When interest in the phenomenon first swept through Western Europe during the Age of Reason, it was not only the aspects of the perverse and risqué that appealed to "reasonable" men but also the sensation of a forbidden, preternatural frisson. While Bram Stoker or Baudelaire may be the first who come to mind in association with vampire fiction, the wide range of poets, philosophers, and painters who have been linked to the vampire, from Byron or Rousseau to Goethe or Edward Munch, amply demonstrates the breadth of interest. On film, the vampire has a graphic reality that is both liberating and limiting. But no amount of rubber bats, stage blood, or plastic fangs can frighten or amaze a viewer without imagination. Many recent portrayals of this creature of the night have attempted to be more tragic than terrifying, focusing on the plight of a being whom, like Tennyson's Tithonus, "cruel immortality consumes." In the end, it is the vampire's humanity, his or her alienation and despair, which most appeals to the Romantic and Existentialist alike. From that combination of rapacity and wretchedness, the image of the vampire often coincides with that of Shelley's Medusa:

> Upon its lips and eyelids seem to lie
> Loveliness like a shadow, from which shine
> Fiery and lurid, struggling underneath,
> The agonies of anguish and of death.

Acknowledgments

As before, the Authors wish to express their appreciation for assistance in researching the films and literature to David Bradley, Ken Dixon, Jim Paris, and Nicholas Odolf Vlad von Blôch [Will Russell Plax]; to Jerry Fiore, Alan White, David Ichikawa, Les Otis, Timothy Otto, and Eddie Brandt for invaluable help with the illustrations; and to Elmer Silver for his aid in preparing the final copy of the first edition manuscript. For the Second Edition a number film industry professionals, including Joel Bender, Manette Rosen, Diana Kaufman, Zane Levitt, and Jonathan Hernandez, helped with references and access to unreleased pictures. For this Third Edition, we are again particularly indebted to a number of filmmakers who have formed an unofficial cooperative of alternative cinema, starting with Kevin Lindenmuth and Ron Bonk who refered us to many others and including Elisar Cabrera, Jerry Feifer, Ron Ford, Michael D. Fox, Bruce Hallenbeck, George Hickenlooper, Leif Jonker, Blair Murphy, Michael Raso, and Gary Whitson. Peter Shiau at Concorde/New Horizons, Kat Scudder at Full Moon Entertainment, Charlie Goldstein at Fox, Victoria Cantrell at Overseas Filmgroup, Carol Davis at Think Entertainment, and Larry Landsman at Showtime previously helped with illustrations. New stills and information for this edition came from many of the filmmakers already listed and also Dan Curtis, Osman K. Ozkaracalar, Bernard J. Taylor, Thomas Muehlbauer, Faye Katz, Steve Florin at Panorama Entertainment, Mark J. Gordon at Wildcat Entertainment, and Bill George at *Femme Fatales*.

For the new Editions, we are also indebted for research assistance to Jon Burlingame, Eric Hoffman, Patricia Arellano, and Tim Lucas. Many hours of research for all the editions were spent at the library of the Academy of Motion Picture Arts and Sciences and the UCLA Theater Arts Library. Gary J. Svehla at *Midnight Marquee* and Tomm Carroll at the *DGA Magazine* published portions of the new material in article format.

Stills are courtesy of Allied Artists, American International, Amicus, Azteca (U.S.A.), Brimstone, Castle Rock, Columbia–Sony–Tri-Star, Concorde/New Horizons, Dimension, Full Moon, Geffen, Hammer, MGM/UA, October, Overseas, Paramount, Republic, Salt City, Showtime, Tigon, Universal, and Warner Bros.

Again for this edition some special thanks:

Mel Zerman at Limelight who agreed to undertake the entire enterprise.

Linda Brookover, Glenn Erickson, Bruce Kimmel, Christiane Silver, and Gyongyver Sóvágo who all proofread portions of the new texts and revised filmographies. Jim Paris and Joel Argenti, who helped lay out the book, devise the illustrative scheme, and print the pages.

The Cover illustration from the original Italian release of Mario Bava's *La Maschera del Demonio* was made possible by Chris Dietrich.

Most of the new illustrations were provided through the courtesy of the Archives of David Del Valle, without whose advice and assistance a considerable amount of additional time and effort would have been expended.

THE VAMPIRE FILM

Christopher Lee's first appearance as the Count in HORROR OF DRACULA

CHAPTER ONE

Sources of the Vampire Lore in Film

When out of all my bones she had sucked the marrow,
And as I turned to her, in the act to harrow
My senses in one kiss, to end her chatter,
I saw a gourd that was filled full with foul matter!
I closed mine eyes, all my body shivering,
And when I opened them, in the dawn's quivering,
I saw at my side a puppet of derision
Who had made of its blood too much provision,
Then fragments of a skeleton in confusion
That of themselves made a mere mist of illusion,
Or of a sign-board at the end of a batten
The winter wind swung, as it seemed, in Latin.

Charles Baudelaire,
"Metamorphoses of the Vampire"

I. THE VAMPIRE IN LEGEND

In a previous study, **The Vampire: His Kith and Kin,** it was my endeavour to trace back the dark tradition of the vampire to its earliest beginnings, until indeed it becomes lost amid the ages of a dateless antiquity, for this remarkable and worldwide belief was very present with primitive man, and is notably significant in the daily customs and practice both tribal and domestic—more especially in the funeral rites and sepulchral houses—of furthest aboriginal and most savage indigene. Nor, owing (as I believe) to the fundamental truth, which, however, exaggerated in expression and communication, essentially informs the vampire tradition did the legend die. As man marched towards civilization it persisted, losing much that was monstrous but none of the horror, for the horror was part of the truth.[1]

Writing in the first half of the century when he might have been considered the foremost authority on the subject, the Reverend Montague Summers clearly suggests that the roots of the vampire myth[2] lie deep in man's

1. Montague Summers, **The Vampire in Europe** (London, 1929)

2. From the beginning it should be noted the the words "myth," "lore," and "legend" are used in their classical sense. For example, the fact that King Arthur may be considered a mythical or legendary figure does not mean that there is no basis in fact for his existence.

17

written and oral history. Vampires and vampire-like phenomena are prevalent in almost every recorded culture with only minor variations in their subsidiary characteristics. In ancient Greece these creatures were given colourful names such as *Lamia, Empusa,* or *Strige.* The first two are most often females who are not only succubi (demons who have sexual relations with humans) but also blood-suckers and ghouls (devourers of corpses). *Lamias* are also associated with snakes. A *Strige,* on the other hand, has the ability to transform itself into a bird after sucking blood. In ancient Assyria and Babylon *Ekimmu* were the souls of the dead who had broken one or more of the numerous taboos and consequently were forced to wander the earth tormenting the living and drawing life from them. In Imperial Rome *Lemures* were like their Assyrian relatives, that is, spirits who tormented the living, often, according to Summers, "absorb[ing] the health and vitality" of their victims. In Druid Ireland blood-suckers were known and called *Dearg-duls.* In India a mythological figure called a *Baital* strikingly resembles the more familiar Eastern European-Balkans conception of a vampire, being a corpse reanimated by the *Baital* demon which can alternately assume a bat-like form. The *Vetala,* also Indian, is simply a blood-suckering hag. China's vampire, *Ch'ing Shuh,* also reanimates bodies and then devours humans, both living and dead, with lightning-like ferocity; it is reputed to be particularly horrifying in appearance. In contrast, Malaysian vampires are almost exclusively women—called *Langsuir, Pontianak,* or *Penaggalan*—and are often extremely beautiful. Africa has its blood-suckers as well—the spirits of dead sorcerers or medicine men *(Asbanbosam, Owenga, Otgiruru).*

In the Christian West, the divergent characteristics and lore that surround the various species of the vampire *genus* begin to congeal into the myths growing out of Eastern Europe and the neighbouring Balkans—myths that ultimately exert the greatest influence on the rest of the West, and through film and literature, the world. The physical aspect, the powers, and the weaknesses of this Western vampire will be dealt with later. A brief list of its names may suggest this creature's proliferation in legend. In Greece: *Vrykolaka* (with variations on that name present also) ; in Bulgaria *Obour;* in Romania *Strigoi* or *Moroii;* in Hungary *Pamgri* or *Vampir;* in Russia *Upir* or *Oupyr* (among other names) ; in Serbia *Vlkodlak* or *Vampir;* in Morlacchia *Vukodlak;* in Germany *Vampyr* or *Nachzehrer;* in France *Vampire;* In Italy and Spain *Vampiro;* in Mexico *Vampiro* or *Ciuatateo;* and in English-speaking countries *Vampire* or in older script *Vampyre.* Even from this less than comprehensive list a sense of the universality of the vampire myth can easily be abstracted. The cultures alluded to above may be distinct in many other aspects but they seem to share an obsession with this figure, as archetype, as super- stition, and as possible reality.

While no definition of "vampire" could encompass all the mani- festations of this creature and its brethren, the best is probably Anthony Masters's in his book **The Natural History of the Vampire.** Drawing on various encyclopedias and dictionaries, Masters generalises that:

> The vampire throughout the world can be divided into two basic manifestations. The spirit of a dead person [or demon] is the first and the second is a corpse, reanimated by his own spirit or alternatively by a demon, who returns to suck at the life of the living, depriving them of blood or some vital organ in order to maintain its own vitality.[3]

Such a definition is succinct yet comprehensive enough to cover the varied types that have been introduced; it is also one most likely to be accepted by researchers in the field.

Hypotheses Concerning the Prevalence of Vampire Legends

In trying to explain the vampire phenomenon and its universality theorists have formulated a number of hypotheses. First, there are those, like Dudley Wright or Montague Summers, who concentrate on collecting legends as well as more documentary evidence about vam- piric phenomena. Though they are often reserved on the question of personal belief in vampires, their careful cataloguing of information, mostly in support of the existence of the "undead," leaves the reader with little doubt as to their view. This explanation of vampiric legends, then, is the simplest and yet for modern man, deprived of a Medieval faith in a cosmos inhabited by demons and angels, the most difficult to accept. In addition, much of the evidence quoted by these researchers is hearsay—based all too often on stories told to the author. There are exceptions, however, instances where the documentation is fairly im- pressive and a materialistic conception of reality most severely tested.

The second explanation, as advocated by more sceptical writers like Anthony Masters, addresses itself to man's traditional obsession in his folklore and art with blood and death. Ornella Volta in **Le vampire** and Masters in his book do a thorough job of tracing the evolution of blood cults. From pre-history, man has made the obvious connection between life and blood, so that the precious fluid has become the focal point of many rituals and taboos. According to Leviticus "the life of a living body is in its blood." In certain societies, women in men-

---

[3.] Anthony Masters, **The Natural History of the Vampire** (New York, 1972).

struation were secluded from the rest of the tribe for fear of the power
of free-flowing blood. In some African tribes the spilling of even a
drop of this liquid symbolic of the "life-principle" required immediate
action. In battle the blood of fallen enemies has been drunk from time
immemorial in order to acquire their strength. Blood has also been
consumed to enhance prophetic powers: in **The Odyssey** the dead
are given the power of speech after drinking the blood of sheep. The
aphrodisiacal "virtues" of this fluid are also evident in ritual and
especially in the cases of historical or natural "vampires," which will
be discussed later. For now it should be pointed out that blood was
often a necessary ingredient for philtres and that haematomania (blood
obsession) is most often related to a sexual need. Organised religion,
however, has probably had more to do with affirming the sacredness
of blood than its more primitive counterparts. In the Old Testament,
Jehovah warns against drinking blood so as not to partake of the life
of a foreign body. In much of Christianity the blood of Christ, in the
form of wine, is drunk to commemorate the Biblical dictate:

> Amen, amen, I say to you, unless you eat the flesh of the Son of Man,
> and drink his blood, you shall not have life in you. He who eats my
> flesh and drinks my blood has life everlasting. (John 6:54-56)

Blood sacrifices have also been common in man's relatively short
chronology. The gods of diverse cultures and eras have been propiti-
ated with blood, and not always that of animals. The Egyptians, the
Aztecs, and Phoenicians, even the founders of Western civilization, the
ancient Greeks, honored the cannibalistic practice of offering human
lives to the gods. Even the therapeutic use of transfusions in modern
medicine subtly re-states the cultural equation of blood and life.

Concomitant with blood cultism is man's natural fear of disease and
dying. To the anthropologist, the vampire is just another mythic transformation that seeks to explain a death from unperceived or misunderstood natural causes. If the plague, pneumonia, smallpox, the "French
pox" or venereal disease, and the contemporary catalogue of fatal
maladies could not be fully comprehended medically in a given society,
they could be feared metaphysically. Accordingly, an epidemic striking
Sixteenth century Europe was not borne of rats or sexual promiscuity
but of demons, witches, and vampires. To the Medieval and Renais-
sance minds in Europe and in many primitive societies today, the
metaphysic of death and its aftermath ("the mysterious land of bound-
less possibilities where all phantasies are realised and all secrets revealed . . .")[4] was and is an impenetrable one that overshadows all

---

[4.] Ernest Jones, **On the Nightmare** (New York, 1951).

Lon Chaney Jr. and Louise Allbritton in SON OF DRACULA

facets of life. As Slochower puts it, "the knowledge of death is the most continuous, most persistent and inevitable, perhaps the most fateful trauma for man."[5] Ornella Volta takes this into consideration in her study and formulates a hypothesis regarding the vampire:

> By decreeing that only the soul has a right to immortality, a position has been created by which the body has also demanded its rights. By refusing to accept the limitations posed by physical death (and by not having the patience to wait for the Day of Judgment for a resurrection of the body) might not the vampire simply be seeking to demonstrate the possibility of survival for a body without a soul? How? By acquiring the soul and life of another through his blood.[6]

Aggravating this fear of death even further is another terror—one that only recently has been allayed by the widespread use of embalming and by medical advances, that is: the fear of being buried alive. Premature interment of plague victims in the Middle Ages and of cataleptics up to modern times was not an uncommon occurrence. Anthony Masters claims that "American statistics in the early 1900's show that not less than one case a week of premature burial was discovered." Masters, supported by Dr. H. Mayo's book **On The Truths Contained in Popular Superstition**, promotes this statistic as one of

[5] Harry Slochower. "Eros and the Trauma of Death," in **Death: Interpretations** (New York, 1969).
[6] Ornella Volta, **Le vampire** (Paris, 1962). (English Translation by Raymond Rudorff).

the explanations for such vampiric phenomena as finding corpses in their coffins so well preserved, in distorted positions, or devouring their shrouds. Still Masters is hard-pressed to rationally explain the reports that these dead leave their graves and return without disturbing the ground or the fixtures of the crypt. He can only dismiss this as part of the mass hallucination symptomatic of vampiric lore.

A final body of conjecture on the origins of vampire legends is constructed by psychologists, most notably by Ernest Jones. They trace the lore back to one or a combination of the following: repressed sexual desires (often bordering on necrophilia); feelings of guilt towards and subsequent dread of the deceased; or a *liebestod* ("love-death") mentality. All of these are expressed, characteristically, in nightmares, many times accompanied by nocturnal emissions. And therein lies, they believe, the root of fantasies in which the dead suck vital fluids.

The Eastern European-Balkans Vampire and His Influence

As mentioned earlier, the image of the vampire which has been generated in the Western world and which dominates its folklore and art is basically derived from an Eastern European-Balkans tradition. For the most part the Eastern European-Balkans type of vampire is an

Herbert Lom as Van Helsing in EL CONDE DRACULA

"undead" (surviving after physical death) human corpse or possibly astral body, animated by the undead's own spirit (or in a few instances by a demon), which leaves its place of rest to visit the living and suck their blood. Further, in returning to the world of the living, the Eastern European-Balkans vampire often preys on his own relatives and loved ones, occasionally while having sexual intercourse with them. This fact is significant in psychological terms in relation to the love-dread attitude towards death and the departed which Jones among others discusses at great length. Adding even more to the ambiguity is the uncertainty as to whether the vampire returns to his loved ones out of affection, revenge, compulsion, simple unmitigated lust, or possibly some combination of these motives.

What can cause a person to turn into a vampire? The answer to this is as varied as the districts and peoples of Europe. The influence of the Greek Orthodox Church's thinking on the subject, even in Roman Catholic areas, has been most pronounced. Although the Roman Church has had no reservations about speaking its mind on the subject of witchcraft—witness the infamous **Malleus Maleficarum**—it has produced few official statements on vampirism *per se*. The obvious reason for this is that Western Europe, the centre of Roman Catholic power after the Schism and the Reformation, and England and North America as well suffered fewer "recorded" instances of vampirism than Eastern Europe and the Balkan countries. Consequently an obsession with eradicating sorcery and the black arts is manifested in these areas rather than concern with vampires. Whatever the case with the Roman Church, Greek Orthodoxy spoke dogmatically about vampirism. As Dudley Wright says:

> The Greek Church at one time taught that the bodies of persons upon whom the ban of excommunication had been passed did not undergo decomposition after death until such sentence had been revoked by the pronouncement of absolution over the remains, and that, while the bodies remained in the uncorrupted condition, the spirits of the individuals wandered up and down the earth seeking sustenance from the blood of the living.[7]

In addition, suicides, murderers, apostates, sorcerers, witches (if not already excommunicated), the unbaptised, a seventh son, a man born with a caul, a man with red hair, and generally debauchers, evil-doers, and blasphemers were considered among others qualified for the ranks of the undead after their human expiration.

The appearance and powers of these creatures is also too varied to

[7] Dudley Wright, **Vampires and Vampirism** (London, 1924).

Christopher Lee as Dracula in TASTE THE BLOOD OF DRACULA

detail; but a general summary of the most common characteristics can be given. Ornella Volta quoting a work ventures an interesting appraisal of the appearance of a vampire: "In his **Encyclopaedic Dictionary of Medical Science**, G. Tourdes enumerates the physcal features of someone with an erotic temperament: 'a tapering face, sharp, shining teeth, an abundance of thick hair, a peculiar voice, aspect and expression and lastly, a typical odour (usually bad).' The Reverend Montague Summers remarks that his description might just as well be that of a vampire." In addition the vampire's skin is elastic and cold; his colour pale; his stare mesmerising; and when finished with a feast his body is gorged with blood. As regards his powers, the vampire is generally reputed to have the facilities of transmogrification—into a wolf, a bat, an insect, moonbeams, etc.—mesmerism, Herculean strength, invisibility, and control over natural forces. Through some preternatural power—possibly by projecting his astral body—the vampire also can leave and return to his grave without disturbing the ground. Vampirism, according to many, is also infectious, that is, the victim becomes an undead like his malefactor.

There are, of course, other attributes of vampires that have become very familiar, chiefly through literature and film, and yet are not catalogued above. The reason is that many of these traits have originated in obscure portions of Eastern European mythology and been developed and emphasised by Nineteenth and Twentieth century writers and filmmakers. For instance, the vampire's inability to be seen in a mirror and his need to return to his earth and coffin at certain times are both primarily Bram Stoker's creative extrapolations from myth for his novel **Dracula**. Later, film-makers continued to interpolate this and have depicted vampires rushing back to their coffins every dawn in fear of destructive sunlight. Although the original Dracula's power could be reduced during the day and his coffin was necessary for transformation and reinvigoration over periods of time, he was a little more potent and flexible in his movements. It is true, however, in most Eastern European-Balkans legends that the apex of the vampires' powers comes during the night hours (effectively setting up the conflict between light and darkness) .

The preventive measures which tradition asserts can be employed against a vampire are chiefly the following:

1. A stake—preferably made of aspen or whitethorn—through the heart
2. Decapitation
3. Consummation by fire
4. The corpse buried face down

5. Holy water or blessed articles (such as the crucifix) , garlic, and thorny roses are considered only temporary deterrents.

II. HISTORICAL AND NATURAL "VAMPIRES"

I am not mad but at the moment of strangling, I understand nothing anymore. Once the deed is done I am satisfied and feel good. The idea never came to me to touch or keep the genital parts. It was enough for me to hold the woman's neck and suck her blood. Today I can't even remember what they looked like.[8]

In this section a notorious coven of criminals who are usually classed as historical or natural "vampires" will be briefly examined. Although it will be apparent in many of these cases that blood obsession *per se,* a usual prerequisite for a vampire, is not a factor (so that they seem closer to simple—if that word can be used—necrophiliacs, psychopaths, or ghouls) most researchers in the field have applied the term "vampire" to them and this categorisation is generally acknowledged.

1. Of all these individuals the most enigmatic is probably Gilles de Rais. Born in France in the early part of the fifteenth century, de Rais, who became a national hero fighting with Joan of Arc, was a noted scholar and a Marshal of France. During his early life his bravery and religious devotion were never in doubt; yet after retiring to his chateau—following Joan's death and the crowning of the Dauphin—he became involved in various bizarre practices. He began by using the blood of children (valued on account of its powers of transmutation) for alchemical experiments but soon was led into blacker rites, sodomy, and lust-murder. When he was finally brought to trial, de Rais neither expressed nor demonstrated remorse, going to the gallows with an untroubled conscience and an arrogance not uncommon to this type of "vampire." De Rais is reputed to have said that "the star under which he had been born destined him to accomplish feats that no one else could have accomplished . . ."[9] Perhaps the most lucid attempt at unraveling de Rais' character occurs in a fictional work, Joris Karl Huysmans' novel **Lá-bas** (1891). The author suggests that de Rais, who plays an important role in the work, came under the influence of Joan's mysticism and was affected deeply by her death. "He is no longer the rough soldier, the uncouth fighting-man. At the same time when the misdeeds are about to begin, the artist and man of letters develop in Gilles and, taking complete possession of him, incite him, under the impulsion of a perverted mysticism, to the most sophisticated

---

[8.] Volta, **Le vampire**, quoting Vincenzo Verzeni.
[9.] Volta, **Le vampire**, quoting the trial records of Gilles de Rais.

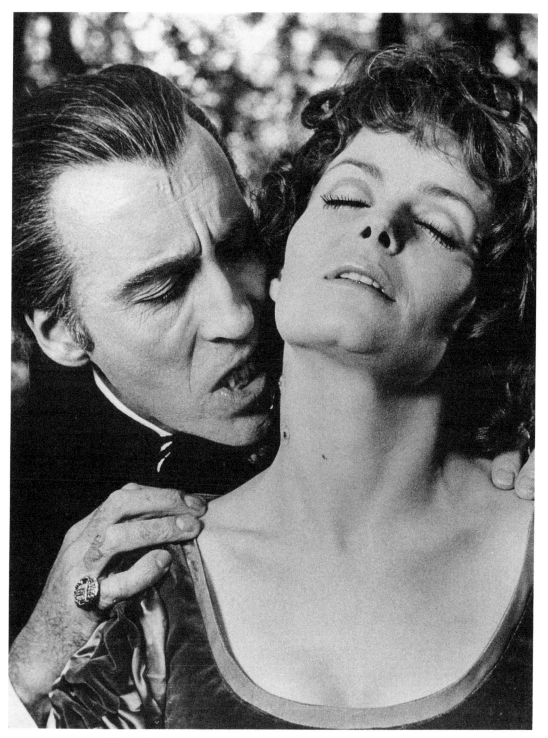

Christopher Lee and Isla Blair in TASTE THE BLOOD OF
DRACULA

of cruelties, the most delicate of crimes. For he was almost alone in his time, this baron de Rais. In an age when his peers were simple brutes, he sought the delicate delirium of art, dreamed of a literature soul-searching and profound; he even composed a treatise on the art of evoking demons; he gloried in the music of the Church, and would have nothing about him that was not rare and difficult to obtain."

2. Gilles Garnier was a French "werewolf" of the late 16th century who was condemned to death for devouring the flesh and drinking the blood of young girls.

3. Clara Geisslerin was a German woman living around 1600 who was accused of drinking the blood of children, of fornication with the devil, and of other crimes of witchcraft. She died on the Inquisitional rack after "confessing" to all these crimes.

4. Elizabeth Bathory was a Hungarian noblewoman of the 16th Cen-

Some of the victims are discovered in COUNTESS DRACULA

tury who became infamous as the "Blood Countess." First introduced into the occult by her manservant Thorko, her high social position allowed her blood obsession—especially centered on young girls— to develop unhampered. It was further aggravated in the later years of her life when she discovered quite accidentally what she believed were certain restorative powers of blood rubbed into the skin. For ten years, from 1600 to 1610, Countess Bathory, with the help of her household servants, slaughtered and "milked" countless young women, reputedly as many as 600. Finally, in 1611, King Mathias II of Hungary investigated rumours of the atrocities and brought her to trial. Countess Bathory refused to appear at the tribunal but the evidence was so overwhelming against her that her appearance was deemed superfluous. She was imprisoned in her own castle where she died in 1614.

5. Antoine Leger, a French rapist and murderer, often ate the heart and drank the blood of his victims. He was guillotined in 1824.

6. Sergeant François Bertrand was known as "The Vampire" although his case is closer to those of lycanthropy and necrophilia. A soldier with a taste for corpses, his violations of graveyards around Paris went unchecked until 1849 when a trap was set for him by an enterprising police officer. He was captured, convicted and sentenced to a year in prison.

7. Vincenzo Verzeni was a young Italian laborer who in 1872 was tried for murder complicated by charges of corpse mutilation and the drinking of blood. He was sentenced to life imprisonment.

8. Dr. Richard von Krafft-Ebing in his work **Psychopathia Sexualis** relates an anonymous case of natural "vampirism." He gives the subject's initials as J.H.:

J. H., aged twenty-six, in 1883 came for consultation concerning severe neurasthenia and hypochondria. Patient confessed that he had practiced onanism since his fourteenth year, infrequently up to his eighteenth year, but since that time he had been unable to resist the impulse. Up to that time he had no opportunity to approach females, for he had been anxiously cared for and never left alone on account of being an invalid. He had had no real desire for this unknown pleasure, but he accidentally learned what it was when one of his mother's maids cut her hand severely on a pane of glass which she had broken while washing windows. While helping to stop the bleeding he could not keep from sucking up the blood that flowed from the wound, and in this act he experienced extreme erotic excitement, with complete orgasm and ejaculation. From that time on he sought, in every possible way, to see and, where practicable, to taste the fresh blood of females.

9. **Peter Kurten**, also known as the "Vampire of Dusseldorf," possessed a classic Jekyll and Hyde personality. By day he was a plain,

well-mannered lorry driver; after dark he prowled the city in search of blood. His victims were usually raped and slashed across the throat so that their blood then gushed into his mouth. In addition, Kurten was infamous for writing macabre letters to his victims' parents. After being jailed for some nocturnal burglaries, Kurten's identity as the "Vampire" was revealed and in April 1931 he was condemned to death. One of his last statements is typical of the insular mania of the "vampire" psychopath: "You cannot understand me. No one can understand me."[10]

10. Fritz Haarmann's early life betrays an unstable and divisive family situation not unlike that of most of the other criminals in this study. Arguments between his parents and violent quarrels with his churlish father drove Haarmann to leave home and join the army. After a short period of service and a subsequent term in an asylum for child molestation, he opened a cook shop in a district of Hanover known for its homosexual inhabitants. With the help of a few friends (most notably Hans Grans), Haarmann began molesting and murdering young boys. What is even more gruesome to relate and what must have proved most unsettling, when it was ultimately revealed to the housewives of Hanover, is that the corpses of the boys he killed were often the source of the fresh meat for Haarmann's steaks and sausages. Haarmann and his accomplices were brought to trial in 1924 and the "Hanover Vampire" was condemned to death

11. We know more about Victor Ardisson, or "The Vampire of Muy," than any other natural "vampire" because of a doctoral thesis by Alexis Epaulard (filed in 1901). Ardisson was for all practical purposes never anything but a necrophile with a misdirected gentleness of manner. Unlike the others in this survey he rarely committed acts of violence. Instead he invaded cemeteries and indulged his fantasies on female corpses, often those of women he had fallen in love with in life. Some of these bodies were even stolen by Ardisson and lovingly preserved. After he was apprehended and confined to an asylum, he became the subject of many studies until his death.

12. In Magnus Hirschfeld's **Anomalies et perversions sexuelles** (Paris ,1935) the author records a case handled by Dr. Craven dealing with a Portuguese female considered an ideal natural "vampire." Here is an excerpt of the text:

> The thoughts and fantasies of the subject all moved around the idea of blood, which she expressed by means of blood-thirsty metaphors and

[10.] Volta, **Le Vampire**, quoting Kurten. See also Karl Berg's **The Sadist**, a study of Kurten's psychopathia based on interviews with Kurten made during his incarceration.

symbols. Blood for her is the symbol of love, hate, anger, and passion. She wants to know in what way human blood is different from animals' blood and has set herself this problem: what aspect would it have if it were to lose its color?[11]

13. John Haigh, "The Vampire of London," is probably the most self-righteous member of this group. A religious fanatic, from a family of puritanically-minded practitioners, Haigh imagined himself as a Christ figure during his trials for murder in 1949. That he had killed and drunk the blood of nine victims did not seem to affect this perception of himself. From childhood he had dreams intermingling religious symbolism and blood lust, and as he grew older he began to enact "rites" inspired by these dreams. When captured and tried he expressed no remorse; quite the contrary, he proposed the erection of a monument to his memory. This admixture of religious fervour and vampiric perversion is eerily reminiscent of the first entry in this coven, Gilles de Rais, closing out the circle of arrogant psychopaths whose delusions of divine or Satanic mission, belief in preternatural powers, and insatiable bloodlust are emblematic of the natural "vampire."

[For more detail on vampires in history and legend see also the sections devoted to the various figures treated above in Montague Summer's two classics, **The Vampire: His Kith and Kin** and **The Vampire in Europe**, Ornella Volta's **Le vampire**—although the English translation introduces numerous errors—and R.E.L. Masters and Eduard Lea's general survey **Sex Crimes in History** (New York, 1963).]

III. THE VAMPIRE IN LITERATURE AND THE ARTS

> When from this wreathed tomb shall I awake!
> When move in a sweet body fit for life,
> And love, and pleasure, and the ruddy strife
> Of hearts and lips! Ah, miserable me!
>   (Keats, "Lamia")

1. Literature: Recognising the universality and antiquity of vampire legends, it is not surprising that some of the earliest literature which has come down to us should contain references to these creatures. In Euripides's play "Hecuba" the plot pivots on a blood sacrifice to the thirsty spirit of Achilles; in **The Odyssey** the dead speak to the hero after drinking blood; and in Summers's **The Vampire in Europe** the

---

[11.] Volta, **Le Vampire**, quoting Hirschfeld. The heroine of Octave Mirbeau's **Garden of Tortures** expresses very similar sentiments.

following dialogue from the "Ecclesiazusea" by Aristophanes is translated:

> SECOND HAG: Come hither.
> YOUTH (to the Girl) : O my darling, don't stand by,
>   and see this creature drag me!
> SECOND HAG: 'Tis the law drags you.
> YOUTH: 'Tis a hellish vampire,
>   Clothed all about with blood, and boils and blisters.

In the early history of vampire literature, the most frequently repeated story is from Philostratus's life of Apollonius of Tyana, a kind of "legendary" biography of the Greek sage including many apocryphal events. The narrative of Menippus and his love for a lamia is such a quasi-fable, made famous by Keats's use of the subject in his dramatic "Lamia" in the early 1800's. In both Keats's and Philostratus's versions Apollonius represents the forces of reason which are in opposition to the lamia's more libidinous and supernatural appeal. The differences between these two works—which are almost as vast as the years between them—are chiefly ones of moral attitude. When Philostratus's Apollonius finally dispells the illusions created by the lamia, breaking her hold over the young Menippus, it is a victory of Greek rationalism over the less sophisticated forces of the universe and the expression of the epistemological prejudices of Greek thought. On the other hand, Keats, rooted in a completely different set of values, makes manifest the more Romantic sentiments of his age and decries Apollonius's narrow rationalism (". . . who look'd thereon with eye severe,/And with calm-planted steps walk'd in austere") while sympathising with the lamia and Lycius—Keats's Menippus—in their search for love no matter how transitory or elusive. While Philostratus's tale concludes when the lamia is exposed as a flesh-devouring, blood-sucking demon who had no thought for Menippus except as victim, Keats's figure is banished like a "foul dream," her real intentions never clear and Lycius dying shortly after her disappearance.

Another ancient source for later vampire tales is recorded by Phlegon of Tralles, a freedman of Hadrian. Phlegon, supposedly speaking as an eye-witness, tells of the return of a young woman named Philinnion from the grave and how she visits a young man named Machates and has sexual intercourse with him until her parents intrude to her dismay and cut short her nocturnal excursions. In 1791 Goethe took this story by Phlegon and developed it into a poem called "The Bride of Corinth." Like Keats, Goethe establishes a dramatic conflict between social repression and sexual instincts. The heroine dies of grief because her fanatically religious mother refuses to let her

Ingrid Pitt as Carla in THE HOUSE THAT DRIPPED BLOOD

marry the man she loves, so she returns to him as a vampire—with death acting as a catalytic release from the sublimations of the living.

Two other fairly ancient vampire stories are "Vikram and the Vampire or Tales of Hindu Devilry" and "A Vampyre of the Fens." The former is a Hindu legend composed in Sanskrit and is, according to the wife of the translator Richard Burton, "the germ which culminated in the Arabian Nights, and which inspired the 'Golden Ass' of Apuleius, Boccaccio's 'Decamerone,' the 'Pentamerone,' and all the class of facetious fictitious literature." Vikram is an Indian hero, not unlike King Arthur, who has promised to bring back Baital (the Indian demon who reanimates corpses and can take the form of a bat) to a Magician or Jogi. In order to delay this abduction Baital proceeds to relate a number of tales, mostly humorous. After these captivating narratives have run their course and the vampire's time is expiring, Baital gives Vikram a warning regarding the treachery of the Jogi (which proves accurate) and is released by Vikram. The second work is an Anglo-Saxon poem to which Dudley Wright alludes but exact information about the text and history of the poem is not available.

Without question, the most prolific period for vampire literature has been the last two centuries. It is no coincidence that this fascination with vampirism coincides with the growth of Romanticism, with that movement's emphasis on the irrational, the instinctual, and the emotional opening the door to the supernatural and its legends. One of the earliest and perhaps best works featuring vampirism in this period is **Thalaba the Destroyer** (1797) by Robert Southey. An epic heroic fantasy in verse, Thalaba's twelve books, which are set in the Near East, look back to stories in **The Arabian Nights**, to **Beowulf** and **Orlando Furioso** and foward to **The King of Elfland's Daughter** and **The Lord of the Rings** in style, structure, and use of myth. It also contains a particularly vivid description of a visitation by a vampire (a vampire who takes the form of the hero's [Thalaba's] love Oneiza) :

> The Crier from the Minaret
> Proclaim'd the midnight hour.
> 'Now, now!' cried Thalaba;
> And o'er the chamber of the tomb
> There spread a lurid light
> Oneiza stood before them. It was She, —
> Her very lineaments,—and such as death
> Had changed them, livid cheeks, and lips of blue;
> But in her eyes there dwelt
> Brightness more terrible
> than all the loathsomeness of death.
> . . . 'This is not she!' the Old Man exclaim'd;
> 'A Fiend; a manifest Fiend!'
> And to the youth he held his lance;
> 'Strike and deliver thyself!'
> 'Strike her!' cried Thalaba,
> And, palsied of all power,
> Gazed fixedly upon the dreadful form;
> . . . He thrust his lance; it fell;
> And, howling with the wound,
> Its fiendish tenant fled,
> A sapphire light fell on them,
> And garmented with glory, in their sight
> Oneiza's Spirit stood.

Coleridge, like Southey, made his contribution to vampire literature in verse form. His vehicle was an unfinished and therefore rather ambiguous poem entitled "Christabel." Its main character is a young lady (Geraldine), who has died before the narrative begins, but returns to torment and/or captivate a maiden (Christabel). The overtones are demonic and erotic, for example:

> So half-way from the bed she rose,
> And on her elbow did recline
> To look at the lady Geraldine.
> Beneath the lamp the lady bowed,
> And slowly rolled her eyes around;
> Then drawing in her breath aloud,
> Like one that shuddered, she unbound
> The cincture from beneath her breast:
> Her silken robe, and inner vest,
> Dropt to her feet, and full in view,
> Behold! her bosom and half her side—
> A sight to dream of, not to tell!
> O shield her! shield sweet Christabel

and as a whole the poem presages J. Sheridan Le Fanu's **Carmilla**.

Carmilla (Ingrid Pitt) and Laura (Pippa Steele) in THE VAMPIRE

Fatal Woman and Fatal Man: above, Ingrid Pitt as Carmilla and Kate O'Mara as her victim in THE VAMPIRE LOVERS; below, Christopher Lee as Drácula and Soledad Miranda as Lucy in EL CONDE DRÁCULA

By far, the most important vampire work of the early 19th Century was dominated by the figure and reputation of that arch-Romantic Lord Byron. "The Vampyre" was conceived on that now legendary June night in 1816 when Percy and Mary Shelley, Lord Byron and his mistress Claire Clairmont, and Dr. John Polidori gathered in a room of their Geneva chateau to amuse themselves with horror tales. On a suggestion from Byron each member of the menage decided to compose a horror story of his or her own. Mary Shelley's contribution became the novel **Frankenstein** while Claire Clairmont and Percy produced nothing of consequence. The situation with Byron and Polidori was a little more complicated. Polidori did publish in 1819 a story called "The Vampyre;" but in its original periodical version it was credited to Byron. Byron denied authorship and Polidori stepped into the void to assert that he was actually the author although he admitted that the original outline was Byron's. Why it was originally credited to Byron has never been fully explained; but the truth of the statement that the outline was Byron's was later verified when the poet published an excerpt from an unfinished novel of his own. This excerpt is unmistakably the core, in plot and characterisation, of Polidori's story. The main character of both the unfinished novel and Polidori's tale is a Byronic hero in its fullest dimensions: a mysterious figure whose magnetism draws people to him but whose secrecy and lonely brooding preclude relationships of any depth. The initial description of Lord Ruthven, the Vampyre, in the Polidori tale illustrates this:

> It happened that in the midst of the dissipations attendant upon a London winter, there appeared at the various parties of the leaders of the "ton" a nobleman, more remarkable for his singularities, than his rank. He gazed upon the mirth around him, as if he could not participate therein. Apparently, the light laughter of the fair only attracted his attention, that he might by a look quell it, and throw fear into those breasts where thoughtlessness reigned. Those who felt this sensation of awe, could not explain whence it arose: some attributed it to the dead grey eye, which, fixing upon the object's face, did not seem to penetrate, and at one glance to pierce through to the inward workings of the heart; but fell upon the cheek with a leaden ray that weighted upon the skin it could not pass.

In the story a young, idealistic man (Aubrey) falls under Ruthven's influence and eventually becomes his friend and travelling companion (the analogy here between the Polidori-Byron relationship and the Aubrey-Ruthven one is fairly clear). During their travels in Greece, they are ambushed and Ruthven is mortally wounded; but before he dies, he extracts a promise from Aubrey not to tell of his demise.

An uncomprehending Aubrey agrees. It is, however, a promise he comes
to rue; for when back in London, Ruthven appears to claim Aubrey's
sister. The half-mad young man is torn between love for his sister
and his innate sense of honour. He only chooses too late. The last lines
are: "The guardians hastened to protect Miss Aubrey; but when they
arrived, it was too late. Lord Ruthven had disappeared, and Aubrey's
sister had glutted the thirst of a VAMPYRE!"

There are a few interesting bits of mythology Polidori draws on or
possibly creates for this story which are not common to Eastern
European-Balkans vampire legend or to most vampire literature and
films. They are the restorative powers of moonlight and the extreme
vulnerability of the vampire, even to ordinary bullets. These bits of
exceptional vampire lore are among the few Polidori uses in the work.
Excepting his need for blood, a certain magnetism, and his revivification powers Ruthven is a most "human" vampire without many of the
demonic qualities and potency of later figures.

Polidori's story was an immediate success inspiring scores of plays,
poems and stories for decades. In fact, the only vampire story, in the
first half of the century, to come close to this tale's popularity was a
"penny dreadful" serial called **Varney the Vampyre**. It was written
by either James Malcolm Rymer or Thomas Peckett Prest (the question is still open) and contains over two hundred episodes which were
released individually during the 1840's. Although, like many of the
other "penny dreadful" serials of that period, it is at times poorly
written and filled with inconsistencies and ludicrous twists of plot,
the main character emerges as an engaging one. **Varney** introduces
us to a tortured compulsive vampire who seems to be driven on by a
will not his own. He is a sympathetic figure doomed to the "life" of
the undead for heinous crimes (which are ambiguously delineated in
the novel). Although he wreaks bloody havoc on a number of victims,
Varney's introspection and sense of guilt are redemptive qualities and
his situation cannot help but elicit empathy. In the final episode
Varney, after a long confession, decides upon a way to end his "life-in-
death." Standing at the mouth of a fissure in Mt. Vesuvius (with a
guide alongside) :

'You will make what haste you can,' said the stranger [Varney], 'from
the mountain, inasmuch as it is covered with sulphurous vapours, inimical
to human life, and when you reach the city you will cause to be published
an account of my proceedings, and what I say. You will say that you
accompanied Varney the Vampyre to the crater of Mount Vesuvius, and
that, tired and disgusted with a life of horror, he flung himself in to
prevent the possibility of a reanimation of his remains.' Before then the
guide could utter anything but a shriek, Varney took one tremendous
leap, and disappeared into the burning mouth of the mountain.

As both the evil and good of Pompeii were indiscriminately swallowed up, so is Varney.

With **Varney** the more intricate myths long associated with the legendary vampire are absorbed into formal fiction. Like Lord Ruthven, he has magnetism, strength, and the ability to be revived by moonlight; but, in addition, the author added elements of colour derived from Eastern European lore. Vampirism becomes infectious in this novel, as the victim too becomes one of the undead, and, more significantly, the stake is introduced as a way of laying a vampire to rest.

At about the same period two Russian writers were also producing vampiric stories. They were Nikolai Gogol and Alexis Tolstoy. Gogol published a story called "The Viy"; written in his usual sardonic style, it is the tale of a young philosopher who must keep vigil beside the coffin of a vampiric witch and who is finally killed by a Satanic monster called a"Viy."Alexis Tolstoy—not to be confused with his more famous cousin Leo—produced a series of stories in a more serious vein (though they are not without their own humour). "The Vampire," "The Family of a Vourdalak," "The Reunion after Three Hundred Years," and "Amena" make up an uneven quartet which is most memorable for flights of expressionistic symbolism. The landscape of Tolstoy's stories is one where dream and reality interplay without regard for territorial rights. For instance, the hero of "The Vampire" is tormented by visions which lead him to suspect his love's relatives of vampirism, while "Amena's" main character, an early Christian, is led by a lamia to renounce his faith and friends in exchange for her illusory charms.

As the sun of Romanticism began its descent in the second half of the 19th Century, a stylistic transformation occured. Out of the ashes of this earlier, more Byronic Romanticism grew a far more morbid and extreme movement in literature and art labeled "Decadence." One of its foremost spokesmen and practitioners was the Frenchman Theophile Gautier; and it is this same Gautier who wrote one of the most intriguing vampire stories of the century—"La morte amoureuse" (known variously in English as "Clarimonde," "The Beautiful Vampire," and "The Dead Leman"). "La morte amoureuse" is a richly textured, erotic tale the style of which is best described by Gautier himself in an essay on Baudelaire's works:

> The poet of the "Fleurs du Mal" loved what is improperly called the style of decadence, and which is nothing else but art arrived at the point of extreme maturity yielded by the slanting suns of aged civilizations: an ingenious complicated style, full of shades and of research, constantly pushing back the boundaries of speech, borrowing from all the technical vocabularies, taking colour from all palettes and notes from all keyboards, struggling to render what is most inexpressible in thought, what is vague

and most elusive in the outlines of form, listening to translate the subtle confidences of neurosis, the dying confessions of passion grown depraved, and the strange hallucinations of the obsession which is turning to madness. The style of decadence is the ultimate utterance of the Word, summoned to final expressions and driven to its lasting hiding-place. Unlike the classic style it admits shadow . . .

"La morte amoureuse" tells of an "obsession which is turning to madness" and towards death. It recounts the "fall" of a naive, young priest who beholds a beautiful woman—Clarimonde, an evil courtesan who has become a vampire—at his ordination and is immediately entranced by her aspect, as conveyed in Gautier's flowing, sensual prose:

> That woman was an angel or a demon, perhaps both; she certainly did not issue from the loins of Eve, our common mother. Teeth of the purest pearl sparkled in her ruddy smile, and little dimples appeared with each motion of her mouth in the satiny rose of her adorable cheeks. As for her nostrils, they were regal in their graceful and dignified shape, and indicated the noblest origin. A lustre as of agate played upon the smooth, glossy skin of her half-bare shoulders and strings of great blonde pearls, of a shade almost like her neck, hung down upon her bosom. From time to time she elevated her head with the undulating grace of a snake, or of a startled peacock, and imparted a slight quiver to the high embroidered openwork ruff which surrounded her neck like a silver trellis work.

This obsession comes to dominate the priest's life, so that he soon finds himself more and more frequently "transported" to a voluptuous world where Clarimonde becomes his perverse and demanding mistress. He continues to live this dual life, unable to determine whether his romantic adventures are dreams or not. The resolution of this dilemma is left, as it is in Keats's "Lamia," to a severe rationalist— here the Abbé Serapion. Serapion discovers the tomb of Clarimonde and destroys her—and the young priest's illusions—with a spray of holy water.

In 1871 a novella entitled **Carmilla** was published. Its author was an Irishman, J. Sheridan Le Fanu, who specialised in tales of horror and the supernatural. **Carmilla**, like its descendant **Dracula**, is very much a product of the Victorian age. It has that same surface optimism, gentility, and balance which was conducive to much of the dull, stodgy fiction of the period. Even when the action verges on the violent or perverse there is always a clear-cut division between good and evil; and, of course, evil is vanquished. But just below that surface, often not very far below, lurks the darker, pessimistic, and sometimes decadent spirit which gave so much of Victorian art and culture its true depth and feeling. Le Fanu's plot centres on a young woman

Ingrid Pitt and Pippa Steele in THE VAMPIRE LOVERS

(Laura) who is visited by a lovely and mysterious dream image (Carmilla). In the course of the first person narrative—the novella operates within a broader tradition of journal fiction—events reveal that she is also Countess Millarca Karnstein, a vampire. In the final scenes her secret crypt is sought out and she is staked and decapitated. Already a set pattern in plot is being followed without much variation; but there is more. There are unusual subtleties here which are only discovered by studying the character of Carmilla. To begin with, Carmilla's victims are almost all females; moreover, she seems to fall in love with her victims beforehand (specifically, Laura and General Spielsdorf's niece). Finally, Carmilla is extremely sympathetic, in that she acts out of compulsion more than will—in this she is somewhat

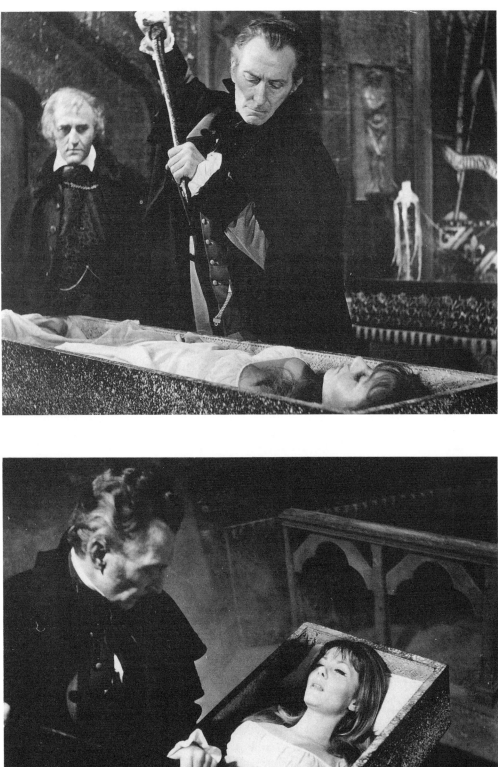

reminiscent of Varney. This compulsiveness coupled with a thinly disguised lesbianism is expressed very well in the following passage:

> She [Carmilla] used to place her pretty arms about my neck, draw me to her, and laying her cheek to mine, murmur with her lips near my ear, 'Dearest, your little heart is wounded; think me not cruel because I obey the irresistible law of my strength and weakness; if your dear heart is wounded, my wild heart bleeds with yours. In the rapture of my enormous humiliation I live in your warm life, and you shall die—die, sweetly die—into mine. I cannot help it; as I draw near to you, you, in your turn, will draw near to others, and learn the rapture of that cruelty, which yet is love; so, for a while, seek to know no more of me and mine, but trust me with all your loving spirit.'

Bram Stoker's novel **Dracula** is, indisputably, the most influential work in vampire literature. With the book's publication in 1897, its predecessors in the genre were immediately overshadowed, and for a number of obvious reasons. "Dracula" represents the most involved interweaving of legends and myths that had been produced in the field. Stoker researched his subject thoroughly, seeking material in Transylvania and from eminent authorities such as Professor Arminius Vambery, who is alluded to in the book. In his research Stoker came upon the person of a Transylvanian ruler of the 15th Century—Vlad Tepes the Impaler, otherwise known as Dracula (meaning "son of the devil" or "son of the dragon"). This rather paradoxical character was reputed to be a mass murderer as well as one of the most celebrated defenders of Eastern Europe against the Turkish encroachment. But his virtues, like those of Shakespeare's Caesar, did not survive his death. They were submerged for centuries beneath a profusion of legends growing out of the facts of his atrocities. He became known within a few decades as a devil incarnate and ultimately a vampire. Building on the historical and legendary elements of this character, Stoker added even more to the myth by creating a Satanic figure who is almost invincible. His control over the elements, his polymorphism, his mesmeric faculty, his all-devouring blood lust can only be checked by someone who has studied his few weaknesses. Here Stoker establishes what has become the archetypal conflict in most of vampire literature and film to follow: between the scientist-doctor-scholar with occult knowledge and the

(Opposite: above and below)
Peter Cushing stakes Ingrid Pitt in THE VAMPIRE LOVERS

Peter Cushing as Van Helsing in DRACULA A.D. 1972

ravaging vampire. Stoker named his vampire stalker Professor Van Helsing and made him familiar with both the vampire and his vulnerability (namely periodic need to return to his native earth, fear of religious articles, and his susceptibility to staking, decapitation, and burning) so that he, in the final chapters, could bring about Dracula's destruction.

The stress in **Dracula**, as in Le Fanu's novella, is again on the erotic. But, as in **Carmilla**, it is an eroticism veiled by Victorian manners and convention. An example of this is in the sensitive area of the author's idealisation of the women in his novel. The two heroines (Lucy and Mina) are representatives of the ideal Victorian woman, who is as J. H. Buckley has characterised her "... the pure ... selfless center of a tightly closed domestic universe."[12] But this is only superficially true, in this novel and indeed in Victorian society itself. For

[12] J. H. Buckley, **The Victorian Temper** (New York, 1964).

when the women come under the erotic-thanatotic spell of Dracula all the sexual drives, which had been so effectively repressed, are released. The attraction between the woman and the vampire in their actual encounters—for instance their fascination with Dracula's bestial *mien* or, more specifically, Mina's initiation drinking blood from his lacerated chest—are described in terms of dominance and submission. In the case of Lucy, the acquisition of a potent eroticism becomes a major factor after her death. The confrontation between the newly undead Lucy and Dr. Seward, Arthur, and Van Helsing gives an indication of the significance of sexuality in the vampire's "afterlife" while serving, incidentally, as an example of the excellence of Stoker's style when he is not attempting to mimic the mannered prose of the day:

> When Lucy—I call the thing that was before us Lucy because it bore her shape—saw us she drew back with an angry snarl, such as a cat gives when taken unawares; then her eyes ranged over us. Lucy's eyes in form and colour; but Lucy's eyes unclean and full of hell-fire, instead of the pure, gentle orbs we knew. At that moment the remnant of my love passed into hate and loathing; had she then to be killed, I could have done it with savage delight. As she looked, her eyes blazed with unholy light, and the face became wreathed with a voluptuous smile. Oh, God, how it made my shudder to see it! With a careless motion, she flung to the ground, callous as a devil, the child that up to now she had clutched strenuously to her breast, growling over it as a dog growls over a bone. The child gave a sharp cry, and lay there moaning. There was a cold-bloodedness in the act which wrung a groan from Arthur; when she advanced to him with outstretched arms and a wanton smile he fell back and hid his face in his hands. She still advanced, however, and with a languourous, voluptuous grace, said: 'Come to me, Arthur. Leave these others and come to me. My arms are hungry for you. Come, and we can rest together. Come, my husband, come!' There was something diabolically sweet in her tones—something of the tinkling of glass when struck—which rang through the brains even of us who heard the word addressed to another. As for Arthur, he seemed under a spell; moving his hands from his face, he opened wide his arms.

Ultimately, **Dracula's** enduring virtues lie in its immediacy, pacing, and in its power to evoke vivid moods. Like **Carmilla** the story is essentially told in first person narrative; but in Stoker's novel there is more than one narrator and so, through a series of letters, diaries and newspaper reports, the events (some of them the same) are recorded from different perspectives. The constant narrative rupture induced by this device is a key to the novel's genuine suspense, as the various perspectives gradually piece together the "reality" of the supernatural and seem to converge on the Borgo Pass for the climax of the

Bela Lugosi greets Dwight Frye in DRACULA (1931)

pursuit and the vampire's dissolution. To reinforce all this Stoker distills the essential mood from the somber style of the Gothic tradition. Dracula haunts medieval castles and abbeys dressed in penumbral attire, seeming to merge with the night; wolves and bats are his familiars and his home a coffin. All that the twentieth century has come to associate with the vampire, from his needle-sharp canine teeth to his retinue of gypsies is present and correct.

Shortly after the turn of the century and only a few years after **Dracula**'s first printing, stories in sharp contrast to the "Stoker tradition" began to appear. First, writers introduced what can only be called "non-human" vampires. H. G. Wells did this in a tale about vampire vegetation called "The Flowering of the Strange Orchid" and so did E. F. Benson in "And No Bird Sings." H. P. Lovecraft went one step further and made his vampire inanimate: the story was "The Shunned House" and featured a "vampire building." In still another direction, writers such as Arthur Conan Doyle and Algernon Blackwood began to play with the idea of a "psychic vampire"— one who feeds off the brain waves or psychic energies of another. The notion was introduced in Doyle's "The Parasite" and in Blackwood's "The

A scene in the abbey from DRACULA (1931)

Transfer" but was not developed to any significant degree in the work
of others. Perhaps the most enduring re-interpretation of the vampire
was through the conceit of the man-eater into the body and soul of the
femme fatale. As a result of a painting by Philip Burne-Jones and an
accompanying poem by his kinsman Rudyard Kipling ("The Vampire"), the term came to represent a very human and non-supernatural
creature who sucked the life out of her male lovers and then ruthlessly
discarded them, a connotation which the word "vampire" has retained
to this day.

There have been a few other landmarks of varying significance in
vampire literature. Guy de Maupassant's frightening tale of mounting
insanity deals with a rather non-substantial and invisible vampire
called a "horla." F. Marion Crawford tells the story of a vampire
suffering from unrequited love in "For the Blood Is the Life." Montague James made his contribution with "Count Magnus"—which
Lovecraft praises highly in his essay on "Supernatural Horror in
Literature"—and "An Episode of Cathedral History." E. F. Benson
in a change of pace from his "non-human" vampires, delineates, in
"Mrs. Amworth," a genuinely "human" vampire of the female sex.

And Luigi Capuana places his fiend in an Italianate setting in "A Vampire." Possibly the most creative use of the vampire myth in the early half of this century has been Clark Ashton Smith's in his tale cycle **Zothique**. **Zothique** is an imaginary and imaginative view of the earth in its last days when "the coal-red sun" is "oblique" and "dead gods drink the brine." In this perishing world man again turns to the occult arts and to the ancient superstitions—vampirism among them. "He who loved the wild girls of Zothique shall come not back a gentler love to seek, nor know the vampire's from the lover's kiss. For him the scarlet ghost of Lilith from time's last necropolis rears amorous and malign." Smith paints with a vivid style similar to Gautier's a portrait of a luxuriant civilization peopled with vampiric succubi and those enraptured by their rapacious love.

Today vampire literature is being produced at a rate which is little short of astounding. Unfortunately, a good deal of this is pulp: paperbacks, comic books, and tabloids dealing with Dracula and/or other vampires are rife and usually of the lowest quality—rarely achieving even the competency of the "penny dreadfuls." There are, as always, exceptions: Richard Matheson in his novel **I Am Legend** has combined science fiction and vampire myths with interesting results. While more satirical writers like Robert Bloch have added touches of humour to the genre (as in "The Cloak"). Some other fascinating twists have been supplied by writers like Fritz Leiber who in "The Girl with the Hungry Eyes" combines a sardonic critique of society's modern advertising techniques with a stereotyped female vampire and Manly Wade Wellman who in "When It Was Moonlight" assumes the point of view of the vampire.

2. The Formal Visual Arts: Vampiric figures do not occur in the formal visual arts of painting and sculpture with the same regularity as in literature. Although there is a Babylonian sculpture of a vampire in the Louvre, most of the art works depicting vampires have been done in the last century—probably as a result of the fairly recent blossoming of surrealism and expressionism. These movements have provided a natural opening for the kind of fantasy treatment vampirism is inherently associated with. For example, Edvard Munch, the Dane, concentrated on sketches of bloody female vampires (e.g. "The Vampire") while his contemporary Max Ernst turned his surrealist leanings to more consciously symbolic paintings (e.g. "Une semaine de bonté"). Felicien Rops and Clovis Trouille, in Western Europe, took a slightly more outrageous tack in their depiction of similarly vampiric subjects. Trouille has been particularly drawn to saturated colours and outlandish humour in works like "Le rêve vampyr" and

"Mon tombeau" while Rops is famous for the eroticism and morbidity which he applied to the genre. The real center of activity in vampire art, however, has been in the pop category. Comic books, in recent years, have flooded the market with vampire issues. Though the illustrations are generally of uneven quality, there are exceptions. The "Vampirella" comics are a particularly good example: their illustrations are usually well-drawn and their multi-colour covers are, according to the publishers, their most important asset in sales. Finally, there are the T-shirts, posters, and even bottle caps which have been distributed in the last few years and which feature a vampire motif. The pop horror art market seems, at present, to have kept pace with the rise in popularity of both the occult arts and vampire films.

3. The Dramatic Arts: As mentioned earlier, Polidori's story "The Vampyre" caused such a sensation in Europe that it inspired a sequel of poems, stories, and plays for the next several decades. The earliest theatrical adaptation was staged in Paris by Charles Nodier and was itself a great success. At about the same time, J. R. Planché in London was producing his own "vampire drama" based more substantially on the Nodier piece than on the Polidori original. Planché, however, employed a more operatic format for his play and called it "The Vampyre or The Bride of the Isles." It, too, was a grand hit and, incidentally, developed a complex stage device known as the "vampire trap" door. In both these renderings, the once very human Lord Ruthven was transformed into a consummate, inhuman villain who receives his just punishment in the form of a lightning bolt. The public responded well to this less Byronic, melodramatic fiend, and adaptations of Nodier's play proliferated. In 1828, in Leipzig, "Der Vampyr" opened. This time Ruthven was an evil Wallachian nobleman who inhabited a Gothic manor and spoke with a thick Eastern European accent. This version was eventually brought to London and is purported to have inspired Bram Stoker's conception of Dracula. In 1851 the incredibly prolific Alexandre Dumas (père), not to be outdone by his contemporaries in any area, added to the list of Ruthven dramas yet another entitled "Le vampire," a play even more excessive and lacking in distinction than its predecessors. Inevitably, this saturation of the vampire theatre with Ruthven and his *semblables* compelled playwrights to seek a new approach to the situation—and satires were the result. A. E. Scribe, the master of the "well-made play," wrote such a comedy and called it, predictably enough, "Le vampire." In it he lampooned the character of Ruthven by having one of his *personae* masquerade as the Lord to the general consternation of the other characters. Similar burlesques were produced around the same time with varying success

—some, in Paris, even competed against each other in neighbouring playhouses.

Stoker's **Dracula** also left its mark in the theatre. The first to produce an adaptation of the novel was Stoker's mentor, the stage luminary, Henry Irving. In 1897, shortly after the novel's publication, Irving presented a version which lasted over four hours and consisted of more than forty scenes. The most famous dramatisation of Stoker's novel, however—one still produced today—came after the novelist's death. The adaptor and director was Hamilton Deane, who premiered his **Dracula** in June of 1924. Much shorter than the Irving version and confined in its action to the London portions of Stoker's story, this play was so successful that in 1927 Deane exported it to America. John Balderston collaborated on the American playscript (which was not significantly different) and the newest **Dracula** had its New York premiere in October of 1927. The actors engaged to portray Dracula and Van Helsing were Bela Lugosi and Edward Van Sloan— both of whom were brought to Los Angeles for the Universal film adaptation in 1931. Although the American production was another financial and critical triumph, Deane preferred to go on tour with a new company, which he did for a number of seasons.

In recent years there have been periodic theatrical versions of classic vampire stories, but none with the impact of the Nodier and Deane plays. One notably innovative and recent exception is the New York E.T.C. Company of Cafe La Mama's staging of **Carmilla**. This multi-media chamber opera with rock-jazz-classical score and an emphasis on the erotic-lesbian elements of the original is remarkably faithful to Le Fanu in characterisation, plot, and dialogue and may be the only adaptation in any medium which has successfully transliterated the dual drives of the novella. The piece is so stylised that only the two principals, Laura and Carmilla, are ever present in full stage reality (the others being incorporated quite literally into the decor, their heads visible as decorative parts of a high-backed sofa on which Laura and Carmilla sit). The sexuality as well as the parasitic aspects implicit in this absence of others is given physical and emotional release in the energetic semi-arias which these two sing from their perpetual stage centre position. In scenes such as the destruction of the vampire (seen on film projected above the actors) viewed simultaneously as premonition and real event (in past and/or future) by the two women, the opera works with time in a manner beyond Le Fanu and accurately captures, where he could at best suggest, the anguish of not merely perpetual life but perpetual re-living which is peculiar to the vampire myth.

The modern implications of the song "Not So Sweet Martha Lorraine" are in the same vein, psychedelic ("The only way that you'll ever get her high/is to let her do her thing then watch you die") as well as erotic. The way this acid rock vampire seems to spring, like Athena, from the brow of Zeus, from those who have gone before her —"She hides in an attic concealed on a shelf/behind volumes of literature based on herself"—is analogous to the way the vampire idiom has been constantly re-adapted to popular styles.

The media which along with film have taken over from the stage in translating the vampire myth into dramatic terms are radio and television. Both have broadcast series and individual shows featuring vampires—some with a sardonic flavour, others in dead earnest. As examples in television: *The Munsters* (1964-66) centred on a zany family of monsters in exaggerated make-up including a vampire grandfather and an undead mother. *Dark Shadows* (1966-71) enjoyed a long run in the afternoon soap-opera market and presented the ongoing vampire character, Barnabas Collins, to daytime audiences.[13] Rod Serling's *Night Gallery* (1970-72) regularly featured vampire vignettes in its series of horror tales. One noteworthy episode, entitled *Death on a Barge,* dealt with a siren-like female vampire imprisoned by the still water surrounding her barge (a bit of Eastern European mythology referred to in Stoker's **Dracula**). Radio produced its own rendering of Stoker's novel via Orson Welles's Mercury Theater. This version, produced in 1938, retains much of the urgency of the original and many of the incidents set in Transylvania that were eschewed both by Deane in his play and Universal in their 1931 film. Relying on sound effects, music, and other aural stimulants to produce a suspenseful, even frightening impact, Welles's necessarily non-visual adaptation demonstrates that the vampire tale can find expression in any form.

---

13. Both The *Munsters* and *Dark Shadows* have spawned a deluge of derivative material ranging from children's lunchboxes with pictures of the former to a series of "Gothic" novels centered in the Collins character and ultimately to several films, comic and serious, designed for regular theatrical distribution.

Lon Chaney as "The Vampire" in LONDON AFTER MIDNIGHT

CHAPTER TWO

The Male Vampire

And day and night she's followed him
His teeth so bright did shine
As he led her over the mountain,
Did the sly, bold Reynardine.

Anonymous Ballad

His face was a strong--a very strong--aquiline, with high bridge of the thin nose and peculiarly arched nostrils; with lofty domed forehead, and hair growing scantily around the temples but profusely elsewhere. His eyebrows were very massive, almost meeting over the nose, and with bushy hair that seemed to curl in its own profusion. The mouth, so far as I could see it under the heavy moustache, was fixed and rather cruel looking, with peculiarly sharp white teeth; these protruded over the lips, whose remarkable ruddiness showed astonishing vitality in a man of his years, For the rest, his ears were pale, and at the tops extremely pointed; the chin was broad and strong, and the cheeks firm though thin. The general effect was one of extraordinary pallor... The hands were rather coarse–broad with squat fingers. Strange to say, there were hairs in the centre of the palm. The nails were long and fine and cut to a sharp point. As the Count leaned over me and his hands touched me, I could not repress a shudder.

Bram Stoker, **Dracula**

I. THE VAMPIRE FIGURE

Character Conventions

It is difficult to synthesize a set of conventional characteristics for the vampire in formal fiction, just as it is difficult to isolate the *sine qua non* of the vampire in "actuality" from the considerable diversity of folk tales and historical figures. As new creators continue to add to the body of work, it is inevitable that many of the standard *genre* assumptions about the vampire

53

be tested, that folk-tales and myths, literary, graphic, and cinematic traditions alike be broken down into component parts and form a nearly infinite range of inexhaustible potential for new combinations. In film particularly, the process of formulating a *genre* type is compounded even further by the medium's inherent multiplicity of verbal, visual and aural expressions. Obviously, the core of the fiction is the character of the vampire itself, whether described as a vortex of malevolence, lust, and savagery or, alternately, as the unwilling victim who becomes a tormented, driven, even tragic figure. But the fairly standard assumption that he or she, or perhaps more aptly it, is "undead" is still qualified by the lore from which the film-makers draw and expanded by the possibilities of narrative invention. As a result, the vampire in film remains a complex and curiously ambivalent figure, and when the usual icons are decomposed or discarded, when the teeth do not shine so brightly as the rakish Reynardine's, as difficult to penetrate as the phenomena surrounding him are rationally inexplicable.

It is equally clear that, in practical terms, the vampire is not that difficult to recognise. The Byronic figure, seductive, erotic, possessing a hypnotic power which makes its questionable charms seem irresistible to its victims is still the starting point for all but a few film characterisations. Most often, as the *revenant* in order to extend its existence

German Robles and Ariadne Welter in EL ATAUD DEL VAMPIRO

offers sexual pleasure and, coincidentally, appeals to the death wish of its prey, the dramatic interplay between the vampire and its lovers becomes a fusion of basic human instincts, not just self-preservative libidinal but also self-destructive, a ritual of "seeking to" as Freud suggests, "bring them back to their primeval, inorganic states."[1] The bride and groom of the vampire are, like the lists of unfortunates who have captured the fancy of the Greek gods, confronted by a potent metaphysical entity and, without the knowledge of ceremonial or symbolic defenses, killed by advances which are overwhelming by their sheer physical and sexual power. The key to the mythical qualities of Reynardine, Ruthven, Dracula and all those who follow after them in film is in this super-humanness. In a totemic sense these undead represent the arch-need of man to purge himself of his severest repressions, they are tokens through which vicariously the most sacred of taboos may be violated and sins that cry to heaven for vengeance committed. They rise up out of men's hidden fears *and* desires, glorying in their revulsive appetites and endowed with an epic quality like that of Milton's striding, primordial Death:

> To me, who with eternal famine pine,
> Alike is Hell, or Paradise, or Heaven,
> There best where most with ravin I may meet:
> Which here, though plenteous, all too little seems
> To stuff this maw, this vast unhidebound corpse.
> (**Paradise Lost** X, 597-601)

Most often then, the vampire is, like Satan, a ruthless stalker of men, attaining the life-blood of the body through the soul, possessing its lover in all senses of the word by instilling a cupidity for love and death in the mind of its object and simultaneously fulfilling it. The very nature of the undead state, willed or unwilled, violates not only the Christian concepts of life and afterlife but the dispassionate, intellectual notions of love as well. Small wonder then that Reynardine requires "concealment all from the pious men," because, for these most basic of reasons, the vampire is unnatural, sometimes definitely diabolical, and by virtue of its loathsome practices necessarily antithetical to society and its values.

Narrative and Visual Conventions

Beyond the character archetype which film has refined from a variety of sources, elements of the narrative and the *mise-en-scène*—from the locales, costumes, and make-up to the lighting and sound effects—have

[1.] **Civilization and Its Discontents**.

also been conventionalised to varying degrees.

To begin with the vampire films are set, almost without exception, over the last one hundred and fifty years, which has come to mean that the action is set either sometime during the Nineteenth century or contemporary to the date of production—the former, as it happens usually being the case with European and Mexican productions (probably because of their more diverse architectural history and easier access to baronial houses, medieval churches, and other older structures) and the latter with American films. The implications of the period setting, which is by far the most frequently chosen of the two, are manifold in terms of specific imagery: Victorian cities with gas-lit, cobblestoned avenues and alleyways alternate with country manors and mountainous castles containing what H. P. Lovecraft has called the "dramatic paraphernalia" of fantasy in general:

> First of all the Gothic castle with its awesome antiquity, vast distances and ramblings, dark corridors, unwholesome hidden catacombs . . . and the infinite array of strange lamps, damp trap-doors, extinguished lights, mouldy hidden manuscripts, creaking hinges, shaking arras, and the like.[2]

Perhaps even more significant than these recognised icons, in relation to the expectations which the average viewer brings to the *genre*, is the notion that there was a general lack of sophistication in the 19th and early 20th centuries. Insulated from the people of that era by this sense of temporal, ethical, and practical distance the audience can accept and participate empathetically in the reality of that time's belief in vampires. Reinforcing this narrative assumption is a rather basic iconography. A traveller's reliance on horsedrawn conveyances, the necessity of passing through long stretches of open country and dense forests where night descends like a blanket, even in the towns and villages where a ground fog turns the high street into a sea of mist—everyday realities like these in a period context are suddenly rife with threatening elements, so that a shift to the still more alien locus of a mountain landscape or the high-vaulted cobwebbed interior of a *schloss* or tenebrous crypt becomes inevitably perilous, a clear sign to those having a minimal awareness of how the *genre* functions of imminent danger and perhaps approaching death.

As much as apprehension of dying or simple dread of the unknown engages the viewer's involvement with the narrative—and again the greater expressive impact of period makes it more acceptable to stage extremely melodramatic occurrences without testing viewer suspension

---

[2]. H. P. Lovecraft, "Supernatural Horror in Literature" in **Dagon** (New York, 1969).

of disbelief too severely—the converse, the fear that the vampire's audacity and power will preserve him from annihilation, has established a catalogue of events which are most likely to define the conflict between the human protagonist and vampiric antagonist. After the presence of the undead has been demonstrated—either directly by including an actual attack in the narrative or indirectly by the discovery of a blood-drained victim or victims—there normally follows an exhibition of the vampire's peculiar attributes (invulnerability to conventional weapons; preternatural strength; and/or metamorphoses into bat, wolf, etc.) common to legend but which only motion pictures, by means of special effects (bullets passing through to explode against the wall behind the figure; men and heavy objects being hurled aside like gimcracks; optical mattes and superimpositions achieving the change in form) can give those ascribed traits the impact of a high degree of graphic reality. After the particular protective devices—cross, wolfsbane, mirror, or whatever—are introduced, film is again uniquely capable of rendering the destruction of a vampire with grisly actuality, and the ritual of staking, burning, or beheading is usually enhanced by a visual contrivance which reduces the once-animated corpse to ashes or dust. Whether it is the illusion or the very melodrama of seeing these things happen on screen—with slight variations from the pattern in the face of innumerable repetitions of the basic scheme—they continue to elicit the most substantial viewer response, to constitute the narrative and visual foundations of the entire genre, which any individual motion picture may play with or against but cannot ignore.

II. DRACULA

Stoker's description of Count Dracula reproduced at the beginning of this chapter is the seminal portrait of that character from which all succeeding interpretations must theoretically be constructed; and yet it is quite apparent that the universally recognised film Dracula, who is in both attire and aspect the epitome of the male vampire, derives from other sources. Of all the incarnations of undead Transylvanian noblemen, from the spectral Max Schreck to the panther-like Christopher Lee, from slender, soft-spoken John Carradine to the heavy-set, belligerent Lon Chaney Jr., from the sinister German Robles in Mexico's *Nostradamus* series to the effete Robert Quarry as the campish Count Yorga, no other has so dominated the role and infused it with his personal mannerisms as the Hungarian, Bela Lugosi. It is somewhat ironic that Lugosi—who moved from the stage production to the film role because of Lon Chaney Sr.'s untimely death—should

Bela Lugosi as "Dracula" on the stage, circa 1928

Top: Lon Chaney as Count Alucard/Dracula with his wife, Louise
Allbritton in SON OF DRACULA

Below: Christopher Lee in DRACULA—PRINCE OF DARKNESS

John Carradine in HOUSE OF DRACULA

so completely *become* Dracula, that the countenance and speech of this quasi-fictional Carpathian boyar[3] should be so irrevocably linked with Lugosi's pallid expressions and peculiar rendering of what Stoker dubbed a "strange intonation."[4] It could be argued that Schreck was more cosmetically terrifying, that Carradine has more grace, Chaney more brute force, Lee more erotic energy and sheer presence, that any of them were closer in some way to Stoker's original idea; but whenever a comic breaks into a vampire parody, the accent and florid gestures, the thick "Good Ev-e-ning," are unmistakably Lugosi's. The perpetuation of the Lugosi Dracula via televised airings of his old pictures and advertising in which mimics sell hair spray, throat remedies, and even hot dogs, and in the face of dozens of later *Dracula* adaptations, is so dominant a factor that a reader of the novel who has experienced all of this may try to visualize Stoker's own version

[3.] For details of Stoker's borrowing from the history of Vlad Tepes see McNally and Florescu's books **In Search of Dracula** and **Dracula: A Historical Biography.**
[4.] No doubt accentuated by the fact that Lugosi's poor English compelled him to read his lines phonetically on stage and in the early films.

Christopher Lee with gray hair and moustache in EL CONDE DRÁCULA

of the character—stockier, older, with bushy grey hair, a moustache, and a "very strong" face—only to have the image of Lugosi, caped and top-hatted, coming out of the fog to mesmerise a doomed flower girl, force its way in.

This very genuine stereotypification of the Dracula figure adds to the list of expectations already associated with the *genre*, so that the dark clothes and full-flowing red-lined cape, the hair brushed back straight and flat from the forehead, the lips extraordinarily crimson and distended in an eerie smile which reveals abnormally long canines are specifically as common to the Hammer productions starring Lee as to the Lugosi vehicles made by Universal. Even Lee's most recent essay of the role in *Count Dracula* (*El conde Dracula*, 1971, directed by Jesus Franco), which claims to be a return to the novel's description, retains many of these aspects. Accordingly, the list of male vampires in motion pictures who adhere to the basic conception represented by Lugosi in the Thirties and Forties and by Lee since the Hammer series began is a lengthy one—Lugosi himself in *Dracula* (1931),

Mark of the Vampire, Return of the Vampire, and numerous cameos; Carradine in *House of Frankenstein, House of Dracula,* and *Billy the Kid vs. Dracula;* Chaney in *Son of Dracula;* Francis Lederer in *Curse of Dracula;* Lee in *Dracula* (1958) , *Dracula, Prince of Darkness, Taste the Blood of Dracula, Dracula has Risen from the Grave, Scars of Dracula, Dracula A.D. 1972, Count Dracula,* and the comedy *Uncle Was a Vampire;* Robles as Nostradamus and Count Duval in a half-dozen titles; Quarry in *Count Yorga—Vampire, Return of Count Yorga,* and *The Deathmaster;* and finally Jack Palance in *Dracula* (1974) to cite only the most widely-seen films and discounting sympathetic portrayals which will be discussed later.

All this is not to say that the typing of the male vampire is total or rigid, that the characterisations of Dracula or the narrative and expressive values of the various films which feature him, by name or by implication, are of an inflexible sameness; but their diversity and invention are perhaps best explored and understood from the context of these well-established and truly world-wide (one has only to glance at the make-up of the title character of Japan's *Lake of Dracula* for confirmation of that) conventions of the genre.

Nosferatu

F. W. Murnau's *Nosferatu* (1922), the first film version of **Dracula**, remains to this day the most imagistically unusual and expressionistic of all the adaptations.[5] The opening is a quote from Van Helsing [Prof. Bulwer] followed by a hazy panorama of Bremen with a church spire in the nearground, and the introduction of Harker [Hutter] and his wife, Mina [Ellen]. Besides the evocation of period, these shots set a tone, in the immediate tension between foreground and rearground and the array of detail in a deep frame, of unseen forces in contention, reinforced by the overt determinism of the dialogue ("Wait, young man—you cannot escape your destiny by running away"). Harker is dispatched by Renfield [Knock], a sinister bald-headed man in a tight fitting tail-coat who reads cabbalistic inscriptions, to Orlof's castle with an equally overt warning: "Do not be surprised if people speak of Transylvania as a land of phantoms." Harker's arrival in the land of phantoms—after he has consigned Mina to the care of Lucy Westenra [Annie Harding] and her husband—resembles the same scene in the novel, but is full of visual novelties from the simple insert of a lurking jackal to the use of under-cranking and a negative image as Orlof's

5. Murnau's Dracula is called Count Orlock or Orlof and the rest of the character names were also altered, which along with changes in the plot was designed to avoid legal difficulties since the producer did not have permission to adapt the Stoker novel then protected by unexpired international copyright. Certain English-language prints restored the original names—Harker for Hutter, Renfield for Knock, etc.—in the titles.

NOSFERATU: the vampire aboard the ship

funereal coach arrives to pick up Harker in a sustained long shot. Besides these manifestly surreal effects, Schreck's make-up—he resembles a giant bat with an oversized cranium, sunken eyes, a beak nose set above long crooked teeth, and tufts of white hair about his pointed ears—the shots of shadows cast by his thin body or gaunt hands with mandarin-like nails and back-lit views of his unnatural frame in Gothic archways become unsettling visual motifs. The many iris shots hint at enclosure, constriction of the image which graphically supports Orlof's unequivocal, "You cannot escape;" moreover, the Count's remark on seeing a miniature of Mina—"Is this your wife? What a lovely throat."—and the parallel montage between Mina's "somnambulistic dream" and Orlof's spectre looming over the hapless Harker combine to suggest the vampire's disquieting ability towards thought projection and mind control. Murnau's stylisation persists long after the plot disjointedly interfaces with the novel: more undercranking as Orlof leaves for Bremen with a load of coffins and slaughters the crew of the schooner that transports him during a gale; Van Helsing lecturing on the Venus fly-trap intercut with Renfield catching flies in a sanatorium; Mina reading a letter from Harker along the beach, where the same onshore winds which carry Orlof towards the city have bent the cemetery crosses to the ground.

The shift away from Transylvania and the intrinsic temporal distortions to the psycho-sexual conflict between the undead and Mina inspires an extrinsic change in pacing. As the plague spreads over Bremen and rats follow in Orlof's wake, Murnau orchestrates his self-styled "symphony of terrors" with fluctuating tempos, employing long takes and compositions of depth and great contrast for the processional lines of dead but shorter cuts as the escaped Renfield is pursued down narrow alleyways and across the rooftops. Orlof watching Mina's room from the window of a house across the street stands rigid and unblinking; while she paces frenziedly, having gained possession of the "Book of the Vampire" which Harker found at Castle Orlof, and prays for strength to sacrifice herself to end the chain of vampiric killings. The film's final effect is pressed into service after Orlof is seduced into remaining with her until after sunrise: he writhes and disintegrates as the light strikes him; Mina expires as well.

Coming as it does at the head of a very long list of films, *Nosferatu* can only be situated generically in retrospect. Thematically, Murnau discovers the potential of narrative distortions and externalised dream states from the beginning, using *mise-en-scène* to alternately condense and expand certain events—both interiorly when he tampers with camera speed and exteriorly in the selection and duration of shots in

NOSFERATU: Nina by the ocean

NOSFERATU: Orlof is caught by the first rays of the sun

his editing scheme—to detach his narrative cleanly from the convention
of realism and relocate it elsewhere. While Murnau's visual contriv-
ances—the undercranking; the negative insertions; doors opening by
themselves; the dissolution of the vampire—have not all become part
of the lexicon of the *genre's* recurring special effects, his choice of an
extra-normal style for such a subject, that was already well-grounded
in the various horror and fantasy films made before *Nosferatu,* bridged
that tradition and all subsequent vampire films. One addition to the
Stoker plot—the vampire's fatal susceptibility to sunlight, whereas the
novel's character was able to emerge during the day suffering only the
impairment of certain faculties such as transformation—has since become a generic constant which is seldom violated. More significantly,
Murnau's expressionistic frenzy demonstrated that an exposition and
treatment of the Dracula figure which is essentially visual can easily be
as dramatic in engendering suspense and eliciting viewer response as
the dialogue confrontations of the popular Deane-Balderston play.

The Expressionistic Tradition in America

Tod Browning's *Dracula* (1931), the earliest sound film in the *genre,*
represents its first synthesis of stage and cinematic traditions. Browning "opens up" the play as soon as the titles fade with a process shot
of a stagecoach in the narrow defile of the Borgo Pass; but the immediate connotations are not particularly ominous. Inside the conveyance
a bespectacled tourist placidly leafs through a guidebook, and the

Bela Lugosi and Helen Chandler in DRACULA (1931)

broadlit location exteriors appear relatively free from threat. Renfield (fulfilling the part played by Harker in the analogous portion of the novel) is isolated visually from the others by a panning shot as he dismounts at the way-station, but this remains undeveloped as a verbal exposition supersedes—"It's Walpurgis Night. The night of evil. Nosferatu," and, "At the Castle there are vampires: Dracula and his wives. They take the form of the wolves and bats and feed on the blood of the living." The peasants' exaggerated warnings and repeated signs of the cross might normally be neutralised by Renfield's undiminished resolve to proceed to Castle Dracula ("That's just superstition . . . it's a matter of business with me") , but for the fact that the evocation of the *genre* has already directed viewer expectations in a certain direction.

The remainder of the prologue is a justifiably classic introduction of the Dracula figure: the emergence of the vampire and his wives from the subterranean coffins; the hovering bat which leads Renfield's carriage up to the Count's fortified mountain lair; the huge oaken door which opens with a cracking sound that suggests centuries of disuse and within the disarray and debris through which rats and armadillos forage; finally, Dracula himself descending the stairs with a candle that casts a feeble light over the massive stonework and solemnly intoning, "Listen to them, the children of the night. What music they make!" Karl Freund's photography—which never manages to hit Lugosi squarely with an eye-light—is remarkably controlled in this and other large interiors, on the one hand rendering the great hall with a somber expansiveness and on the other creating a suffocating intensity in the chambers upstairs, as Dracula hungrily watches his prey squeeze a drop of blood from a cut finger, a sequence which ends in a sustained shot after the stifled Renfield faints and the wives approach only to be turned back by Dracula who then bends to the prostrate man's neck.

Little of the rest of the film compares with this first portion. Visually, the few conspicuously stylised usages—the shadow of the dead schooner captain lashed to the wheel, reminiscent of *Nosferatu*; the craning shot across the sanatorium lawn up to and through the window of Renfield's room; the glimpse of Dracula and Lucy, after she has become "the bloofer lady," prowling in the park hedges—stand out without much effect, dispersed as they are between long dialogue scenes staged in medium and medium close shot. Even the return to architectonic vastness in the concluding sequence at Carfax Abbey is flattened by full-light and lenses of greater focal-length. Throughout the narrative, the most extraordinary events are reported rather than visualised—"He came to me; he opened a vein in his arm and made me drink"—as Browning is content to cutaway at the critical moment of every attack and indulge in ironic touches (as when Harker seeing the wounds on Mina's throat asks, "What could have caused them, Professor?" or the maid announces "Count Dracula" in voiceover before Van Helsing can reply). The ability to hypnotise and assume a bat-like shape are givens which are never reinforced by means of convincing optical work—the bat hovering outside Lucy's window returns to human shape through the benefit of a cut to the sleeping woman and a pan back to Lugosi at the foot of the bed—and never achieve even the understated impact of the simple device earlier in the film that has Dracula slip through a cobweb on the stairs of his castle, which the corporeal

Renfield cannot penetrate, to occasion a sardonic observation: "A spider spinning his web for the unwary fly. The blood is the life, Mr. Renfield." Even the hint of weariness which Dracula lets slip at the opera—"To die, to be really dead, that must be glorious . . . there are worse things awaiting man than death."—bespeaks a certain consciousness of lingering humanity on his part which is never amplified in later scenes. In a film which is already excessively verbal, Dracula, given increasingly to casual observations rather than action and more often spoken of than he is present on screen, assumes an off-handed haughtiness in his encounters with Van Helsing; although the latter interpreted by Edward Van Sloan with stolid determination and armed with wolfsbane, mirrors, and crosses is more than a fair match and wrests an admission of that ("Your will is strong, Van Helsing") and a wry compliment ("For a man who has not lived even one lifetime, you are wise, Van Helsing") from his adversary.

Perhaps the root difficulty with this *Dracula* is that even though modern (1931) London and Transylvania are thoroughly camouflaged, Van Helsing's dismay that "the strength of the vampire is that people will not believe in him" and his assertion that "yesterday's myth is today's science" are too insistent, too much the pronouncements of a Nineteenth century man undercut by a contemporary context of which he is markedly unaware. His single-minded combat with the undead is encapsulated but unable to carry the entire film. Mina's precipitous eroticism, transferred from Lucy in the novel, is introduced in the last reel; the laying to rest of "the bloofer lady" is not even included in the narrative. After an overabundance of static scenes, the film is stripped of a climax as Van Helsing stakes Dracula off-screen, with only a dull thud and a groan bearing witness to the event.

Browning followed *Dracula* with *Mark of the Vampire* (1935). Again there are the Eastern-European setting, the knowing professor, and some exquisitely Baroque images of dark figures moving through obscure passageways or of Luna flying with ragged silk wings like some decayed waterfowl, photographed by James Wong Howe with as much bravura as the menacing prologue of the earlier film. Again also there is reliance on expository dialogue, unavoidably so in the disclosure that all of it has been an elaborate sham to trap a commonplace murderer, which dissipates almost totally the iconic potential that has been built up.

In many ways, Robert Siodmak's *Son of Dracula* (1943) represents the liberation of the Dracula figure from these traditional, stagebound constructions. To begin with, the vampire itself is reduced to a subordinate role; but vampirism as a moral and ontological question becomes thematically central. While Count Alucard—a crude Dracula anagram—is treated more as a phenomenon than an actual personage, his scenes remain the expressive core of the film. His initial appearance is part of an elaborate craning shot, which—in contrast to the example of this technique in *Dracula*—pulls back from a dance in a country estate, travelling across a terrace and garden and stops abruptly on a high angle medium close shot of Alucard gazing at the house, a revelation which is sudden and startling despite the anticipatory camera movement, almost as if the figure had drawn attention to itself or somehow intruded into the frame while remaining immobile. Established by the dynamic of this shot as a force to be reckoned with, Alucard momentarily spreads his cape, compresses his massive form into that of a bat, and departs. The vampire's first nocturnal rising is equally impressive: a coffin breaks the surface of the swamp water, a mist seeps out from beneath the lids, congeals, and becomes the vampire who then propels the strange vessel forward by some psycho-kinetic command towards an eager victim awaiting him on the bank (the shot is taken from over Alucard's shoulder, floating silently with him across the pond).

Kay Caldwell, Alucard's willing victim, is less obsessed with him than with the freedom from death which he symbolises. Inheriting a Southern plantation house after her father is killed by Alucard, she rejects her former lover and marries the Count in order to become undead and immortal herself. After Frank Stanley, the discarded suitor, inadvertantly shoots her, when the bullets he intends for Alucard pass through his insubstantial "body" and into hers, she is reanimated and appears to him, in jail for her murder, to explain the premeditation behind her actions ("Frank, isn't eternity together better than a few years of ordinary life?") and to convert him to vampirism. This sequence of impacted narrative ironies which reduce the Dracula figure to something of a cipher for Kay Caldwell's aspirations towards eternal life speculates ambitiously on the notion of immortality so pivotal to the myth of the vampire.

Eventually, Frank eliminates Alucard by burning his coffin full of native earth hidden in a viaduct, then he immolates Kay in an upper room of her house. As the natural equilibrium of a complete and genuine cessation of life is restored, the staging which concludes the film—cross-travellings to underscore the once arrogant vampire's impotent terror on descrying the fiery coffin; a close shot of him rim-lit by the flames as he screams, "Put it out!"; a pan, after he staggers and collapses, from the sunbeams which penetrate the sod roof down to his skeletal hand. Or in the final scene, the tissue of gauze draped

Robert Paige mourns his love Louise Allbritton in SON OF
DRACULA

around the bed and framed in the foreground, which is parted by the
fire and falls away to reveal Frank flanked by men who have followed
him from jail before a travelling forward moves in to isolate him in
close-up staring desolately at the pyre, also draws back from the
qualified reality of special effects to the more natural expressions of
lighting and camera movement, from the myth itself to the tragic
dimensions of misguided belief in the promise of that myth.

While both *Dracula* and *Son of Dracula* are contemporary in their
setting, so that strictly speaking they initiate the tendency towards up-
dating traditional material peculiar to U.S. productions, a condition
roughly analogous to that of a period locale is achieved in these
pictures not only through stylisation of image and decor but also by
avoiding many temporal indicators. Little more than an occasional auto
horn on the soundtrack or the fashion of the costumes betray the 1930
London *Dracula*, and the situation of the action in the back country
and marshland of the South similarly insulates *Son of Dracula* from the
pressing realities of war-time 1943.

When the expressionistic approach fostered in pictures such as these

by Universal studios ended in the late Forties, the vampire film in
America went into a dormant stage. Curious *genre* experiments such as
the vampire Western, *Curse of the Undead* (1959) in which the title
figure, dressed all in black, is vanquished in a gunfight by an opponent
with silver bullets in his revolver; quasi-science fiction in films like
The Vampire (1957) ; or the "shadow-of-a-doubt" vampirism of *Return
of Dracula* (1957) in which a Dracula figure impersonates the Eastern-
European cousin of a small-town family to gain a secure base of operations but is unmasked by a suspicious teenage daughter—all these con-
tributed to a confusion and breakdown of *genre* expectations built up
by earlier releases. Not until the 1970's—ten years after the revival of
the vampire film began in Europe and Mexico—did the undead return
to the screen in the United States in sufficient numbers to reconstitute
a *genre* identity.

Count Yorga, Vampire (1970) relocates an undead Transylvanian
nobleman in the conspicuously modern precincts of Los Angeles, opening with a title sequence which follows his coffin from a docked freighter
onto a flatbed truck, then over freeways and through business districts
to his new home. Although that home is a large estate surrounded by
park land, and the vampire himself recalls in dress and make-up the

Michael Pate as the vampire with Kathleen Crowley in CURSE
OF THE UNDEAD

Above and right:
The Two Faces of
Count Yorga, Vampire
(Robert Quarry)

prominent features of Lugosi, Chaney, or Carradine, the narrative consciously plays against both the anachronism of his appearance and speech and the obvious fact that he "looks," as someone is made to remark early in the film, "like a vampire." The challenge to his antagonists when faced with the realisation that he is precisely what his stereotyped aspect would suggest then becomes not merely to find the wherewithal to defeat him—their skepticism about the "normal" methods, about the efficacy of garlic or a cross makes them hesitant to rely on such silly or apocryphal remedies against a being which had been classed with unicorns and dragons in their belief—but also to remain convinced themselves while persuading others of the accuracy of their perceptions. "You've got to be kidding—a vampire!" is the kind of modern response which must almost of necessity occur somewhere in the course of the dialogue. *Count Yorga* approaches this inherent problem of having to address viewer disbelief, undiminished by any sense of pastness in the narrative and undistracted by a strong, mythic iconography, rather obliquely by retreating into parody and puns and by exploiting the alternate distractions of sex and violence—typified in Yorga's unexpected assault on a couple in a parked van. The characters' own disbelief continues to make them self-conscious, so that along

Roman Polanski and Jack MacGowran in clothes stolen from two vampires in DANCE OF THE VAMPIRES

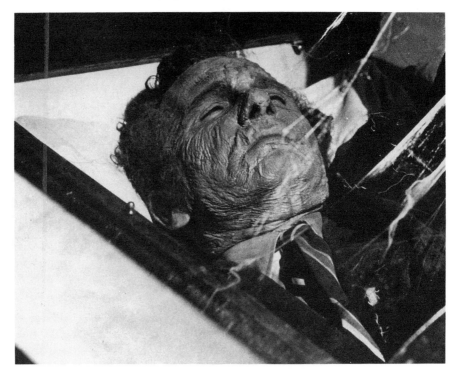

Michael Pataki before rejuvenation in GRAVE OF THE VAMPIRE

with the audience they cannot fully shake the impression of being only a step away from the ridiculous, from absurdity and buffoonery such as that of the inept Prof. Abronsius and Alfred in Roman Polanski's *Fearless Vampire Killers* (*Dance of the Vampires*) (1967). Ultimately, this vacillation between seriousness and satire in *Count Yorga* (which is common to other titles such as *Blood of Dracula's Castle* or *Scream, Blacula, Scream*), this situation of the picture being midway between the clear comedy of a film like Polanski's and a straight treatment reduces its integrity both as drama and as genre piece to the point where it loses its interior reality.

A more direct confrontation of the paradox of the modern-day vampire is illustrated in recent productions like the made-for-television *The Night Stalker* (1972) or *Grave of the Vampire* (1974). The former retains the essential demonic Dracula figure, "Janos Skorzeny," whom the plot eventually discloses as a Rumanian of relatively recent (1899) birth who also happens to be a voracious undead. His powers, in terms of *genre* precedents, are literally awesome. Equally invulnerable to a hail of police bullets or a battering with nightsticks, he overcomes dozens of men in a raid on a blood bank and in a later pursuit

through surburban backyards. In both instances, the juxtaposition
within the frame of helmeted, uniformed police with the gaunt, dark
form of the vampire, illuminated by gunbursts as he throws men aside
like rag dolls, sets up an opposition of iconic readings—that is, prag-
matically omnipotent police versus mythically omnipotent vampire—
which simultaneously tests and supports this hybrid of *genre* types.
The viewer encounters this vampiric presence like the used-car dealer
in the film does—"Something inside says don't mess with this guy. He's
a creep . . . with those red eyes and that voice"—on a visceral level of
raw strength and graphic violence.

The Night Stalker like *Son of Dracula* is less concerned with the
persona of the vampire than it is with the abstract, mythic implications
of his existence. The narrative framework—an ostracised reporter's
diary-form recollections which flashback to a series of murders in Las
Vegas—assumes a point-of-view which is already convinced of the
authenticity of that existence; and yet Kolchak, the reporter, has both
a detached precision—his voiceover account introduces scenes with a
detailed journalistic chronology ("Sunday, approximately two-thirty
A.M., the corner of Fremont and Central . . .") and description of
events—and a sardonic style (one victim is simply "125 luscious pounds
minus twelve pints of blood") to go with his straw hat and brash
manner, to guarantee a minimum of continuing viewer identification
with his predetermined perspective. While the narration and dialogue
play with the question in the abstract (can vampires exist? if so, how?)
during the press conferences and Kolchak's arguments with his editor,
the visuals treat the actual attacks or the coroner's examination as
occurrences without need of qualification, as things real because they
are on the screen, while preserving the referent of Kolchak's point-of-
view for certain puzzling details (the viewer like him can never do
more than speculate, not having seen the action, on whether the
second woman's body was thrown a hundred yards into a dry creekbed),
so that the film's own base reality of image never questions the
verisimilitude of vampirism. And while the plot may be full of modern
conceits (the blood bank; the vampire keeping a hostage alive on
plasma in order to have a ready supply of blood in his house), it is by
and in the presence of more traditional objects (cross, stake, the coffin
of earth, even the isolated rented house heavily-curtained against the
intrusion of sunlight) that the vampire is finally trapped and executed.

Grave of the Vampire (1974) restores to the title figure a character
function equal in importance to that of the non-vampire antagonists.
Again the fact that it is contemporary—the film has a prologue that
takes place in the Forties but is predominantly set in the present—

compels a certain amount of self-consciousness about the subject matter but not much compared to either *Count Yorga* or *The Night Stalker*. The undead of this film was a sorcerer and premeditated murderer in his first life and continues so in his vampiric phase, which he camouflages by working as a professor of the occult (night classes only), who occasionally practices what he teaches on his women students. The more interesting personage, however, is his son, conceived in rape, half human, half vampire (he is weaned on his mother's blood and survives to adulthood by eating raw meat), and bent on finding and killing his father in a situation charged with Oedipal connotations. By underlining the character conflicts and, fatalistically, by delaying the full inheritance of the son's proclivity to vampirism until after he has overcome his sire, this motion-picture, like *The Night Stalker*, succeeds to a great degree where *Count Yorga* and other productions fail, in transcending and reinterpreting many of the more rigid conventions of the genre.

Nostradamus

In 1956, the Mexican film industry began production of a cycle of vampire films which carry on the eclectic and extravagant expressionism of Universal studios. Beginning with *The Vampire* (*El vampiro*, 1956) the films freely recruited elements from the catalogue of both sublime and ridiculous *genre* conventions. Dense ground fogs and manor houses flanked by spectral forests are the locations for the operations of such undead noblemen as Count Duval in *The Vampire* and Count Swobota in *World of the Vampires* (1960). While the former portrays the vampire as a blood-sucking gigolo who uses his erotic appeal to captivate and live off the maiden aunt of the heroine and who is easily reduced to smouldering remains by a semi-comic doctor, *World of the Vampires* imposes its particular lore on a revenge narrative—the vampire has come to the new world to annihilate the descendants of a family which persecuted his ancestors in Hungary—including a Transylvanian melody with "certain combinations of notes" which raise the dead and play as much havoc with a vampire's senses as the sight of a cross. Both Duval and Swobota wear the classic make-up and the formal suit with high-collared cape, which inspires admiration for their "mysterious" good looks in women and contempt in men ("Jealous? Of a man who dresses as if he were at a carnival"). While there is generally a competent deployment of standardised visual usages in these films' art direction and cinematography—a travelling into a victim in bed and pan to her window is followed by a shot of Count Swobota standing amid some ruins and summoning her hypnotically; continued intercutting as she rises and walks, windswept and anxious, through the woods, while he waits with a keylight on his eyes reminiscent of *Dracula*—there are also glaring lapses in production value, such as the ludicrous, over-sized rubber masks and gloves worn by Swobota's fur-covered bat-like minions.

This dichotomy between levels of expression, between the imaginative and the banal, is nowhere more apparent than in the Santo series, featuring a masked wrestler in a succession of real-life matches with vampires and associated fiends. *Samson Versus the Vampire Women* (*Santo contra las mujeres vampiras*, 1962) , for example, focuses on a blood cult of female undead who dress in white robes (resembling the gowns of the wives in *Dracula*) which mysteriously change colour to black when they enter their coffins. Interspersed with scenes in which Santo single-handedly overcomes these vampire women and their henchmen—including a finale in which he takes a torch and incinerates a line of them lying in propped-up wooden boxes in a sustained medium shot accentuated by the fetishistic use of flame which has been a motif throughout the film—are shots of the hero driving to the rescue in his sports car and even a number of prolonged bouts between Santo and human opponents in the arena, which bear no relation to the rest of the plot.

The most detailed and consistent of the Mexican Dracula prototypes is Nostradamus, also featured in a series of motion pictures in 1960. Fully as arrogant as any American or European vampire, Nostradamus dresses with a continental flair, sporting a black homburg and a neatly-trimmed steel-grey moustache and van dyke and with the lining of his cape folded back over his shoulders like small white wings. In *Curse of Nostradamus* (*La maldicion de Nostradamus*) , the first of the films, the vampire introduces himself under the pseudonym of Erikson to a Van Helsing analog named Professor Dolenz whose assistance he requests for a "revindication" of the prophesies of the 16th Century astrologer Michael Nostradamus, later revealed to be his father. The repeated zoom-ins to the face of this figure as he promises to commit a dozen murders to extort Dolenz's cooperation and warns him that "You know nothing of my power, power to destroy the whole world," imply in an energetically visual way that he may indeed have more than an imposing presence to back up his threats.

While the plot of *Curse of Nostradamus* wanders through the first half of the proposed killings (the rest are consigned to a sequel entitled *Blood of Nostradamus* [*La sangre de Nostradamus*]), the *mise-en-scène* displays a remarkable consistency in supporting characterisation and exploiting *genre* expectations. Repeated low angle shots of the vampire sustain the feeling of his dominance over men and events introduced in the first scene. In his second meeting with Dolenz, close-ups of Nostradamus are countered with medium close shots of the professor, making him physically larger within the frame as he scoffs at the gun held by his human opponent: "You haven't got the courage . . . you will find that I'm invulnerable to petty human aspirations." More derisive laughter is followed by extra close shots of Nostradamus's mouth ("So fire!") then the gun as it explodes, cutting back to medium shot as Dolenz empties the revolver and a reverse of the room with only the billowing draperies betraying the vampire's departure, unscathed. On a less complex level, a recurrent use of low-light and side-light for "unnatural" effect; the deceptive point-of-view travelling camera into the bedroom of Dolenz's daughter which the viewer takes to be the vampire but turns out to be the professor; the optical device which allows Nostradamus to assume a bat shape when repelled by the Antioch cross; even the simple close-up of the undead's eyes as he takes possession of a bookseller ("My spirit will enter your body") to whom he had brought a first editon of his father's book—all these visualisations produce an expressive ambience which distinguishes the film from the stale, strictly conventional images of most Mexican entries in the *genre*. Although Nostradamus is eventually reduced to crawling rat-like through the sewers and buried in a cave-in after Dolenz and his assistant have pursued him with platinum bullets through torch-lit stone corridors and pillared anterooms, this cultured, impeccably-groomed, and extremely conceited vampire who discusses the ineffable qualities of time and space as well as "petty human aspirations" proved different enough from the pasteboard Duval and Swobota to merit a resurrection so *Curse of Nostradamus* was followed by three sequels in the same year: (*La sangre de Nostradamus* [*Blood of Nostradamus*], *Nostradamus y el genio de las tinieblas* [*Genie of Darkness*], and *Nostradamus y el destructor de monstruos* [*The Monsters Demolisher*]) By the time of *Genie of Darkness*, the novelty of the characterisation had worn thin. The professor continued to track him and the vampire acquired new assistants to replace the collection of dwarves and hunch-backs lost in prior outings; but the critical pieces of parchment, the theft of the vampire's ashes, even the transformations have a mechanical sameness about them which merely accentuates the exhaustion of the character's potential. Only a scene in which he stands by laughing as a woman burns to death recalls some of the striking arrogance of the first film.

Christopher Lee in DRACULA—PRINCE OF DARKNESS

The Hammer Dracula

The only incarnation of the Dracula figure on film to have appeared
in more productions or to survive more intervening years than Lugosi
or the Robles Nostradamus is the Hammer Film version of Stoker's
Count as played by Christopher Lee. Debuting in Terence Fisher's
Dracula in 1958 Lee's interpretation has restored the demonic and
bestial aspects of Dracula lacking in the Universal pictures, without
diminishing the cunning and evil intelligence of the character.
Hunted by a succession of able vampire-killers—most notably Fisher's
Van Helsing in the first film and Father Sandor in *Dracula, Prince of
Darkness* (1965, also directed by Fisher)—Lee's Dracula possesses a
primitive and instinctual dynamism which severely tests the rational
foundations of these men's belief. Although the vampire usually
receives but a fraction of the screen time allotted to his opponents,
he manages to create an aura of menace with his limited presence that
hangs over the whole of the various films.

   In his *Dracula,* Fisher indicates a return to the narrative organisa-
tion of the book (rather than the stage play which formed the basis of
the 1931 adaptation) with a deceptive introduction of the Count
himself. Appearing suddenly at the head of a broad flight of steps,
he strides down threateningly towards Jonathan Harker who is aghast at
what seems to be the prelude to an attack, only to proffer words of

greeting and conduct him upstairs. Dracula's second appearance is more unsettling: as Harker is about to be bitten by one of his wives who has asked his help in escaping, the vampire emerges from a secret passageway, red-eyed and snarling, and flings the woman viciously to the floor. To complement what can only be termed, particularly when compared to the stylised rendition of the same scene in Browning's *Dracula*, this explicitness of action, Fisher discards the conventions of expressionistic lighting and the amorphous cobwebbed expanses of earlier films, choosing to break up his frame instead with the variations of colour and detailed furnishings.

In other respects, Fisher retains and embellishes the pre-existing iconography of the *genre*. The Van Helsing of *Dracula* logs his notes onto a crude dictaphone carried over from the novel, which machine specifically records his serious doubts as a scientific observer about the undead's ability to change his shape or dematerialise. However by *Brides of Dracula* (1960, directed by Fisher) the professor is forced to concede that the bat which assails him may be the altered form of a vampire. Van Helsing's caution, however, is based equally on his fear of the vampire as an entity and his academically-grounded reluctance to hypothesise on the limitations of the known and the unknown. Integral to Fisher's conception of Van Helsing is both a ruthless pragmatism and a troublesome curiosity about ontological secrets. His professor is a Nineteenth Century forerunner of modern para-psychologists whose enthusiasm for the unexplained carries him into the occult and whose questing disregard for risks is fortunately protected by a physical dexterity and an uncanny ability to improvise, so that in *Brides of Dracula* he finds the means to cauterise a vampire's bite by heating an iron in the forge of a stable and in the climax of the earlier film he defeats Dracula himself first by feigning a loss of consciousness when in the vampire's grasp and, after breaking free, by fashioning an improvised cross from the base of two candlesticks. This destruction of the undead at the end of *Dracula* is particularly striking in contrast to the anti-climactic finale of the Universal production: after the vampire is transfixed by the makeshift icon, Van Helsing lunges at a nearby window and tears down the curtain. The shaft of light outlined by the disturbed accumulation of dust catches Dracula's foot and reduces it to a mass of putrid flesh; Van Helsing circles around and forces the whole body back into the killing light, so that the corpse buckles and collapses like a punctured air bag then crumbles to a fine ash (as Stoker describes the dissolution) to be scattered by the wind. Everything is rendered with a careful attention to the graphic details of image and sound in a convincing mixture of physical combat and ritual far removed from the

Christopher Lee threatens his guests in DRACULA—PRINCE OF
DARKNESS

Michael Gough and Peter Cushing find a victim in DRACULA
(1958)

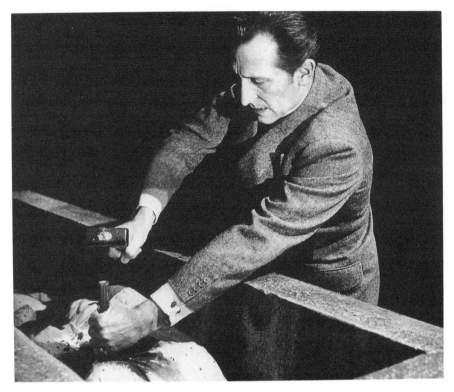

Peter Cushing at work in DRACULA (1958)

subdued, off-screen efficiency of Browning's Van Helsing. Moreover, the destruction of Dracula in the Hammer version comes after two earlier on-screen executions, the first by Harker of Dracula's wife (a staking which transforms her into a wizened corpse) and the second by Van Helsing of Lucy (the novel's erotic "bloofer lady," who the film's Van Helsing drives back into her crypt by branding her forehead with a cross and stakes her after sunrise), both of which are similarly direct in their use of special effects not to mention stage blood to underscore the grisly reality of piercing an undead—which screams out its hatred at the vampire-killer—and laying its soul to rest. But Fisher's violence is not gratuitous, not just a titillating bit of *grand guignol*. Like the savage eroticism which he associates with the vampire in *Dracula* and which Lee and later directors refine to the point where the responses of the young women in *Taste the Blood of Dracula* (1969) unmistakably suggest orgasm, the violence in the Hammer productions is a psychic release, an incontrovertible breakdown of the rational processes of the world and a substantive displacement of the filmic reality, throwing it and the viewer into a chaos which only ritual for the characters and catharsis for the spectators can restore to order.

Perhaps the most successful synthesis of the various generic elements among all the Hammer Dracula films is Fisher's *Dracula—Prince of Darkness*. Opening with a reprise of the last moments of *Dracula*, (vignetted by a diamond-shaped wedge of fog), this "prologue" incorporates a voiceover statement on Van Helsing's triumph:

> Here at last was an adversary armed with sufficient knowledge of the vampire to destroy him . . . thousands had been enslaved by the obscene cult of vampirism—now, the fountainhead himself perished.

Fisher's evolving notion of the vampire as a kind of aberrant but essentially natural phenomenon, as the germ of "an obscene cult" is introduced directly by means of this title and restated on several expressive levels. To begin with, the recapitulation of the concluding moments of the earlier film combined with the dispassionately-read commentary strips the event of almost all its mythopoeic potential, declines to romanticise or elevate Van Helsing's act to the level of anything more than execution of a criminal. In *Brides of Dracula*, the young male vampire is a spoiled son of aristocracy; his profligacy and licentiousness eventually degenerate into what Van Helsing terms the "disease" of vampirism. In *Dracula* the emphasis on the bestial—low angle shots of the Count framed against the rapacious gargoyles which crown the battlements of his castle, Lee's hissing and growling—also hinted at a deteriorative or atavistic cause underlying the vampirism. In *Dracula—Prince of Darkness*, the narrative exposition and expressive imagery re-confirm this naturalistic point-of-view.

The film proper opens with a funeral procession for a young woman. In a long take around her bier, Fisher builds up tension as the dead woman's mother argues with several villagers and a local priest over the disposition of the body, as figures move from foreground to background then the camera pans with the crazed Frau as a man positions a stake over the girl's heart and raises a hammer. Before he can strike, a shot reverberates on the soundtrack. At the moment of maximum anxiety caused by the men's action and the unseen report of a firearm and sustained by the unbroken continuity of image, there is a cut to a low angle long shot of a mounted figure. This stylised introduction of Father Sandor as he rides out of the shadows to accuse the townspeople of "blasphemous sacrilege . . . and superstition," identifies him instantly as a dominant figure and, the viewer anticipates from convention, the representative of reason. Sandor is unusual in that he combines the function of priest (evident from his monkish garb) with those of hunter (the gun he carries) and scientist (his contempt for

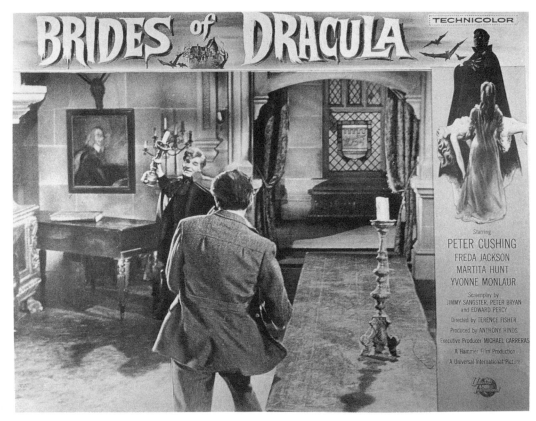

From Terence Fisher's BRIDES OF DRACULA

the villagers' hysteria). While he scoffs at the local people's folk-tales and quaint defences against the unknown ("Garlic to keep out the bogie man"), he cautions the English tourists at the inn who plan to travel on to the next town at night to "at least, stay away from the castle." Such a warning, coming from a man who has confessed that "I enjoy shocking people's sensibilities, but I can be serious" becomes doubly portentous.

As the narrative focuses on two English couples—they have been abandoned by their coachmen at the crossroads near the castle which Sandor counseled them to avoid, and the brasher of the two men convinces the others to board a driverless carriage sent out to meet them— the indications of impending death become more overt. Despite this, Fisher pushes the viewer back into uncertainty by a misleading *mise-en-scène*. The dark silhouette which looms suddenly in the doorway inside the castle is revealed, when it steps into the light, to be nothing more than a servant of Dracula, however sinister. The supper and dialogue are full of ironies—the servant explaining that Dracula made provision to entertain guests after his death because "my master died without issue, sir . . . in the accepted sense of the word;" or the toast proposed by the Englishman, "Here's to him. May he rest in peace"— but Dracula fails to appear, and the expected attack on his guests is withheld. Eventually, the disturbingly "objective" travelling shots which explore the upper corridors after the visitors have retired—objective because they represent no character point-of-view, although the viewer may again be deceived into suspecting that it is the vampire moving down the halls—cedes to a subjective perspective as one of the men follows the servant through a hidden passage down to a cellar where he does discover the crested sarcophagus of Dracula. The camera moves with him as he walks around and examines it, finding it empty, then wanders into an adjoining room where he is stabbed.

Fisher's staging up to this moment has been consistently naturalistic —even the carriage without a driver is treated with an objectivity and lack of manipulation which differs markedly from analogous sequences in both *Nosferatu* and the Lugosi *Dracula*. Further, the handling of the re-animation of Dracula which ensues is the culmination of this detached expositional method, as the servant suspends the dead man's body over the ashen residue of the undead reposing in the funerary stone, punctures the neck, and lets the blood flow out and mix with the dry dust until a blue mist gathers in the well of the sarcophagus and a reformed hand with a red ring abruptly gropes out of it.

Having bridged the gap between the physical and metaphysical in this sequence, the succeeding events fall momentarily into a regular generic pattern. The wife of the sacrificial victim becomes Dracula's bride, while the other couple manages to escape under the protection of the cross; but the vampire pursues them to Sandor's monastery and in a context of increasing violence and defiance of conventional strictures on his behaviour, Dracula penetrates the consecrated building, forces the younger woman to drink from a self-inflicted wound in his chest (transposing a scene with Mina from the novel), and abducts her. In a precipitous conclusion, Father Sandor and her husband destroy his first victim who has become undead, his human servant, and the vampire himself as the monk's gun breaks the icy surface of the castle moat and the caped figure disappears beneath a floe.

Throughout *Dracula—Prince of Darkness*, Fisher refuses to reduce the conflicts to a level of abstraction. Sandor and the Dracula figure are opposed along a number of parallel lines, some of which are symbolic or allegorical, others moral or ethical; but neither impinge on the basic material reality of the frame. If anything the reverse is true,

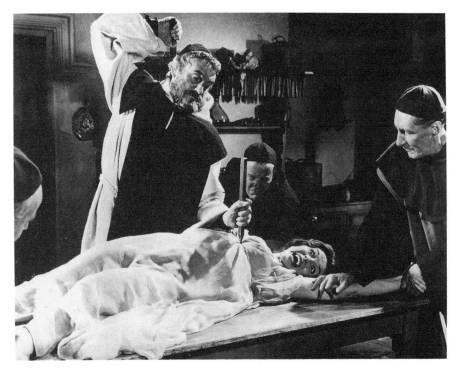

Andrew Keir stakes Barbara Shelley in DRACULA—PRINCE OF
DARKNESS

as Fisher's characters may produce the critical symbols from objects
without inscribed meaning—as in Van Helsing's crossed candlesticks
or the even bolder stroke at the end of *Brides of Dracula* in which a
huge, fiery cross is fashioned from the burning blades of a windmill.
Consequently, the struggles between the characters themselves cannot
be generalised, for, developed as they are through a matter-oriented
interpretation of the *genre's* iconic constructs and actualised in the
minds and bodies of the participants, they define the Hammer Dracula
and his antagonists with an immediacy and concreteness unparalleled
in the *genre*.

Dracula 1974 Vintage

Dracula (1974, directed by Dan Curtis and written by Richard Matheson) is in many ways the most faithful and at the same time the most
innovative film treatment of Stoker's novel. The earliest sequences
between Harker and Dracula in the latter's castle are strikingly similar
to the original both in their naturalness of exposition (Dracula recounting his personal history long into the night; or his very appearance, dressed in a simple grey frock coat and silk tie) and in their use

Christopher Lee and Peter Cushing in DRACULA A.D. 1972

of portents of impending disaster (the pack of wolves which surrounds the castle in the opening shots; the ghostly carriage ride). This sets up an immediate tension between surface appearances and what the viewer familiar with the *genre* knows are the sub-surface realities. Additionally, certain aspects of the novel which are rarely transliterated to the screen—for instance, Mina serving as a medium to track Dracula in the race back to the security of his homeland—are included, while other events are purely the invention of Curtis and Matheson (such as Dracula's freeing a wolf from the Scarborough Zoo to attack Arthur Holmwood).

Stylistically, the tone of the film is naturalistic. The use of titles ("Bistritz, Hungary, May, 1897") over shot to establish time and place suggests a quasi-historical or journal-like progression which resembles the novel. The images themselves are of interiors which are mostly full-lit, crypts where the detail of the Gothic arches and stonework is visible and not lost in *chiaroscuro*, and exterior scenes photographed under cloudy skies (Harker's arrival in Bistritz; the "Vesta" aground on the beach at Whitby), rain (Lucy's funeral), or a simulated moonlight—little which recalls the expressionism of previous adaptations. The acting as well is subdued, lacking in broad gestures or strange intonations. The unusual effects which are present become, in context, the more dramatically unsettling. The tilted angles which introduce numerous sequences become an unavoidably disturbing motif—particularly when the tilted shot is constructed from the strong, tipped verticals of a corridor or passageway—which figuratively externalise the metaphysical imbalance that hangs over the film as a whole. The elaborate camera movement when Dracula arrives in England—a side-travelling and pan around a dead sailor lashed to the schooner wheel in the foreground then a zoom into Dracula standing alone and windswept on the beach below with a single box of native earth at his feet—becomes in contrast to the earlier visual treatment of him doubly ominous.

Undoubtedly, what makes this film Dracula exceedingly different from both the Stoker conception and the other adaptations is the sympathy with which the title figure is treated. This is not to say that his demonic characteristics are underplayed. His blood obsession (typified in the scene in which Mina is compelled to drink from self-inflicted wounds in his chest) ; his arrogance ("So, you play your wits against mine, me who commanded armies hundreds of years before you were born") ; his herculean strength (he overpowers at least a dozen men in his attack on an inn) ; his bestiality (he howls like a wolf, although he never transforms himself into any animal) ; and his mesmeric abilities (over both men and animals) are all present, true to certain conventions. But this Dracula suffers from a kind of existential anguish which draws him closer to the vampires treated in the next section than to Stoker's creation *per se*. He is to a great extent a Romantic figure, not merely in the Byronic mould but in the ironic suggestions of the large portrait of him (as Vlad Tepes) in the midst of battle astride a white horse and brandishing a scimitar (strongly reminiscent of Gericault's "Mounted Officer of the Imperial Guard") and in the flashbacks, from his point-of-view, to a woman who died during his natural life. In a very real sense, it is the burden of this past rather than his present vampirism which inspires Dracula's violent and irrational actions. He is distressed at the sight of blood when Harker cuts himself shaving less from any repressed desire to drink it than, it seems, from the realisation which it forces upon him that he is no longer human. A truer loss of control is evidenced in the mental disturbance of the flashbacks, which are brought on by the sight of a photograph of Lucy Westenra who resembles the woman in his fixated memory.

Dracula's "tryst" with Lucy on the lawn of her home in England combines the dynamic of cross-tracking (intercutting between a receding camera travelling back from her as she walks and a forward track from her viewpoint in towards him), which suggests in a direct visual way something of the magnetism of his being, the sexuality of their embraces, and her clearly orgasmic reaction to his bite with the sentimental associations of the music-box theme on the soundtrack, a melody first heard over his flashbacks and represents his former love. Consequently, his seduction and murder of Lucy is as much an attempt to recapture this lost love as it is to fulfill the needs of his "disease." When she becomes undead. he tries to rejoin her only to discover that she has been staked by Van Helsing. In a rage of despair—intercut with a final flash of memory back to the death of the woman in his first life—he demolishes the crypt then circles around inside it in a moment of impotence and frustration reminiscent of the closing shot of *Scream, Blacula, Scream* (both photographed from a high angle emphasising the futility of the figure's gestures). Even the final scene of his destruction—he is debilitated by sunlight and speared by Van Helsing but does not, as is traditional deteriorate into dust—ends with a travelling shot past his corpse into the portrait on the wall accompanied by a fanfare of martial music and a title explaining Dracula's historical "actuality" which mitigate the monstrousness of the character.

III. THE SYMPATHETIC MALE VAMPIRE

Africa, the dark land where voodoo drums beat in the night, where the jungles are deep and full of secrets and the moon that lights them is still a mystic moon. Africa, where men have not forgotten the evil they learned in the dawn of time. I always come back to Africa; but even here there is no rest for me. The path of time is curved upon itself like a circle, without beginning, without end. I must follow it forever. I cannot die. I cannot rest. I cannot rest. I cannot rest.

Webb Fallon in *The Vampire's Ghost*

"And I was once happy," he said mournfully, "once happy because I was innocent. Oh! gracious Heaven, how long am I to suffer?"

Varney the Vampyre

In distinct contrast to the Dracula figure is a much smaller group of male vampires whose roots go back to Lord Ruthven in "The Vampyre" and Varney in **Varney the Vampyre**. Like Ruthven and Varney, these figures are driven by a disease of mind and body; and no matter how sedulously they try to rid themselves of the curse of the undead, they are always unsuccessful. One of the earliest examples of this type of vampire in motion pictures appears in *House of Dracula* (1945) Lawrence Talbot (the wolfman), Frankenstein's monster, and Dracula are all brought together in this, one of the last gasps of the Universal monster factory. The film-makers, in a final gesture, even allow Talbot

From Erle C. Kenton's HOUSE OF DRACULA

to be cured and redeemed. Although Dracula is not granted such an indulgence and perishes at the conclusion, the vampire is characterised as seeking a remedy for his affliction. But while undergoing the protracted treatment the "call of Thanatos" becomes too strong. Dracula's second fall into darkness comes as a woman plays Beethoven's "Moonlight Sonata," which he finds "breathes the spirit of the night . . ." Nonetheless, until the moment when the Romantic music precipitates a regression, this Dracula is portrayed as genuinely longing for release from his vampiric "malady."

In the same year Republic Pictures released an exceptional small-budgeted film called *The Vampire's Ghost*. Despite the limitations of minimal production values the filmscript (written by Leigh Brackett and John K. Butler) is an intelligent and restrained re-working of the vampire myth. *The Vampire's Ghost* disregards almost completely the immeasurable influence of the Dracula figure returning instead—much more decidedly than *House of Dracula*—to a pre-Stoker conception for its inspiration. Webb Fallon has, like Varney, suffered through several centuries as a vampire in reparation for a heinous crime. In his present "incarnation" he is the proprietor of a cheap bar and gambling hall in an African outpost. While he is generally liked and respected by the inhabitants, they are, needless to say, unaware of his periodic nocturnal wanderings in search of blood. Viewer empathy with Fallon is established from the first scene, when he breaks up a fight in his bar using his powers of mesmerism and thereby saves the life of the conventional hero (Roy). Despite the violent surroundings Fallon (as underplayed by John Abbott) is soft-spoken and unassuming; he is, in fact, a much more appealing character than the ostensible protagonist (Roy) to the point where Roy's fiancée begins to prefer Fallon. On a narrative level, there are further parallels with the histories of Varney and Ruthven. For instance, Fallon seems to operate equally well during the day or night with only his dark glasses suggesting any sensitivity to light. In addition, he has no need to return to his coffin for periodic resuscitation, although he is conventional in that he is impervious to bullets and can only be destroyed by fire, the stake, or a silver blade. However, when Fallon is stabbed with a silver lance by one of the more superstitious natives during a hunt in the jungle, he does not crumble to ashes like Dracula. Rather, like Ruthven, he enlists the aid of Roy—whose life he has saved a second time in the underbrush—and he is carried to a mountain-top where he can be revived by moonlight. This faculty of revivification by moonlight is something rarely seen in vampire films—a striking anomaly to say the least—which Fallon accomplishes by bringing the delirious Roy, like

Aubrey in "The Vampyre," under his hypnotic influence. Unfortunately for Fallon his all-too-human infatuation with Julie leads to his
end. He kidnaps her and is followed into the jungle by Roy and a
priest figure, Father Gilchrist. There he is slain by them in a traditional manner.

The title character of *The Vampire* (1957) is probably the most
pathetic and unwilling vampire in film or literature. Combining the
Fifties vogue for science fiction with vampiric blood lust, this picture
features a humanitarian doctor (Paul Beecher) who accidentally consumes some "vampire pills" developed by a fellow scientist, a situation
made even more pathetic in that his young daughter unwittingly gives
them to him. In the grip of an ironic, drug-induced personality split—
killing by night and saving lives by day—his "angst" is like that of Talbot the wolfman in that, despairing of a cure, he seeks death.

Finally, this premise of the vampire himself as unwilling victim has
been recently revived in American-International's Blacula films—
Blacula (1972) and *Scream, Blacula, Scream* (1973). "Blacula" is the
rather cynical sobriquet adopted by an African prince named Mamuwalde, who has been infected with vampirism after an encounter with

John Abbott as Webb Fallon, one of the earliest sympathetic vampires in
THE VAMPIRE'S GHOST

Above and below, the two faces of John Beal as the title character in THE VAMPIRE

William Marshall and Pam Grier in SCREAM, BLACULA, SCREAM

The power of the cross in BLACULA

Dracula himself. Like his predecessors, Blacula is caught in a double bind between a desire for release and a compulsion to spread the vampiric plague, complicated in both films by the presence of love objects whom he does not wish to become his victims. In *Blacula*, he does turn the girl Tina into a vampire, but not until she is shot and vampirism seems the only way he can save her from complete death. When she is finally destroyed by those hunting Blacula, his instinct to continue "living" is so severely undercut that he walks out into the sunlight, and becomes a suicide in the manner of Varney.

In *Scream, Blacula, Scream* Mamuwalde is resurrected into a world even more alienating and unfamiliar than the one in the previous film. In one scene in particular, as he wanders the city streets and encounters two black pimps who laugh at his reprimands for exploiting their brothers and sisters and are as a result ruthlessly slaughtered, Blacula's outrage at society is explicitly stated. He does initiate a new search for a cure, participating in a voodoo ritual which the priestess Lisa—whom he has fallen in love with—performs, and nearly completes, before the police invade his house. In the final scene Blacula is found and staked. As he feels around the room in an agonised circle of frustration and despair, a freeze-frame from a high angle externalises his sensation of suspended, unending rage.

Judith Lang as Erica after a visit from Count Yorga

CHAPTER THREE

The Female Vampire

"I remember everything about it—with an effort. I see it all, as divers see what is going on about them, through a medium, dense rippling, but transparent. There occurred that night what has confused the picture and made its colour faint. I was all but assassinated in bed, wounded here," she touched her breast, "and never was the same again."

"Were you near dying?"

"Yes, very—a cruel love—strange love that would have taken my life. Love will have its sacrifices. No sacrifices without blood."

Joseph Sheridan Le Fanu,
Carmilla

None of these women approaches, so far as depth and sophistication of sadistic sexual perversion is concerned, Elisabeth Bathory... astonishingly white flesh, almost translucent, through which one could see clearly the delicate blue veins beneath; long shimmering, silken hair, black as the plumage of the raven; sensual, scarlet lips; great dark eyes, capable of doelike tenderness, but sometimes igniting into savage anger, and at others glazing over with the abandoned somnolence of intense sexual passion.

R.E.L. Masters and Eduard Lea,
Sex Crimes in History

I. ELISABETH BATHORY

Only recently has the Sixteenth Century Hungarian Countess described by Masters and Lea been reincarnated in motion pictures. The earliest of several motion pictures based on her life and legend was released in 1970. The historical Elisabeth Bathory (or Elizabeth or Erzabeth, various spellings are used; she was also occasionally known as Nadasdy, the surname of her husband, Count Ferencz) was briefly detailed in Chapter One. What is most pertinent to this book is that, among the other practices in which she and her followers engaged, was the systematic kidnapping and torture of hundreds of young women culmintaing with the Countess "milking" them

Ingrid Pitt as Countess Elisabeth Nadasdy reverts to her aged state
at her wedding in COUNTESS DRACULA

of their blood to daub on her skin and restore its "translucence."[1]

Countess Dracula (1971, directed by Peter Sasdy) is not, despite its
title, a conventional vampire film. For while it centres on the Countess's
reputedly successful use of blood as an elixir of youth, Sasdy's
adaptation of Bathory's life is a most literal and logically developed one
which depicts her as a living woman rather than a blood-sucking vampire. Accordingly, *Countess Dracula* does not exploit the usual icons of
the *genre* or adopt its pervasive style of expressionistic lighting and
decor, deploying those elements instead as a general reinforcement to
the authenticity of the narrative events and reserving the more extra-

---

[1] Masters and Lea record that in the dungeons of her stronghold, Castle Csejthe, law
officials eventually discovered a "herd" of young women quartered like cattle and kept
ready to satisfy the Countess' obsession.

Ingrid Pitt with her lover Nigel Green in COUNTESS DRACULA

ordinary handling for moments such as the Countess's transformations or to suggest her growing madness. The medieval art works
which appear under the titles,[2] the portraits of Nadasdy ancestors,
the scenes in the kitchen with their Breughel-like detailing (servants
in drab homespun around the breakfast table, a pig being dressed and
milk churning in the background), even the doddering scholar
Fabio puttering in his library or the sequence in the tavern where light
filters through grimy windows to cast broken patterns on the walls and
white-painted men from the travelling circus carouse in turbans,
feathers, and red capes—all these form a context of tangible reality, a

2. Including one of the real Elisabeth, called "The Blood Countess' and painted by
   St. Csok.

The rejuvenated Countess

verisimilitude which contrasts with the diffused landscapes and soft interior key-lights associated with the Countess's presence. As the grey-haired, deeply wrinkled woman of the opening scenes, garbed in faded black with veil and high collar, is transfigured by her fortuitous discovery of the power of blood, she is at the same time carried imagistically farther out of that reality, emerging from behind a screen of variously-coloured glass after her bath, golden-haired (strikingly contrary to descriptions of the actual countess) and attired in a blue peignoir which reveals a flesh that is indeed "astonishingly white."

Ultimately, in effects such as the montage of the old Countess stabbing a gypsy girl followed by a sudden red toning, freeze-frame, and dissolve to the young Elisabeth riding out of the castle or the simple tilted angles as the re-ageing woman frenziedly begs her discarded lover for help, Sasdy's stress is on the psychology and not the metaphysics of Elisabeth Bathory's aberration. Aside from the clear prerequisite that the blood be taken from a virgin—established when that of the local whore fails to have effect—nothing is specified of the alchemy which miraculously restores her beauty. Further, her personal vampirism is depicted as conditioned by aristocratic insensitivity rather than any incipient inclination to evil, so that she may even pray to God and finger a rosary while she waits anxiously for a new "object" to ritually immolate. With this preference for realistic detailing and visual understatement already demonstrated, Sasdy's staging of the final scenes becomes an effective mixture of ceremony and slaughter. The movement from the placid Titian blues and ochres of the wedding altar and the Latin reading of the priest to the sudden ferocity of the decaying Elisabeth's attack on her daughter and the stabbing of her youthful paramour externalises the opposing states of her mind. From a pan across the faces of village wives chanting "devil woman" below the castle ramparts, a cut inside reveals the Countess for the last time, walled up in her chamber, clad again in black, her visage more devastated by time than ever before, neither demon nor vampire, simply a madwoman.

A second adaptation of the Bathory character—produced in the same years as *Countess Dracula*—is more explicit in that it treats the Countess both as vampire and as sexual criminal. The central premise of *Daughters of Darkness* (*Le rouge aux levres*, 1970) is that the "Scarlet Countess"—the script's epithet for the historical Elisabeth—has somehow survived her incarceration up to the present time. Her face layered with heavy white make-up and sanguine lipstick (a visual pun on the French title), this Countess uses her real maiden name (Bathory) and makes little attempt to conceal either her inexplicable

A sadistic couple in LE ROUGE AUX LEVRES

longevity (she tells the constable of a resort town she had visited forty years before that her secret is "diet and lots of sleep") or her proclivity for young women both as victims and sexual objects, even pausing midway through the film to discuss her medieval persona and how she drew "the blood of three hundred virgins to bathe in and drink." "To drink," because *Daughters of Darkness* describes Elisabeth Bathory as a vampire in the traditional sense, and while it emphasizes the erotic aspects of her blood lust, it concedes a sensitivity to water (her servant Ilona reacts violently to a shower) and daylight as limitations of her power. Elisabeth seduces rather than attacks her prey, gradually drawing the blood from a young bride she meets at the resort and hoping not to destroy her but to make her a companion undead. When the Countess herself "perishes," by being thrown from a car while racing home to avoid the sun and impaled on a tree branch, she evidences a faculty of metempsychosis very similar to that of Carmilla in Vadim's *Blood and Roses* which permits her to take possession of the body of her latest victim, who in turn assumes the pallid aspect and voice of the Countess and initiates a new cycle with another newly-wed couple as the film ends.

Ritual of Blood (Ceremonia sangrienta, 1973), as yet unreleased in the United States, restores the Bathory character to a period setting but obscures the question of her vampirism in much the same way as *Countess Dracula.* Although the film opens with the discovery of an authentic undead, who is staked and decapitated in hopes of terminating a plague of killings, the Marquise Elisabeth Bathory of this film is again fixated on blood only as a restorative of her youth. While her husband Karl does expire and become a *revenant*, she remains alive, entering into an arrangement with him whereby they "share" the young women he abducts to fulfill their respective needs. Eventually she destroys him out of jealousy, and, ironically, this murder cuts her off from the virgin blood. With a genuine emphasis on ritual—the narrative contains many scenes of incantations and castings by the Marquise and her counsellor sorceress as well as grisly stagings of blood-draining and torture eschewed by Sasdy in his version—and a stylistic stress on rich colours and *chiarascuro*, the overall portrait of the Bathory figure falls midway between the psychological realism of *Countess Dracula* and the unabashed eroticism of *Daughters of Darkness*.

II. CARMILLA KARNSTEIN

In 1871, Sheridan Le Fanu created in his Gothic novella of sixteen chapters the Countess Carmilla Karnstein. Under the guise of being a "discovered manuscript," it is not only an antecedent of the alternating first-person "diary" form which Stoker was to employ in **Dracula**, but also the first major treatment of a female vampire in literature. Possibly Le Fanu knew of Bathory, for there are some resemblances between the two Countesses, but the noble rank and need for the blood of young women are of a superficial sort at best. The anagrammed antagonist of Le Fanu's fiction, Carmilla/Millarca/Mircalla is not a slayer of men. On the contrary, her conflicting impulses towards narcissistic love and annihilation compel her to seek out victims of her own age and sex, reflections of herself. The irony of Carmilla's affliction is not merely of one trapped in perpetual youth simultaneously forced to shun the daylight and to forego the patterns of normal existence, but, Le Fanu might allow, of a former victim caught in a cycle of having to relive with each new killing her own psychic destruction—an irony compounded by her awareness of playing a role.

Carmilla elucidates that dilemma in the lines cited at the beginning of this chapter, speaking of the "cruel love" which, later revelations make apparent, murdered her and issuing with a languorous fatality a warning to her "intended" of the impending re-enactment. That act of confession places Carmilla, at least in terms of the novella, with Lucy Westenra and others both male and female in a class of unwilling

Annette Vadim as Carmilla in BLOOD AND ROSES (ET MOURIR DE PLAISIR)

revenants, objects to be pitied rather than despised, to be executed but consolingly.

There have been a number of dramatic adaptations of Le Fanu's tale, each of them revealing different prejudices towards the original characters and themes. Le Fanu used understatement and pressed the reader into identifying with the somewhat innocuous Laura for suspense and *frisson*. The connotations of fatality and sexuality are not blatant but present nonetheless; and the images of bestiality, of breasts being pierced by two huge needles, were probably more acceptable to Victorian audiences in the context of supernatural horror. Beyond that, Le Fanu permits varying interpretations.

Consequently, in his film *Et mourir de plaisir (Blood and Roses,* 1960), Roger Vadim chooses to underscore the aspects of transference ("I live in you; and you would die for me . . . You must come with me, loving me, to death"). Vadim's Carmilla suffused with an incestuous energy that may lie hidden behind masks or explode in a fireworks display, never dies but draws the soul from a body and replaces it with her own in an eternal, parasitic transmigration. Although *Blood and Roses* uses only fragments of Carmilla's narrative line, the first-person viewpoint is carried over. It is, however, from Carmilla's perspective,

Elsa Martinelli and Mel Ferrer watch over Annette Vadim in ET
MOURIR DE PLAISIR

Ralph Bates repels Yutte Stensgaard in LUST FOR A VAMPIRE

becoming Georgia's—the equivalent of the novella's Laura—only after *she* has become Carmilla.

Excepting the one pursuit of a servant girl through the forest or the sight of Carmilla impaled on a fence post, Vadim avoids the *genre's* tendency towards violence and blood images; but ten years before *Countess Dracula,* he does evince a fascination with the psychology of vampirism as keen as Sasdy's. The dream states are not of "monstrous cats" but of women waiting listlessly in white corridors and of modern surgery, of fears not connected with distant castles and dungeon racks but with hospitals and operating tables, subverting the institutions of life-preservation and addressing death in a form that is most tangible to the viewer. Lacking the period setting, the present is stylised via the Italian manor with its antiques and faded oils and the forest with its night mist and carpet of leaves. On a narrative level, the costume ball and the visualisation of Georgia's nightmare in the unusual black-and-white waiting room produce moments of surrealism and anomaly within the assumed sense of contemporary actuality. These shifts in both narrative consciousness and expression, the displacement of reality by both masques (the ball) and reveries, the

Carmilla (Annette Vadim) revisits her crypt in ET MOURIR DE PLAISIR

change from colour to a world of greys, undercuts the stability of appearances in which the characters seek refuge in much the same way as vampirism being superstition threatens the rationalism of science. These events propel the film backwards figuratively into a dark age,

While the Carmilla of *Blood and Roses* pertains more to Vadim than to the novella; *Terror in the Crypt* (*La cripta e l'incubo*, 1963, directed by Camillo Matrocinque) transliterates it more exactly. The graphic, black-and-white aspect of the *schloss* and the ruined church, the cautious subjectification of Laura's dreams in slow, circular tracking shots, the emphasis of her fear of going insane—all expand the Gothic imagery and ambivalence of the original. The tension between Laura's fantasies and apprehensions and what Carmilla really is, belied by her moments of "normalcy," is restored—the final resolution is the revelation of the latter's true nature.

Terror in the Crypt begins in the midst of nightmare, a rapid montage as a woman leaps from a coach and pivots around a tree frightened by the vehicle's black shape: a close-up as she lies dead with her eyes open is followed by an extra long view of a castle, then a medium shot as Laura suddenly awakens in her bedroom and a fast zoom-in as she screams. The instantaneous effect is one of disjunction and continues as each succeeding dream is introduced into the narrative without any visual or aural qualifier to indicate that it is anything other than real. There is a confusion of the same sort of night-visions which Laura experienced in the novella with her waking state, coloured and made half-mad by those experiences.

The Carmilla-figure, here called Lyuba, arrives—again as in Le Fanu—in a runaway carriage and immediately is woven into the texture of Laura's dreams; but the audience as much as the dreamer is cut off from any indication of their cause. Visually, Laura alone and awake is linked with a kind of stasis (she is constantly introduced by high angle shots) and repressed energy (the dynamic yet limited action of the zoom shot), while Lyuba's presence—physical or psychic (when she impresses herself onto Laura's mind) —inspires movement in the form of pans and tracking shots. Laura and her governess turn to spells to try and rid her of her ailment; Lyuba remains a detached observer, playing a larger role in Laura's nightmares than in the rest of the film. This schematisation of Laura's growing insanity restores some of the subjective quality of the original work. Not only the dreams but nearly all the scenes which centre on Laura somehow reflect her inner thoughts and fears. The morbidity ("It's so beautiful here . . . here one could come for pleasure or for death") and sense of displacement ("In places like this, the past still seems to flourish . . . and I live more in the past than in the present") which surround her find equivalents in both the words and images, in a shot selection which fixes her to the ground but permits Lyuba to float over it, which externalises the former's sensations in the shock of quick cuts, the entrapment of tight close shots, the imbalance of off-angles, and the chaos of broken patterns of light.

In a way, the spectre of Lyuba and death represent freedom for Laura, a release from worldly care epitomised when both women hurry down the path to the ruined church at night, windswept and backlit, cutting a bold diagonal across the face of a dark landscape in

Douglas Wilmer revenges himself on Kirsten Betts in THE VAMPIRE
LOVERS

their white nightdresses. The fact that Lyuba like Carmilla in *Blood and
Roses* is suffocating her victim with the strength of her will is implicit
in the narrative—*genre* convention tending to cast viewer suspicion
on others than the stated heroine—and in the symbolic transformations
of Laura's dream. The resolution, then, may be more confirmation
than revelation. Appropriately all that remains of Lyuba, who has been
more a stifling ghost in Laura's fantasies than anything substantial,
after she has been shot with a wooden bolt and disintegrated, is an
empty cloak which Laura removes from the earth.

Although both *Blood and Roses* and *Terror in the Crypt* have a
highly developed narrative point-of-view, which filters the sexuality

Mike Raven and Yutte Stensgaard in LUST FOR A VAMPIRE

and mania of the sourcework through the subjective perceptions of predator as well as prey, both suffer the insertion of a male figure, which—
even though the witch-hunter of the second film is drawn from the
novella's "picture cleaner from Gratz"—is not present in the original
and who to some extent in each film defocuses the sexual exchange
between the two women. Self-love becoming love of the other, the
projection of the potent vampiric consciousness onto the object and
the latent carnality of that action, are treated mostly in a stylised or
symbolic way in *Blood and Roses* and *Terror in the Crypt*. The former's
close shot of the women's rain-wet faces as they kiss or, in the
later film, the hand-holding strolls through the gardens and hesitant
caresses are their strongest manifestations of the sexuality which is at
the core of Le Fanu's work—clearly so in style and equally in the
dramatic causality, past and present, of the narrative—and also of the
most recent film adaptations.

Carmilla's lesbianism and Laura's qualified reciprocation of it is
partially de-eroticised in all the film versions, but—in terms of scenes
of physical interaction between Carmilla and her lover-victims—is
least ambiguous in the two latest of them. Hammer's *The Vampire
Lovers* (1970) and *Lust for a Vampire* (1971) represent in their way a

Mike Raven and Barbara Jefford in LUST FOR A VAMPIRE

modern transliteration of the tradition in which Le Fanu laboured. Carmilla, as embodied by Ingrid Pitt—who portrayed Countess Dracula in the following year—is, more than the blondes Annette Vadim and Ursula Davis who had the role in the earlier productions, physically dissimilar to Le Fanu's description: "she was slender . . . her features were small and beautifully formed; her eyes large, dark and lustrous." But despite the fact that the Hammer Carmilla is full-bodied and lacking the sloe-eyed features of the verbal portrait, she possesses a consummate sexuality which she depends on more heavily than any cunning or unnatural strength to acquire blood and guard the secret of her affliction. Unlike the Carmilla of *Blood and Roses* or *Terror in the Crypt,* her communion with her victim is based more on a physical than mental control. Her blood-drinking begins as she bares and strokes the young woman's breasts, desensitising them to the sharpness of her fangs by inducing a quasi-orgasmic haze in the classic manner of the male undead. This Carmilla's prideful self-image, the view of herself as both master and malefactor, is also a state of mind more conventionally found in the male of the species.

Once having become what she is, the Hammer Carmilla seems to spends less time in remorse than in the pursuit of pleasures which are still available to her. In one sense, this kind of characterisation is farther removed from the novella than any previous, accentuating hedonism above compulsion as the principle motivating force and undermining much of the irony of the situation; but in a scene such as the observation of the village girl's funeral procession, in which Carmilla complains of how discordant the burial music is and deprecates the whole process ("What a fuss! Why *you* must die everyone must die. And all are happier when they do"), the emphasis shifts, so that her discomfiture may be caused either by the religious icons and chanting of the cortège or by the memory of her own death and melancholy over her loss of that "happiness" so that the ambiguity of the original is retained. Even with the added scenes of seduction and the overt staging of what remains essentially Le Fanu's plot, *The Vampire Lovers* is not purely exploitative. Carmilla's bath, for example, is not a *de rigueur* nude scene but a narrative event which sets up a situation in which Carmilla can first display her body then have her unwary host disrobe to try on one of the dresses she had laid out, insisting that to get the feel of the fabric she must wear nothing underneath, so that this episode ultimately becomes the first in the pattern of sensual manipulation which the vampire practices throughout the film.

Alhough the Hammer Carmilla is staked and beheaded at the end of the first film, she survives that quietus to return in a sequel; and this may, in the most pragmatic terms, account for why she is the least covert of female vampires, relying on her powers to seduce and destroy anyone who discovers her undead condition taking few other precautions. In turn, this arrogant and extravagant behaviour may explain why, of all the film versions of **Carmilla**, *Vampire Lovers* most consistently brings the enigmas engendered by Le Fanu to melodramatic fruition.

III. OTHER DAUGHTERS OF DARKNESS

"I'm going out hunting vampires. Ha, ha, ha."
"Vampires, sir? I thought one hunted them with checkbooks."
"Don't be facetious, Hobbs."
                                        Dracula's Daughters

While the historical and literary traditions represented by Elizabeth Bathory and Carmilla have only been brought to the screen in the last dozen years, the female vampire as the main character of a motion picture goes back considerably farther in time and, as with the male figure, includes both demonic and sympathetic characterisations.

Dracula's Daughter (1936) is, as the year and title may suggest, an

Gloria Holden hypnotises her young model in DRACULA'S
DAUGHTER

informal sequel to Universal's *Dracula*. Although the Count's daughter,
Maria, murders for blood—an early sequence demonstrates her mesmeric powers as she attacks a young man in the street—she is indifferent
to her victims as sexual objects and considers herself an otherwise
normal woman possessed by an hereditary disease. When the distractions of painting and a direct attempt to exorcise the influence of
Dracula's parentage by stealing and burning his body in a moonlit
ritual of elaborate incantations and rubrics prove unremedial, she
seeks the help of a psychiatrist, planning to inspire either his love
or his scientific curiosity ("There are more things in heaven and earth
than are dreamed of in your psychiatry, Mr. Garth") to insure his silence.
Because Maria is so painfully aware of her uncontrollable bestiality
but so naive as to its necessary consequences—her conversations with
her manservant underscore the futility of her attempts to sublimate
and her hopes for a cure ("Sandor, what do you see in my eyes?"
"Death") —and because the actual assaults are so stylised (she uses a
ring to hypnotize her prey and the two sequences end before any actual

blood-drinking with a subjective blurring as Maria advances on the man and a pan to the African mask on the wall of her studio when she attacks a young woman recruited by Sandor to pose for her), the female figure in *Dracula's Daughter* is more sympathetic than most.

The notion in film of the vampire as a demon or as a victim of its own evil desires finds an example much less frequently in women and then usually only in the form of minor or supporting characters. Such diverse titles as *Santo vs. The Vampire Women,* (see Chapter Two), *Vampyr,* and *Twins of Evil* constitute the isolated instances of female antagonists who are unmitigatedly evil. *Twins of Evil,* in particular, breaks down the schizophrenic impulses which often plague the unwilling vampire into two mentally opposed but physically identical

An aristocratic bloodline, Gloria Holden as Countess Zaleska aka DRACULA'S DAUGHTER

The village beauty, played by Madeleine Collinson, finds an unsuspecting victim in TWINS OF EVIL

personages and develops as a central premise the assertion that "those
who are truly dedicated will not die from a vampire's bite—they will
become one of the undead."

At one point in *Dracula's Daughter* a police inspector has the
brief conservation with his butler reproduced at the head of this
section. In his own way Hobbs reflects the popular disbelief which
underlies all films of the horror and fantasy *genre*, and against which
many specific pictures from *Dracula's Daughter* to *The Night Stalker*
have consciously played. As with the male figure, films centered on
women which operate outside the normal iconography have an added
burden in maintaining suspension of that disbelief. *Blood of Dracula*
(1957) is, like *The Vampire*, a film which takes certain characteristics
of the traditional undead and places them in a science-fiction context,
specifically centering on an extraordinary situation at a girl's prep

school where a chemistry teacher experiments on a pupil and changes her into a bat-faced monster who sucks blood, with whom a minimal amount of empathy is possible.

The Velvet Vampire (1971) is more of an analogue to *Count Yorga,* interesting both because the antagonist has no compunctions about the practice of her vampirism and also because it parodies certain aspects of the *genre*—ranging from simple homages such as an art exhibit in the "Stoker Gallery" and naming the woman vampire Diane Le Fanu to the more elaborate novelties of having her make her home in the desert or demonstrate a taste for raw chicken. The eclectic style of this film—day-lit desert landscapes and a final chase through downtown Los Angeles providing a contrast with low-lit interiors full of unnatural colours—encompasses some imaginative narrative turns (the vampire using her strength to overpower and kill an unsuspecting mugger which antedates a similar scene with the two pimps in *Scream, Blacula, Scream*; her body "floating" down an escalator in the chase scene in a manner reminiscent of *Son of Dracula*) but like *Count Yorga, The Velvet Vampire* never really comes to terms with the broader implications of the *genre,* never makes the female figure's vampirism more than an inexplicable aberration or, like her fondness for velvet, a fetish.

Celeste Yarnall as Diane Le Fanu in **THE VELVET VAMPIRE**

Celeste Yarnall seduces Sherry Miles in the VELVET VAMPIRE

IV. VAMPYR

Whether Carl Dreyer's *Vampyr* should even be classed with the other films of this chapter is unclear. Although the titles credit Le Fanu's **In a Glass Darkly** (a volume of tales containing **Carmilla**) as a source, the conception of the female vampire which Dreyer brings to the screen bears little relation either to Le Fanu and the adaptations already discussed or almost any other figure in the whole of the *genre*. The entire film lies under a kind of expressionistic veil, much thicker than that of *Nosferatu* or *Dracula,* as the vampire (an old woman), the doctor in her service, and the various protagonists move with dance-like deliberation through a series of disconnected scenes. The very idea of the undead woman as a white-haired crone borrows more heavily from the lore of witchcraft and sorcery than that of vampirism—the figure in the film closely resembles the witch who is burned at the stake in Dreyer's *Day of Wrath*—and, excepting such secondary characters as the Baroness in *Brides of Dracula,* is without parallel in film.

Despite the fact that this withered succubus is more than anything else a personification of evil, a decaying body feeding on the young,

The skeletal hand in Gray's dream from VAMPYR

The vampire peers at Gray in the coffin from VAMPYR

Vampyr itself is less a horror film than a vivid nightmare of unforeseen images and events cut from the same fabric as the dream in *Blood and Roses* but less explicit, an ontology of terror which constricts and obscures material reality causing the viewer to puzzle over what traces of it do filter through. Characteristic of Dreyer as much as of the genre, the viewpoint is again that of the victim; for although an image like that of a skeletal hand poised to pour out the contents of a small vial may seem nothing more than an emblem of sensory delight—in having animated this bony thing or of intellectual delight in having the "magic" to animate it, when put in the context of an overall visual delirium, the shot reacquires a "sense" of its own. There are more direct examples of this subjective rendering of a vague, metaphysical malaise: a victim lying fully conscious inside a coffin and being carried to a gravesight; shots repeated to generate an aura of *déjà vu*. Even a static shot such as that of a women bound to a wrought-iron bench can be staged to suggest the rupture or perhaps transcendence of being caught in the vampire's grip: her black dress is set off from the white wall behind her; the uneven texture of that wall is accentuated by the shadow of the bench and unlit grey areas. Her hands are jerked behind her, bound and held to the iron by a two-foot length of rope which she

Leone bound to the bench from **VAMPYR**

The Doctor perishes in a deluge of flour from VAMPYR

is drawing taut for no apparent reason. Her body lurches forward but her head is erect and she gazes ahead. What is most remarkable is that none of her discomfiture is apparent from her expression. Her body, which is alive, is reduced to a kind of inanimateness or numbness, even though her arms are twisted into angles not unlike the clawlike fingers of the bony hand. On the surface, her face and its serenity contradict her situation. Simultaneously, she cannot foresee and yet does foresee being untied, has a presentiment of such clarity that when she is freed she need not even glance at her rescuer. Like the bony hand the image requires penetration: it is not merely unreal but illusionary.

Accordingly, the conclusion of *Vampyr* is a perpetuation of all the earlier paradoxes. While a young couple wander through the woods, the doctor perishes. As the scenes shift back and forth, the light diffusing through the branches clutches at the couple annihilating the sharp line of their silhouette as it envelops them in hazy long shot; the flour tumbling down through an overhead sifter (shot subjectively so that the white powder pours through the wire mesh like the sun's ray through the branches outside) and clinging to his hair and whiskers envelops the doctor. Both move lethargically: he because of the physical impediment of the flour; they for unspecified reasons. The noise of the machinery alternates with the calling ("Halloing") on the lake, with the drums and violins on the soundtrack. From the low angle of the man with the lantern who sets the mill wheels in motion and traps the doctor, the scene cuts to a high angle of another man on a bank helping the couple to beach their boat. Finally, both are isolated, he in his white cage, they on the lake with its oppressive dimness, isolated from "land" as surely he is in his torrent of flour; and throughout, the facile symbol of the wheels grinding, reoccurs curiously explicit in the middle of it all. If this and, to a certain extent, the entire film deviate from the *genre* conventions in both narrative and expression, it is because Dreyer has gone beyond concerns of terror. The only terror is in the "dream in dream" tone of *Vampyr*, which goes beyond fantasy into a world where the fantastic imagines the real.

Christopher Lee as Dracula and Caroline Munro as Laura in
DRACULA A.D. 1972

CHAPTER FOUR

Emerging Traditions

I. HAMMER AND THE VICTORIAN PSYCHOLOGY

None of the group of beliefs here dealt with is richer or more overdetermined than that in the Vampire, nor is there one that has more numerous connections with the other legends and superstitions. Its psychological meaning is correspondingly complicated, and in the analysis of it we shall proceed from its most typical form. It may be said at the outset that the latent content of the belief yields plain indications of most kinds of sexual perversions, and that the belief assumes various forms according as this or that perversion is more prominent.[1]

The release by Hammer Films of a new version of Bram Stoker's **Dracula** in 1958 is something of a landmark in the history of the horror film. Ninety percent of the vampire films produced to date throughout the world have been made since the Hammer *Dracula*, and its influence continues to be felt both creatively and economically. Because it generated substantial grosses worldwide off of a modest budget, Hammer itself, and other production companies and independent producers which it inspired, resurrected the vampire film from the comic clutches of Abbott and Costello to which Universal had consigned it and made it, once and for all, a staple of the horror *genre*. Without Hammer's *Dracula*, this study's lengthy filmography would likely be much shorter. As important as the financial success of Hammer in the horror market may have been, there is another consideration even more central to this book: Hammer's overt and even emphatic introduction of violent and sexual elements into the narrative of *Dracula* and its immediate successors. The depredations of the Universal Studios Dracula in the Thirties and Forties could be curtailed either by the sight of a cross *or* a memorandum from the Hays office. Whether the motivations were aesthetic or exploitive, in probing these violent and sexual aspects of the vampire myth, Hammer restored the psychological sub-text and the emotional integrity of the source work. As a result, the world of the Hammer vampires was, from the first, one to which psychologists and devotées of Nineteenth Century literature alike could more fully relate. The male vampire figure, especially as he was most frequently to be portrayed by actor Christopher Lee, became a tall and virile demon with none of the posturing or artifice which tainted some of his

1. Jones, **On the Nightmare**

123

predecessors, while the female vampires of his retinue became voluptuous and voracious succubi. "Desire" and "obsession" became the key words as Thanatos and Eros were intermingled in victim and oppressor, translating into dramatic terms Friedlander's observation that "the active impulse to die is based on a libidinal impulse."[2] The Lucy of the Hammer *Dracula* awaits her deadly leman in bed, breathless and eager. Even the quintessentially Victorian Mina has her repressions dissolved as Dracula bestows kisses and caresses on her before indulging his vampiric thirst. Jones's analysis of the vampire phenomenon is particularly relevent here:

> The explanation of these (vampiric) phantasies is surely not hard. A nightly visit from a beautiful or frightful being, who first exhausts the sleeper with passionate embraces and then withdraws from him a vital fluid: all this can point only to a natural and common process, namely to nocturnal emissions accompanied with dreams of a more or less erotic nature. In the unconscious mind blood is commonly an equivalent for semen, and it is not necessary to have recourse, as Hock does, to the possibility of . . . 'wounds inflicted on oneself by scratching during a voluptuous dream.'

It does not involve much extrapolation to appreciate that views such as this must have affected the creators at Hammer Studios.

Hammer's introduction of colour to the vampire film also had a specific effect. On the one hand, it increased the realism of the productions (something Hammer was to aim for continually) : vampires with blood-streaked fangs and breasts and the richly coloured tones of the sets create a mood of unsettling actuality far different from the black and white, neo-Gothic expressionism of Universal. On the other hand, colour could suggest quite the opposite of realism, could enhance the sensual, dreamlike quality of the films, as in the blue moonbeams that float through the air on the balcony of Lucy's room when she awaits Dracula's fatal embrace or the vivid red—traditionally associated with the devil and eroticism—which becomes a colour motif for the title figure in many of the films, to the point where some of his close-ups are completely suffused with that colour. Ultimately this use of colour is most effective in amplifying the nightmare state of these films. While most black-and-white productions do achieve visual distortions in camera angle, lighting, and set construction which are suggestive of nightmare; while allegorical conflicts and terrifyingly surreal events still abound, colour is uniquely able to add a layer of ineluctable, visceral immediacy to the image.

Watching a horror film, an audience probes the periphery of its unconscious—propelled through suspension of its disbelief toward a

---

2. Kate Friedlander, "On the 'Longing to Die'." in **Death: Interpretations**.

Dracula (Christopher Lee) decomposes in the now classic finale of HORROR OF DRACULA

moment when repressed desires and psychological struggles are clarified in symbolic terms and then just as suddenly distanced and forced to consider the "reality" of what is on the screen in terms of their own dreams and fantasies. What became the Hammer style and was imitated by other companies worldwide was an exploitation of a general audience's susceptibility to fantasy and horror and a stress on psychological realism, eroticism, and natural detail in both performance and decor. Michael Carreras, Jimmy Sangster, Terence Fisher, and Anthony Hinds were among the most important forces behind this development, with Fisher and Hinds as good examples of radically different contributions made to the synthesis of the Hammer style.

Fisher in *Dracula, Brides of Dracula* (1960) and *Dracula, Prince of Darkness* (1965) relies heavily—particularly in relation to other Hammer products—on understatement. By means of finely-drawn characters and a flexible visual style, Fisher employs shifting moods to elicit tension. Van Helsing's arduous, fascinating struggle with his arch-enemy is the vortex of Fisher's Dracula films: he is a cool, methodical man (incarnated by Peter Cushing, with certain mannerisms carried over from his Frankenstein portrayal for Fisher) using modern scientific instruments as proficiently as he uses garlic and the crucifix, and in that very close to the original conception. On the other hand, Anthony Hinds, writing under the pseudonym John Elder, has scripted films which are far more hysterical and deviate in plot, temperament, and characterisation. In works like *Kiss of the Vampire* (1963), *Dracula Has Risen from the Grave* (1968), *Taste the Blood of Dracula* (1969) and *Scars of Dracula* (1970), Hinds initiates an exploration of the classic dichotomies of vampire fiction. Living and dead, light and dark, bestial and human, chaotic and ordered, good and evil are but a few examples of these dichotomies. The allegory is simple and direct like that of a Medieval morality play. The vampire is a creature of the night, an accomplice of the devil who is finally, and often quite literally, defeated by the forces of light in the form of men with faith, knowledge, and good purpose. Hinds, however, goes beneath the surface of the myth and draws out the more obscure, psychological oppositions inscribed in it. In the process the conflict becomes more of a struggle between the ego and the unconscious. Not unlike the counter-impulses of "Lamia" or "La morte amoureuse," the contest in films like *Kiss of the Vampire* is between the "reasonableness" of repression—the Victorian temper itself—and libidinous irrationality.

Hinds, then, associates the vampire myth in his films with the same psychic material which Jones speaks of:

> The love motif can, however, especially when in a state of repression, regress to an earlier form of sexuality, particularly to the sadistic-masochistic phase of development. It was remarked above that the masochistic side of a personality tends to regard the idea of Death as an aggressive onslaught, and the same is even truer of the idea of a dead person. A dead person who loves will love forever and will never be weary of giving and receiving caresses.

> On the other hand the dead being allows everything, can offer no resistance, and the relationship has none of the inconvenient consequences that sexuality may bring in its train in life. The phantasy of loving such a being can therefore make a strong appeal to the sadistic side of the sexual instinct.

> It [vampirism] evidently signifies a reversion to the most primitive aspects of sadism, both of the oral and anal kind.

The cult in *Kiss of the Vampire*—headed by a handsomely gaunt roué named Ravna who, with the help of an incestuous son and daughter,

Noel Williams introduces Jennifer Daniel to the vampire cult in
KISS OF THE VAMPIRE

lures young men and women into their group of corrupt devotees—exemplifies the reversion which Jones isolates. Ravna's orgies and black rites, for all the manorial splendor which surrounds them, are primitive enactments. One of his victim/disciples, a daughter of the local innkeeper, typifies the cruel frenzy of one who has become a ravenous

Isobel Black prepares to vampirise Edward de Souza in KISS OF THE VAMPIRE

undead. The oral-sadistic complexes connected with her vampirism could hardly be more explicit than in the scene in the graveyard where she bites the hand of Professor Zimmer who has interrupted her in the midst of an orgasmic summoning of a corpse or the later languorous assault/seduction of Gerald. The pleasure these aggressive actions give her is entirely manifest and forms a strong contrast to the morose and self-mortifying (in both his physical self-abuse and his drunkenness) demeanour of the bearded, black-clad Zimmer. The loss of his own daughter to Ravna has made him a monomaniac concerned only with the destruction of the cult and driven to adopt the elaborate ritual means which turn the forces of evil upon themselves and accomplish his end.

Hinds's Dracula films introduce a severe reversal of traditional roles. In *Dracula Has Risen from the Grave*, one of the king-vampire's followers is a priest and his antagonist, an agnostic. But the film in which

Christopher Lee menaces Barbara Ewing in DRACULA HAS RISEN FROM THE GRAVE

Hinds seems most conscious of the underlying hypocrisy of moral pos-
tures is *Taste the Blood of Dracula*. Here, Hinds's vision of the Vic-
torian-Edwardian family is focused on an overbearing father secretly
indulging his sexual aberrations while restraining his children's natural desires. The Dracula figure is subsumed into this scheme as a cata-
lyst, a ritual projection who leads the children to patricide and sexual
fulfillment with him as their master.

In 1970 Hammer released the film adaptation of Le Fanu's **Carmilla**
under the title of *The Vampire Lovers*, it perpetuated the studio
tradition. Eroticism and attention to the period and intent of the original were, as with the male figure embodied in the *Dracula* series, a key

to the psychology of the female vampire typified by Carmilla. While preying on men as well as women, the compulsive, carnivorous sexuality of the Hammer Carmilla in this film and *Lust for a Vampire* is tempered by her sentimental attachments to members of her own sex, which results in a double bind between affection for the love object and the need to consume it. *Twins of Evil* (1971 and written by Tudor Gates, who has worked on both *The Vampire Lovers* and *Lust for a Vampire*) contains a characterisation of a female undead who, as in Hinds's films, is the dramatic centre of a struggle between Puritanism and libido. Peter Cushing as the witchfinder Weil assimilates much of Hinds's Professor Zimmer, developing a portrait of a fanatic anti-Satanist who resembles a character from a Hawthorne tale.

Vampire Circus (1971) —a dense film containing sufficient personages to populate an expansive Victorian novel and consequently quite complex and difficult to follow—addresses the conflict of good and evil on a more obviously allegorical level than most Hammer productions. In a prologue, a young woman entices a child into the castle of her lover, the vampiric Count Mitterhouse. He is destroyed by a throng of frenzied villagers, and she is stripped and made to run the gamut. Like Weil, the vampire hunters are excessively Puritanical and sadistic,

From TWINS OF EVIL

Adrienne Corri supervises the diabolical rites in VAMPIRE CIRCUS

Robert Tayman is destroyed by a group of angry villagers in VAMPIRE CIRCUS

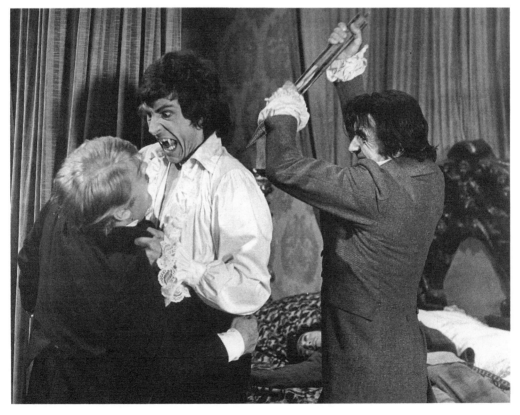

Linda Hayden as Alice visits the Master (Christopher Lee) in TASTE THE BLOOD OF DRACULA

villifying her as much for her adulterous love as for participation in the murder of the child and obviously taking pleasure in the beating which they administer as a group. The remainder of the film takes place fifteen years later in the midst of a plague which the more super-stitious townspeople believe is the result of Mitterhouse's dying curse. After the local doctor (the voice of rationalism: "Old wives' tales. The vampire exists only in legend nowhere else") has left in search of serum, a circus arrives promising "a thousand delights" to which the distraught villagers willingly surrender. The ritual aspects of this seduction of the entire town are externalised in both the calliope-like score of the film and the tricks of the circus performers—tumblers turn-ing into bats; a panther becoming a man; the "mirror of life" which acts like an extra-spatial passageway (reminiscent of Cocteau's *Orpheus)* —all contribute to a scheme of explicit non-real or symbolic events which haze the distinction between the material and the illusionary, a distortion which is exploited for suspense in later scenes when the vampires are pursued by the townsmen or for a more immediate, Lew-tonesque *frisson* when a pair of jewelled boot buckles are taken for a pair of deadly animal eyes. Simultaneously, the stylised sexuality of the prologue (the beating or the image of a bat emerging from the

eye of a skull) becomes more overt, containing implications of bestiality as the panther-man seduces the young daughter of the *burgermeis-
ter* and incest as the headmistress of the circus is revealed to be the
woman of the prologue who now sets her undead twins (fathered
presumably by Mitterhouse) on her mortal daughter.

Finally, *Countess Dracula* concentrates, as in Sasdy and Hinds's
earlier *Taste the Blood of Dracula*, on the psychological cannibalism
and latent incest of family life. Countess Elisabeth enters into her
relationship with Imre Toth after having figuratively devoured and
assimilated her offspring's personality. Constrained by the enactment
of child murder and the fantasy of recaptured youth fulfilled, the
Countess vacillates schizophrenically between the role of mother and
jealous lover, alternatively cradling Toth to her breast or rocking him
like an infant and reprimanding him for bringing a whore into the
castle. H. F. Searles characterises such a relationship—which on a more
general level is typical of the ambivalent response of a victim to a
vampiric predator—in this way:

> We have records of the parent of the schizophrenic patient who behaved
> in an inordinately seductive way towards the child, thus fostering in the
> latter an intense conflict . . . between, on the one hand, his desire to
> mature and fulfill his own individuality, and, on the other hand, his
> regressive desire to remain in an infantile symbiosis with his parent, to
> remain there at the cost of investing even his sexual strivings . . . in that
> regressive relationship.[3]

II. MARIO BAVA AND THE BAROQUE IMAGE

> What man that see the ever-whirling
>   wheel
> Of Change, the which all mortall things
>   doth sway
> But that thereby doth find, and plainly
>   feele,
> How MUTABILITY on them doth play
> Her cruell sports, to many mens decay?
>   Spenser, "The Faerie Queene,"
>   VII, i, 1-5

A carved sarcophagus reposes in a high-arched, tenebrous crypt. After
a montage in which the corpse/woman within it has undergone a metamorphosis from the bony remains of necrosis to new-moving flesh, the
camera has pulled back to medium long shot. From this vantage, the

3. Harold F. Searles, "The Effort to Drive the Other Person Crazy" in the *British Journal of Medical Psychiatry*.

Barbara Steele watches over her father's corpse in BLACK SUNDAY

Unwary visitors to the crypt of the reanimated Asa in IL MASCHERO DEL DEMONIO

spectator familiar with the constructs of the genre may anticipate a hand stretching out painfully from the enclosure (cf. a similar resurrection in *Dracula—Prince of Darkness*). Instead, the virulent energy which has reformed the ashes into unnatural life is suffused into the cinerary stone itself. There is a crack; an explosion: granite fragments break away and crumble into heaps on the floor of the vault. The thin cloud of dust, newly disturbed after hundreds of years, settles again and reveals the body still lying, unmoved, on the catafalque.

This sequence from Mario Bava's Black Sunday (*La maschera del demonio*, 1960) illustrates some of the expressive power of Bava's *mise-en-scène*, suggests something of the scope and invention of his Baroque imagery which in turn defines his approach to the genre, an approach that, to borrow Coleridge's terms, "dissolves, diffuses, and dissipates . . . is essentially vital, even as all objects (as objects) are essentially fixed and dead."[4] Here the "fixed and dead objects" are the conventions of the vampire film (some overused to the point of stereotypification and cliché), which for many filmmakers become suffocating restrictions. Bava's tactic is a heavy reliance on visual expression which externalises the metaphysical implications of the subject matter. The unseen energy postulated by the intricate series of dissolves as the skull in *Black Sunday* begins to reacquire flesh in slow, barely perceptible stages, as each layer of skin reappears and the punctures left by the demon's mask close into fine circles and vanish, as the black, empty sockets gradually disclose the whites of eyes enraged by centuries of death, until finally the nostrils flare, the neck muscles constrict, and the whole body arches up under the sting of renewed life—that energy (and the expectations it engenders in the viewer) builds to the point where it can no longer be contained, where the stone itself must rupture and release it.

Coming as it does in the forefront of scores of vampire films which have been produced since 1960, compared to the relatively few made before that date, *Black Sunday* simultaneously recalls the seminal expressionism of Murnau in its iconography—the sophisticated optical devices which create the graphic reality of the vampire's revivification are differentiated from the earlier filmmaker's undercranking and negative images principally in terms of technological advances—and anticipates the psychological realism of many later films in its characterisations. More importantly, perhaps, all of Bava's films are staged with a consistency of viewpoint inapparent in other European productions. While a motion picture such as the German *Cave of the Living Dead (Der Fluch der grünen Augen,* 1963) may project shadows of a vampire onto

4. "Biographia Literaria," XIII.

Above, BLACK SABBATH (I TRE VOLTI DELLA PAURA) with Susy Andersen and Mark Damon; below, Boris Karloff as Gorca, the vampiric grandfather with one of the family victims

Barbara Steele and the Mask of the Demon

white walls in a manner reminiscent of *Nosferatu*, the insertion of such highly stylised shots within the context of a modern setting causes an iconic confusion, a disintegration more appropriate to parody than straight dramatic treatment. While *The Last Man on Earth* (made in Italy in 1964) may adapt the science-fiction vampirism of Matheson's **I Am Legend**, its final scenes of the killing in the church lapse into quasi-religious symbolism and deific myths, which are barred from Bava's *Planet of the Vampires* (*Terrore nello spazio*, 1965), being instead a more rigorous synthesis of the two *genres* which draws its novel and bizarre sense of horror from such juxtapositions as dead astronauts rising from their shallow, slab-covered graves to tear through their airless shrouds of transparent plastic. Most basically, the world which Bava conveys in his films is a mutable one, composed of shifting contrasts and colours, of complements and atonalities, a world which moves like Spenser's "ever-whirling wheel" from real to unreal and back again, from life to death and death to life in an unstable landscape of phantasmagorical sights and sounds. Bava's characters are often thrust into the mutable middle-ground between these two existential extremities, where figures glide through misty, opulently-decorated yet insubstantial and illusionary settings, a universe of semi-darkness where shadows and hallucinations are as graphically actualized as the personages, a spectral passageway linking the natural and supernatural where the way forward or back is uncertain. The oracle Medea in *Hercules in the Haunted World* (*Ercole al centro della terra*, 1961) typifies one stranded in this limbo. The masked form of the woman is merged with an eerie, laboured voice on the soundtrack, modulated as if she were calling up from a chamber deep below ground; she is separated by a curtain of glimmering beads from the camera's (real world's) plane of view and is caught in a flood of changing lights of green, blue, and gold which spin through the frame alternately striking her body and falling behind her to throw her into silhouette, while she sits swaying between intangible polarities.

While many of these expressions are rooted in a photographic style which Bava may have developed earlier in his career, as a cinematographer, the mood and quality of the images in his own films seem dictated by an underlying conception of life as an uncomfortable union of

Christopher Lee as Lichas in HERCULES IN THE HAUNTED WORLD

Barbara Steele as Katia in BLACK SUNDAY

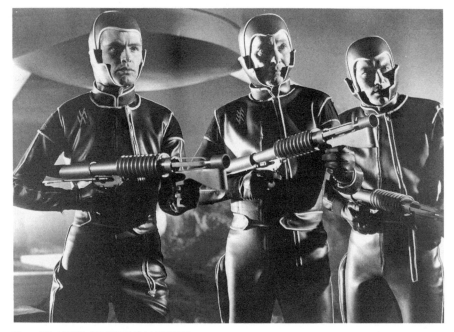

From PLANET OF THE VAMPIRES

illusion and reality and are fused into a dramatic conflict which is primarily psychological as his characters confront the dilemma of distinguishing between the two perceptions. In *Black Sunday,* the protagonist is faced with a choice between a seductive vampire and a virginal young woman who happen to be identical in appearance and who, to further confound his recognition of one or the other, can exchange souls; in the conclusion of *What!* (*La frusta e il corpo,* 1963) the heroine dies without resolving the ambiguity over whether she has genuinely been haunted by the ghost of a murdered former lover or simply conjured up his aspect out of her guilt-ridden subconscious; in *Hercules in the Haunted World,* the travellers to Hades are explicitly warned about the power of illusions by the Hesperides—"Do not believe in what you think you see"—which counsel is verified visually when Hercules and Theseus dive into a sea of flames to discover it is only water.

Just as Bava evokes the *genre* on a formal level—of stylistic resonances with both antecedent and subsequent films—he adds detail to it in his own motion pictures via a specific visual and figurative usage. The cold blue light which envelops the father returning from killing the Turkish vampire, and now undead himself, in the final episode of *Black Sabbath* (*I tre volti della paura,* 1963) makes it instantaneously clear that his family's and his own fear that he might become a *vourdalak* have been realised, that the pall of light which grips him is the equivalent of an aura of death. The apprehension of a character moving down a corridor in *Black Sunday* is transmitted by a shifting side-light, which strikes first one half of the face then the other in an equation of fear and curiosity driving the figure hesitatingly forward (an equation only partially complete in the black-and-white frame of *Black Sunday*, which Bava compounds by also changing from blue to red light with their respective connotations of cold and warmth in analogous sequences in later colour films). Equally informing is the red mist through which Hercules and his companions drift unconsciously, a visceral premonition of the rust-coloured tangled trees and crimson lakes of lava which await them in the underworld. Bava often recruits mythic and social codes as well as purely filmic conventions to instill a sense of anxiety in the viewer based on "misreading"—the two mastiffs which accompany the entry of Barbara Steele playing a dual role in *Black Sunday* hint incorrectly that in this instance she might be the vampire come back with two bestial familiars, who turn out to be mortal pets; or the plot twist at the end of *Planet of the Vampires* which indicates that the astronauts seen throughout the film have not been of the earthly origin which the audience supposed from their speech and human features.

Ultimately all these elements are united to maximise the chances of a positive, emotional response from all viewers—both the novice and the sophisticate in the *genre*—as, for example, in the dissolution of the female *revenant* in *Black Sunday* or in the last combat in *Hercules in the Haunted World* in which the mythic hero uproots a grove of petrified trees to dispatch a cohort of stone-men in garments that resemble cobwebs and overpowers the vampire, Lichas, who wields a knife formed from the fingers of a skeletal hand. When the witch returns to ashes in *Black Sunday*, when the figure of Lichas bursts into flames and falls to dust, neither the event nor its context are new—it is only the rendering, which in these cases and countless similar ones, in films by Bava and scores of others, can transmute both the particulars of narrative and the generalisations of *genre*, can make yet another recounting of the vampire myth as fresh as the oldest of its tellings.

Winona Ryder as Mina and Gary Oldman as Dracula, the "Prince," in BRAM STOKER'S DRACULA

Dracula A.D. 1992

It was enough to make an Old World monster go back into the earth, this stunning irrelevance to the vast scheme of things, enough to make him lie down and die.

Anne Rice, **The Vampire Lestat**

In the prologue of Anne Rice's *The Vampire Lestat*, the members of a rock band observe that "everybody was sick of Count Dracula." Nearly a hundred years after its publication and despite the influence of Rice's series of best-selling novels and other New Age creatures of the night notwithstanding, the title character of Bram Stoker's *Dracula* remains the definitive vampire. But the remorseless predators incarnated by Max Schreck, Bela Lugosi, and Christopher Lee have given way to more thoughtful portrayals, many of whom seem to take their inspiration from the record of Dracula's destruction in the final entry of Mina Harker's Journal where she notes that "even in that moment of final dissolution, there was in the face a look of peace, such as I never could have imagined might have rested there."

I. THE NEW AGE DRACULA

CAPITAL EXCITEMENT! ! !
A YOUNG VIRGIN *DEVOURED*
BY THE AUTHENTIC VAMPIRE FROM PETERWARDEIN
WHO WILL DRINK SEVERAL PINTS OF BLOOD...
WONDERFUL ATTRACTION INDEED! ! !

Paul Feval, **La Ville-Vampire**

The 1974 *Dracula* starring Jack Palance emphasized certain sympathetic aspects of the Count and underscored the Romantic nature of his affliction by linking a past love interest with present victims. Many subsequent versions from the shoestring budget, porno film *Dracula Exotica* (1981) to

Francis Ford Coppola's most recent and most costly *Bram Stoker's Dracula* (1992) have made the same link and reinforced it through flashbacks and actresses in dual roles. The two final adaptations of the 1970s, however, with Louis Jourdan and Frank Langella reverted to earlier prototypes.

The three-part BBC *Count Dracula* (1978) addresses its subject with a restrained, almost documentary style. The opening, sunlit departure of Jonathan Harker for "Bohemia" complete with sandwiches from Mrs. Westenra owes as much to Browning (Robert not Tod) as to Stoker. As with Browning, the irony of God being in His heaven is that all is not right with the world. When he greets Harker, Dracula wears a dark frock coat that closes around him like a cassock and strikes a prayerful pose when he asks that Harker "leave some of the happiness you bring." Like a cleric fallen from grace Louis Jourdan's understated characterization, from the barest trace of an indeterminate accent to the clean-shaven face of an aged matinee idol, suggests horror that lies just beneath the surface. The use of solarization, mattes, step-printing and other optical effects whenever Dracula's vampirism manifests itself visually reinforces the sense of a parallel world of unnatural urges and behavior existing side-by-side with well-mannered, Victorian society. Dracula's coy, white-gowned wives have an almost pre-Raphaelite demeanor when they first approach Harker, an image in marked contrast to their red eyes and fangs or Lucy's erotic behavior after she has joined the vampire's harem. Similarly, the everyday aspect of the breakfast at which Lucy reads aloud the newspaper account of the grisly events aboard the ship that has run aground near Whitby, represents one reality, while her trance-like dance merged with the surreal image of Dracula's face represents quite another. The graphic impact of the actual bat perched on Lucy's bed, precisely because it is not the rubber kind usually favored by filmmakers, is as disquieting as the red, solarized eye superimposed over the sequence.

This tension between the living and the "undead," between propriety and eroticism, is at the core of Stoker's novel. The filmmakers may proclaim in the main titles that this adaptation is "A Gothic Romance based on Bram Stoker's Novel"; but in asking "can one take a life without being responsible for the soul?" the thematic ground is clearly that of early Romanticism. Such a question links this narrative more closely to Mary Shelley's **Frankenstein** than to the truly Gothic ilk of **Varney the Vampire**. What runs counter to this and to Mina's assertion of "that poor soul is the saddest one of all" is the compressed arrogance of Jourdan's performance, as when he remarks: "We must survive all of us. Blood for me, a cooked bird for you. What is the difference?" Because his character has long balanced the disbelief of the civilized society with the actuality of his undead state, he has avoided being "held responsible" either for the tormented

Below left, Louis Jourdan and, below right,   Frank Langella as Dracula

Peter Cushing as MacGregor in TENDRE DRACULA

souls of his victims or, as he asks Harker early on, "for a vivid imagination." It is as if Jourdan's Dracula has survived for centuries by consciously
exploiting the truth of Van Helsing's observation that "evil will not disap-
pear simply because we disapprove of it."

The Langella *Dracula* (1979) was, like Bela Lugosi's, motivated by the
popularity of the actor's Broadway stage version a few years earlier. This
revival of the Balderston-Deane play was, also like Lugosi's, touted for its
star's erotic appeal to women. The film opens in the Hammer tradition:
wolves howl over a black screen; red main titles with dripping letters are
underscored by John Williams with a flourish of minor chords; step print-

ing sends a full moon racing preternaturally across the night sky. There is no Transylvanian castle, no wives, no introduction of the Count behind a cobweb; rather the movie opens with the arrival of the doomed ship carrying Dracula and his boxes of earth. While these omissions streamline the narrative, other changes, such as combining and rearranging character names and traits so that Lucy is Dr. Seward's daughter and engaged to Harker while Mina is the first victim *and* Van Helsing's daughter, may disconcert viewers familiar with the novel. To further romanticize Langella's impersonation, his face is never seen until a fateful dinner party at Dr. Seward's; but given the obvious genre expectations and the publicity used with the picture, the effect of this conceit is minimal. There are other subtle shifts: in setting, to Tintagel in the West of England, and in dramatic emphasis, with lines such as "the children of the night-what *sad* music they make."

Like the melancholy Grandfather Dracula in *La Saga de Los Dracula* (1972), Langella's Count also presents himself as "the saddest, the kindest of all." Unlike Mina in *Count Dracula*, the victim here perceives the sadness of a Romantic Fatal Man, not a doomed creature of the night. Ultimately, the "traditional" staging overwhelms such pointedly clever touches as Lucy's remark that "I love to be frightened." Certain visual effects, like the candle flames optically intertwined with plexiglass pieces and beams of light in Dracula and Lucy's tryst or the solarized point-of-view of the murderous sunlight as Dracula is hoisted skyward at the end, add a sense of anachronism rather than irony. By the time the final chase is underway and the staging of the action has Harker's roadster dodge wagons and carts before crashing, the tension seems more akin to *Fantomas* than Stoker. The unique aspects of this adaptation's ending in which Van Helsing perishes, a sun-blistered Dracula flies off like a black-cloth kite, and Lucy is not cured may be part of a conscious attempt by the filmmakers to be different from all previous versions. In that regard, *Dracula* 1979, looks back to *Dracula A.D. 1972* and forward to *Dracula* 1992; but lacks the inventiveness of either.

Between 1972 and 1992 many if not most of the treatments of Dracula were seriocomic. From the French farce *Tendre Dracula* and *Andy Warhol's Dracula* (both 1973) to *Monster Squad* (1987) and *Nightlife* (1989), the comic mode has proved an effective way for filmmakers to reach an audience. In fact, until the success of *Bram Stoker's Dracula*, the parody *Love at First Bite* (1979) had been the highest-grossing vampire film ever released.

Tendre Dracula, using icons ranging from a dank castle by a lake shore to Peter Cushing, as the horror film star "MacGregor" satirizing the Hammer productions and playing a Dracula figure for the first and only time, is ostensibly a plot by a French producer to "get MacGregor back to horror not moonlight and roses." While it may ultimately be revealed that the white-sheeted ghosts are actually a movie crew recording the events on film, MacGregor's statements, such as "it is romance that separates man from beast," strongly anticipates an important aspect of the Palance and Langella characterizations.

The parody in *Monster Squad* is visual. The opening shots travel sideways from a graveyard to a matte shot of a castle then into a torch-lit crypt where an armadillo scurries past in an obscure homage to the Browning version (Tod not Robert). In the end the playfulness of t-shirts that read "Stephen King Rules," a misunderstood message that "Alucard called about Van Halen's diary," or Dracula's face burned by the garlic on a pizza undercuts both the visual nuances and the straightforward staging with confused results. While neither this film nor *Tendre Dracula* is as overtly comic as *Love at First Bite*, all use the horrific aspects to underscore the comic tension. George Hamilton's dress ball Dracula in *Love at First Bite*, dancing to strains of "I Love the Night Life," parodies *Saturday Night Fever* and the vampire genre with equal aplomb. Meanwhile the would-be vampire killer/psychiatrist, unable to convince the authorities that the undead are anything but his paranoid delusions, perseveres as mightily as any antecedent "Van Helsings" but with hapless results.

The title shot of the variously named *Andy Warhol's Dracula* or *Blood for Dracula* effectively summarizes the viewpoint of the filmmakers: vampirism as camp, something that is at once chilling and comedic, decorative and disgusting, the same kind of ghoulish sideshow that Paul Feval conjured up in 1875. The diverse hands of Andy Warhol, Paul Morrissey, and Antonio Margheriti represent different approaches to the genre that came together in this film for a diffracted result. The title shot begins in close as

George Hamilton in
LOVE AT FIRST BITE

Robin Krause © 1978

the pale and gaunt Udo Kier applies eye make-up and rouges his cheeks then pulls back as he takes up a brush and blackens his hair. Finally, the camera pans to a mirror to reveal that there is no reflection. The initial implication is traditional: no reflection therefore the character is a vampire. Given that the title of the picture and the actor's appearance have already supplied the audience with ample cues about the nature of the figure before them, the shot has more figurative than narrative value. But without a shot from Dracula's point-of-view, it leaves unanswered the mocking question: can a vampire see himself in the mirror when he needs to apply his make-up? Unfortunately, little in *Blood for Dracula* fulfills the promise of its initial shot. The visual impact of the sustained shots of the first bite on the neck that seems to go on for over a minute (actually 39 seconds) or moments later the sequence of Dracula sprawled by a shining white porcelain tub and regurgitating the tainted blood dissipate rather than underline the eroticism or horror of the moment. Other shots such as the wide angle from the foot of Dracula's wheelchair as he reenters his room are unmotivated visual flourishes. The equation of Dracula's search for virgin blood with the political "vampirism" of aristocrats over workers is also thin. "That class stuff...it's a thing of the past," remarks Mario, the gardener who deflowers all the Marquis Belfiore's daughters, in an aside that is meant to be more wry than radical. In the end, the intention to create parody from exaggeration, whether Dracula is vomiting blood or having his arms and legs chopped off, sputters as feebly as the character himself when he laments that "the blood of these whores is killing me."

Nightlife combines aspects of *Love at First Bite* or other overt parodies of the vampire tradition with elements of the new age mythology; or as the sympathetic vampiress Angelique observes, "This is a new and wonderful century. We're no longer monsters. We're simply diseased." In a tactic reminiscent of Anne Rice's Lestat, Angelique buries herself for 100 years

Udo Kier
in
BLOOD
FOR
DRACULA

to escape from Vlad, the one who made her a vampire and who is, of course, relentless in pursuit of her. In fact, when Vlad reminds Angelique that "there was a time when you reveled in being a murderous monster" or when she drinks blood from a wine glass, *Nightlife* is more a parody of Rice than Stoker. Like *Monster Squad*, *Nightlife* opens with a visual treatment that recalls the icons of the genre: mummified corpses in the catacombs of Mexico City and nocturnal gravediggers unearthing a coffin as wolf howls fill the soundtrack. Angelique's discovery of the modern world is evoked with optical effects to simulate her point-of-view and through her encounters with the unfamiliar from elevators to discos. For the sympathetic physician, Dr. Zuckerman, who revives her after her abortive visit to a blood bank, Angelique is the victim of some unknown disease. Zuckerman is as fascinated by Angelique as by her disease, by her blood which swirls "like some kind of intricate and delicate ballet." Because of this fascination he remains equally unperturbed when he cuts his finger and she sucks it sensually or when she tells him that she can feel the presence of others who have her disease who "form a cult with rules and rituals...they kill for blood." Zuckerman makes two key discoveries: that ultraviolet light makes vampire plasma react like plastique explosive and that the endorphins released into the bloodstream by the victim's fear sustain the vampires. These "scientific" explanations are part of the serious side of *Nightlife*, as is Vlad's affirmation of his vampire credo: "To be diseased in this culture is to be a monster... what your century has produced in greater quantities than the past is arrogance... Well, I cannot be squeezed into the small box of your reality. I exist beyond the realm of your imagination." In saying that there are more things in heaven and earth than are dreamt of in Zuckerman's philosophy, Ben Cross' black-clad Vlad reasserts his genre kinship with the Dracula of Louis Jourdan.

The mixture of comic and dramatic aspects in *Sundown: the Vampire in Retreat* (1990) yields a similar result. In a plot that has Dracula altering his name to Margulak ("I was getting a little too famous. I had to change my name") and starting a town of vampires called "Purgatory" in the desert, where sun block, shades, and parasols are *de rigueur*, the aspects of parody and atonement are equally in play. Again the rest of the narrative–which hinges on efforts to manufacture a vile-tasting, synthetic blood and the uprising of a "traditional" faction that wants to drink the real thing and arms itself with automatic weapons that fire wooden bullets– overwhelms the slender pretext. Stylistic understatement, such as having vampires and humans alike drive vintage cars, subtly reinforces the underlying anachronism; but by the time Van Helsing's great-grandson is turned into a vampire, that point has been blunted if not lost altogether. The culmination is a pitched battle and the erection of a huge wooden cross that burns or

sunders the bodies of the traditionals but leaves the repentant Margulak and his followers unscathed. Because Margulak himself has been a subsidiary character, the cause for his transformation is never clear. Without that information to counterbalance against the genre archetype, much of the ironic impact is diminished.

The very concept of vampire towns like Purgatory, Salem's Lot in *A Return to Salem's Lot* (1987) or Allsburg in *Children of the Night* (1992) test the limits of suspension of disbelief. In a tradition that revolves around secrecy and concealment, how can a town full of undead bloodsuckers hope to go unnoticed by vampire killers? The eccentric Romanian played by Samuel Fuller in *A Return to Salem's Lot*, who casually goes about staking the denizens of the town during daylight, is as much a descendant of Van Helsing as his great-grandson in *Sundown: The Vampire in Retreat*.

It is only when anger reveals their "true form" that the vampires of Salem's Lot resemble Murnau's bat-like title character from *Nosferatu*, albeit via a rubber prosthetic that calls to mind a cheap Halloween mask. Despite collaboration with actors as diverse as Michael Moriarty and Samuel Fuller, *A Return to Salem's Lot* is like most horror films directed by Larry Cohen a mixture of odd characters in even odder circumstances. At times, in other Cohen films such as *Q* or *God Told Me To*, displaced myth and modern ennui interact for an emotionally effective result. Despite an incongruous opening which finds its protagonist filming a documentary on human sacrifices in the Amazon jungle, the results in *A Return to Salem's Lot* are more irregular than intriguing.

In terms of the Dracula figure, the original *Salem's Lot* (1980), Werner Herzog's *Nosferatu*, and *Bram Stoker's Dracula* all represent a kind of neo-traditionalism, i.e. a return respectively to Gothic, Expressionistic, and Romantic conventions. The early Stephen King novel, *'Salem's Lot*, was a seminal work in the New England, neo-Gothic style which that author was to popularize. While it seldom focuses on vampirism, King's other work is in contrast to the neo-Romanticism of Anne Rice and typifies the new fright novel. The adaptation of 'Salem's Lot follows that tradition.

In his critical study of "the entire horror phenomenon," **Danse Macabre**, Stephen King himself acknowledges that the snarling performance of actor Reggie Nalder in *Salem's Lot* as a baldheaded, pale-skinned, yellow-eyed and rat-fanged Mr. Barlow "brings us full circle to Max Schreck again." King's own prose description of Barlow is quite different, in tone as much as in detail: the "face was strong and intelligent and handsome...hair swept back from his brow in the European manner...red, lurid eyes...long and sensitive fingers like a concert pianist's..." even "a wine-colored tie." More significantly King's vampire addresses his victims in "a rich, powerful voice" with a formal *hauteur* unmistakably derived from Stoker; he even leaves taunting letters detailing abominations he has planned for them to endure. For the filmmakers, Barlow is a speechless monstrosity, a glowering elemental whose lines are given over to his human associate, Straker. While James Mason's portrayal captures the same tone of condescension towards the vampire's pitiful victims, the words coming from him rather than Barlow create a very different irony.

After discussing the psychological sub-text of Stoker's novel in **Danse Macabre**, King asserts that "when I wrote my own vampire novel, I decided to largely jettison the sexual angle." Despite this King's town doctor, James Cody, gives a graphic account of the sexual connotation of the vampire's bite. King also expresses his admiration for Stoker's manipulation of the narrative in which Dracula is all the more menacing because he appears infrequently, a method employed in **'Salem's Lot**. Images of the film Barlow's bared fangs are similarly spread throughout the picture; but Barlow's leering victims seem to pop-up constantly, dissipating the impact. In fact, the filmmakers seem content to use shock cuts and musical stings for cheap scares rather than sustain viewer apprehension. For instance when Susan Norton follows Mark Petrie into the evil Marsten House and he suddenly leaps out at her, the viewer is hammered into her shocked point-of-view. The montage of scurrying rats and stuffed bobcats seems equally arbitrary. The medium close shot which follows and holds Susan and Mark in a long take as they are assailed by sounds from all over the house is a much more subtle and effective externalization of their trapped tension.

The actual vampire manifestations in the film *Salem's Lot* are staged against a prototypical background of natural disturbances: the cold emanating from the mysterious crate, the wind that sweeps through the woods and startles a child before a black form blots out the frame, the dark storm clouds that pass over Marsten House casting ominous shadows. When an undead boy floats up to Mark Petrie's window in a blue cloud, it is like a grotesque variant of a cherub. Crucifixes, wooden stakes, and other standard paraphernalia are in evidence from when Mark chases off his former playmate to the destruction of Barlow. The issues of faith and evil, issues central to King's concept, are also at play in the film with varying degrees of explicitness. "Do you believe a thing can be inherently evil?" Ben Mears ask his old high school teacher. "I think that an evil house attracts evil men." In both novel and film, against such evil but with faith, Mears can effectively wield a cross made out of tongue depressors; without it, Father Callahan's heirloom crucifix is useless.

As might be expected, Werner Herzog's direct remake of Murnau, *Nosferatu: Phantom der Nacht* (1979), also recreates the look of Max Schreck with actor Klaus Kinski. In Herzog's muted color scheme, the pale skin, black eyes, and bat-like ears combine in a way that also recalls the appearance of Conrad Veidt as the Somnambulist in *The Cabinet of Dr. Caligari.* Where the filmmakers of *Salem's Lot* synthesized the King book into a variant on American Gothic, Herzog's appropriate cultural option is for neo-Expressionism. Both the dreamlike long shots of characters wandering the city streets under a hazy light that seems neither day nor night and the synthesized rumblings, screeches, and exploding chords of Popul Vuh's electronic underscore sustain the Expressionistic mode.

For Herzog as for other self-conscious filmmakers, the political implications of *Nosferatu*, of vampirism itself, go back to the Age of Reason. After the sudden surge of interest in Eastern European reports of the undead during the first part of the Eighteenth Century, Voltaire wryly summarized the political ironies of the phenomenon that "a large part of Europe was infested by vampires for five or six years, but there are no more" in his **Philosophical Dictionary**: "One never heard speak of vampires in London, nor even in Paris. I admit that in these two cities, there

Below, Klaus Kinski recalling the make-up of Max Schreck in Herzog's NOSFERATU

were...business people who sucked people's blood in broad daylight, but however corrupted they were never dead." Voltaire's analogy was picked up and extended more than a century later when Karl Marx referred to "dead labor that, like a vampire, lives only by sucking living labor"; and it continues to apply in Herzog's view, in which a proletarian fervor compels Lucy Harker to sacrifice herself in order to destroy a parasitic aristocrat. Without the oratory of *Blood for Dracula*'s Mario, Herzog's neo-Brechtian, alienated staging leaves the political statement unresolved.

Herzog's plague of rats, like Browning's armadillos, takes its iconic inspiration from Stoker's original. Both within and without the Expressionistic tradition, not just in Germany or the United States, many filmmakers have relied more heavily on production design and/or acting style than on cinematography to evoke the genre. Universal's recently restored, Spanish language *Drácula* (1931) exemplifies the best and worst of this tradition. Using the same script and sets and borrowing several of the most evocative shots from Browning's film as described in Chapter Two, this version, in particular, plays out many scenes with the mad Renfield that Browning abridged, most notably a brief assault by Drácula's wives. From Drácula's first appearance out of a white mist that spews from under the coffin lid, the supernaturalism of the piece is not as understated as its English language counterpart. *Drácula* also eschews understatement in its acting style and permits its lead actor, Carlos Villarias, a wide array of melodramatic leers and poses. Least understated is its eroticism from the cape-covered kisses of the vampire to the suffusion of sexual energy emanating from Eva after she has drunk Drácula's blood, which prompts Juan Harker to exclaim that she "looks marvelous." While Browning staged the final scenes in Carfax Abbey with an incongruous languor, director George Melford derives appropriate suspense by intercutting Harker's frenzied assault on the abbey door with Drácula bending over Eva and the unforeseen intrusion of the sun's rays.

The first Japanese adaptation of Stoker *Chi o Suu Me (Lake of Dracula)* (1971) is so loosely derived from the novel that it only retains the Mina and Lucy analogs (here, sisters) and other odd bits and pieces. It does effectively restage the ending of Fisher's *Dracula* and invents a prologue in which the Mina character, as a little girl, visits the local old dark house. As was suggested in Chapter Two, the Dracula figure itself, with slicked-back hair, ubiquitous white scarf, and bizarre golden eyes, is an insoluble blend of Western and Eastern elements, just as the shots of the Lucy figure wandering through the Japanese woods with back light and low hanging mist is a graft of different Expressionistic traditions. There is one shot which strikingly synthesizes the Japanese scheme of stylized violence and the "Old World monster." The Cinemascope frame is fixed tightly on the vic-

Above: Keanu Reeves as Harker and Gary Oldman as the Old Dracula

Above: Gary Oldman in armor as Vlad; below, Van Helsing confronts the vampiric Lucy

tim's neck. Her dark hair and the vampire's black cloak cut diagonally across the the left and right sides of the shot. Neither face is seen but at the image's center are the ruffled edges of her nightdress and the bare throat, down which a single drop of blood draws a bright red line. The chilling image recalls an observation of Goethe's *Faust*: "How strange that such a lovely neck/A single band of crimson must bedeck./A knife's edge scarcely seems less wide."

Sixty years after the Universal versions and twenty years after Hammer's *Dracula A.D. 1972*, *Bram Stoker's Dracula* ostensibly takes the audience back to the original concept. Originally entitled *Dracula: the Untold Story*, the final version is both the highest budgeted and largest grossing vampire film ever made. Francis Ford Coppola's adaptation has literally taken Stoker's material to new heights and single-handedly revitalized the vampire film in much the same way that Anne Rice's first vampire novel startled the literary community. Because it derives as much from grand opera and the Romantic literary tradition as from Stoker, Coppola's film, as forcefully as Rice's books, represents neo-Romanticism in the genre.

While the narrative of *Bram Stoker's Dracula* does attempt to be just that, faithful to the plot line of the novel, two key elements seem to come from Richard Matheson's script for Dan Curtis' 1974 version: that Dracula is Prince Vlad Tepes and, as already mentioned, the identification through flashbacks of Lucy as the reincarnation of the love of his (human) life. In the novel, Dracula does tell Harker of "one of my own race who as Voivode crossed the Danube and beat the Turk on his own ground. This was a Dracula indeed!" Much later Van Helsing posits that their adversary "must, indeed, have been that Voivode Dracula, who won his name against the Turk." Stoker's research source never identifies the "Voïvode," or Count, Dracula as "Vlad the Impaler"; but the books by Anthony Masters and McNally and Florescu published the year before Curtis' production do make this connection. Reputedly, the first such link in a film adaptation was made by the Voïvode's old enemies in the Turkish production, *Drakula Istanbulda* (1952); but that film was never released in the West. The concept that a current victim of the vampiric Voïvode resembles a past love does seem to be Matheson's invention. In any case, given the number of other pictures since 1974 which have also made these links to Vlad and lost loves, the makers of *Bram Stoker's Dracula* would be hard pressed to claim that these concepts are original to this adaptation.

There are a few visual resonances to the Curtis *Dracula* also, most notably in the use of superimposed titles or an occasional, elaborate camera movement; but on the whole the very multiplicity of Coppola's effects from transparent, stage-like backings to layered lap dissolves forcefully separate *Bram Stoker's Dracula* from any previous adaptation. Coppola's treatment of the opening scenes combine the battle poses of *Alexander Nevsky* with the ominous colorations of the Gothic interiors from *Ivan the Terrible*. The first shot, as the narrator tells of the fall of Constantinople, is of the dome of an Orthodox cathedral surrounded by billowing black clouds of smoke as the city burns. The cut is directly inward to a tighter composition, again recalling Eisenstein's method of montage. The next shot of the Maltese-shaped stone cross falling in slow motion is an expressionistic treatment. Finally, the image of a map over which the shadow of an Islamic crescent slowly spreads recalls the expositional graphics of pre-War American cinema.

Ultimately, Coppola's style is much more reminiscent of Mario Bava in its Baroque opulence than any English or American filmmakers. The battle scene staged in silhouette against a red sky and ending with hundreds of the Turks impaled on spears is both an effective and economical staging that lays out the past events like a fiery Bayeaux tapestry and captures metaphorically the way in which the physical "dimension" of scenes from the more distant past is reduced by time. If there is a deficiency in the early expositional scenes of *Bram Stoker's Dracula*, it is that Coppola does not exploit the genre expectations of the viewer. By opening with past occurences and using the same actress to portray both Mina and Vlad's wife, Elisabeta, the filmmakers substitute certainty for suspense. As the audience participates in the narrative development, they know the key fact of Dracula's doomed romance with Mina. This supports the creative choice of the filmmakers to emphasize the "love story"; but the first third of the motion picture also contains some verbal asides and visual effects that do not fully support the narrative direction. When Dracula tells Harker that "I was married once, ages ago," the irony is one which only Dracula shares with the audience, since they are already aware of the double entendre and Harker cannot possibly perceive it. Clearly the parallel cutting encourages viewer identification with Mina, not Dracula or Harker. When Harker explores the castle, finds the strange bottle of amber fluid that drips up, and is attacked by the wives on a surreal bed, the special effects develop neither the narrative nor the character identification. After Dracula floats in and proclaims, as in the novel, that "This man is mine," the filmmakers add a second line to his response to the wives' protests: "Yes, I, too, can love. And I shall love again." Again the implication is already clear to the audience from genre expectation but has no meaning for any other characters in this scene.

Coppola himself has stressed the importance of the costumes. (In fact, on that subject, he co-authored with the costume designer one the many books published in conjunction with the film's release.) The elaborate hair style and blood-red dressing gown in which the white-haired Count greets

Anthony Hopkins as Van Helsing in BRAM STOKER'S DRACULA

Harker, for instance, is a new conception, at variance with the novel's "clad in black from head to foot." When Harker sees the Count crawl out "lizard fashion" in this costume trailing a long red tail of fabric, it makes for a remarkably different effect than "his cloak spreading out around him like great wings" as staged in the Hammer, Jourdan, and Langella versions. However striking Vlad's red suit of armor might be, bringing imagery from both Gray's **Anatomy** and samurai films into a medieval setting, it pushes the viewer over the brink of suspension of disbelief into a state of stylized dread.

In Coppola's extremely active symbolic scheme, Messianic allusions can be interposed with sexual imagery, as when the Dracula figure kneels with arms outstretched on Mina's bed in a crucified posture. When Dracula renounces God, symbols overlap amd a phallic sword pierces the center of a cross and draws blood. A more elaborate mise-en-scene accompanies the return of Mina and Jonathan to London. As she tells the viewer, "Now that I am married I begin to understand the nature of my feelings for my strange friend," a cut across the square brings a craning move down a phallic column which reveals Dracula standing in the right foreground. More confusing is the externalized sexual frenzy as Lucy and Mina dance in a maze during the rainstorm that arrives with Dracula's ship. The camera even pivots dizzily at the end.

As in the ending of *The Godfather*, Coppola also intercuts a sacrament with savagery. Instead of a baptism and mob murders, Mina and Jonathan's Orthodox wedding ceremony parallels Dracula's last attack on Lucy, the final shot of which is a literal explosion of blood. Blood itself, its swirling cells captured through microphotography and resembling Zuckerman's description of an "intricate and delicate ballet" in *Nightlife*, is repeatedly superimposed over the shots. Besides astral projection, it would seem that Dr. Zuckerman's spiritual forebear, Dr. Van Helsing, has the ability to smell this blood, to catch the scent of the vampire as when he suddenly waltzes with Mina on the terrace.

Throughout the picture, step-printed shots from the vampire's point-of-view speed up the motion to confirm, as Rice's characters already have, that "the dead travel fast." For Coppola, the movement represents not only a preternatural power but also, whether through a wrought-iron gate at the zoo or up the steps to Lucy's bedroom, a release of pent-up sexual energy. While symbolic overtones are just that, *overtones*, certain plot points imperil the credibility of the narrative. The first encounter of the young Dracula and Mina, when he tells her that "I have crossed oceans of time to find you," is a multi-layered staging culminating in his temptation and refusal to "vampirize" her immediately, as the escaped wolf arrives and the insistent, mellifluous love theme enters its lowest register through the cellos. This darkly romantic moment follows a black-and-white peep show, which must leave the viewer wondering why Dracula would risk taking Mina to such a place. Bringing the sexual tensions of Stoker's novel forcefully to the surface, as when Lucy and Mina giggle over a pornographically illustrated volume of **Arabian Nights**, creates a literalism that is at odds with the figurative elements. By the time Dracula and Mina drink absinthe and an extreme close shot through a glass isolates the "SIN" from the label, the film has moved well beyond Stoker's fiction.

Like the overlaid maps and miniature trains, optical devices such as the St. Elmo-like blue fire on the road to the castle are alternately effective and intrusive. The composite of a train on a red clay roadbed riding at the top of the frame over Harker's diary at the bottom, while a voiceover provides the essential information, adds needless distraction. Some of the dissolves, however, from the peacock's feather or the circle of fire to the dying sun or from the bite marks on Lucy's neck to the eyes of a wolf, are chillingly evocative of the 1890s mixture of decadence, primordial power, and Victorian gentility that is inherent to the novel.

II. THE SENSITIVE MALE VAMPIRE

One evening a vampire rises and realizes what he has feared perhaps for decades, that he simply wants no more of life... And that vampire goes out to die. No one will find his remains.

Anne Rice, **Interview with the Vampire**

Graveyard Shift (1987), not to be confused with the better known *Stephen King's Graveyard Shift*, exemplifies the way in which newer filmmakers combine aspects of the vampire legend with the traditions of other film types.

In a contemporary setting "Stephen Tsepes" is a taxi driver on the grave-yard shift, a characterization that harkens back simultaneously a few centuries to Vlad the Impaler and a few years to Travis Bickle. Christopher Frayling notes in his excellent new study **Vampyres**: "In folklore the vampire was likely to hurl himself at the victim's chest–to smother as well as to suck. In fiction, the preferred erogenous zone was invariably the neck." Tsepes is not one of these Victorian vampires but bites his female victims on the breast. Like other taxi drivers, he drinks coffee, smokes cigarettes and even eats catsup-covered french fries. Unlike them, it is blood which he wipes from his mouth with the back of his hand.

Like the Curtis and Coppola Draculas, Tsepes encounters Michelle, someone bearing a striking resemblance to a woman seen in flashbacks whom he loved in life. Tsepes seduces but does not "turn" her to vampirism. As an early sequence reveals, Tsepes uses his job to find sick or suicidal women who are already doomed. He explains to Michelle "that is the time I come to my lovers, when they are in the cycle of death." Although Tsepes' powers tell him when they first meet that Michelle is terminally ill, she inspires him to end his own life rather than hers. He avers that "I have been here for centuries. I am tired" and that previous attempts to expire failed because he "did not have the courage." The intervention of Michelle's philandering husband, whom she first describes to Tsepes with unwitting irony as "quite the lady-killer," brings about the quietus which Tsepes desires. In the process, Michelle *is* vampirized by one of Tsepes' "wives"; and the ending reveals that the entire narrative has been a flashback from a present time in which she now drives a taxi in search of prey.

Although it features the same actor as the lead vampire, *Graveyard Shift II: the Understudy* (1989) is neither a sequel nor a treatment of the vampire as a confused predator. If anything, the female protagonist's mixed emotions about becoming a vampire and attaining immortality recall *Son of Dracula. To Die For* features yet another low-budget "Vlad Tepish" (the spellings change but the allusions remain the same) and yet another woman torn between predatory and erotic desires but without any of the thoughtfulness or originality of *Graveyard Shift*. In the sequel, *Son of Darkness: To Die For II*, the same screenwriter presents a revived Vlad who has changed his name to "Max Schreck." Unlike his silent film star namesake, Dr. Schreck is an emergency room physician and as such has access to a blood bank which can sustain him and his vampiric underlings Celia (also resurrected from part one) and Tom. Unlike Angelique in *Nightlife*, neither of these "adolescent" vampires are excited about biting into plastic bags to feed their blood hunger. While he toys with mortal love *To Die For*'s Tepish is, unlike *Graveyard Shift*'s Tsepes, not drawn to self-destruction.

If any of these modern incarnations of Vlad is "sensitive," it is more to the pointlessness of their unending lives than to the suffering of their victims. The coven of vampires in *A Return to Salem's Lot* feed on cattle for their own safety. As their leader observes, "Human blood is still the best, but the way things are going nowadays, it's not quite good for you, what with drugs, alcohol, hepatitis, and the AIDS thing going around." Rice's Louis in **Interview** preys on rats "rather than go through the world bringing misery and death to human creatures"; but Louis still revels in his "vampire nature...the greatest adventure of my life; all that went before it was confused, clouded." Unlike **Interview with the Vampire**, *A Return to Salem's Lot* never speculates on the feelings of either its vampire children or its vampire senior citizens. Clearly for any human outsider, like the grown man who returns to find the lover of his adolescence still a teenager, the vampires living in Salem's Lot are freaks. Equally freakish are the half-human, half-vampire "drones" they want him to father; and yet in their enclosed society, the very old and very young help the vampires eternally to mimic human life. To what end? For characters such as these, it is the lack of self-consciousness that keeps them from despair, from the existential anguish that Steven Tsepes shares with Travis Bickle or Raskolnikov or countless other fictional characters.

Anne Rice's four-part *Vampire Chronicles* contain a portrayal of vampirism that readily draws from the full breadth of the myth. Both in its narrative structure and visual style, *Dance of the Damned* (1989) is the most faithful of the unofficial adaptations of Rice's work. Like her characters, the nameless vampire in *Dance of the Damned* has extremely sensitive vision and hearing. Rosy-colored shots externalize this vampire's point-of-view as he peers through the darkness to see and hear private conversations in back rooms. When Rice's Louis flicks an ash from his interviewer's sleeve, the movement is barely perceptible. All of Rice's "immortals" overpower their victims with astonishing strength. In *Dance of the Damned*, optical stepprinting propels this figure effortlessly around mortal characters and a snap of his wrist can drive a flower stem through an human eye. Besides sporting the long hair and black garb which the vampire Lestat favors, this nameless predator also tries to avoid "innocent blood." And, of course, he is in mortal peril from the rays of the sun.

During the course of the night in which this elemental tries to communicate his feelings to his next victim, he explains that he is, unlike Lestat, not an "Old World monster": "I'm not supernatural. I'm a separate species. I was born not made." While it may be of little consolation to his victims, also unlike Rice's creatures who prowl every night, this vampire asserts that "I rarely feed and when I do I only take the ones that have given up." What really links *Dance of the Damned* to the ethos of Rice's Chronicles

The vampire (Scott Valentine) and the victim (Charlie Spradling) as soul mates in
TO SLEEP WITH A VAMPIRE

is the attitude of this vampire. Despite knowledge, money, power, endless life, he yearns to understand mortals and their feelings as powerfully as he yearns to see the sun. Jodi, his latest prospective victim, is a despairing, young mother, deprived of her child by her ex-husband's wealthy family and reduced to performing in a topless bar for a meager living. Like Tsepes in *Graveyard Shift* or Rice's Louis, this character can not only hear her words but also read her thoughts to learn that she is pondering her own destruction. Because he has never been human, never died and returned to prey on his own kind, he has neither the guilt of Louis nor the cruelty of Lestat nor the world weariness of the New Age Draculas. His melancholy is because, as he tells Jodi, "you'll never understand the emptiness of living forever."

Although she is unhappy, Jodi is anything but a willing victim. When she agrees to show her captor what the sun is like and takes him to a local beach to evoke the mood, she is hoping for an opportunity to escape. In the course of playing out her part, she comes to sense the truth in the vampire's declarations about his feelings. Unlike the dozens of Lucys, Minas, and other women who are enthralled by the preternatural eroticism of their attackers, Jodi's empathy is entirely human. It is this quality which gives the ending of *Dance of the Damned* its tragic overtones and makes the nameless vampire closer to the Fatal Man of Mary Shelley than most others of his ilk. In his gratitude for "showing" him the sun, just minutes before he must drink her blood or perish himself, he gives her a taste of his nature. Like a potent hallucinogen, his blood alters her perception and momentarily gives her the power to break free. As she flees to a locked bathroom and tears out the material blocking the window, the sunlight filters in. She implores him twice: "Please don't come in," as much out of fear for him as for herself. Despite seeing the rays of light seep under the door, in an act of human self-immolation, he does enter. "It is beautiful," he says and perishes.

To Sleep with A Vampire (1993) is a remake of *Dance of the Damned*. While the plot and dialogue changes are so minimal that entire scenes are simply restagings with different actors, the overall tone of the film is subtly different. To begin with, the nameless vampire is not stylishly coiffed and attired, but unshaven and threadbare. As in *Dance of the Damned*, he is introduced as he approaches the strip club; but *To Sleep with A Vampire* has an almost surrealistic prologue. In the alley he encounters a woman around forty and a boy around twelve, who are watching a bunch of white balloons float up into the sky towards the full moon. The vampire is clearly hungry for blood, as revealed by a shot of the boy's neck from his point-of-view–rendered in this film as slightly over-exposed black-and-white with accompanying rumblings on the sountrack. As he bends towards the white flesh, the woman says, "Please, don't." Oddly, he staggers and falls to the pavement next to a shard of a mirror which reflects his face, as if the filmmakers were underlining the fact that this is not a typical vampire.

After this unusual opening, *To Sleep with A Vampire* loses its stylistic focus. When he watches his intended victim, here named Nina, dance, her open-mouthed crawl up the runway is a cat-like or vampiric pose that antcipates the transference theme; but when not performing, she is harder-edged than Jodi. The encounter on the bus from *Dance of the Damned* becomes a rumble in the alley where would-be motorcycle thieves are tossed aside; and there is another, rather pointless bar fight later. Where *Dance of the Damned* isolated its characters in a shared, nocturnal interlude, *To Sleep with A Vampire*'s night world is populated by many others. The vampire's impoverished state, colorless visions, and relentless hunger humanize him more in this version; and Nina's desire for him to appear human is evident as she repeatedly asks him to reveal his name. In fact, when he perishes, unlike *Dance of the Damned*, she cradles his head on her lap, and he does tell her his name. For all its stress on the vampire's humanity, *To Sleep with A Vampire* never evokes the Romantic grandeur typical of Rice's figures, which *Dance of the Damned* had at least partly captured.

Roger Corman's other recent production, *Dracula Rising* (1993) features two vampires with conflicting codes of conduct in a shallow variant of Rice's Louis and Lestat. *Dracula Rising* goes so far as to use the beer advertisement parody from Zuckerman's nightmare in *Nightlife*, "Blood Light," as straight dialogue. Its extemely sensitive protagonist is quite literally the son of Dracula, having been both physically sired and metaphysically vampirized centuries before by Vlad the Impaler himself. In another variation on recent conceptions from Matheson/Curtis to Coppola/Hart, flashbacks reveal that this Vlad (Junior?) actually sought vampirehood because the peasant girl who seduced him away from his monastic vows was burned at the stake, and he hoped to remain alive, or at least undead, until she was reincarnated. "I embrace what I am. You cannot," his fellow monk-cum-vampire lectures Vlad Jr. Because he is ambivalent about his vampirism, when his evil cohort does lure the reincarnated girl whom he consigned to the flames to Romania, Vlad refuses to "turn" her. After destroying his antagonist in a climactic, low-budget confrontation that mimics the stylized battle scenes in *Bram Stoker's Dracula*, the blond, white-clad Vlad immolates himself by waiting for sunrise.

Perhaps the best illustration of the conflict between traditional and sensitive figures is *Subspecies* (1991), since it features two vampiric half-brothers. One, Radu, is a virulent killer who suggests *Nosferatu*'s Schreck before undead alopecia removed his hair. The other, Stefan, is a reluctant bloodsucker who "follows his father's way" and controls his vampirism by taking nourishment from a "bloodstone." In a somewhat irrelevant sub-plot (which accounts for the film's title) Radu escapes from his father's cage by breaking off the tips of his extremely long fingers, which turn into small beasts that do his bidding. At the same time, three young women arrive to do graduate study on the folklore of the area. From various sources they learn of the legend of the vampires who saved the town centuries ago from a siege by the Turks; but for some reason there are no references to the ruins of a nearby castle where the locals still believe the vampires are confined. Stefan, who is ostensibly an anthropologist, suggests in his first conversation with the young women that this omission is because such ruins are "invisible to all but the most sensitive eyes." With these words, the character self-identifies with "sensitivity"; and the visual treatment, from

Anders Hove as the remarkably unattractive Radu in SUBSPECIES

close-ups of the actor's face to long shots as he prowls the ruins in his black leather overcoat, reinforce this characterization. Because Stefan is "unliving" proof of his belief that "there is good and evil among the vampires as there is among men" and because he can survive without victims, he is less conflicted than Steven Tsepes or the non-human vampire of *Dance of the Damned*. Although the last shot of the beheaded Radu smiling at his little minions suggests that he may yet devise a way to rise again (which he does in *Subspecies II* and *III*), it is Stefan's very sensitivity which permits an unusual, happy ending. Michelle (which seems to be a popular name for the consorts of sensitive vampires), who is the only woman to survive and the one to whom Stefan is most attracted, has been bitten by Radu. Because she is terrified that she may die and, like her friends, become one of his ilk, she pleads, "I don't want to be like him, Stefan. Make me like you." Although he had never planned to turn her to vampirism, Stefan now makes her his bride and they lie down together in his coffin.

The Romanian setting with its stone ramparts and ruins both in *Subspecies* and *Dracula Rising* creates a context of modern characters in antique locales where superstitious beliefs are common. Like Harker in the opening chapters of **Dracula**, the outsiders encounter locals who speak in hushed tones of "creatures" and demons. As already discussed, other filmmakers have prefered the situational irony of *Graveyard Shift* or *Dance of the Damned*, where "Old World monsters" lurk in coffee shops. The plot of *Pale Blood* centers on a psychopathic videographer who kills and drains women of blood in hopes that the publicity will attract an authentic vampire "lonely" for his own kind. Michael Fury, who comes from Romania to Los Angeles for exactly that reason, is almost as sensitive as Stefan. He "hasn't killed for years" and discourages the local investigator, whom he hired, from her fascination with him. The way in which Michael finally finds a soulmate lacks any of the impact of *Subspecies*, but *Pale Blood* does

Michelle (Laura Tate) pleads with the sensitive Stefan (Michael Watson) in SUBSPECIES: "Make me like you."

create a most unusual prop: a garment bag that opens into a zip-up coffin, the perfect accessory for the modern, jet-setting vampire.

Alexander d'Hiver, the lead character in *Tale of a Vampire* (1992), is the most recent example of the admixture of the Eastern European and Anne Rice traditions. Although he does haunt a research library during the day, Alex is a night prowler. In the title sequence, he demonstrates an affinity with Rice's Louis when he takes a black cat, which the viewer might have mistaken for a vampiric familiar, bites into the animal's neck, and fairly gargles with its blood. From the staccato montage immediately following the titles, the viewer learns that a man has been killed in a car explosion; a young woman, Anne, tearfully identifies the charred body; Alex is a vampire haunted by flashbacks to a past love who resembles Anne; and a bearded man in a black hat is somehow involved. This man, in fact, writes a letter which leads Anne to a job at the library where "Alex is writing a thesis about religious martyrs, people who were burned at the stake."

The screenplay by Shimako Sato, co-written from her story, opens with a voice reading from the poem "Annabel Lee" and contains a fairly novel twist, in which the Man in the Dark Hat, named Edgar, is ultimately revealed to be E.A. Poe, likely undead himself and pursuing Alex through the decades to avenge the seduction of his child bride, Virginia Clemm. The visual emphasis by Sato, the director, is on the details of composition and design. When Alex follows Anne, the Virginia Clemm look-alike, home from the library, a long establishing shot watches her going into a market. Then a cut into a close up of very red tomatoes, like the red clothes of Virginia and Anne, imagistically reaffirms the blood theme. Sato treats the blood itself, whether pouring from a slashed throat or as a single drop falling from Alex's lips onto Anne's cheek, as a symbolic substance and makes Alex's stealthy visit to her bedchamber a chilling paraphrase of a traditional vampiric visitation.

Sato's style, with its penetrating, sustained shots, creates an atmosphere seldom evoked in earlier Japanese-made vampire films. The girl school principal-cum-vampire in *Chi o Suu Bara (Evil of Dracula)* (1975) with his anachronistic black coat, pale make-up, and comic opera fangs is a misdesigned and misplaced Western icon. Under Sato's direction, Alex D'Hiver's London echoes the visual traditions of Japanese cinema and almost becomes the dark side of Yasujiro Ozu's Tokyo

As the flashbacks reveal, Alex, like Rice's Louis and his child "bride" Claudia, had turned Virginia to vampirism because she was dying. He did so uncertainly and at her behest: "Virginia, you must choose. You can die a human death or live on forever an immortal beast." After Anne has fallen in love with the mysterious and sensitive Alex, even as he preys on the citizens of London, Edgar reveals Alex's true motives to her: "He can-

Amanda Bearse as the once virginal girlfriend in FRIGHT NIGHT

not help it, it is his nature... To kill is the greatest sensual delight, he knows... they devour the living in a vain attempt to assuage their hunger. He will devour you, that is what the vampires call love." Anne goes to his lair, where he lies on a brass bed in an industrial annex surrounded by figures that emerge from plaster columns like tortured ghosts, but cannot bring herself to kill him. Like the tormented plaster figures Alex would welcome death and tells her to "Go on...you would be doing me a great service." With a Romanticism reminiscent of Rice, the vampire's own desire for death is his most seductive aspect. Anne professes her love and wants to join him in immortality but he has "made this mistake before." In the end the Poe character, who has disfigured and imprisoned the immortal Virginia, unwittingly extracts a most terrible revenge by killing Anne and condemning Alex again to an eternity alone.

III. I WAS A TEENAGE VAMPIRE

Of Course. You have to invite them inside. He knew that from his monster magazines, the ones his mother was afraid might damage him or warp him in some way.

Stephen King, **'Salem's Lot**

Do you want to hear a secret? You were my first.

A Polish Vampire in Burbank

While it may not be clear at which point in the span of a theoretically endless life a vampire may experience adolescence, there are possible indicators. For New Age undead the first kill, like the first sexual experience, might be regarded as a rite of passage. Although it is not entirely clear in *Subspecies* whether Stefan has sucked blood from a neck before, his experience with Michelle could well be both a sexual and vampiric first time.

While such an association is entirely earnest in *Subspecies*, a parody like *A Polish Vampire in Burbank* (1986) is entirely facetious. The same association is less absolute in *Fright Night* (1985), which opens as teenager Charley Brewster tries to convince his girlfriend finally to go all the way while the local horror show, "Fright Night," is on television in the background. Before long, the neighborhood vampire has changed his virginal steady into a voluptuous creature of the night.

Fright Night also typifies the dilemma of those who first notice the bloodsuckers next door, i.e. overcoming the complete incredulity of those who have not. Van Helsing himself points out that the true power of the vampire is that people do not believe in its existence. From Anne Rice's predators who exploit this truism or King's Mark Petrie, another "boy who cried wolf," to *The Lost Boys* or *Buffy, the Vampire Slayer*, the cry of "It's unbelievable" echoes from Salem's Lot to the San Fernando Valley. Peter Vincent in *Fright Night*, has spent too many years as a fictional vampire killer to believe Charley Brewster's story until he sees the bared fangs for himself. By mixing irony with graphic violence and hideous make-up, *Fright Night* tips the balance away from comedy but offers the viewer no new insights.

The Lost Boys (1987) is even more ambitious than *Fright Night*. From its opening aerial shots over a fictional Northern California town, "Santa Carla," the interplay of the chilling and the comic is quite self-conscious. The Emerson family, mother Lucy (thanks to Stoker, still a more popular name than Michelle in modern day vampire films) and teenage sons Michael and Sam arrive to live with Lucy's father. "Is it true Santa Carla is the murder capitol of the world?" Grandpa does not explain why that is; but that evening, after displaying his knowledge of collectible comics at a local store, Sam gets a free sample entitled "Vampires Everywhere" from a pair of odd young brothers, Edgar and Alex. "I don't like horror comics," he tells them derisively. "You'll like this one," they reply. "It could save your life."

As in the opening of *Fright Night* and like the reference to "Vampirella" in King's **'Salem's Lot**, the acknowledgement of vampirism and its place in popular culture within the context of the narrative creates a tension between the audience's shared awareness of vampire comics, cartoons, etc. outside of the film, its identification with the characters, and its suspension of disbelief. There are several "facts" about vampires which Mark Petrie in **'Salem's Lot** does not remember reading in "his monster magazines" until a one actually comes to his window: the undead cannot come in until you invite them and crosses confound them. Alex and Edgar make a litany out of these concepts. Although the first two attacks in *The Lost Boys*, on a security guard and a punk couple in a convertible, are staged through a combination of quick cuts and point-of-view shots from overhead, so that the viewer never sees the vampires, there is no question from genre expectation about what manner of monster is responsible for these attacks. But keeping them unseen and referring to them indirectly through remarks about "murder capitols" and comic book covers does inject a question about just exactly what sort of vampires these are.

Besides invoking both the vampire genre and Peter Pan ("You never grow up, Michael"), *The Lost Boys* alludes even more strongly to the "troubled youth" film. Michael is the new adolescent in town; and Jim Morrison singing "People Are Strange" on the soundtrack forcefully reminds the audience what it is like "when you're a stranger." But rather than merely underscore his alienation with brooding portrayals such as Stefan's in *Subspecies*, Michael and David, the head of the Lost Boys, engage in a motorcycle chicken run right out of *Rebel without a Cause*. Stephen King remarks on the irony of the concurrent release of films like *Rebel without a Cause* and *I Was a Teenage Werewolf* in **Danse Macabre**; but, in a new generation, filmmakers now make the direct connection and create clear allusions in their narratives and stagings.

What the background of the vampire genre provides in *The Lost Boys* is a much broader range of visualization and allusions than a simple story of "troubled youth." Although these rebels offer him a leather jacket and invite Michael to "be one of us," they first confuse him with their hypnotic power, so that he imagines rice and noodles are maggots and worms. After they trick him into drinking their blood, he becomes a "half-vampire" initiate in the manner of Mina Harker. Then they complete this New Age initiation and reveal themselves by hanging under a railroad bridge and falling through the clouds. Still when Michael falls from the bridge and lands on his own bed, he has not separated weird dream from vampiric reality.

If *The Lost Boys* has a significant shortcoming, it is in lacking the resolve to follow through on the serious aspects of its own allusions. Instead it uses visual *bon mots* for cheap thrills and avoids the risk of a viewer's contemptuous laughter by repeatedly mocking itself as, for example, when Sam discovers Michael's plight and tells him that keeping this secret is "not like getting a D in school, you know." The antics of Edgar and Alex, the teenage vampire hunters, particularly in the dinner scene where they conspire with Sam to determine if Lucy's new boyfriend is the head vampire, are quite amusing; but to what end? From this perspective, a concept like the vampire child, so profoundly ironic for Anne Rice and weirdly frightening for Stephen King, becomes in *The Lost Boys* a glib aside: "It's the attack of Eddie Munster."

Like *The Lost Boys*, *Children of the Night* contains many elements of parody, starting with the very name of another middle American town in which vampirism will rear its undead head, "Allsburg." The opening

THE LOST BOYS: worshipping Morrison and indulging in acrobatic hijinks

scenes are darkly comic: a converted van topped with loudspeakers and a cross fringed with Christmas-tree lights cruises for souls rather than warm bodies down the main street. The widescreen frame pivots back and forth while a small-town doctor and small-town ambulance-chaser argue over a dead patient/live client to the discomfort of the mayor. Finally, the van knocks over the town drunk, Matty, as he crosses the street causing him to cry over his spilled wine, like a red omen of blood to come.

In a waterlogged crypt beneath the old church lurks Czakyr, another atavistic, Nosferatu clone, whose very name is ugly. When two teenage girls, Cindy and Lucy (yes, another one), visit the crypt they inadvertently

rouse him. As the plot meanders about, the comic moments become gris-
lier, from Grandma dropping her dentures before she tries to put the bite
on the young hero, Mark, to a drain spout arranged to funnel blood into a
punch bowl. By the time Mark drives up to Allsburg with a couple of bags
of stakes in his back seat to rescue his Lucy, the tone of the film has shifted
again. In a parallel plot, Czakyr's first victim, Cindy's mother, has become
a voracious vampiress and finally seduces the priest who imprisoned her.

At the Bloodsucker's Ball, comic and horrific are fully intermixed. Most
of the locals have been "turned." Drunk on blood and emerging from
vampiric·cocoons, they capture and plan to sacrifice Mark and Lucy to
their new ruler. While Matty commandeers the preacher's van to help the
young couple elude the pursuing townspeople, Czakyr smells out Lucy's
virgin blood. Elsewhere Karen's daughter stakes her cocooned mom to
undead oblivion before she finally gets Lucy to help her free Czakyr's flock
of crypt kids. The ending wryly reaffirms all that has gone before. Allsburg
goes back to what it calls normal: "I got half the town lined up over at my
clinic," the de-fanged doctor laments to the mayor, "Been pulling splinters
out of their chests all day long!"

Like Julian Sands as Alex in *Tale of a Vampire*, the bloodsucker in *Midnight Kiss* (1993) has long blond hair. His sleeping arrangements also recall
Pale Blood in that he zips himself into a black body bag. The resemblance
ends there. This unnamed creature of the night is anything but sensitive;
or, as he says to a would-be victim, "I told you, I like it rough." Although
it features a portrait of the vampire as a kind of psychotic, L.A. surfer
gone amuck–one shot captures him traipsing along Melrose Avenue under
a neon "Wacko" sign–*Midnight Kiss* is not "Vlad's Excellent Adventure."
Instead it focuses on a policewoman who becomes a modern day Mina
Harker when she is infected by the vampire's bite. Lacking a host of Victo-

Below left, another version of the vampire as cleric (Gregory Greer); below right, Michelle Owens
as the policewoman who becomes a "half vampire" in MIDNIGHT KISS

rian protectors, aided in fact only by an unbelieving ex-husband, this female protagonist knows that if she ever wants to go out in the sun and lose
the sudden craving for raw meat, she will have take care of business herself.

While *Children of the Night* and *Midnight Kiss* also feature plenty of atmos-
pheric, low-key lighting, George Romero's *Martin* deliberately plays
against the expressionistic imagery typical of the genre. The 16mm film,
with the contemporary scenes in color and, in the manner of *Blood and
Roses*, Martin's dream memories of the old country in black-and-white,
yields a grainy, quasi-documentary quality to the visuals. Within this context Romero intercuts for "subjective" effect. When Martin pauses outside
the door of the train compartment before assaulting his first victim, he
imagines a black-and-white scene in which he enters and is warmly
greeted by the glamorous woman inside. The reality is quite different. She
emerges from the bathroom with her face whitened by cold cream and,
despite being injected with a tranquilizer, struggles fiercely with her assail-
ant. Halfway through Martin's second attack, more flashbacks and voice-
overs of his call to a radio talk show reveal the rest of his story. In this instance, the soundtrack's echo effect, which simulates the several second delay between speaking into the phone and hearing one's voice over the radio that a caller would actually experience, accentuates the documentary
tone. For all his insistence that "there is no magic" to his vampirism and
the flashbacks which suggest a self-image of being persecuted for an irresistible impulse, Martin is not really a sympathetic figure.

It is never clear why Martin comes to stay with "Tata Cuda," his cousin
from the old country who ultimately fulfills his promise to destroy him;
but when he tells Cuda's granddaughter, who thinks both her relatives
need psychiatric help, that he is 84 years old, the seemingly adolescent
Martin is certainly one of the most ingenuous of vampires. Despite a bizarre electronic score that works against the hyper-realistic staging,
Romero's spare style means that Martin's work as a delivery boy and his
two vampire attacks receive the same detached exposition. The second attack, in which Martin is surprised to find the woman he has stalked enter-
taining a lover during her husband's absence, is in stark contrast to the
"easy" kills of most vampire fiction, recalling a similar treatment in Hitchcock's *Torn Curtain*. While the black-and-white flashbacks may seem to romanticize 19th Century vampirism with its low-key shots of canopied bed
chambers and torch-bearing mobs of pursuers, Martin's discussions with
the all night radio deejay trivialize its modern day practice. Martin the
vampire plods on, more out of habit than conviction. Even the suicide of
the woman who provides the carnal love, which he may or may not have
experienced in the flashbacks, is more confusing than disheartening to

John Amplas in
George Romero's
MARTIN

him. Despite the mocking interlude when Martin dresses in a black cape
to frighten Cuda or the dubious exorcism which his relative arranges,
Romero's treatment is relentlessly anti-sensational. Martin survives the
random modern violence of a shoot-out between drug dealers and police
only to be staked in his bed by a superstitious old man whose garlic and
crucifixes he had ridiculed. In his destruction, in its gritty, almost off-
handed realism, *Martin* captures some of the Old World vampire's "stunning irrelevance" to which Lestat alludes.

If *Martin* has a comic equivalent in terms of style and budget, it must be
A Polish Vampire in Burbank. An ultra-low budget parody made in Super
8mm for a few thousand dollars, *Polish Vampire* nonetheless manages to
conjure up a "castle" for its Burbank-based bloodsuckers. Like *Monster
Squad* et al., the film easily invokes the genre with organ music, a castle
that is part model, part location, and part gargoyled set pieces, and hand-
held "tracking" shots past coffins in its title sequence. The hapless teenage
hero, Dupa, is a vampire virgin who has never bitten a victim and is content to suck blood from a straw out of the ziplock bags that his father and
sister bring back for him. Given its extremely limited budget, *Polish Vampire* does manage moments of visual parody of the genre, most notably in
its own black-and-white sequence, staged like a vampire wet dream: eye-
light captures Dupa in a high-necked cape, sporting pancake makeup and
darkened eyebrows as he prepares to bite a peignoired blonde. Dolores,

the vampire film fan ("I must have seen *Horror of Dracula* twenty times"), is the blonde whom Dupa hopes will overlook his vampiric shortcomings (she likes "large fangs") and offer him his first neck. In fact, while Dolores may initially "sleep" with Dupa in his coffin because she thinks he has gone to all this trouble to impress her, the experience makes her, like so many straight victims, eager for more. Unfortunately, Eddie Deezen as the skeletal brother, Sphincter, or Dolores' roommate and ex-boyfriend doing a Sonny and Cher imitation at a pool party, are more typical of the level of humor which *Polish Vampire* can afford to offer its viewers. For all of its shortcomings, in terms of addressing the genre and its icons, this film is certainly as inventive as *My Best Friend Is a Vampire, Beverly Hills Vamp* (both 1988) or *Rockula* (1990), all produced on limited budgets but nonetheless costing many times more than *Polish Vampire*.

Unlike the "Teenage" Werewolf, Frankenstein, Caveman, etc. films of the 1950s, few of these teenage vampires take themselves seriously. The cheaply-made-for-video *Teen Vamp* (1988) replays the familiar story of a teenage nerd who acquires animal magnetism in the manner of the feature *Teen Wolf*. *Love Bites* (1993) is a the most recent of vampire comedies, adapted by Malcolm Marmorstein from his stage play, with Adam Ant as Zachary, a sensitive, young (only three hundred years old) vampire who awakens after a century-long repose. A groggy Zachary falling out of his coffin, then being introduced to modern self defense techniques by Kendall, the woman who now owns his house; her fiancé mistaking the catatonic vampire under the covers for her; even a bumbling private detective named Vinnie Helsting–all these moments of broad comedy clearly harken back to *Love at First Bite*, which obviously inspired the title change from the play's "The Reluctant Vampire." The subtler comic moments range from a disco "Dies Irae" on the soundtrack to Kendall cleaning the cobwebs out of the crypt to innocuous double entendres: "I wouldn't touch a woman, if I could get it from animals." "You're sick!" "I'm not sick. I'm dead." Like Angelique in *Nightlife*, Zachary has a former vampire lover, Nerissa, who made him what he is and now, of course, conveniently reappears. What novelties there are in *Love Bites*, from Zachary's discovery of the 1990s to his decision to humanize himself, are sidelights in what is essentially a romantic comedy that is less about vampirism than sensitivity; and the ultimate plot twist is that, after a yuppie-ized Zachary has taken over her ex-fiancé's insurance firm, Kendall wants her loveable vampire back.

The latest of "teenage" vampire comedies is *Buffy, the Vampire Slayer* (1992). Although it picks up many of its cues from *Salem's Lot* and *The Lost Boys* and drives shafts through hearts with more relish than Cupid on Valentine's Day, *Buffy* is unabashedly comic. Buffy herself, the last in a long line of slayers, has already had dreams of a past-life experience (hers are in color) and knows what every teenager should about the undead ("They can't come in unless you invite them, can they?"). Given the press of cheer leading practice and senior dance committee, she initially doesn't feel she can fit vampire killing into her schedule. Even after the death of her mentor, Merrick, her commitment is still suspect: "Here the world is under attack by legions of the undead, and you're going to a mixer." Of course, her antagonist, the vampire Lothos, has his own problems with his number two man, Amilyn, played by Paul ("Pee-Wee Herman") Reubens: "1,200 years old–you behave like a child." When these legions of teen vampires come to the dance (they can't be kept out because "they're invited. They're seniors"), Buffy, her schoolmates, and her rebel boyfriend, Pike, dispatch them all, Lothos included.

Comic or not, one questions the origins of Buffy. Even though it was made before *Bram Stoker's Dracula* demonstrated to the major studios that the public could turn out in large numbers for a straight vampire film, a big budget bloodsucker comedy like *Buffy* is itself somewhat "retro." That a Valley Girl should become "way lethal" and appreciate the non-conformist attitude of someone like Pike may have liberating overtones; but why must it take a plague of vampires to obtain that result?

Below, the classic pose of the vampire hunters: Peter Vincent (Roddy McDowall) and Charley Brewster (William Ragsdale) in FRIGHT NIGHT

Above, Buffy (Kristy Swanson) and her "rebel without a cause" boyfriend, Pike (Luke Perry). The tag line says it all

Julie Carmen bares her fangs in FRIGHT NIGHT PART 2

CHAPTER SIX

Countess Dracula A.D. 1992

Even the least vampirish woman of the third part demands to be courted in... the grand manner.

H.L. Mencken

For Mencken, like Hobbs in *Dracula's Daughter*, the female vampire sought lucre rather than blood. Even now when that era of liberation has been tempered by the reality of sexually transmitted diseases, the preternatural daughters of darkness still have little difficulty finding willing victims. While Dracula, Lestat, and other well-known males of the ilk in A.D. 1992 can become objects of forlorn Romanticism, the sensuality of the female vampire still means that her story is likely to end in destruction with a subtext of repression by a male-dominated culture.

I. CARMILLA: THE NIGHTMARE CONTINUES

The good ones are those who dream what the wicked actually practice.

Plato, quoted in opening epigram of
La Novia Ensangrentada

Through the decades, J. Sheridan Le Fanu's novella, **Carmilla** has continued to nourish the creative appetites of horror filmmakers. Second only to Dracula, Carmilla has maintained her position as a primary Victorian archetype of the vampire. Her resilience can be attributed to several elements. First, the overt eroticism of the original story, with special attention being paid to the lesbian aspects, have fit the sensationalistic nature of the vampire film. Second, there is the story's dialectical construction with Carmilla, the vampire, and Laura, the "victim," acting as reflections of each other in their loneliness and repressed desire. Finally, there is the implicit feminism of the story. The two females who suffocate literally, in Carmilla's case, and figuratively, in Laura's case, within a Victorian, patriarchal system provide the basis for a very modern context and has been a foundation on which filmmakers have built their adaptations.

Blood and Roses, Terror in the Crypt, and *The Vampire Lovers* were all fairly straightforward adaptations. Even Vadim's contemporary setting in the earliest film was sustained by a timeless, oneiric quality. However, the feminist slant to the story has been particularly emphasized in two other versions of **Carmilla,** one by the Spanish filmmaker Vicente Aranda in 1972 (*La Novia Ensangrentada*) and the second directed by Gabrielle Beaumont in 1989 (*Carmilla*). Aranda's film is by far the most idiosyncratic and riveting of the two. Coming out of the tradition of Buñuel and Dali, Aranda has chosen to eschew all Gothic or Expressionistic stylization in favor of modern day settings and naturalistic backgrounds. Rather than set the film in the medieval castle of the original, Aranda has relocated it to the Spanish countryside, filled with blinding sunshine and adjacent beaches. Like Buñuel, Aranda creates his nightmare world by the juxtaposition of incongruous images. For example, Carmilla/Mircalla is discovered buried in the sand in full snorkel gear. As the sand is slowly brushed away from her body and her mask, snorkel, and naked breasts are revealed, she comes to resemble a Dali goddess more than any Gothic vampire. The unexpected intrusions of the female victim's (here she is called Susan) nightmares also intensify the surrealistic mood. Because of their naturalistic aspect, the viewer is at least temporarily unsure of whether or not they are dreams.

The dreams of the heroine are, in fact, the key to this film's feminist preoccupations. On her wedding night Susan dreams of being raped by a masked man who resembles her husband. This nightmare turns into reality as her husband (significantly, he is never given a name) evidences his own preference for rough sex. Over several weeks he rapes his wife; tears down the door of a pigeon cage, in which she has locked herself, to reach her; forces her to perform fellatio on him in a forest; and shoots a female fox in a trap while thinking of her.

In response to these indignities the figure of Carmilla, the avenger, rises from the sand. Much as the original Carmilla relieved the loneliness and isolation of the original Laura, this Carmilla enlists Susan in a full-fledged attack against the patriarchal power symbolized by her husband and his friend, the doctor (also with no name). In an orgasmic ritual in an abandoned cathedral, Susan and Carmilla pledge their undying devotion while chanting insults directed at her husband: "He spat inside your body to enslave you." In dream form, they castrate the husband; in reality, they do the same to the doctor.

In the final scene the patriarchy does murderously reassert itself as the husband, finding Carmilla and Susan nude in each other's arms and asleep in the coffin, riddles their bodies with bullets and mutilates them. However, Aranda is not satisfied with this rather conventional ending. In order to reinforce his thesis, he has the husband go further. He shoots and mutilates the gardener's young daughter because he believes she has inherited the "worm in the bud," as Ronald Pearsall in his book on Victorian sexuality calls it, of female sexuality, the real power of Carmilla's curse.

Carmilla (1989) is somewhat more traditional in its rendering of the classic. Although it does change the location to the post-bellum South and the heroine's name to Marie, the structure, tone, and mood is more familiar. The isolated plantation, particularly during the cold, blue nights, is an effective substitute for Le Fanu's *schloss*. The plot points are also faithfully rendered: Marie is frustrated and lonely; a beautiful visitor is deposited on her doorstep via a carriage accident; she and the strange visitor become inseparable friends and "lovers," but in the end Carmilla is violently separated from her newest companion.

Within this familiar structure, the filmmakers have added some significant touches which bring material that was subsumed in the original story to the foreground. As in Aranda's version the two women are Januses: each mirrors the other in appearance and often in dress. While in *La Novia* they were blondes, in this film they are brunettes whose sultriness underscores their duality. In many ways Carmilla is but a projection of Marie's longings, symbolized by the doll house with which she plays. Carmilla preys on her ennui, growing out of her relative isolation, and her re-

Below, the most recent adaptation of CARMILLA: Ione Skye as Marie and Meg Tilly as Carmilla

Left, Marie (Ione Skye) and her overprotective father (Roy Dotrice) in CARMILLA

Lynn Houston, Showtime © 1989

sentment towards her father, who has kept her locked away in this Tara-like mansion, away from any possible friends.

After Carmilla's arrival Marie begins to sever the ties with her father. As they stroll hand in hand through the grounds, dressed in identical outfits, as Carmilla hangs from a tree like a bat, sucking blood from her special friend, and as they conspire to ignore the advice of her father, Marie gains newfound strength. She defies her father and defends Carmilla against his suspicious questions. She is no longer the pouty, little girl, doting on her father's moods. She has seen his frailties and his obvious sexual attraction to Carmilla. She has even gained enough strength to dispatch Carmilla herself. For in a significant departure from any other version of the story, Marie stakes her friend, releasing her spirit. This final action is filled with ambiguity for Marie as well as the viewer: how could she kill the one she loved? What will she do now that her source of strength is gone: revert to the control of her father or strike out on her own? It does at least leave open the possibility of a more positive future for this nightmare-plagued heroine.

A Filha de Dracula (1972), directed and written by Jesus Franco, might be subtitled "Carmilla Comes of Age." In many ways, it is the filmic equivalent of a *bildungsroman*, relating the story of how Carmilla, here called Marie Karnstein, became a vampire. Set in modern-day Portugal, in the deserted seashores, mountains, and castles Franco often favors, Marie Karnstein is called to her dying mother's side to learn the family's darkest secret: that their ancestors were vampires. At Castle Karnstein, Marie visits the crypt of those ancestors and confirms the source of her suspected predilection for vampirism and young girls. Marie now begins a reign of terror, picking the most attractive women in the environs as her obscure objects of desire.

Franco's handling of Marie's attacks are both novel and revealing. He alternates between a subjective camera, indicating Marie's POV and an extreme close-up of her eye as she spies on prospective victims. In this manner he forces the audience to identify with Marie while exposing her voyeuristic tendencies. He has Marie dress as a man in several attacks, again with dual purpose: it reinforces her transgression into traditional male territory and it redirects suspicion from her onto someone else.

Like the other Carmillas this young woman has a fatal flaw: she falls in love with her victims. Marie restrains herself from killing her childhood friend. Instead they become lovers while Marie satisfies her blood lust with other women. Eventually she can no longer control her desire and vampirizes her friend who dies from the loss of blood. The Carmilla figure has tried to combine love and survival, and found, as she may find again in future incarnations, that she has failed.

II. ELISABETH BATHORY: STILL THIRSTY AFTER ALL THESE YEARS

I earnestly wish an end would come to this bloody race I am forced to run.

Countess in *La Comtesse Noire*

Countess Elisabeth Bathory is an equally resilient archetype of the vampire film. Her obsession with blood as a source of eternal youth, her inevitable confluence of blood and sexual desire are, at least in the film versions if not in the historical record, qualities which inspired the filmmakers of *Countess Dracula* and *Le Rouge aux Lèvres*.

Probably the most hallucinatory adaptation of the Bathory legend is Jesus Franco's *La Comtesse Noire* (1972). As with so many of Franco's films there are several versions of this movie, which makes sorting through various prints an hallucinatory experience in itself. Typically Franco jumbles his archetypes so haphazardly that no amount of cross-referencing can fully explicate. For example, the Countess in this film is sometimes called "Karlstein," a bastardization of Carmilla's last name in Le Fanu's story. She is joined by horror figures from earlier Franco films, like Dr. Orloff, who seem thrown in for good measure. Over and above all this silliness and beyond the blatantly sensationalistic treatment of the subject, there is a serious and personal core.

With a few exceptions like *Jack the Ripper* (1978), Franco abandoned the more Gothic trappings and Baroque style of his 60s films like *Succubus* (1967), the Dr. Orloff duo (1962 and 1964), *Venus in Furs* (1969), and *El Conde Drácula* (1970) to begin a minimalist period. Often acting as writer-director-cinematographer and star, often using pseudonyms, he adopted a style relying heavily on roving camera and zoom lens, allowing him to explore ceaselessly the terrain of his films, whether the human body or the physical landscape.

In *La Comtesse Noire* the camera lingers lovingly over both the body of the mute Countess (played by the uninhibited Lina Romay, also known as Candy Coster, who would be his creative collaborator in numerous films) as well as the cliffs and beaches of the island of Madeira. In this isolated hideaway, the Countess, starved for sex and fluids, searches out new victims whom she can drain of their "essence." Rising from the fog, like a Botticelli Venus on a half-shell, blending with the terrain by the flattening effect of a telephoto lens, the Countess seeks her prey, hunting for the responsive stranger whom she can use as source of nourishment.

As with so many of the male vampire films, there is character ennui beneath this purely exploitive facade. Like various male counterparts this Countess is weary of her life of constant hunger and need. "I earnestly wish an end would come to this bloody race I am forced to run," she laments in voiceover as her car winds down the mountain path. A seagull hood ornament with its wings extended plays against traditional iconography. Associating the Countess Irina not with a bat but with a sea bird creates more positive associations. In this empty landscape, highlighted by long pans over vacant cafés, unoccupied luxury hotels, forlorn mountains, the Countess tries to assuage her boredom as much as her blood thirst.

As in the Hammer *Countess Dracula*, romantic love is this Countess' undoing. On the island she meets a writer who wants her to take him "behind the mist" of her eyes, knowing full well that death waits there. His avowal that "Even if I had not met you, I would have left this world" precipitates an emotional exchange similar to that of Tsepes and Michelle in *Graveyard Shift*. The Countess leaves her world of bored socialites who practice Sadean acts in darkened dungeons to relieve their *anomie* and blind doctors who yearn for "true darkness" and reluctantly takes her suicidal lover into her arms of death. After he is gone, she takes one final bath in his blood, drowning herself in the fluid that once gave her beauty and life.

The Bathory blood-bathing motif is central to the 1973 film *Il Plenilunio delle Vergini*. Rosalba Neri plays the Countess, here called de Vries, with a dark sensuality as she seduces two brothers and bathes in the blood of virgins, her nude image rising up from the steaming blood, her bathtub a ro-

Patty Shepard as The Countess in LA NOCHE DE WALPURGIS

coco fantasy of sculpted figures. Other films which feature the Bloody Countess include two films with Paul Naschy [Jacinto Molina]: *La Noche de Walpurgis* (1970) and *El Retorno de Walpurgis* (1973). In the first film, although her name is changed, the central figure clearly is the infamous Countess. In a flashback to the Inquisition she is accused of bathing in virgin blood like her infamous role model. In *La Noche* and its sequel, *El Retorno*, Patty Shepard plays the Countess as she faces off against the Wolfman, limned by Molina. Their battles are often bloody and sometimes ludicrous.

Contes Immoraux (1974) is a series of ribald tales, one of which recounts the story of Elizabeth Bathory. The episode is at least initially satiric with the Countess visiting her lands in search of virgins. A town crier announces her arrival, promising "eternal joy" and a life "better than the king himself" for the girls who sign up. The townspeople seem none too impressed, choosing to hide their daughters rather than share them with the Countess. As the captured girls are lined up like so many cattle, Bathory, dressed in a gown of black lace and pearls, examines her potential donors.

When the virgins are taken to the Castle, the film shifts to an erotic, religious ritual. The girls are bathed and perfumed in a Baroque setting. Medieval choral music and chamber pieces alternately play in the background. When the Countess appears in a transparent dress covered with pearls, the girls frenziedly rip it to pieces and fight among themselves for the spoils. As part of the plan, the guard, also a woman, then fulfills her role by slaughtering the girls and collecting their blood for the Countess' bath. The bath is prepared and Bathory luxuriates in it, her beauty preserved for another year or at least until the authorities arrive to put an end to her depredations.

In the Italian/Hungarian co-production *A Zsarnok Szíve* (1981) the Bathory figure returns literally and figuratively to her native land. Belgium hosts a modern-day Countess in *Mama Dracula* (1979). In this low-budget pastiche of *Dance of the Vampires* and *Andy Warhol's Dracula*, the cast mugs its way through endless slapstick routines, as a naive scientist goes to the Bloody Countess' mansion to find a way of synthesizing virgin blood. There he encounters the Countess, played with an anomalous dignity by Louise Fletcher, and her twin vampires. Neither flashes of self-conscious technique nor the presence of Fletcher can raise this film above the level of its sophomoric humor and mediocre plot.

Thirst (1988) does posit another twist on the Bathory myth. While on vacation a successful businesswoman is kidnapped by a cult of blood-drinkers who operate a modern, scientific "dairy farm" for blood extraction. While in their clutches, she discovers that she is the descendant of the Bloody Countess and that her captors want her to marry the scion of another ancient blood-drinking family.

The eroticism associated with various films that featured Bathory in the 1970s had considerably diminished by the time *Thirst* was released. In an enclosed social situation reminiscent of the blood farmers of *Return to Salem's Lot*, the cultists of *Thirst* use blood in a ritual that is unconcerned with either vampirism itself or the collateral risks of AIDS and other diseases.

III. STILL OTHER DAUGHTERS OF DARKNESS: THE SCORNED

> Heav'n has no rage like love to hatred turn'd,
> Nor hell a fury like a woman scorn'd.
>
> William Congreve, "The Mourning Bride"

While Dracula may be considered the most powerful and vicious of the vampire figures, his sister vampires, especially in the last two decades, have struggled to match the Prince of Darkness blow for blow and bite for bite.

In *Fright Night 2* (1988) Julie Carmen portrays the demonic Regine, literally a sister of the vampire from the original *Fright Night*. Out for re-

venge against the young man, Charley Brewster, and his horror-film host
cum vampire-hunter mentor, Peter Vincent, who destroyed her brother,
Regine is a vampire worthy of her name. She combines diverse talents: a
performance artist, who utilizes vampire iconography in her seductive
routine; a television personality, who takes over for a terrified Peter Vincent; and a dominatrix. She and her servants perform sadomasochistic sex
acts with Charley's best friend to the horror and barely suppressed fascination of the voyeuristic Charley. When Charley and Peter Vincent finally
muster the courage to fight her, she transforms herself into a demonic
monster with the strength of any Dracula, capable of destroying her physical environment as well as any humans who inhabit it.

Among the most carnal and animalistic female vampires are those who
appear in *Vampyres* (1974), *Nocturna* (1979), *Vamp* (1986), *Dracula's Widow*
(1989), and *Def by Temptation* (1990). More than any other film of its period, *Vampyres* is credited for the shift in the genre to explicit sex and violence. Although both Terence Fisher and Jesus Franco had laid the
groundwork with films from *Horror of Dracula* to *La Comtesse Noire*, *Vampyres* mixed delirious eroticism and violence within the context of "traditional" vampirism. The eroticism is introduced in the prologue of the film
as the two women intertwine in a lesbian interlude for which a man, possibly a husband, shoots and kills them. They become vampires and typify a
preternatural dialectic of light and dark reified in the persons of the

Marianne Morris as Fran (left), Anulka as Miriam, and Murray Brown as her love-obsessed victim

blonde and brunette, Fran and Miriam, still locked in orgasmic embrace after death. The atavistic quality of these vampires is also established early as they run through the woods like animals in heat, in search of unsuspecting motorists whom they will lure into their den then vampirize for their blood. That blood flows freely and they lap it up like frantic cats. Even their hibernation underscores this animalistic ethos, as they sleep entwined in their capes like bats in a wine cellar.

One victim does finally fall under their spell so completely that he willingly becomes a source of blood. He is attached romantically only to one of them, Fran, but as he grows weaker and weaker, his obsession with her grows stronger. Only when he senses that he is dying does he gather enough strength to break this bond and escape into the rising sun.

Def by Temptation features a vampire-succubus as sensual and animalistic as the pair in *Vampyres*. Set in the African-American sub-culture, the films pit Temptation, the vampire-succubus, against a rural boy, Joel, raised by his grandmother and his minister to battle evil in all forms. In the early scenes his religious training is intercut with Temptation's seduction of various pickup artists with trite come-on lines such as, "Haven't I met you somewhere before. I remember where it was...in my dreams." After politely listening to their rap, she leads them to her canopied bed where their sex dreams turn to nightmares. They die in a torrent of blood or are infected with her evil, in a none-too-veiled reference to AIDS.

Deciding to expand his horizons, Joel goes North to stay with his friend, "K," in New York. There he is exposed to the urban African-American milieu. "K" teaches him the newest hip-hop idioms and shows him the "defest" fashions. Unwittingly, "K" takes him to a bar where Joel encounters the alluring Temptation, who has eyes for no one else, as she forms her plan to seduce and destroy this paragon of virtue. The film as a whole alternates between two contexts. One is naturalistic, consisting of the streetwise banter and hip-hop humor of "K," the satirical pickup rituals of the males in the bar, and the graphic seductions by Temptation. The other context is Joel's increasingly nightmarish world, half-dream, half-real, where the local hangout turns into a denizen of zombies, where his grandmother defends him against Temptation, and where "K" is sucked into the maelstrom of a liquid TV set. Although Joel's final victory is predictable, his struggle seems to reaffirm a fundamentalist morality with which his grandmother had so effectively inculcated him.

Although *Dracula's Widow, Vamp,* and *Nocturna* center on vampire-succubi similar to Temptation, the resemblance ends there. Sylvia Kristel as the widow of Count Dracula, searching for the remains of her husband in exotic locations like the Hollywood Wax Museum, Grace Jones as Katrina, performance artist in a vampiric club catering to moronic teens, and Nai

Is it really the vampire's kiss? Nicolas Cage as Peter Loew and Jennifer Beals as the mysterious Rachel in THE VAMPIRE'S KISS.

Bonet as a disco vampiress have little more dimension than their distorted shadows on the screen. Genre-conscious humor does little to mitigate the banality of the plots.

Vampire's Kiss (1989) is a much more ambitious narrative, constructed around a central ambiguity. Is the vampire to which the protagonist, Peter Loew, becomes enslaved real or imagined? While this survey does not consider many "imaginary" vampires, in the case of Peter Loew's vampire-seductress, the line between reality and dream is so blurred that neither viewer nor protagonist may be able to distinguish between them.

Loew is a callous womanizer who cannot spend the entire night with any woman and a compulsive, yuppie supervisor who abuses and harasses his employees. His newest victim at the workplace is Alva, a Latina secretary, whom he sends on futile searches for obscure, unimportant documents. One night while in the midst of a new sexual conquest, a bat flies into his apartment, resulting in *coitus interruptus* as well as a severe case of the shakes. The next evening he meets the beautiful and exotic Rachel in a disco. During sex later that night, she puts the bite on Peter. Rachel continues to visit him intermittently, aggressively taking her pleasure while, he thinks, initiating him into the world of vampirism. He never grows fangs, so he purchases cheap plastic ones which he tries unsuccessfully to use. He never obtains his own coffin, so he sleeps under an overturned couch. He is even visible in mirrors, although he believes that he is not. He does, however, have other symptoms: he grows paler, is sensitive to light, has telltale marks on his neck, and becomes even more arrogant and overbearing. He continues to persecute Alva mercilessly. He pursues her into the bathroom, then laughs about her sexual harassment complaint with his fellow employees. He hounds her at her home on her sick day and even tries to rape her in the hallway.

Like other quasi-satires of the genre, *Vampire's Kiss* works on several different levels. On the surface it is a black comedy buttressed by a truly expressionistic performance by Nicolas Cage as Peter Loew. Whether raving about his lost contract to his psychiatrist ("I've never misplaced anything, not once, not one thing."), practicing his Nosferatu looks in the mirror, chasing pigeons in the park, or standing on a corner with a stake of wood under his arm philosophizing to an imaginary listener, Cage's performance dominates the film. The clear sub-text of *Vampire's Kiss* is a critique of both male chauvinism and an oppressive capitalist society. Rachel is in many ways an embodiment of vengeance, evening the score for the women Peter has mistreated, most particularly Alva. Significantly, in the scene when Peter is raping Alva, she turns into Rachel. Moreover, it is not accidental that he has picked an Hispanic woman to abuse. As he himself says to her, in the corporate world, "you are the lowest." As a result,

Rachel, the "angel" of vengeance, demands total devotion from him, forcing him to abandon all other women, making him confess his love and subservience, driving him into a frenzy, then leaving him to search for death and an end to the vampiric state he imagines himself in. The politics of the film are never compromised. In the final scene Peter is staked by Alva's outraged brother, confirming for Peter his own vampirism as well as functioning as a revolutionary act. In the hands of the filmmakers of *Vampire's Kiss,* the vampire tale is given a novel political reading.

Vampyros Lesbos (1970), made a year before *El Conde Drácula,* is like *El Conde* a transition film from Franco's Baroque period to his minimalist one. A woman, Linda, becomes fascinated with a descendant of Count Dracula, Nadine, played by Soledad Miranda. While visiting her, Linda becomes her newest victim, giving her blood and her sex to Nadine. Although the story is rather mundane, Franco adds texture to it through his set design, cutting, and unusual soundtrack.

The film opens with an elaborate striptease-performance piece, with Nadine, a brunette, before a tilted mirror. She is dressed in black stockings and red scarf, caressing a blonde mannequin which surprisingly turns out to be real. Inside her mansion on a secluded island, the dominant colors of red and black are repeated. She sleeps on a black bed with a red fringe; she wears black outfits topped off with a red scarf. The design of her mansion is modern, symmetrical, cold, an anomaly, like Nadine herself, in this Byzantine-Islamic city of Istanbul.

The editing scheme creates metaphor by associative montage: Linda is

The striptease in
VAMPYROS LESBOS

associated with trapped insects like moths, grasshoppers, flies while Nadine is juxtaposed with scorpions. When Nadine is killed by Linda, with a pin through the eye, the film cuts to the same scorpion drowned at the bottom of a pool, the same pool in which Nadine herself had earlier floated, catatonically. The stylization of the soundtrack also enhances the disorientation of the film. The filmmakers use a combination of jazz organ, reversed dialogue loops, and synthesized sound effects. This unsettling aural barrage, particularly when juxtaposed with the spare dialogue, creates an appropriately oneiric mood.

Spermula (1976) and *Lifeforce* (1985) both showcase female space vampires who are not simply interested in blood. In the former film the females, led by Dayle Haddon, arrive from another planet to feed off men, drawing out their "essential fluids" during the act of sex. In *Lifeforce*, based on Colin Wilson's novel, **The Space Vampires**, Mathilda May portrays a voluptuous vampire who drains her victims by means of an electrical transfer of fluids and energy. Although *Lifeforce* has expensive special effects and *Spermula* none, both fixate on the one aspect of the sex vampire to the exclusion of any narrative novelty or stylistic dimension.

In contrast, Jean Rollin has sustained over the last three decades his single-minded obsession with erotic and evil female vampires who perform perverse acts of sexuality in surrealistic settings. Like Franco, Rollin has tested the limits of this sub-genre. His series of films from *Le Viol du Vampire* (1967), *La Vampire Nue* (1969), *Le Frisson des Vampires* (1970), and *Lèvres de Sang* (1975) to *Fascination* (1979) and *La Morte Vivante* (1982) have combined deviant behavior with such bizarre imagery as beast-headed men, victims whipped with seaweed, and living tableaux of Magritte paintings. His most consistent themes are the evil lesbian vampire and the concomitant oedipal struggle for power involving a weak male.

Lèvres de Sang is a vampiric rendering of the mythic story of Siegmunde and Sieglinde. A young man is haunted by a childhood image of a beautiful girl in white who comforted him when he was lost in the woods. Now grown, but still tied to his grasping mother by a tautly-pulled, psychological umbilical cord, he begins to see the girl from his childhood everywhere: astride the rails of the Metro; in a theater, eerily merging with the bride in the movie projected on the screen; in the Montmartre cemetery, beckoning him to her crypt. Defying the warnings of his mother, he pursues this *amour fou* with an obsessive passion worthy of Proust. Even the revelation that the girl is his sister, a vampire who destroyed their father, does nothing to dampen his ardor. Instead, in conjunction with the girl, he instensifies his efforts to escape his mother's influence.

Enlisting the aide of her vampire sisters, the girl in white rescues her brother-lover several times. As he follows her through the nightscape of the city, he is hounded by assassins. In an empty Metro car he dodges the bullets of a killer. In a sculptural fountain the vampire girls flood the area with lights to blind his pursuers. In a sterile sanatorium where his mother has locked him away, they dress as nurses and set him free. Through the night these delirious visions in diaphonous gowns are his guardian angels until he can be delivered to their queen, his sister. When their mother finally does track them down, she initiates a slaughter of the vampire girls and orders her son to do the same to his sister. Instead he stages her decapitation, using the head of a doll-like effigy located in the crypt. Free of the oppressive influence of the mother, the incestuous couple becomes one, naturally and supernaturally, as she vampirizes him. In a culmination of their insular love, the couple takes refuge in a coffin near the edge of the ocean, embracing ecstatically as the coffin drifts out into the arms of their new mother, the sea.

In *Fascination* Rollin again develops this oedipal struggle, this time within the confines of a picturesque French chalet. There a coven of female vampires congregate periodically to partake in orgies that culminate in the death and exsanguination of an unsuspecting victim. Although they prefer women, their newest ceremonial object is a handsome thief named Marc who is using the chalet as a hiding place. During his stay, this amoral drifter has quickly seduced the two guardians of the house, Eva and Elisabeth. Eva is a murderous vampire and takes delight in her slaughter of the

family who pursues Marc. Elisabeth is a melancholy creature who wants to flee this eternal cycle of sex and blood. After falling in love with Marc, she tries to arrange their escape; but the pull of the coven, particularly the motherly Countess, has a primal power too strong to resist. She kills her lover and returns with his blood on her lips to the embrace of the Countess.

The surrealistic imagery of this film is typical of Rollin. The film opens with a high-angle shot of two women dancing along a jetty as nearby an old Victrola scratches out a dance tune. When all the women vampires have been revealed, they are dressed in similar outfits of varying colors and are arranged in the landscape like mannequins on display. When Eva, played by European sex star Brigitte Lahaie, wreaks her vengeance on the neighboring family, she is naked under a black cape and carries a scythe, creating an image of death that is both sensual and terrifying.

Another individualistic director with a predilection for the savage and carnal female vampire is Argentinian Leon Klimovsky. In the previously mentioned *La Noche de Walpurgis* Klimovsky uses the sepulchral aspect of actress Patty Shepard to create a strikingly evil Bloody Countess. Dressed in a black gown and veil, resembling a satanic wedding dress, the Countess conducts stylized rituals involving the blood of young women. In a plot twist reminiscent of the Universal films of the Forties, the Countess battles the psychologically tormented Wolfman, for the blood and soul of Elvira, a virginal researcher. As the brooding Wolfman awaits the full moon, the Countess and her newest disciple float in slow motion through the windswept woods and attack innocent travelers. The psychological ambiguity of the film extends beyond Naschy's quasi-masochistic suffering. Elvira herself has erotic dreams about the Countess and her acolyte in which she imagines them piercing her with a phallic instrument and dancing in a langourous embrace as they drink her blood.

In *La Noche de las Orgias de los Vampiros* (1973) a group of travelers are stranded in a small Transylvanian village. The village is inhabited by vampires, but a very unique blend of them. In a naturalistic style Klimovsky carried over into other films, particularly *El Extraño Amor de los Vampiros* (1975) and *La Saga de los Drácula*, the vampires vary in type as much as real people do. One is a hypertrophic servant who feeds the tourists the limbs of unlucky townspeople. Some are aged and barely able to walk. Some are peasants; others, nobility. There is, of course, the *de rigueur* lustful female vampire who attempts to "dine on" a stereotypically beautiful and often naked blonde. For the most part, not unlike the townfolk of *Return to Salem's Lot*, this village of vampires reflects the demographics, if not the culinary habits, of any Eastern European village of that period. There is even a child vampire *à la* Anne Rice, a rarity in the annals of vampire

Cheryl Smith as the child victim Lila with her "vampiric mother," Lemora (Lesley Gibb), above, and imprisoned, below, in THE LEGENDARY CURSE OF LEMORA

films. He becomes attached to one of the traveler's young daughters and in a particularly harrowing scene suffocates her and then buries her half-alive. The total effect of this naturalism is an almost anti-erotic quality, robbing vampirism of its sensual, glamorous facade.

The Legendary Curse of Lemora (1973) has, like so many of the films in this book, several titles as a result of a checkered release history. Of its various designations, the one that is most indicative of the style and the mood of this work is *Lemora–A Child's Tale of the Supernatural*. From the pre-titles sequence where a gangster breaks into a darkened room and blasts his wife and her lover with a shotgun, the film, like *The Night of the Hunter* and *The Company of Wolves*, conjures up the look and the feel of a child's nightmare. Subjectified from the point of view of the murdered woman's thirteen-year-old daughter, Lila Lee, all that follows reflects her frightened vision.

Lila is an innocent child who, as promoted in the local minister's announcements, sings "like an angel." One night she receives a letter from a mysterious woman named Lemora who claims to know of her father's whereabouts. Wishing to forgive her father and to escape the sexual advances of the minister, she sets out on a journey to Lemora's house. Like Little Red Riding Hood, she must brave a treacherous forest in order to reach her objective.

Using a wide-angle lens, saturated primary colors, and stylized set design, the filmmakers heighten the surreal quality of her journey: first in the city where prostitutes sit beckoning behind windows bathed in red light; where ticket sellers lasciviously offer candy to little girls; and where buses are deserted except for deranged drivers who accept whatever fare is offered. The stylization becomes even more extreme when Lila reaches Lemora's abode. There the lady in black, Lemora, adopts her, coddles her, sensually bathes and dresses her, all in preparation for her to take her place as Queen of the Vampires. While outside mutant vampires battle each other, inside, in a plot twist reminiscent of Carmilla, Lemora seduces the young girl away from her fundamentalist religious beliefs.

At this point in the film the other aspects are subsumed by the subversive nature of the work (which earned it a condemnation from the Catholic Legion of Decency). Lila tries to escape through the nightmare world of vampire mutants, but seems only to go in circles, ending where she began, Lemora's house. As she wanders through the house, voices tell her that she is the one who has wished all of this. She has willed this world of sensuality and violence. After staking her father in a moment of oedipal agony, in which he calls her his "princess" as he dies, she finds herself in the arms of her new mother, Lemora.

In order to confirm Lila's bizarre rite of passage, she now must find the preacher who has been so desperately searching for her. Locked in her embrace at last, he admits his desire for her and calls her his "princess," as her father had. And like her father she puts an end to his life. In the final shot of the film Lila is seen singing again in the choir, the preacher significantly absent. The "angel" Lila has now quite possibly transformed herself into the vampire Lila, closing the film on an ambiguous note.

IV. STILL OTHER DAUGHTERS OF DARKNESS: A TOUCH OF SYMPATHY

It is the secret sympathy,
The silver link, the silken tie,
Which heart to heart, and mind to mind,
In body and in soul bind.

Sir Walter Scott

Endemic to the vampire myth, as it has developed over the decades in film, is its perception as a curse. In seminal films like *House of Dracula*, *The Vampire's Ghost*, and *The Vampire* (1957), a strain of vampire films have explored the existential anguish of the undead.

In *Mary, Mary, Bloody Mary* (1974) the vampire of the title is a decadent artist living in Mexico who paints Dali-esque canvases which express her deep alienation and disorientation. Although she tries to bury her emotions behind transitory bisexual encounters, objectifying her lovers as she turns them into victims, and although she coins flippant epigrams like "eat or be eaten," Mary is nevertheless tormented. She is haunted by the memory of her father from whom she inherited this curse.

When she does meet a man whom she can actually love, she becomes truly vulnerable. Her lover tries to understand her alienation and assuage her fears while blissfully unaware of her "sickness." The oedipal dimensions of the story are brought to the foreground when her lover is enlisted in the battle against a "man in black," who has pursued her throughout the film and who turns out to be her father. Mary resists vampirizing her lover in order to maintain his much-needed support in overcoming her "disease" as well as her father.

Her resolve to escape the curse of vampirism is broken when she discovers that her father is the one tracking her and that he wishes to kill her to release her from her state of misery. In a feeding frenzy Mary vampirizes not only her father but also her lover. Turning to her father's body she proceeds to devour it, as if, as in many ancient rituals, she can partake of his spiritual power by digesting his body. She has truly fulfilled her motto, "eat or be eaten."

The Devil's Mistress (1966) is in many ways a low-budget remake of Ingmar Bergman's *The Virgin Spring*, set in a Western context. Four outlaws traverse the arid landscape of New Mexico in search of food and supplies. In the middle of the desert they stumble upon a "minister" and his wife who have transplanted themselves there from Salem in order to avoid persecution. Although the outlaws find it strange that anyone could survive so isolated, deep in the desert, they accept their hospitality. In gratitude they kill the "minister," kidnap and rape his wife, Leah, only to find that she is a vampire. On their trek back across the desert, each one is killed by the avenging Leah.

The film is notable for several reasons. First, its visual style, like *The Virgin Spring*, is spare. The compositions are simple but evocative, the outlaws shot with a telephoto lens flattened against the windswept desert and imposing mountains. Leah with her dark hair and black cape is framed against the bleak terrain.

Second, the film is very precise in establishing its characters. Two of the outlaws are brutal and savage. Around the campfire they talk about raping women. When sharing the food of the "minister," they refuse to speak, devouring their meal like wolves. Leah, too, is drawn with care. She is mute, but conveys much with her large, dark eyes and innocent expressions. Moving from victim to avenger, she is by far the most sympathetic of the characters. Even in the midst of her attacks, her retribution remains just.

Finally, the film subtly mixes eroticism and savagery. After Leah is viciously raped, she regains her strength, seducing all the men and in the process either sucking their lives from them or causing their death through her power over nature. Leah's most difficult challenge is the final one. The virginal outlaw resists her temptation. She crawls to him like a snake, flicking her tongue, licks his skin like a cat, all reinforcing her association with animals and the forces of nature. Finally he surrenders. Leah vampirizes him and cuts out his heart to devour it. Her revenge is complete.

The Hunger (1983) is a stylish, high-tech film based on the novel of the same name. Its centerpiece is Catherine Deneuve as the bisexual vampire

Catherine Deneuve and David Bowie as the vampire couple in THE HUNGER

Miriam. She repeatedly falls in love with her consorts and promises them eternal life through blood; but gradually, unlike her, they age. She keeps her "loved ones" in the cellar of her fashionable penthouse, whispering to them affectionately as if they were still alive. Miriam and her newest consort, John, approach Sarah, a doctor who is experimenting with blood disease and how it relates to aging. However, John's aging is accelerating too rapidly for any cure. As he sits in the clinic waiting room, the film intercuts the tape of a prematurely aging monkey with John's own rapid disintegration.

After John's death Miriam falls in love with Sarah and they begin an affair. Like so much of the film, their affair is photographed and edited in the slick style of a television commercial. There is non-linear cutting, sensual textures of skin and fabric, and glamorous actresses (Susan Sarandon plays Sarah opposite Deneuve). As Sarah grows more frantic and evidences symptoms of vampirism, Miriam's concern grows. She promises her eternal life, like the others, but before she can bring it to fruition, Miriam's jealous, enraged former consorts rise up from the cellar and kill her. In the end Sarah takes Miriam's place in the penthouse, a new vampire queen staring desolately out at the city below.

Although the film is a fairly serious treatment of the vampire mythology, its focus is softened by its voguish, music video visuals. The opening is typical, beginning in a disco and ending in Miriam's *moderne* penthouse, as Miriam and John pick up two New Wave denizens of the club. Cut to the dance beat of the music, the couple is seduced and exsanguinated, with Miriam using an ankh, the Egyptian symbol of eternal life, as a weapon.

The Hunger is not the first film to treat vampirism as a blood disease. As discussed earlier *House of Dracula* and *The Vampire* used this premise. In *Bram Stoker's Dracula,* Van Helsing delivers a lecture on syphilis and other blood diseases, implying that there is a relationship between them and vampirism. *The Hunger,* however, is in the forefront of a series of AIDS-era vampire movies whose plots link vampirism with a deadly malady. In *Red Blooded American Girl* (1990) a clinic, headed by the vampiric Dr. Alcore, is set up for the purpose of studying this vampiric contamination and finding a cure. When Paula, the red-blood American girl of the title, is infected at the clinic, she becomes a nymphomaniac. Even when she is cured, through the traditional blood transfusion, her sex drives are not lessened as she and the hero, Owen, embrace passionately among the tubes and needles, again establishing a connection between sex and this mysterious, ravenous malady,

Near Dark (1987) is a redneck version of the vampire legend. The film showcases a clan of violent "good old boys," including two women and a lecherous dwarf, who terrorize country bars, listen to hard rock, guzzle

As with most vampires the sun kills in NEAR DARK

liquor, steal cars, curse profusely, and survive shootouts right out of *Bonnie and Clyde*. This vampiric Hole in the Wall Gang is on a crime spree through the Midwest, showing no mercy in their violent depredations.

At one of their stops a disaffected young man, Caleb, falls for Mae, the youngest vampire, and is vampirized or, as the others refer to it, "turned" by her. In spite of the objections of the clan, Mae takes him under her wing, feeding him from her own blood as she would a baby until he is able to make his own kills. As he sucks from her open veins, Mae becomes both his mother and his lover. Although Caleb can never bring himself to vampirize anyone, he is finally accepted by the clan when he performs a daring escape which saves them during a shootout. He is given a set of spurs as a symbol of their trust.

Near Dark is among the more violent of vampire films from a woman director, Kathryn Bigelow, better known for straight, action-oriented films like *Blue Steel* and *Point Break*. The movie reinterprets the vampire as a "thing of violence" that can slit throats, rip off faces, crush heads, burn vehicles, and single-handedly destroy diesel trucks. One confrontation follows another at breakneck pace, all to the incessant beat of Tangerine Dream. These vampires actually seem to thrive more on violence than on blood.

The only force these bloodsuckers fear is sunlight. They race to shelter every sunrise, before a ray of sun can sear their flesh. In the climactic battle between Caleb, who has been cured by a transfusion, and the clan, the vampires spontaneously combust as the sun burns into their bodies. Caleb does rescue Mae and returns her to her original state by means of another blood transfusion. The final shot of the film freezes on the two lovers basking in the warmth of a sun Mae has not felt for years.

At the opposite end of the spectrum from *Near Dark* is *La Strage dei Vampiri* (1962). This film evokes Gothic and Romantic moods with its camera style. Scene after scene is punctuated by gliding camera movements, a chiaroscuro black-and-white patina, and piano themes in the style of Rachmaninoff and Tchaikovsky as the underscore. The central character is Louise, an aristocratic woman deeply in love with her husband; but when a mysterious Count arrives, she is drawn to his Byronic aspect and his poetic musings on love and death in the tradition of 19th Century Gothic fiction. The imagery of the sun and moon, light and dark, life and death, are used to epitomize Louise's conflicting impulses, which make her vulnerable to the Count. As an example, after being vampirized by the Count, she is bed-ridden. Before her husband leaves to find assistance for her, she begs him to place her in the rays of warm sun so that she might resist her tormentor's influence. This he does, but soon the sun sets and Louise finds herself bathed by the cold light of the moon and even more vulnerable to the Count's power. Her husband is so distraught that he considers joining her in a vampiric "life in death"; but ultimately, through the intervention of his doctor, he comes to his senses and embraces the "light of God's love." The dialogue interacts with the imagery as he abandons his wife to the darkness of night.

Like *La Strage, Ganja and Hess* (1973), written and directed by artist-actor-writer-filmmaker Bill Gunn, is designed with an acute painterly eye. Even in its many butchered versions the vigor of the original film is apparent. Shooting in golden, misty hues, Gunn paints his cinematic canvas not only with colors which amplify the mood of the scene but also with objects which reveal the central conflicts of the story. Gess's house is photographed in dark hues as the camera pans over his collection of Christian icons intermingled with African artifacts from the blood-drinking Myrthian tribe which he is studying. By means of this juxtaposition Gunn underlines the central conflict of the film, i.e. the battle between Christianity and Paganism. When his assistant Meda (played by Gunn) shoots him-

Graziella Granata as Louise plays a theme from LA STRAGE DEI VAMPIRI

self, after infecting his friend Hess via a Myrthian dagger, he falls flat onto
the green tile floor. His red blood seeping over and eventually obliterating
this expanse of green. When Ganja, Hess's new wife, takes her first victim,
their passionate bout of lovemaking, followed by her exsanguination of his
body, consists of a montage of flesh flecked with gold (a recurring motif in
the design of the film), stained with her victim's red blood. Finally, the cut-
aways to the Myrthian queen, shot in slow motion against a pastoral landscape, her huge body laden with feathers and trinkets, symbolize not only
the power of vampirism but in addition the pull of the mother culture on
both Hess and Ganja.

Although *Ganja and Hess* starts out as Hess's story, ultimately Ganja's
presence comes to dominate the mise-en-scene. Her regal stature, her
authoritarian yet loving manner in dealing with Hess, her physical link to
the Myrthian queen, instensified by intercuts to the queen when Ganja is
featured in a scene–all force the viewer to concentrate on her as Hess fades
into the background. When Hess finally abandons his mother culture and
accepts the "slave religion" of Christianity and its iconic cross in order to
end his vampirism, Ganja refuses. In a particularly evocative scene, Hess
hangs a swinging cross in a backlit room and is destroyed by its shadow
while Ganja, wrapped in a black garment, avoids its spell. She survives in
order to maintain her identification with the ancient queen, even though
she has lost the man she loved.

Even in the most violent and serious films, such as *Bram Stoker's Dracula* or *Near Dark*, iconography, archetypes, lines of dialogue are sometimes played for their camp value. How many times can one hear "The children of the night, what music they make" or see a vampire cringe in the shadow of a cross before these conventions become clichés? The film which most effectively satirized these conventions of the vampire movie was Polanski's *Dance of the Vampires*. Others have used a contemporay setting with varying degrees of success. In *Once Bitten* (1985) the Countess must drink the blood of virgins in order to live forever, as in *Andy Warhol's Dracula* and the Elizabeth Bathory legend. The Countess, accompanied by her wise-cracking assistant, played in deadpan by Cleavon Little, scour Hollywood and its environs for a prize virgin. When they finally find one, it turns out to be a teenage boy, a comic reversal of the of the usual sex of the victim. Mark is a naive, sexually frustrated teenager who is overwhelmed by the sexual advances of this older woman. Taking him back to her den, she wastes no time, tearing his buttons off with her teeth, and mounting his tense body. That night he is deflowered while he is vampirized.

Like other "teen vampire" comedies, *Once Bitten* plays off the adolescent male's insecurity about sex. As in *Teen Vamp* or *Teen Wolf*, the preternatural context is ready-made for the transformation of a virgin into a self-assured stud. Of course, the vampire genre is an apt milieu for this transformation with its existing convention that vampirism goes hand in hand with heightened sexuality, as with so many prior victims from Lucy Westenra on. In this case, Mark acquires a new licentiousness that makes him a suave roué and leaves his awkward days behind.

Vampira (1974) also tries for satire mode but is less accurate in its trajectory. Relying on tired jokes and vulgar racial humor, it brings little to the tradition of vampire parody. *Innocent Blood* (1992), like John Landis' earlier, influential *An American Werewolf in London,* is informed by a dark, violent, and, at times, puerile sense of humor. Anne Parillaud, best-known to American audiences as the programmed killer of *La Femme Nikita*, portrays Marie, a mysterious vampire-cop who only victimizes "bad guys." Not only does she vampirize them, but she also "blows them away" with her arsenal of weapons. Ironically, when Sal, a Mafia chief, escapes her destruction, he finds his new state of vampirism advantageous to his criminal career. He initiates a reign of terror to which Marie must put an end.

Marie is the cornerstone of the film and a prototype of the new female vampire. She is a violent, sexual being who is supposed to draw on the viewer's sympathy simply because she fights on the side of the law and because she can care for a man, her partner. Robert Loggia as Sal, however, is the darkly humorous center of the comedy, exaggerating every line, overplaying every gesture in an over-the-top performance.

Frank Langella as Dracula in the revival of the Deane-Balderston play.

CHAPTER SEVEN

The Multimedia Vampire

I. STRANGER THAN FICTION

I think people who drink blood should be able to go to blood banks to buy blood, blood that's safe and has been tested for AIDS. I'd buy that kind of blood, if I knew it was safe.

The Vampiress "Monique," quoted in **Bloodlust**

As Carol Page observes in **Bloodlust**, her collection of interviews with "actual" vampires, "Vampires are simply people who drink blood. There are about as many reasons for drinking blood as there are vampires, but generally the reasons fall into two categories: intimacy and power." Like Peter Kurten or John Haigh, Page's subjects cannot turn into bats and cannot live on blood alone. Unlike the sociopathic killers of earlier decades, a New Age natural vampire may take an ascetic approach to his or her blood need, may like Monique be a Buddhist. Their desire to drink blood leads them to form a "communion" with others who think likewise. As with Celia in *Son of Darkness* or her sound-alike Angelique in *Nightlife*, the real-life Monique would not mind taking her blood from a plastic bag. Life also imitates art in Page's interview with her own "Vlad," a rock singer whose band may not be as popular as Lestat's but, at least, it's real.

While its low-budget and uneven performances greatly hamper its dramatic effectiveness, *Vampire at Midnight* (1988) is one of the few films since Robert Hossein's *Vampire of Dusseldorf* (1964) or Ulli Lommel's *The Tenderness of Wolves* (1973) to depict a natural vampire. Unlike the period pieces of Hossein and Lommel, which dramatize the actual exploits of Peter Kurten and Fritz Haarmann, *Vampire at Midnight* presents itself as a "genuine" vampire movie, i.e. the filmmakers use and even play against the viewer's expectations of the genre to obscure whether its predator is preternatural or merely psychopathic. In its title sequence the body of a young woman with two puncture marks in her neck is dumped out of a Jaguar in the Hollywood Hills. From a brief conversation between a detective and a uniformed policewoman in a comic book store, the viewer learns that Los Angeles is being plagued by someone whom the media has dubbed "the vampire killer," and that, like this policewoman, some are even beginning to wonder if there might not be "something to it." The killer's identity is never a secret from the audience; and "Dr. Victor Radkoff," a hypnotherapist by profession, has the necessary mesmeric ability and Eastern European accent to qualify as an authentic bloodsucker. In addition he sleeps during the day, actually drinks blood, and makes wry comments to prospective subjects like "Don't worry, I won't bite you." In fact, he doesn't bite people, but slices their necks with a knife. The filmmakers leave the question of whether or not he is a vampire open until the last scene, when Radkoff is shot dead with ordinary bullets and the detective removes the plastic fangs from his mouth. Still, another cop's early observation lingers: "We know our boy is no vampire. So what the hell's he doing with all the blood?"

Below, films based on real-life vampires Peter Kurten and Fritz Haarmann

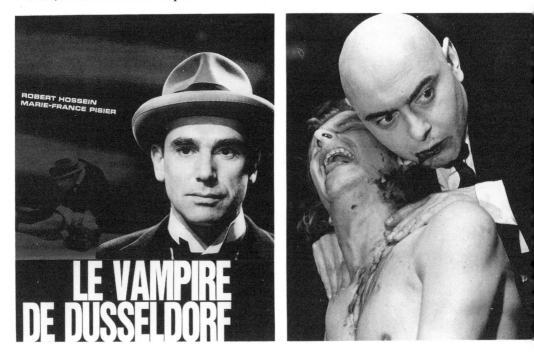

ROBERT HOSSEIN
MARIE-FRANCE PISIER

LE VAMPIRE
DE DUSSELDORF

II. I SING THE BODY VAMPIRIC

I was caught in this life like an innocent lamb.

Sting, "Moon over Bourbon Street"

Vampirism in all media refuses to die. Its many incarnations in book, tele-vision, theatrical, even musical form continue to flourish. As previous dis-cussion has made clear, the most significant and influential work to date has been Anne Rice's *Vampire Chronicles* series, which includes four books: **Interview with the Vampire**, 1976; **The Vampire Lestat**, 1985; **Queen of the Damned**, 1988; and **The Tale of the Body Thief**, 1992. It is no coinci-dence that Rice is also the writer, under the pseudonym A.N. Roquelaure, of erotic novels, for her vampire tetralogy is highly charged with Romantic sensuality and perverse sexuality. There are very few taboos in Rice's world. Pedophilia, sadomasochism, homosexuality are all touched on as part of the vampire milieu which she constructs.

What is most remarkable about Rice's vampires is the empathy through which she entices the reader to share their perspective of their world. She presents them as alienated, existential wanderers who are cursed by their isolation, even as they search out fellow vampires. Although Rice's work influenced many filmmakers, her own books long resisted adaptation to the screen. **Interview with the Vampire**, her most famous novel, was op-tioned several times and was the object of litigation over those rights. At one time Paramount announced the book as a television mini-series. Ac-tors linked to the project were as disparate as Sting and John Travolta. In fact, Sting's song "Moon over Bourbon Street" from his album *The Dream of the Blue Turtles* is inspired by Rice's work. In 1993, the Geffen Company again announced production of *Interview with the Vampire*. After a brief cast-ing controversy when Rice and many of her fans objected to Tom Cruise (rather than Daniel Day Lewis) as Lestat, the film was finally shot [see Chapter Eight]. After seeing the movie, Rice tooks out ads to reverse her-self and praise Cruise's performance.

Few best-selling vampire novels have, like King's **'Salem's Lot**, depicted vampirism in a traditional manner, as did its 1980 television adaptation. Whitley Strieber, best known for the novel **Communion**, wrote the high-tech fiction, **The Hunger**, in 1981. In it he associated vampirism with blood disease and relied heavily on lesbian eroticism for sensationalistic ef-fect. In the area of science fiction, Colin Wilson wrote **The Space Vam-pires** in 1976 which was also adapted into the movie *Lifeforce*.

Comic book publishers continue to churn out *Vampirella* and *Dracula* comic books by the score, the latest addition being a vampire hunter named Scarlet. Book publishers like Ace and Dell spew out serial novels featuring celebrated undead and their clones and descendants including, but not limited to, Dracula and Barnabas Collins. Even the children's book market is not safe from the vampire's bite as evidenced by Deborah and James Howe's series of tales of a vampire bunny, **Bunnicula** (1979) or Daniel Pinkwater's ginger-ale drinking **Wempires** (1991). Non-fiction studies of vampirism, real and imagined, also abound and have considerably lengthened the bibliography of this book.

The most notable stage production with a vampire theme since the original adaptation of Stoker's novel was the revival of the Deane-Balderston play on Broadway in 1977. As designed by Edward Gorey, the play approached the original "war horse" with its tongue firmly planted in its cheek. After Frank Langella brought a suave sensuality very different from either Lugosi or Lee, which he carried over into the screen adaptation in 1979, Raul Julia took up the title role.

Television has rivaled movie theaters as a fertile ground for vampires, not merely as an outlet for the Universal pictures of the 30s and 40s but also with original programming going back to the *NBC Matinee Theater* version of *Dracula* in 1957 starring John Carradine. There have been two British television productions, one already discussed in 1978 with Louis Jourdan as Count Dracula. In the mid-60s Denholm Elliott sported a Van Dyke and sunglasses as the Count, in an adaptation which went even further than the Browning version and completely blended the Harker and Renfield characters. There were also solarized optical effects which anticipated the Jourdan version. Not to be outdone, the Canadian Broadcasting Company sank its teeth into the classic in 1973 just before the Dan Curtis *Dracula* premiered on American screens. Dracula also found himself reemerging very briefly in the U.S. on *Dracula 90*, a television series for teens, as the vampire down the block and as a sit-com character in *Mr. and Mrs. Dracula* in 1980. Television Draculas and other vampires have been serialized as well in France, Italy, and Japan, where small screen bloodsuckers seem to overcompensate by sporting fangs that resemble mini-walrus tusks.

The Dan Curtis series *Dark Shadows* was briefly brought back to life in 1991 with Ben Cross in the starring role. The series flashed back and forth between the present and the past, leaving the heroine quite perplexed as to her identity. Barbara Steele added the presence of a genre icon to the proceedings in portraying a doctor treating the vampire. *The Munsters* featuring the vampiric grandpa and Lily was also revived in cartoon form, in several television movies and as a short-lived syndicated series *The Munsters Today*. Another comic short was the episode of *Tales from the Crypt* featuring Malcolm McDowell as a night watchman at a blood bank who sleeps by day in a coffin that folds up like a Murphy bed. *Forever Knight's* (1992) vampire, introduced in the movie-of-the-week, *Nick Knight*, is the most fascinating of the batch on television. As the title implies he is a vampire with an aristocratic past who is trying to live up to a code of chivalry at odds with his vampiric curse. As a detective he is confronted not only with quests in which he can vanquish criminals, but also with temptations to revert to vampirism, particularly carnal temptations. Children's programming which has long had a fang-toothed and monocled Muppet Count on *Sesame Street* has now added another vampire puppet on *Eureeka's Castle* and the animated vegetarian hero, Count Duckula.

As with *Salem's Lot* and *Nightlife*, the movies-of-the-week format has been the usual one length for both straight and serio-comic vampire tales on television. In *Vampire* (1979), co-written by Steve Bochco before his *Hill Street Blues* fame, Richard Lynch gives an appropriately menacing performance as Anton Voytek, a vampire at large in the city. In *I, Desire* (1982) vampire hookers are hunted by obsessed detectives, and in *The Midnight Hour* (1985) a group of teens raise the dead and die to regret it. In *Daughter of Darkness* (1990), a young woman returns to Eastern Europe to search out her father, a vampire, played with great panache by Anthony Perkins.

While the original *Night Stalker* has become the classic vampire movie-of-the-week, the series which spun off from it featured the same wire service reporter, Carl Kolchak, overcoming the skepticism of his boss and the local authorities to reveal a different unexplained horror every week. While such a premise for a series, as might be expected, was not fated to last very long, one of the show's episodes, *The Vampire*, was an informal sequel to *Night Stalker*. A hooker from Las Vegas, likely to be an unaccounted for victim of the original's Janos Skorzeny turns up as a vampire in Los Angeles and leaves a trail of "bodies missing an inordinate amount of blood." While it is burdened with a sub-plot in which Kolchak used the pretext of interviewing an Indian mystic to get to Los Angeles, Kolchak's sardonic narration, as it did in the original, sets the tone: "She was no longer missing, nor could she really be considered a person." In the conclusion, Kolchak single-handedly (as usual no one believes him, so no one will help) flushes the vampire from her lair then lures her up a hillside where he has poured out gasoline for a circle of fire to entrap her. When he also ignites the giant cross that is a landmark of the Pilgrimage Theater, she is sufficiently disturbed and distracted for him to stake her as the police arrive. As per formula, they momentarily charge him with murder then release him without admitting that his victim was a vampire; and he is left to ponder the coroner's report on the plane trip home: "Female, species human, who had been dead at least three years. This is a medical conundrum for which I have no explanation."

Undoubtedly the most remarkable vampire MOW since *Night Stalker* is *Blood Ties* (1991). Directed by Jim McBride, the film posits vampires as an oppressed subculture trying to maintain their traditions in the face of a hostile mainstream society. These vampires are no longer supernatural, only more powerful physically and sexually than humans. Nor do they live forever, only longer. They are not even vulnerable to the traditional weapons like the cross, garlic, etc. Instead the emphasis in this film is on the culture of this "Carpathian-American," as they call themselves, population. At a party in one of their wealthier members' mansions, the vampires dance traditional dances, share stories of their homeland, honor their elders, and enjoy their future, their young children.

Even within this idyllic setting, a conflict lurks and with it the traces of the negative side of vampirism. The vampires are being pursued by a right wing, fundamentalist group who wants to exterminate them. On a talk show one of the leaders of this group accuses the vampires of taking "our wives," stealing "our jobs." How to react to this persecution is the question which gives rise to the central conflict of the film.

On one side are those who preach bloodletting as a defense, including Eli, the industrialist, and his brood of motorcycle toughs, the Shrikes. The other side is led by Harry, a journalist and an "assimilationist," who preaches legal remedies and working within the dominant culture while holding on to their beloved traditions. It is an argument which has gone on in the ranks of almost all cultures when threatened with extinction by a more powerful force. The extremism of the vampire hunters ultimately forces a violent resolution to the problem. In the final scene the vampires destroy their enemies in a bloody battle. Harry does join them in order to avoid a pogrom against his people and to save a former lover. *Blood Ties* is an obvious metaphor of contemporary American social ills. The political intentions of the film are never soft-pedaled but speak out loudly for multi-cultural tolerance.

Television, more than any other medium, reflects the popular myths of the day. That the vampire has been a constant visitor to that medium speaks to the myth's strength. Whether it is a serious reworking of the vampire legend as in *Blood Ties* or the ultimate commercial Count, where Dracula becomes a celebrity endorser, sinking his fangs into a can of Coca-Cola, the vampire as icon and myth still strikes a responsive chord.

Bram Stoker's Dracula has become the highest-grossing vampire film ever made. The irony, of course, is that Dracula is no longer Stoker's, or anyone else's, possession. As the centenary of his birth (in fiction, that is) and a new millennium approach, still more incarnations of Dracula and his ilk will doubtless appear. Dracula, Carmilla Karnstein, Elizabeth Bathory, all of these figures long ago transcended the limitations of their original appearances. In the process, they have acquired new powers and new weaknesses, new desires and new anguishes. There have been vampire dogs and moths, vampire turkey men and trees. They have come from outer space, from Shangri-La, from Burbank, and to Kobe to make beautiful women. As to the future, it might be best to heed the caution from Ray Bradbury's vampire tale, "The Man Upstairs":

> We don't know what a hobgoblin or a vampire or a troll is. Could be lots of things. You can't heave them into categories with labels and say they'll act one way or another. That'd be silly.

Below, Ben Cross in the short-lived revival of the series DARK SHADOWS.

Above, Kathleen (Lili Taylor) prowls the night in *The Addiction*.

CHAPTER EIGHT

The Vampire at the Millennium

My perception of mortals has changed vastly since my vampiric induction.... To me you are all prey. Simple easy prey. I bear no grudges and hold no court over mercy and reprieve. When darkness falls, I rise, kill, feed, and return to my place of safety before the blistering sun rinses my kind from the earth.

"D.P.E." in **Vampires the Occult Truth**

As the year 2000 approaches, the vampire film reflects the same apocalyptic concerns informing all of late Twentieth Century culture: epidemics of new pathogens, urban blight, alien invasion, factional warfare, and natural disasters. In many cultures a coincident rending of the traditional social fabric–family values, rules of civility, organized religion, trust in the government–has created an ethos of decay and anxiety prevalent in all forms of media.

The vampire film of the Nineties has surpassed even the "Euro-trash" of the Seventies (mirrored in the work of directors like Rollin and Franco) in melding the erotic film with the violent action movie. This phenomenon is certainly not confined to the vampire genre. Hollywood product in general has become more and more exploitational using graphic violence, based on sophisticated and now relatively cheap special effects and unabashed eroticism to sell mainstream, A-budget films like the *Robocop* and *Terminator* series, *Basic Instinct* and *Showgirls*. Because the vampire film draws its strength from more atavistic cultural and psychological sources, from collective myths and the collective unconscious, it has always been a more fertile ground than mainstream films for tracking cultural trends. As the lines between fact and fiction blur more frequently than ever, vampire cults commune over the internet and self-professed "real" blood-drinkers prowl for willing victims in the occult nightspots of the neo-"goth" scene. While the Seventies and Eighties were marked by the emergence of sensitive and sympathetic vampires, not just Anne Rice's tortured Louis but variant views of Dracula as a quasi-victim from Dan Curtis and Francis Ford Coppola, the past few years has seen the return of the unrepentant predator, not just Rice's Lestat but *The Vampire in Brooklyn*. The anonymous male true-believer who writes about himself in the book **Vampires the Occult Truth** relishes a fantasy that involves murder and hemophagy. In the face of such spreading cultish beliefs, the traditional vampires imagined by past filmmakers may seem a bit old hat.

I. DRACULA'S NIGHTMARE

You have known what it was to be in a nightmare in which you feel that there is some all important thing for which you search and which you know is there, though it remains forever just beyond your reach.

Arthur Conan Doyle, "Lion's Mane"

For an instant I didn't know where I was. I'd been dreaming something desperate which was threatening to vanish completely without the slightest clue to what it had been...

Interview with the Vampire

More than two decades after *Young Frankenstein* (1974), writer/director Mel Brooks tackled Stoker's novel in *Dracula Dead and Loving It* (1995). The scenes themselves are most often played straight, so most of the humor de-

Below, Dracula (Leslie Nielsen) menaces Mina (Amy Yasbeck) in *Dracula Dead and Loving It.*

rives from skewed renderings of generic set pieces, and the plot line relies as heavily on Balderston and Deane as on Stoker. In the ending, for instance, Van Helsing (played by Brooks) rips away a board from a window to expose Dracula (Leslie Nielsen) to the sun in the manner of the Hammer *Dracula*. But the first part of Dracula's body struck by the light is his shoe, which results in his hopping around suffering from a preternatural hot foot. Brooks does concoct one very unusual scene. Dracula awakens and discovers that it is daylight, but he is unaffected by it. Thinking that drinking Lucy's blood has cured his sensitivity, he wanders out in a park where he encounters some picnickers who offer him a chicken leg and a glass of wine. After a moment's hesitancy and parody of Lugosi ("I never drink...wine"), this comic Dracula decides to imbibe after all. Moments later Renfield wanders by and tells his master that he is starting to smolder. As a panicked Dracula despairs of finding shelter in time, he awakens in his coffin and realizes it has all been a "daymare."

While Brooks' broad lampoons do not really inquire metaphysically if vampires dream of fang-toothed sheep, the act of dreaming gives the preternatural predator a sympathetic almost vulnerable aspect. While essentially silly, running gags such as Dracula and Van Helsing squabbling over who will have the last word in Moldavian (a disembodied Dracula gets that, right after the end credits) debunk the pomposity of the characters.

Eddie Murphy's portrayal of Maximilian in *Vampire in Brooklyn* (1995) is less humorous than Nielsen's Dracula and truly beset by the nightmare sense of seeking something which is just beyond reach. In director Wes Craven's world view, the grisly can be funny-strange or funny-humorous; but, while Murphy's Maximilian has a wry smugness entirely appropriate to a Dracula figure, the plot extrapolates freely from the vampire canon, moving quickly from a Dracula-like arrival on a ghost ship to a Blacula-like encounter with some wise-guy thugs to a Brooks-like pun ("I just had Italian.") without ever clarifying why Maximilian must find a bride. In his unabashed rapacity and elegant aspect, Maximilian is a throwback: cunning, charming, and guiltless. But the narrative, the complex make-up and effects, and Murphy's performance as Max never probe beyond the surface. In fact, the make-up used to make Murphy/Maximilian into other characters has more dramatic impact than the vampiric transformations.

Since Maximilian has no inner conflict, the more dramatic characterization in *Vampire in Brooklyn* is Rita (Angela Bassett), the half-vampire police woman who has never known why she has always been "more of a night person" and whom Max has come to Brooklyn to find and make his bride. But, while the plot contorts itself to make it seem that she may succumb to Maximilian's enticement, in the end, she refuses to feed on the living and rejects her vampiric half. The dramatic development of Rita's

Above, Julius (Kadeem Hardison) interrupts Maximilian (Eddie Murphy) as he prepares to transform Rita (Angela Bassett) in *Vampire in Brooklyn.*

conflict is constantly derailed. Scenes with Maximilian are sandwiched between cop scenes involving Rita's partner, Justice (Allen Payne), and broad comic relief from Max's decaying ghoul, Julius (Kadeem Hardison), and landlord (John Witherspoon). Neither Maximilian's demise nor Rita's return from the brink offer any real resolution, so it all ends with a cross-genre parody of Murphy's *48 Hrs* as Julius proclaims that "there's a new vampire in town."

There is also an element of parody in *From Dusk Till Dawn* (1996), although the generic identity of this picture is somewhat confused. Most vampire films introduce the undead characters in the first half of the narrative—not so, *From Dusk Till Dawn.* As a parody, the initial reference points are director Robert Rodriguez's own *El Mariachi* and writer/co-star Quentin Tarantino's *Pulp Fiction* with snickering allusions to *The Wild Bunch* and *Seven Samurai* thrown in. The first portion of this film follows in the wake of destruction left by the Gecko brothers (George Clooney and Tarantino) as they try to slip from Texas into Mexico, abducting an agnostic ex-minister named Jacob (Harvey Keitel), his family, and his motor home in the process. Once out of the country, the narrative is over, except for their encounter with the vampire proprietors of a unique truck-stop-cum-girlie-club. After the ragtag band of reluctant believers discusses what they know about vampires, they set about a systematic extermination of their hosts. No hint of how the vampires came to run this smorgasbord of low-life victims is ever given, except for a last high-angle matte shot that pulls back from the gutted nightclub to reveal a Mayan pyramid at the rear. In the dynamic of *From Dusk Till Dawn,* where threats of violence alternate with violence itself, little matters except the stylized destruction. It is as Seth Gecko remarks an "unfortunate business," an encounter with unbelievable but undeniable creatures from hell. The obvious irony is that the Gecko brothers are themselves such creatures, as the body count displayed on a mock newscast established early on. The encounter with the Geckos does help restore Jacob Fuller's faith, for as Seth points out "if there's a hell, then there must be a heaven." After this last serious moment, the humans arm themselves with outrageous weapons salvaged from the truck cargoes of earlier victims: a jack-hammer stake, a cross bow, a super-soaker filled with holy water. Of course, the minister just makes a cross out of a bar club and a shotgun, in a manner which another character noted "worked for Peter Cushing." The orgy of dismemberment which follows leaves but two survivors: Seth and Fuller's daughter Kate (Juliette Lewis). Dawn restores equilibrium, and the film itself now becomes a variant of *The Getaway.* For a moment, in explaining to his dubious Mexican contact that "psychos do not explode when sunlight hits

Below, Seth Gecko (George Clooney) prepares to face the vampires' assault with a stake-tipped jack hammer in *From Dusk Till Dawn.*

them," Gecko is forced to confront the preternatural nature of the night's events. Then he just uses complaints about his brother's death and his own ordeal to barter a lower price for his criminal cohort's services and drives off, back to a life of real monstrousness.

When *Interview with the Vampire* (1994) was finally released nearly two decades after the novel's publication, the adaptation of Anne Rice's novel came at the crest of resurgent interest in the genre. Originally dismayed by the casting, Rice reversed herself and extolled the film and Tom Cruise as Lestat in a rambling essay written for the Vampire Lestat Fan Club newsletter. The film became the highest grossing vampire film of all time. This was balanced, of course, by the fact that it was the highest budgeted vampire film of all time. Just three years after *Interview* and five after *Bram Stoker's Dracula* the ranks of $20 million plus vampire films have more than doubled. Among them in mid-1997, *Blade,* starring Wesley Snipes as the Marvel Comic half-vampire who hunts his undead kin, is in post-production; *Vampires,* to be directed by John Carpenter from John Steakley's novel, is about to begin shooting; and a third adaptation of Richard Matheson's **I Am Legend** is being contemplated by Ridley Scott and Warner Bros. to star Arnold Schwarzenegger. If it is made, this picture would easily eclipse the budgets of all its vampire film predecessors.

The anticipation that surrounded *Interview with the Vampire* was rooted not merely in the original novel but the entirety of Rice's "Vampire Chronicles," which spans several books, and the new perspectives she brought to the vampire genre. Although the film carries the sub-title *Vampire Chronicles*, Rice deems the Chronicles to have begun in 1985 with the successor book, **The Vampire Lestat**. While Lestat may be the one with the fan club, it is the enigmatic and tortured Louis, the interviewee of the first novel, that ignited the phenomenon of vampires from New Orleans. And while producer David Geffen pondered a succession of possible actors and directors, other filmmakers, as discussed in the previous chapters, wasted no time in borrowing liberally from Rice's mythos.

"It was a vampire that accepted." So Louis (Brad Pitt) tells the interviewer (Christian Slater) about the creature that fulfilled his death wish. From the harshly lit, ill furnished room in present day San Francisco, where Louis begins his story, the cut back to a matte shot of the 18th Century delta spans several distances at once: between now and then, here and there, and real and imagined. Once in that world, the black and white textures and sparse decor of San Francisco are overwhelmed by the painterly aspect of the period setting. The gestures and performances become melodramatic and, as Lestat vampirizes Louis and they fly up into the rigging of a schooner, the events become fantastic, and the underscore Wagnerian. If this evocation of the supernatural seems closer to *Der Fliegende*

Holländer than Murnau's *Nosferatu,* it does fit with Rice's troubled view of the world. "Romance is a divine word which has never really been denigrated by the drugstore novels with the swooning ladies on the cover," Rice has asserted in discussing the film *Interview,* "Romance will be with us for all time." For most critical commentators, the "romantic" elements of "The Vampire Chronicles" like the tinges of sado-masochism overtly part of Rice's erotic novels (written as A.N. Roquelaire) have been subsumed by the overwhelming angst of Louis.

The strategy for director and uncredited screenwriter Neil Jordan and his key collaborators–cinematographer Phillippe Rousselot, designer, Dante Ferretti, and composer Elliot Goldenthal–was to separate the two worlds which Louis inhabits. Modern San Francisco, first seen in aerial shots under the main titles with an ominous choral motif in the underscore, is a sea of lights. Passing through the stream of pedestrians, the camera moves across an urban street and pans up a window. A reverse cut reveals Louis, in a plain black suit, hair tied back in a pony tail, posed against a window and the city lights outside. The surroundings belie the outrageousness of his assertion: "I'm a vampire." He demonstrates his preternatural powers to the incredulous interviewer without special effects. The editing creates his movement to the light switch to illuminate the

Below, Lestat (Tom Cruise, left) and Louis (Brad Pitt) posed in their finery in *Interview with the Vampire.*

room "too fast for you to see." Without music, the loudest sound is the scrape of the chair as the startled interviewer recoils. Although Louis tells the tale, the final cut of the introductory scene is back in time, from a close-up of the interviewer smoking nervously to the sun setting over a period quay.

Even more palpably than in the novel, the physical beauty of Louis and Lestat on screen, even without the embellishment of the make-up and costumes, masks the fact that they are monsters. While the vampire king of *Bram Stoker's Dracula* may suffer over his long-dead bride and pitiful existence, the special-effects transformations of that character reveal not just his bestial nature but the decay of his soul. In *Interview with the Vampire,* this dual nature of the vampire is split into two characters. But while Louis may bemoan his condition, he is still a vampire by his own choosing. However ill-informed his choice, his fate is the result, and his torments are not entirely undeserved. While the vampires of both novel and film are technically celibate–in fact, Rice has commented in articles about the androgynous nature of Lestat–there is certainly a sexual aspect to Lestat's "feeding." Detached from human appetites–a scene of Louis and Lestat pretending to eat dinner for the benefit of appearances ironically underscores that they, too, "never drink...wine"–Lestat clearly exults in his other sensuality. When Louis laments about the pretense of "dining on empty plates and drinking from empty glasses," Lestat remarks that "the Paris opera is in town, we could try some French 'cuisine'."

Whatever he may claim, there is also a sexual dimension to Louis' appetite. At one point, Lestat stages an elaborate scene for Louis' benefit. He "seduces" a prostitute (Indra Ove) with talk of seeing her on a satin bed. Of course, where he really envisions her is on a serving tray. As Louis enters, Lestat kisses/bites the woman on the breast. One close shot reveals that the sensation is, for her, clearly pleasurable, then another captures Louis' mixed emotions about what he is witnessing. Moments later, the woman realizes that the warm sensation coursing down her torso and between her legs is her own blood. As she screams, Lestat fills a wine glass with her blood. When Louis brushes it aside, Lestat shouts, "Do not doubt, you are a killer, Louis!"

The most troubling aspect of any vampire/hero for a viewer is that, as Lestat constantly reminds Louis, he or she is a predator, a killer. The prostitute had pleaded with Louis: "I cannot die like this. I need a priest." Louis did not help and may have resented the implication in her plea of how easily she could find absolution. While sympathy is possible for anyone caught in the grip of a powerful compulsion, would the vampire be quite as Romantic a figure if he or she were a child molester? Accordingly, perhaps the most daring and original character of the novel is the child

Above, Lestat (Tom Cruise) prepares to vampirize a prostitute (Indra Ove) in *Interview with the Vampire*.

vampire Claudia. After refusing to drink the prostitute's blood from Lestat's glass, it is Louis who flees and then initiates the creation of Claudia (Kirsten Dunst) by "molesting" a child.

Lestat transforms Claudia into a child/lover for Louis; and, indeed, as he tells the interviewer, "She slept in my coffin at first, curling her little fingers around my hair," a two shot reveals them nestled together. While Lestat may indulge various impulses in his killing, may objectify men, women, and children alike to satisfy his rapacious hunger, what could be more perverse than a child who kills? For under Lestat's tutelage Claudia, too, is soon killing men, women, and children without hesitation. Because her nature and a residue of human ethics prohibits consummating her love for Louis, a mentally mature Claudia is so infuriated by her unending childhood that she kills Lestat. "Louis, my love. I was mortal till you gave me your immortal kiss," Claudia whispers to lover/father. Only Lestat accepts Claudia for who she is. "I hope it's a beautiful woman with endowments you'll never possess," Lestat taunts minutes before Claudia cuts his throat.

In Paris, where Louis and Claudia flee after the killing, the anomalies continue, and they discover "vampires pretending to be humans pretending to be vampires." The stage on which a coven of vampires perform a snuff theater is presided over by Armand (Antonio Banderas), an ancient immortal. When the vampires strip and ravage a young woman as part of the act in the Théâtre des Vampires in the novel, the action is described by Louis in terms that are more sensuous than savage. In the film, the same action is a disturbing prelude to the appearance of Armand. As he comes forward in his "star" vampire outfit and whispers the hypnotic incantation, "No pain," the young woman finally surrenders. Unfiltered by Louis, the moment where she "embraces death" is unromantic and pitiful.

In the period world recollected by Louis, death is indelicate and bloody. After slashing Lestat, which unleashes a veritable torrent of blood from his throat, Louis must lift Claudia onto a chair before the red tide reaches her shoes. While some of the usual myths are inapplicable or inoperative, for example, the reflection of Louis and Claudia in the parlor mirror as they recoil from a reanimated Lestat, others are in place, most notably the searing effect of the sun. The pantomine horse and mock explosions on the stage are more dynamic events than the subtle predation of Armand. But the real drama in the theater of vampires is the execution of Claudia and her new mother, Madeleine (Domiziana Giordano). Freed from his responsibility, Louis is finally permitted the catharsis of fury and destruction.

Below, Louis (Brad Pitt) and Claudia (Kirsten Dunst) recoil in horror from the disfigured Lestat in *Interview with the Vampire*

His story ends with allusions to the power of cinema, where Louis can watch Murnau's *Sunrise* and *Nosferatu*. The images are a stark contrast to Louis' richly-colored and orchestrated recollections. In a major change from the novel, where the interviewer merely plans to visit the place where Louis rediscovers Lestat, the indomitable predator is lurking in the back seat and springs to action as the interviewer drives across the Golden Gate Bridge. At the wheel of the car, the music of choice is not Handel or Hadyn but Guns N' Roses singing "Sympathy for the Devil."

In the pre-title sequence to *Cronos* (1993) as a narrator solemnly intones the history of the device of the title: "In 1536, fleeing the inquisition, the Alchemist Umberto Fulcanelli disembarked in Vera Cruz...," the viewer sees the notebook and prototype sketches. The *Citizen Kane*-like exposition continues, as the audience witnesses the Alchemist's death in a 1937 accident, then a series of slow craning shots and pans explore his mansion, where bowls collect blood dripping from an anonymous victim. According to the narrator, the inventory of goods eventually sold at auction does not include the Cronos device.

From the muted wedges of color of this somber introduction, the title sequence features modern Mexico City and the family of antique dealer Jesus Gris (Federico Luppi) at breakfast. The bright red carries over in the sweater of his granddaughter Aurora (Tamara Shanath) and is amplified by the vibrant color of the orange juice pitcher. At the end of the sequence Gris and Aurora reach his antique shop, where a rough-looking customer is soon examining a plaster angel. When the man leaves, cockroaches emerge from the angel's eye socket, and Gris discovers a golden object in its hollow base. The echoes of *Kane* mixed with Howard Hughes return in the next sequence, which introduces invalid industrialist Dieter De La Guardia (Claudio Brook) as a gloved and surgical-masked nephew Angel (Ron Perlman) wheels a breakfast cart down a corridor of plaster angels encased in plastic. Reluctantly Angel agrees to follow up on the report of another angel.

The true horror of *Cronos* is not in its supernatural events but in the sense of lurking evil beneath the everyday. Angel's name is powerfully ironic for under the gray suit and blue mask are the spiritual aspect of a demon. The white-haired Jesus and the young Aurora are the angels; but even in the balanced and painterly clutter of his shop, there is no true sanctuary. The underlying decay is evoked as much by images of the scavenging insects as by Angel moving through de la Guardia's factory and handling the supposedly antiseptic stainless steel breakfast tray. After Angel buys the statue, he asks Gris and his granddaughter what they think of his new nose, which he plans to get through plastic surgery, by holding

Above, the antiquarian Jesus Gris (Federico Luppi) shows his granddaughter Aurora (Tamara Shanath) the gold bug they have found in the hollow plaster angel in *Cronos*.

cut-outs up to his face. The metamorphosis Angel plans in this scene anticipates the involuntary change which will afflict Gris.

The ultimate symbol of decay is the device itself. The legs and siphon which extend from the case like a grotesque beetle are still gold. When Gris suffers his first affliction after being "bitten" by the gold bug and yields to the impulse to let it feed on him again, close-ups of the inner workings give the viewer of a glimpse of the shriveled parasite housed inside. For Gris, whose meticulousness is evoked in the title sequence where he carefully takes the cover from his vintage car, the descent into darkness has irrevocably begun. The next morning, as he sits in the shop which Angel and his men have torn apart, he notices one unbroken item: a small bell jar. In an attempt to restore his shattered equilibrium, he reaches over and tips it onto the floor. By the next evening, Gris' bloodlust has led him to licking up spilled blood from the marble floor of a men's room. As he placidly presses his face to the surface, its texture is another visual precursor, as it mirrors what his skin will soon become.

Knowing who must be searching for the device, Gris goes to confront Angel and meets De La Guardia, who explains how the parasite in the Cronos device gives life but whose parable confirms Gris' worst fears. "Maybe insects are God's favorite creatures. Christ walked on water, like the mosquito. And as for resurrection, it's not an odd concept for the spider or the ant, who can remain in a rock for hundreds of years until some-one sets them free." Indeed, as Gris and Angel move through the mecha-nistic interiors of De La Guardia's factory, they are as trapped by fate as the parasite inside the device.

In developing the perception of the ancient vampire as weary and want-ing to die, in the manner of Varney the Vampyre, *Nosferatu in Venice* (1981), alters the physical aspect of Klaus Kinski, reprising his role from the Werner Herzog remake of Murnau two years earlier. Instead of being bald and dressed in black, he sports a shock of unkempt hair and an 18th Century frock coat as he prowls the quays and canals of Venice. But as he ravages a new generation of women from a Transylvanian/Venetian fam-ily, the effect is the return of an elemental in a decorative setting. In easily overcoming a local doctor, whose fiancée had summoned him via a séance, and a dying vampire hunter (Christopher Plummer) who believes that "vampires are everywhere," this Nosferatu is listless and disaffected; but he still destroys humans without a second thought. There is a similar conflict in the recent, low-budget *Vampire Journals* (1997) which pits a reluctant un-dead turned vampire hunter against a powerful, ancient predator. Clearly derived from Anne Rice's Louis and Lestat, the two characters here are not bound together like the half-brothers Stefan and Radu in same film-makers' *Subspecies*. Ash (Jonathon Morris), the elder undead, runs a gam-bling house to maintain his extended family where the patrons are un-aware of their hosts' true nature in the manner of Rice's Theater of the Vampires. Flashbacks reveal the vampiric induction of Zachary (David Gunn) and his voice-over colors the entire narrative in the manner of Rice's first novel. But in his rage over the loss of his own life and that of the woman he loved, Zachary is as ruthless as the vampiric kin he would all destroy. He does overcome Ash but too late to thwart his attempt to in-itiate a young pianist, Sofia (Kirsten Cerre). Another variant of *Subspecies* finds her and Zachary huddled together in the end away from the killing rays of the sun, condemned to live in eternal night.

Perhaps the most dazed and confused of Gen X vampires is the figure in *Blood & Donuts* (1995). As the flippant title suggests, the mood of the film is off-beat. Earl (Justin Louis), a cab driver who owes money to some local hoodlums, picks up a newly reanimated Boya (Gordon Currie), a vampire who does not want to hurt anyone. Unlike Kinski in *Nosferatu in Venice* the youthful appearance of this character belies his fatigue with his condition. The tongue-in-cheek narrative actually opens with shots of a moon land-ing and the image of a ghostly astronaut cavorting on the surface. A title reads: "In 1969 man walked on the moon and Boya crawled into a bag." In the title sequence, a stray golf ball disturbs the garment bag in which Boya has entombed himself. Compelled to walk the earth again, Boya is a disoriented, burnt-out undead, more intent on digging up a suitcase of memorabilia and pasting a picture of his latest "gal" in his photo album. The oddest thing is, he uses a little of his blood as glue.

As a vampire parable, *Blood & Donuts* is more parody than pretense. Tilted angles and thunder on the soundtrack may externalize Boya's disorientation as he checks into a rat-infested hotel, but they also mock the seriousness of the genre where rats scurrying along the baseboards can be a plus. Still, the next scene where Boya pokes his fist through the cheap wall and pulls out dinner has a certain preternatural charm. When the shaggy-haired, leather-coated Boya stumbles into Bernie's Donuts, even the smart-mouthed counter-girl Molly (Helene Clarkson) succumbs to that

Below, Annabella Sciorra as the vampire seductress Casanova in *The Addiction*.

charm. Shortly after walking her home, Boya is psychically coupling with her from his bathtub.

As a possibly reluctant undead, the shuffling and grinning Boya is truer to his convictions than the whining Louis or any other self-pitying vampire. Why he saves Earl from the strong-arm men is unclear. Perhaps the cabbie's moans and whimpers were disturbing Boya's sensitive hearing, which another sequence renders in aural point of view; perhaps he just wanted a friend. In the end, rather than completely return to the "field where I worked for some years, extermination," Boya chooses self-immolation.

II. NOSFERATU'S DAUGHTER

This young lady indeed, to do her justice, was but little addicted to the use of conventional terms.

Henry James, *Portrait of a Lady*

While the male vampire has grappled philosophically with his affliction, the female undead in recent films have often embraced their state with a mix of fervor and repulsion. With the elemental power of the Nosferatu figure, they prowl the dark passages of the urban world to slake their hunger. *The Addiction* (1995) is perhaps the best example in clearly expressing the millennial angst through female protagonists. The film was made by Abel Ferrara, the philosophical director of low-budget classics like *Ms. 45*, *Bad Lieutenant*, and *The Funeral* whose previous statement on modern vampirism was a scene of Asian gangsters watching Murnau's *Nosferatu* in *King of New York*. Opening with a lecture and slide show on the My Lai massacre, Ferrara immediately sets the mood and amplifies the theme briefly introduced in *King of New York*–vampirism as metaphor for the evil in human nature. But Ferrara's vision of evil is not abstract or religious but palpable: the inhumanity of man to man. Throughout the story of Kathleen (Lili Taylor), a socially aware graduate student in philosophy who becomes a vampire, Ferrara interweaves examples of human cruelty on a massive scale–the Holocaust, massacres at My Lai and in the Middle East–with individual acts of cruelty: drug addiction and vampirism itself. In one scene Kathleen's mouth still drips with the blood of a recent victim as she watches a news report of a mass killing. In this context when the vampire holocaust occurs at Kathleen's academic dinner party at the end of the film, the viewer has been prepared psychologically, intellectually, and emotionally for this particular interpretation.

Interwoven with theme of "man's inhumanity" is the motif of moral responsibility. When Kathleen first encounters her vampire-inductress (Annabella Sciorra), she is given a chance to escape. The vampiress whispers as she clutches her neck, "Tell me to go away." But Kathleen only mutters a feeble "please." In Ferrara's violent universe, silence becomes consent. The theme of refusing to deny evil recurs several times in the film. For example, a hungry Kathleen picks up a girl in the library. After siphoning off some of her blood, she says to the outraged girl, "It was your decision," emphasizing again the dimension of free will so vital to Ferrara's concept of evil. From those who fail to resist with vigor, the evildoer obtains social consent for his or her evil whether it is on the natural level of murder, genocide, and drug addiction or on the supernatural plane of vampirism. In Ferrara's ethical construct these evils are all equal, all involving willful violence to oneself and/or others. The tracking shots down urban streets past addicts making deals parallel the vampires drawing blood.

When Kathleen meets Peina (whose name is a homonym for "pena" or "emotional pain" in Spanish, portrayed by Christopher Walken), she discovers a philosophical vampire who has "controlled" his desire for blood. Like Anne Rice's Louis, he is tormented by this unending thirst but limits it as much as he can. "...Like the Tibetans," he says, "You learn to survive on a little." He takes her to his industrial style dwelling and there attempts

Below, Kathleen (Lili Taylor) meets the master vampire Peina (Christopher Walken) in *The Addiction*.

to indoctrinate her into his method of "becoming human" while taking her blood. He is more Nietzschean in outlook when he speaks of will conquering desire and of how he has learned to eat solid food, defecate, and even diet. He is ultimately unsuccessful with his recalcitrant student, as Kathleen goes off to initiate the final blood bath. For as she comes to realize in the end: "Our addiction is evil."

In *The Girl with the Hungry Eyes* (1995), based on a story by Fritz Leiber, evil is punished by a beautiful model-vampire Louise (played with sensuality and humor by Christine Fulton), who is an unlikely cross between Cindy Crawford and Nosferatu. Her full mouth and statuesque figure epitomize a model in one instant while her stooped posture and claw-like hands mark her as a descendant of Max Schreck in another. In one shot the filmmakers pay explicit homage to *Nosferatu* by showing Louise's enlarged shadow creeping along the walls of downtown buildings. Beginning in a Miami art deco hotel in the 1930s, the film establishes Louise's back story through voice-over and montage. Louise herself, dressed in a period evening gown, speaks of her love for the hotel as she walks through its hallways. Suddenly the sounds of her arguing with her faithless lover interrupt her reverie. Then a hand places a picture of her and a newspaper clipping about her swindling boyfriend on a white surface. Next she drops a key onto an ashtray. She enters her room. The camera cuts to a shot of a spinning ceiling fan. Her hand touches her jewelry, the blades continue spiraling slowly. Then a pan of the room reveals the spasmic movement of legs as she dangles from linen woven into a rope.

The narrative moves to modern-day Miami where the now decaying hotel, cursed throughout the decades by Louise's suicide, is about to be taken over and demolished. The building itself, in an act of self-preservation, establishes a symbiotic relationship with Louise–raising her from the dead in a reverse motion shot of her original hanging. An electronically altered voice, that of the hotel, accuses her ("You did this to me.") and then sends her off on a quest to find the key to a safe deposit box in which the deed to the hotel has been placed, a deed made out to her.

Louise's mission turns out to be more extensive than finding a lost key. On a metaphysical level she becomes an avenging angel, punishing a series of male evildoers, miscreants not unlike her dead lover. In each of her sexual encounters with these men, she physically and psychically connects with them by becoming what they most desire. She is a rural, Southern girl, replete with accent, for a first victim, Henry (portrayed by the director, Jon Jacobs), who committed rape while still a child (Louise: "How old were you when you first raped?"). Subsequent encounters involve a young boy whom the macho gangster Johnny (Leon Herbert) violated ("Where's that boy? Did he kill himself afterwards?" she asks as he enters her from behind.) and a weeping model with a scarred face whom an agent named Bud (Bret Carr) callously deserted after her accident. In each case she vampirizes her victims in the middle of a sexual encounter.

The one shiftless, alcoholic, womanizing male she cannot bring herself to destroy is the one who most reminds her of her dead lover. He is Carlos (Isaac Turner), a photographer like her fiancé. Instead in classic obsessive fashion she relives the emotionally torturous experience, hoping this time to succeed where she once failed. In many ways her obsession parallels that of the sympathetic Dracula figures in Dan Curtis' *Dracula* and *Bram Stoker's Dracula*. While the gender-bending Nineties may typically reverse the sexual roles, the emotional thrust, the pangs of the vampire for its human past, is the same. Carlos eventually eschews his weak-willed ways and obtains the key to the safe deposit box. He wins her over by this act of love and his declaration: "I don't care what you are. I love you." She then asks him to "commit," something he has never been able to do. He agrees, and in the next sequence they are entwined, blood covering their bodies as they writhe in an apocalyptic, erotic embrace. Louise has found a faithful lover and gained a hotel in the bargain. In this sense, Louise's quest to relive her past is far more successful than the any of the Draculas.

Nadja (1994) is a post-modern rendering of *Dracula's Daughter* (1936). Like its antecedent the film tells the story of the child of the most celebrated undead, as she wanders the urban streets at night looking for victims. "Nights...nights without sleep, long nights in which the brain lights up like a big city," she intones as her sad face is superimposed over a shot of the lights of the city at night. Nadja (Elina Löwensohn), daughter of Dracula, resembles her cinematic ancestor from the Thirties, Countess Zaleska: both share dark hair and eyes, a tall, languorous frame, a predi-

lection for hooded capes and female victims, and a melancholy expression evidencing a weariness with eternal life. Plot elements like the seduction of a young girl, the presence of a protector-servant, the theft of her father's body reverberate from the original film as does her hypnotic stare used to spellbind victims.

What makes this film most effectively post-modern is its sense of humor and its unique visual style. *Nadja* resonates with the style of its Executive Producer David Lynch,

particularly in its use of humor, understated and ironic. When Van Helsing (Peter Fonda) tells of Dracula's desertion of his two children (Nadja
and her twin brother Edgar, played by Jared Harris) he describes
Dracula's mood this way, "He was tired, lost. He was like Elvis in the
end...drugged, surrounded by zombies. The magic was gone." The appearance of an equally post-modern Van Helsing enhances the irony. He
is a long-haired, burnt-out hippie who often mumbles incoherently, chases
phantoms on his bicycle, and falls inexplicably asleep in the oddest places,
including inside a piano. When Lucy (Galaxy Craze) tells her husband Jim
(Martin Donovan) that his uncle Van Helsing was arrested for staking
Dracula, he says flatly, "A stake in the heart? I can't picture it." This is
then followed by a fast cut of the staking itself as if in answer to his doubt.
Lucy responds with, "I can," as if she could see the cut preceding her line.

The visual style of the film recalls *The Addiction*. Both pictures are shot in
black and white, unsual today even in vampire films; but in further push-
ing the visual anomalies the director of *Nadja*, Michael Almereyda, intercuts video footage shot with a "toy" video camera (a Fisher-Price PXL
2000). The extreme graininess of the image gives the film an emotionally
unsettling texture. Almereyda uses the video format for Nadja's POV
shots, often from an out of body perspective; in the disturbing death of
Nadja's father, in the flashbacks to the Carpathian mountains; and in several other scenes where a quickly altered mood is appropriate. The mixed
visual formats, including a more traditional use of slow motion, add a surreal quality to the film compounded by details like the Dracula Christmas

Opposite, the title character of *Nadja* (Elina Löwensohn) walks the night. Below, Van
Helsing (Peter Fonda).

ornament–also part of the ironic humor–which emits a high-pitched chant.

Nadja's character conflict is about change. She tells her servant, after her father's death, "He's gone. I'm free...I want to change my life...I'll find someone. I'll be happy." The one she finds is Lucy, the niece of Van Helsing. But just like her father who fell in love with Nadja's human mother but ultimately could not break his predatory pattern, Nadja cannot really change. Wounded, she returns to her ancient home in the Carpathians. She summons her brother to her telepathically ("a psychic fax," she calls it), knowing he will bring Lucy. And, as she planned, he does. Aided by Van Helsing and Jim, they hunt her down. But by this time she has reverted to the vicious animal her father was. Unable to change her life, she fights back by taking over another's, transferring her spirit to that of Cassandra (Suzy Amis) via transfusion ("No one suspected that I was now inside her.")

Family conflict adds a further dimension to the thematic tableau of the film. Jim accepts the burden of his crazed uncle with sulleness and a barely repressed irritability. He listens patiently to his uncle's rantings on vampires but is always on the edge of separating from him. For her part Nadja calls her father "a bastard" for deserting them and rejoices at his death. Nadja's twin brother Edgar fears and loathes his sister, hiding from her as he assuages his blood lust with Mexican baby shark plasma. Threatened by Nadja, Edgar ultimately agrees to lead the expedition which will destroy her, because, as he says "She's a monster." This quasi-incestuous mingling of two families–even Edgar's nurse Cassandra is related to Van Helsing–

Below, with revolver cocked, Rafe (Dennis Miller), private detective/vampire hunter, confronts Lillith (Angie Everhart) in *Bordello of Blood*.

Above, really "Lost Boys" Reggie (Matt Hill, left) and Caleb (Corey Feldman) in *Bordello of Blood*..

creates an insular world which gradually loses contact with normality altogether. Nadja's possession of Cassandra adds a final twist to this "incestuous" tale as she marries her own brother. For as Nadja tells her brother, "Family is all that really matters."

While *The Addiction* deals with apocalyptic violence, *The Girl with the Hungry Eyes* with derangement and sex, and *Nadja* with alienation, there are mainstream films which present the female vampire in a less complex context with an emphasis on blatant humor, comic book antics, and hi-tech special effects. In *Tales from the Crypt Presents: Bordello of Blood* (1996) the filmmakers eschew subtlety in order to capture the all-powerful adolescent market. There is little style to the violence or true irony to the humor. *Bordello* tells the story of a televangelist (Chris Sarandon) who has raised a vampire-succubus named Lillith (played by supermodel Angie Everhart) from the dead in order to set up a bordello in which vampire-hookers lure sinners to their destruction as punishment for their sins. Lillith, provocatively garbed and brandishing a mane of red hair, seduces her prey in one shot and then literally rips out his heart in the next, while tossing off sarcastic *bons mots*. She is also not above making men her slaves, including brash teen Caleb (Corey Feldman). She meets her match, however, in cunning and in quips in the detective-turned-vampire-hunter (portrayed by social humorist Dennis Miller). She wants him as a paramour, but he brandishes pump guns filled with holy water. In a holocaust of special effects, the bodies of the vampires explode all over the walls of the tacky bordello, leaving Lillith defeated, for now.

Red Lips (1995), directed by Donald Farmer (*Vampire Cop, Red Lips II*), is particularly subversive. Like many vampire films before it, particularly the Carmilla adaptations, it elicits sympathy for a "sexually deviant" character. *Red Lips* opens with a simulated sex scene between two women. As they writhe in ecstasy and one of the women–Caroline (Ghetty Chasun)–moves into a position for oral sex, the camera modestly cuts away. In the next shot, Caroline's head slowly rises into the frame, her lips covered with blood. As in the seduction scene between Lucy and Nadja, the female vampire draws its strength from the female repository of menstrual blood–invoking images of birth as well as the traditional ones of death.

Caroline's lesbianism may be inborn but her vampirism is an aberration of science. In order to earn money, the glam Caroline, with her tattoos, pierced body parts, dyed jet black hair and funereal garb, sells her body to a doctor (Mandy Leigh) who experiments on her, creating a virus which results in Caroline's blood thirst. This experimentation precipitates a rampage of vampirism, which is not confined to females, as Caroline's blood hunger does not discriminate based on gender. Each encounter is progressively more violent and deviant. Like Carmilla before her, Caroline's fatal flaw is her humanity, her ability to fall in love. The object of her obsession becomes Lisa, portrayed by a "butch" Michelle Bauer (ubiquitous "scream queen" of B-horror), who cares for Caroline by helping her through an episode of withdrawal on the streets of New York. Lisa becomes Caroline's caretaker in a classic co-dependent relationship. She disposes of her victims, chopping one to pieces and storing her parts in the refrigerator. She even helps her find victims. When Lisa is finally killed by the outraged boyfriend of one of her victims, Caroline is left alone. Sitting next to the river, she screams out her agony in the final poignant shot of the film.

Below left, Caroline (Ghetty Chasun) flashes an impressive array of canines and body piercing in *Red Lips*. Right, a more contemplative vampiress, Monica (Rachelle Packer) in *Jugular Wine*.

Red Lips has the style of the Lower East Side punk-glam amateur film movement of the late Seventies and Eighties. Like *The Right Side of My Brain* (1985, Lydia Lunch-Richard Kern), or *Geek Maggot Bingo* (Nick Zedd), the film has a grainy immediacy, enhanced by its video format. The film's lighting tends, by necessity of format, towards the unsubtle, with intense reds and greens created by gels, predominating. The Manhattan "downtown" ethos pervades the movie–cheap apartments, performance art clubs, graffiti-covered streets, pervasive drug use. Also recalling the Lower East Side films, *Red Lips* amplifies moments of sex and violence. As the film progresses, the wounds of the victims become larger and the blood flow more ample. One victim is merely chopped to pieces but another is submerged in a bath of his own blood. Partially because of budget, partially by choice, *Red Lips*, like its Lower East Side predecessors, uses mostly non-professional actors, giving it the unfinished and improvised feel of a documentary.

Two films which link alien invasion paranoia with the undead are *Vampire Vixens from Venus* (1994) and the Showtime *Vampirella* (1996), featuring Talisa Soto as the scantily clad vampire from another planet. While the vixens in the first film drain humans for their own purposes, Vampirella fights for humanity against the evil Vlad (Roger Daltrey) and his clan of nasty bloodsuckers. Both films are tongue-in-cheek but even as parodies lack the inventiveness of the more creative films they mock.

A more serious rendering a world overrun by vampires is *Jugular Wine* (1994). A low-budget movie which nevertheless features locations as disparate as Alaska, Philadelphia, Louisiana, New Orleans, and Arizona, *Jugular Wine* creates a world in which vampires have infiltrated all levels of society from underground nightclubs to high-priced art auctions, Southern funeral homes, corporate businesses, and the Alaskan fishing industry. They have become a species unto themselves with warring factions, not unlike the vampires in Anne Rice's novels or in Jim McBride's engrossing *Blood Ties*.

The film opens, markedly like Mary Shelley's novel **Frankenstein,** aboard a steamer in the barren reaches of the North latitudes with a journal-like narration by its main character, the anthropologist James (Shaun Irons). As the "vampire queen" Alexandra (played by Alexandra), naked under white fur like Sacher-Masoch's **Venus in Furs**, caresses the protagonist's body, she explains his primary obligation to her: to protect her from a rival vampire named Legion. The narrator's face registers erotic pleasure as well as fear as she bites his neck, creating a blood tie between them but not turning him into a vampire. For that he needs to drink of her blood. This erotic episode is interrupted in mid-act by Legion and his minions. The furious master vampire proceeds to rip the heart out of Alexandra and devour it before James's eyes, thereby absorbing his rival's strength.

This brutal act propels the inconsolable narrator on his "odyssey" of revenge and discovery, searching not only for the slayer of his queen-lover but also for the "biological source" (James's own words) of vampirism. As the film progresses, the audience comes to the realization that James is lost without Alexandra and so a more desperate, if hidden, motive for his journey is to find a replacement for her. Because of his relationship with Alexandra, he can no longer relate to his wife and even his young daughter Meghan (Meghan Bashaw) can only reignite his incoherent emotions as he tries to explain the new "frontiers" he is exploring. Meghan does not understand intellectually but accepts him emotionally with an unconditional love his wife cannot give him.

The narrator's odyssey does lead him to a replacement for Alexandra– Monica (Rachelle Packer) who first appears as a nondescript student of his and only later reveals herself to be a dark reflection, in both appearance and mood, of Alexandra. After they make love in her *moderne* apartment replete with indoor pool and abstract art, the camera catches her posed by the reflection of the pool on the wall. She is half-naked like Alexandra in the first scene but she has a much darker aspect. Her jet black hair, her dark eye make-up, her black lipstick all recall the vamps of silent films. Even her words betray a spirit much less comfortable with her vampiric state than Alexandra: "You're trying to make me feel...You're going to be dead tonight."

But Monica's dark beauty is not enough for the narrator as he continues to be haunted by images of

Below, "Legion" in *Jugular Wine.*

Alexandra, so he continues his odyssey to find Legion. As he explains to the viewer while watching a long-haired, muscular vampire from Eastern Europe seduce a Creole beauty in New Orleans, he seeks those entities "beyond evil and still in the order of nature." Soon he becomes "intoxicated" by this underworld and, as he wanders through New Orleans, the film takes on that point of view and becomes hallucinatory in its fast-motion traveling shots through the tenderloin areas of "the Big Easy". The sequence ends echoing *Vampyr* as James awakens in a silk-lined coffin. This style is extended as he heads for Arizona, there encountering vampire clubs decorated with green lights and aluminum foil and populated by transvestites.

This phantasmagoria climaxes where it began in Alaska, coming full circle as in Shelley's landmark novel. On the frozen tundra, under a full moon, the huge eye of Legion tells James that he must become "new" again, become one of them. In a vampiric ballet, silhouetted naked dancers entwine James in a series of black, transparent scarves emblematic of his entrapment. Before him on a throne of leaves, like an ancient European goddess of nature, appears Monica, dressed in a black sheath dress. Before her is an offering, wrapped in a white coverlet–James's own daughter. He watches horrified as Monica vampirizes his daughter in slow motion, heightening the tension of the scene while externalizing his agonized point of view. Finished with her rite of initiation, Monica then unexpectedly attacks Legion, ripping his heart from his chest and feeding it to a prone James. In low angle she spreads Legion's blood on her face as below her James devours Legion's heart. In a final series of shots James stands in the shadows, born again, "new," as Legion had predicted. Above him is his queen, Monica, and next to him, holding his hand, is his daughter, now all united in their vampirism. For they have "embrace[d] the unknown" (Legion's words) and passed through "the frontier" James had sought in so many different places.

The overlapping of the erotic film genre and the vampire genre has led to several other changes in female vampires facing the millennium. In a post-feminist era where Camille Paglia can write in **Vamps and Tramps,** "I want a revamped feminism. Putting the vamp back means the lady must be a tramp," the erotic film has become as oriented towards the female audience as the traditional male one. Not only paying more attention to the physical pleasure of female characters on screen, and by extension their counterparts off screen, filmmakers have also added the conventions of the Romance novel to the fabric of the genre. While they may not fully agree with Anne Rice's pronouncement that "Romance is a divine word which has never really been denigrated by the drugstore novels with the swooning ladies on the cover. Romance will be with us for all time," producers have responded to what they believe women want in erotic films, with results such as Zalman King's long running *Red Shoe Diaries* series for cable. While most erotic films still retain the traditional patriarchal and objectifying perspectives, the female point of view does dominate the discourse of some of these newer examples.

The vampire film has long featured films revolving around females such as the vampire characters Carmilla, Elizabeth Bathory, and Dracula's Daughter, and also the controlling heroine in *Son of Dracula*. These vampiresses were determined and aggressive in their pursuit of their desires which were not only physical but most often emotional as well. They were, in many ways, prototypes of the post-feminist woman.

Embrace of the Vampire (1994), directed by Anne Goursaud, starts off with a male vampire (played by Martin Kemp) as its protagonist. In flashback the spectator witnesses his seduction in a forest by three vampire-succubi, a scene derived from *Bram Stoker's Dracula*. After the subsequent death of his love, there is another reworking of the Curtis' *Dracula*, as he begins a search for a woman to replace her. The Vampire ensconces himself in the tower of a Renaissance-style university where he enters the dreams of Charlotte (Alyssa Milano) in order to bring her to him and relieve his eternal torment. The focus then shifts from the male vampire to the female, a repressed, deeply religious virgin. Charlotte, unlike her more "modern" school sisters, dresses conservatively, surrounds herself with religious artifacts, including a cross around her neck and a crucifix on the wall, and allows her horny yet patient boyfriend, Chris (Harrison Pruett), to sleep beside her but not with her. Although her hipper friends and classmates scold and deride her–from the solicitous "Check out the field" to the hostile "She needs to get laid"–Charlotte clings to her chastity. When sorely tempted by the beautiful bisexual photographer Sarah (Charlotte Lewis), who disrobes her during a photo shoot, Charlotte almost succumbs to the atmosphere created by the erotic photography around her and the power of this new experience of exhibitionism. Only at the last moment does she pull away. In Freudian terms, her superego overcomes her wandering id; in terms of the vampire genre she preserves herself for the undead predator. The Vampire uses the dream doorway to her psyche to extend his influence. As her dreams become more and more erotic featuring both men and women, Charlotte begins to take on the behavior of a vampire herself, a vampire who has released all inhibitions. She replaces her cross with a pagan ankh, adopts more alluring costumes, smokes filterless cigarettes, drinks, uses foul language, and alters her make-up to emphasize her sultry qualities. She becomes a vampiric predator, for although she does not draw blood, she does take away men from the taunting "bad girl" Eliza (Jordan Ladd). She also reverses roles with the photographer and becomes the aggressor, biting Sarah's lip in a vampire's kiss. More overtly than in vampire myth, literature, and early film, vampirism becomes a metaphor for long repressed natural and "unnatural" sexual desires that suddenly come forth. And the proto-vampire herself is but an externalization of that inner sexual conflict.

Tied to this theme of sexual repression, that is a staple of Romance novels, is that of Romantic love. After a brief tryst with a bar-hopping, tattooed vampire in black leather (played by Jennifer Tilly), Chris confronts the Vampire in the bell-tower as he is about to

Above, Illyana (Julie Strain) in *Blonde Heaven*.

possess Charlotte totally, body and soul. Chris cannot defeat a vampire; only Charlotte's will can do that, As she turns from the sensual and thrilling Vampire to confess her love for the safer, mortal Chris, this act of will on the female's part destroys the male vampire and his hold on her. She has purged herself through idealistic love and now can begin a life of more "appropriate" sexual behavior, freed of inhibitions but chastened by her unbridled expression of desire.

In *Blonde Heaven* (1995) the female vampire is an unabashedly Nineties creation, a shapeshifting, gender-bending character Illyana (played by six-foot-tall erotic star Julie Strain). She is able to take the form of either sex, depending on the desire of her victim. She first enters their minds and then their bodies, like more traditional vampires. Although the film was directed by B-movie specialist David DeCoteau (*Sorority Babes in the Slime-ball Bowl-o-rama, Nightmare Sisters*, etc.), he takes credit under the pseudonym of Ellen Cabot and maintains this persona even for interviews. This masquerade reaffirms the desire of erotic filmmakers to appeal to the female spectator. In this film, which centers on an escort agency with a predilection for nubile blondes, the filmmakers take overt eroticism to the point of parody, as the director boasts in interviews that the film "has eleven sex scenes in it, surpassing anything else."[1] Whether this dubious claim is accurate or not, the intent speaks for itself.

Supplementing the erotic scenes in which Illyana shifts from male to female personas are carefully designed sets and lighting. The offices of the agency and the mansion are moderne with an emphasis on heavily contrasting neon blues, blacks, and reds. There is a slickness and sensuality to the look which is also carried over to the designer clothes the female vampires wear. As in *Embrace of the Vampire* the filmmakers also introduce the element of romance. Illyana falls for a prospective employee, Angie (Raelyn Saalman), because she resembles her dead male lover, a painting of whom Angie finds while hiding in a closet in Illyana's rooms. Although Angie claims not to know any better, she protests too much. When Illyana first seduces Angie by taking the form of her boyfriend, she does not keep that form throughout the lovemaking. She turns back into herself while maintaining the traditionally aggressive posture of the male. Angie, for her part, does not seem to notice or feigns not noticing the change, leaving the audience to doubt her innocence.

In a by-now familiar formula *Night Shade* (1996) opens with a couple in the midst of sexual passion. But unlike *Blonde Heaven*, which introduced Illyana aggressively ravishing her victim-lover, the lovemaking of this couple is far more tender and traditionally romantic. The lighting and photography of this scene and the entire film contrast with *Blonde Heaven's* hard blues, blacks and reds. There is a warm amber tone in most scenes and, during flashback love scenes between Scott (Tim Abell) and Jennifer (Teresa Langley), a diffusion filter invokes the visual cliché for artful sex. Such stylistic devices place this film–although told from the perspective of a male, Scott–in the tradition of the Romance novel. In the back story, Scott has recently lost his wife to a medically unexplained illness. He continues to be haunted by images of his past with her when they made love in various picturesque locations. At the same time, he is receiving strange e-mail from a woman with the screen name Electra. Intrigued by the messages, he decides to follow her directions to a nightclub.

At this point *Night Shade* adopts the conventions of the stripper-vampire movie, established in films like *Vamp* and *Dance of the Damned*. The private club he finds himself entering is, unbeknownst to him, run and staffed by vampires, led by a vampire-stripper-queen named Charmagne (Tane McClure). The acts the customers witness feature sado-masochistic themes common to many vampire films: bondage, pleasure linked to pain, fetishistic use of objects. In one act a blonde stripper (Jennifer/Electra, who is masked) threatens another semi-naked brunette caught in an over-sized

1. *Femme Fatales*, Spring, 1994, p. 54.

spider web. The blonde's jabs with the knife alternate with caresses of the captive brunette. In another routine Charmagne crawls around the stage transforming herself into a wolf and then back into a woman, to the astonishment and fear of the men watching, who are nonetheless enthralled. In a back room select men are taken and distracted by lap dances which culminate with an orgasmic draining of their blood.

In this den of evil and "ecdysiasm" Scott finds Electra, a stripper who reveals herself, after removing her mask, to be his dead wife. As the film cuts from one of the vampire-strippers seducing and then vampirizing a customer in a back room to Electra's gaudy dressing room in order to maintain suspense and establish the milieu Jennifer has found herself in, Jennifer/Electra tries to explain to her disbelieving husband that she died but was resurrected as a vampire and is now a prisoner in this club. She asks her husband to forget her and go on with his life. Already obsessed with his lost lover, Scott cannot do so. He rejects the advances of a seductive co-worker Allison (Jennifer Leigh Burton) and spends his time trying to prove to his private investigator friend, Jack (Don Scribner), that Jennifer is "alive." It soon becomes clear that this obsession is not one-sided: Jennifer continues to visit her husband against her better judgment. Unable to detach emotionally, they make love, a dangerous act considering her physical and emotional state. And she *is* tempted to vampirize him, but the sight of a photo of herself in her human form, lovingly placed by his bedside, causes her to retreat from her purpose. Jennifer's obsession ultimately turns to jealousy as she pursues the sexually persistent Allison through an abandoned parking lot, appearing and disappearing at will, and then destroying her.

Below, Rachel (Laura McLauchlin) in *Addicted to Murder.*

After alienating the police and causing Jack's death, Scott returns to the club, this time armed with a crossbow and revolver; but he is unable to save his wife. Instead she dies in the process of rescuing him from the clutches of Charmagne, stabbed by an arrow Charmagne has caught mid-air and then planted in Jennifer's breast. Echoing the sentiments of many male vampires finally released from their undead state, Jennifer says "I'm already dead...It's better this way...I'm finally free." After her death, a frenzied Scott dives out a window he has broken to let the purifying sun in, thereby destroying Charmagne.

Milliennialism has also produced a growing obsession with serial killers, from the high prices paid for John Wayne Gacey's grotesque clown paintings to Richard Speck's bootleg prison tapes to Jeffrey Dahmer's murder by a fellow inmate acting as "an angel of vengeance" to the elevation of the fictional Hannibal Lecter to icon status. Even Charles Manson has resurfaced for a new generation who listen to Marilyn Manson and wear t-shirts displaying his image. *Addicted to Murder* (1995), directed and co-written by Kevin J. Lindenmuth, mixes genres by combining vampirism and serial murder to produce an unusual study of the mind of someone "addicted to murder." The film opens in black and white with a subjective camera, as a young Joel (played as an adult by a beefy Mick McCleery) runs into the forest and witnesses the vampirizing of a man who is distracted by Joel before he can overcome a beautiful, young vampire named Rachel (Laura McLauchlin). In low angle point of view, Joel and the audience watch Rachel's bloody depredations. From the background the audience hears the commanding voice of his mother. Joel is frozen between the demands of two women, Rachel asking seductively not to be revealed ("I owe you one...") and his mother beckoning forcefully to him. This traumatic childhood incident is the key to Joel's psychological dysfunction–his obsession with murderous women. Lindenmuth follows this scene with a shot of the adult Joel listening to an answering machine, where a disembodied voice leaves a chiding message after his mother's funeral. Then a television interviewer and expert discuss a serial killer. In a semi-parody of the Freudi-

Below, Kevin (Mick McCleery) and the remains of Rachel in *Addicted to Murder*.

anism that would deem Joel to be locked in an unresolved Oedipal struggle, which plays itself out in misogyny and murder, the psychologist discusses the unknown killer's need for violence, his addiction to murder.
What the expert does not know is that Joel *is trapped* in a double bind,
caught between women making demands on him he cannot or is psychologically unable to meet, because of his encounter with a vampire.

Like Peter Loew in *Vampire's Kiss* Joel takes his frustrations out on
women while seeking to serve his vampiric Mistress Rachel (the same
name as the character played by Jennifer Beals in *Vampire's Kiss*). The
audience learns through flashbacks which are part of the complex non-linear structure in *Addicted to Murder*, that the vampire Rachel became Joel's
only childhood friend, protecting him from an abusive mother who
dressed him like a girl to punish him and from a sexually aggressive baby-
sitter who masturbated him when she found him spying on her and a
lover. In another effective use of subjective camera, Joel watches his baby-
sitter and her boyfriend making love until he is discovered and then mo-
lested by the baby-sitter, all done from his POV which puts the audience
into the mind and feelings of Joel. Ultimately Rachel kills Joel's tormen-
tors, as much to control him and become his new tormentor as out of any
affection for him. For Rachel is the one who initiates him into the game of
murder. When she says, "This is the way I need your love," she means
through deadly violence in which she compels him to "kill her" repeatedly.
In one scene her love-making consists of forcing herself onto his knife
(read: phallus) in orgasmic ecstasy in which she dies then revives herself
into undeath. This act is repeated in varying forms, including a very gruesome scene where he penetrates her over and over again with a chain saw.

Eventually Rachel tires of Joel and sets him free to be a "human predator" on his own. Joel is not turned into a vampire until the very end of the
film. Rachel refuses to perform the transformation even though he begs
her. She is the one who forces him to go out into the world saying simply,
"I don't need you anymore." She consigns him to the alienating New York
city streets to search for the image of his second mother–Rachel–in the
faces and bodies of other women. Joel marries but divorces his wife out of
fear that he will harm her. Losing control, Joel reverts to the behavior
Rachel inculcated. When he finds the proper subject, to recreate the form
of lovemaking Rachel taught him, Joel kills. Ultimately he does find a perfect replacement for Rachel in the person of Angie (Sasha Graham). He
meets her at a club called "The Hungry" (reminiscent of the one in *Night
Shade* and the titles of the novel and film *The Hunger*) and literally, in a
short insert close-up, sees Rachel in her. Angie is also a vampire and
comes to dominate his life, playing the same bloody games as Rachel, waiting for him like his mother when he comes home late. She takes over

where Rachel left off and even tells him tauntingly, "Rachel gave you to me. Now you're mine forever." Angie is not reluctant to share her powers and grants him his wish–to become a vampire.

Joel does finally resolve his Oedipal double bind he has found himself in. Ten years later he returns to hunt down his primal mother Rachel. He has now become a much sleeker, more attractive individual, sporting a leather jacket and shades. He presents himself with a new found confidence as he confronts his mentor and stakes her to the ground, decapitating her for final effect. He stands before the mirror, holding her head in his hand, and delivers his cryptic last line, "Why do we feel so much?" The line acts as a contrast to an earlier contemplation before a mirror in which he had bemoaned his lack of feelings after murdering a girl. The final line makes the resolution even more open-ended. Do vampires feel more than humans, an echo of Anne Rice, or has Joel exorcised his torment through this bloody catharsis?

The female vampires in *Addicted*, like those in most of the vampire films approaching the millennium, radiate an aggressive sexuality and an emotionalism typical of Nineties female icons from Madonna through Sharon Stone to Cindy Crawford. They are post-feminist archetypes who herald a new century.

III. VAMPIRES NEXT DOOR

I myself do not get into blood drinking, but I know people who do. You have your different vampires: there's psychological ones and the Anne Rice vampires. I'm mainly the dressing-up kind...

"Blue" quoted in *The Los Angeles Times*

BATON ROUGE (AP) -- Five teen-agers believed to be members of a Kentucky "vampire cult" were being held in jail Friday in connection with the bludgeoning deaths of the parents of one of the youngsters.

As Dracula turns 100, vampirism as fiction has become equally familiar as pop phenomenon, sometimes via campy club scenes, sometimes as a game played with deadly earnestness. Still, in their neo-Gothic costumes and their rules of engagement, the filmic image of the vampire is the predominant influence on these activities. For some, who may even be the teenagers next door, internet games such as Vampire the Masquerade can be twisted to take on a fatal reality.

While the Seventies and Eighties often found vampires on television in syndicated series and movies-of-the-week, the Nineties have seen a feature revival that ranges from major studio projects to a spate of ultra low-budget, direct-to-tape features. Many, shot in "film-looked" video, explore novel concepts of how vampires are created or why some chose self-de-struction rather than turn on loved ones, in the manner of such cheaply-made antecedents as *Vampire's Ghost* and *The Vampire*. Such already dis-cussed, under-$100,000 features as *Jugular Wine* (shot in 16mm film) and *Addicted to Murder* (shot in Beta SP video) would have been difficult if not impossible to make in the technology of five years ago.

Vampyre (1990) is an unofficial remake of Carl Dreyer's *Vampyr*. Report-edly shot on a budget of less than twenty thousand dollars, it demonstrates many of the problems inherent in minimal budget: amateurish acting, ill-fitting costumes, unfinished sets. But what are defects in other films work to an advantage in *Vampyre*, as the film's model, Dreyer's classic, also fea-tured stiff acting and minimalist set design, though in Dreyer's case it may have been a matter of aesthetic choice not necessity.

Whatever the historical case, the filmmakers of *Vampyre* recreate the dreamlike mood of Dreyer's original. David Gray (Randy Scott Rozler), a melancholic vampire hunter since childhood who speaks with a deliberate cadence, arrives by boat to an isolated rural town. He is called there tele-pathically by the villagers who are in the midst of a plague of vampires. There he discovers an evil witch-vampire named Marguerite (Cathy Sey-ler). In a possible appeal to modern sensibilities, the witch is a nubile, top-less vixen rather than a hoary crone of *Vampyr*, and her accomplice, a cor-rupt doctor, is named Dreyer in homage to the master director. Gray's power in this metaphysical battle rests in his innocence of spirit. Because of this rather than in spite of it, he is ultimately victorious over the clutch

Below, David Gray (Randy Scott Rozler) and the witch-vampire Margeurite (Cathy Seyler) in *Vampyre*.

Below, Sam Heller (Jason Walsh) makes a stand in *City of the Vampires*.

of vampires, floating back out of the town much as he had entered, this time with the woman he has rescued.

Remaking *Vampyr*, however, requires more than similarity in plot points. The filmmakers of *Vampyre* impose a measured, oneiric pace, interspersing unexplained or incomplete scenes, often in slow motion, and utilizing disconnected, poetic dialogue, with shocking images, which wake the spectator from his reverie into the a vampiric nightmare. The bloody attacks of the vampires are particularly unsettling when the victims are children, as is the protagonist's voyage in his own coffin shot with a claustrophobically subjective camera (again lifted from Dreyer) or David's spirit rising from his sleeping body to be seduced and vampirized by the voracious Marguerite.

Heartstopper (1989), adapted by George Romero protégé John Russo from his own novel, features an unusual narrative structure as it cuts back and forth over time from the colonial era to contemporary Pittsburgh. Its vampire protagonist is as non-traditional as Romero's Martin: Latham (Kevin Kindlin) is a colonial physician whose experiments with blood cause him to be hanged as a vampire and who rises two centuries later when his burial site is disturbed to become what he was falsely accused of being. After inadvertently killing a child with his poisonous saliva, he considers killing himself, seeks absolution from a priest, but finally finds a companion and settles into a low-profile lifestyle much like Rice's Louis.

City of the Vampires (1994) combines the haphazard peril of *2,000 Maniacs* with the plague of Matheson's **I Am Legend** in which an urban landscape becomes an unfettered hunting ground every night. While the film's snarling vampire (Noel Bonk) proclaims himself to be "Legion," his followers are actually a bit rag-tag. Still the images of abandoned buildings in upstate New York and the shed full of discarded tires where the young protagonist's girlfriend is taken to be vampirized do evoke a sense of urban decay where vampires could prowl like over-sized rats. Guilt-ridden over fleeing, he finally comes back to find her. She has become a vampire but,

Above, Randi (Amber Newman) about to give new meaning to the term red neck in *Deadly Dreamgirls*.

as in *Vamps Deadly Dreamgirls* (1995), nonetheless attacks her creator to save him. The Ohio-based, female undead of *Deadly Dreamgirls* are, like the vampire coven in *From Dusk Till Dawn* and their low-budget sisters in *Night Shade*, proprietors of a topless bar. In an opening scene a redneck mistakes the intention of the buxom vampiress Randi (Amber Newman) who promises "to suck him dry" and dies with his boots on. There are allusions to *Fright Night* and Elvira in the mock television show the priest/hero watches and from vampire films on his wall as well as an invocation of the Hammer tradition in the flashback/dream which the head vampiress has about her initiation; but the attempts at style cannot overcome the limited abilities of the cast. The same holds true, with English accents, for another shot-on-video feature *Demonsoul* (1995), in which a confused woman's past

Below, Selena (Eileen Daly) and her monk-like disciples capture the hapless Alex (Drew Rhys Williams) in *Demonsoul*.

Above, a pack of vampires savage their prey in *Darkness*.

life/childhood encounter as/with a vampire is recalled through hypno-therapy wherein the trance state triggers her own transformation into a bloodsucker and a confrontation with a vampire coven in a desanctified church in the heart of London. Is it real or a dream? In the end she sits babbling in an asylum locked in a state of perpetual nightmare.

Leif Jonker's *Darkness* (1992) is shot in Kansas and also posits a sort of vampire plague with allusions to *Children of the Corn*. In the title sequence a young man runs down a dark highway to a gas station convenience store. "He is coming," he tells the policewoman and clerk; and soon all inside are dead. Outside a woman is taken while she fills her car with gas. Tobe (Gary Miller), the lone survivor, runs off into the night, where he stalks the Lestat-like master vampire throughout the hours of darkness. A sub-stantial portion of *Darkness'* minuscule budget must have gone for the blood, which spurts from countless teen-age victims. While Tobe hunts them with guns, a chain saw, and a soda bottle full of holy water, the infes-tation of vampires replicates itself in the manner of *Night of the Living Dead*, and soon packs of teenage undead prowl the suburbs like feral dogs savag-ing all whom they encounter. As with *City of the Vampires*, most of the ac-tion is set in a single night at the end of which Tobe tries to help a van full of concert-goers. One of the them, Jodie (Steve Brown), is tracked to a movie theater where the master vampire (Brian Caldwell) traps him. "The night takes care of its own. And we are the night," he explains as he sets him against the vampire hunter: "I am darkness." When the sun finally rises, punctuated by the sound of shotgun blasts on the soundtrack, the vampires dissolve into pools of bloody flesh on the highway. Only Tobe and Kelly (Cena Donham) are left alive. They amass a fresh cache of weapons before nightfall, when the master vampire rises from the earth again to renew the cycle of destruction.

Despite their technical limitations, the restricted time frame and spare visual style of *Darkness* and *City of Vampires* help create a much more oppressive mood than in *Vamps Deadly Dreamgirls* or *The Vampire Conspiracy* (1995), which co-opts the millennial fear of invasion or covert operations sweeping through mainstream films and predicates a scheme to dominate the world by alien vampires who control minds via sexy videos and then impregnate nubile women to produce a race of super vampires. With a premise outrageous enough to evoke *Plan Nine From Outer Space,* this fear of "The Other" recalls countless B-movie science fiction films of the Fifties but adds a Nineties spin of gratuitous nudity and graphic violence. *The Vampire Conspiracy* endlessly repeats shots from music videos featuring vampire centerfolds and cuts frenziedly between disconnected scenes using distorted video effects for transitions until it becomes mind-numbingly redundant. *Witchcraft VII: Judgment Hour* (1996) is equally unabashed in its use of sex scenes as pure filler. While there are occasionally some imaginative scenes–police watching a surveillance camera of a victim writhing in the embrace of a vampire who is invisible on video or that same victim running out of an emergency room naked under a hospital gown which lures a jogger to his doom–*Vampire Conspiracy, Witchcraft VII* and titles such as *Sleepover Massacre* or *Caress of the Vampire* bear more relationship to *Dracula Sucks* than to *Vampire's Ghost.* The just completed *Mark of Dracula* (1997) features a Count reanimated after scores of years when a geneticist

Below, a reanimated-via-cloning Count Dracula (Mark Allen) renews his acquaintance with Lucy Westenra (Roxanne Coyne) in *Mark of Dracula.*

Above, Ivan (Bill White) a "good" vampire who closes up gateways to the underworld leads Kirsten (Wendy Bednarz) through a corridor of grasping demon arms in *Vampires and Other Stereotypes*.

reconstructs him from a residue of tissue on the stake that reduced him to ashes. Weary of the cycle of death and rebirth, this Dracula wants to be made human again, but cloning proves easier than curing.

While there is some intentional humor in *Deadly Dreamgirls* and even *Witchcraft VII,* most low-budget filmmakers eschew comedy. An exception is the "Hungry Like a...Bat?" episode of the trilogy *Twisted Tales* written and directed by Kevin Lindenmuth. With a self-consciousness manifest in the title of his first feature, *Vampires and Other Stereotypes*, and in the best Corman tradition, Lindenmuth uses his cast from *Addicted to Murder* in a "twisted" parody which finds a reluctant vampire dating a succubus. When these immortals exchange bodily fluids the results are not pretty. While the humor in the earlier *Vampires and Other Stereotypes* is limited and the performances marginal, the concept of vampire security guards protecting the world from demons permits a free range of imagery, such as as allusion to Polanski's *Repulsion* with a corridor of grasping arms.

The romanticization of the Dracula figure continues to find new expression in other media as well. A revival of Heinrich Marschner's 1827 operatic rendering of the Polidori short story, *Der Vampyr*, became a five-part BBC mini-series, whose creators added the tongue-in-cheek sub-title, *A Soap Opera* (1992). Certainly, the carryings-on in *The Vampyr*, with each episode ending in a "cliff-hanger" and which features a craven Ripley (Omar Ebrahim) roaming London in designer suits and shades, are a far cry from Polidori and overwhelm Marschner's early Romantic music. The contemporary *Dracul the Musical* (1996) uses the model of Curtis/Matheson and Coppola so that its title character sings of again finding his lost love Helene in the form of Mina. Although Mina is a willing victim, in the end Dracula opts to die rather than turn her into an undead. Another musical, Bernard Taylor's *Nosferatu the Vampire*, takes a *Phantom of the Opera* approach to the Murnau Dracula. "I did not do it for humanity, what I have done I did for him," Mina sings to Harker after surrendering her virtue to Nosferatu: "I've never known a man so wretched and alone." Like his namesake in *Nosferatu in Venice*, this vampire finds his quietus as much from weariness as from entrapment. In the last two years there have also been Czech and German *Dracula* musicals, and in 1994 the Houston Opera produced *The Dracula Diary* by Robert Moran and James Skofield. For the Dracula centennial, Houston has produced a ballet using music by Franz Lizst which opens with a score of vampire brides dancing through ground fog around Dracula's sarcophagus. Not content with twenty brides, Dracula kidnaps another young woman from the nearby village, but in the end rescuers invade his castle and pull down heavy draperies exposing him and his harem to the killing sun.

The pop scene of many of the "goth" clubs around the country features "vampire" bands in the tradition of older gothic groups like The Cure. Alucarda lead singer, Azra Medea, is a cross between Theda Bara and Barbara Steele, who rises from her coffin on stage. Her full-bodied voice renders mystical lyrics with a trance-like quality in songs such "Metamorphosis of the Vampire" based on the Baudelaire poem. Alucarda is also influenced by Italian horror films and has produced an album based on Lucio Fulci soundtracks.

Anne Rice's fifth vampire novel, **Memnoch the Devil**, again features. Lestat, whose literary primacy is challenged each year by scores of pulp vampire romances. As for female undead in print, two anthologies edited by Pam Keesey, **Daughters of Darkness** and **Dark Angels**, feature mostly lesbian vampires in such stories as Elaine Bergstrom's "Daughter of the Night," a clever retelling of the Bathory legend, and Pat Califa's "The Vampire" which focuses on connections between vampire mythology and the world of S&M. There are several graphic novels derived from Rice's fiction and an extremely popular comic book called "Embrace." Modeled after MTV-star Carmen Electra, Embrace is a Gen-X Vampirella, whose dark hair, sultry features, and sexy outfits make her a likely candidate, like comic-book hero Blade, to inspire a film version.

Where the trail of the internet vampire will lead is uncertain. Hundreds of web sites and scores of discussion groups are already well established. Between this and future editions of this book, you can even visit ours at "http://members.aol.com/vampyrfilm."

Anna Massey poised to terrorize a restaurant with fangs and a switchblade in VAULT OF HORROR

Filmography

In this revised and updated Filmography, we have still confined ourselves for the most part to "genuine" vampires in the Eastern European tradition discussed in the first chapter. Most of the films which merely feature the word "vampire" in the title but that deal with *femme fatales*, criminals (as did many films films of the silent era, most notably Louis Feuillade's 1914 *Vampires*), or other "non-human" vampires are excluded. Unless the twist is that they happen to be "real," as in *Graveyard Shift II*, plots in which actors play vampires as in *Body Double* are likewise excluded. Because "Dracula" is known world-wide, there are films such as Disney's *Mystery of Dracula's Castle* which feature the name but not the vampire. Similarly, while it may feature Lugosi's farewell appearance and an actress named Vampira, the legendary *Plan Nine from Outer Space* does not become a vampire film by association. Given the profusion of brief appearances by Dracula and his fellows in recent years, we have also eliminated such cursory moments as the musical number in *Damn Yankees*, the dream sequence in *Paris When It Sizzles*, and the Christopher Lee/Peter Cushing cameo in *One More Time*. While we have included selected television productions, we also decided to omit short films such as *Upior* or *La Fée Sanguinaire*.

We have made occasional exceptions. (1) We do include certain historical or natural vampires of the type described in Chapter One, most notably the Blood Countess, Elizabeth Bathory, and her various filmic alter egos, although many filmmakers have transformed her into a traditional, supernatural vampire. Besides Fritz Haarmann and Peter Kurten, some fictional, psychopathic vampires are included. (2) We also list certain "sci-fi" vampires such as the extra-terrestrials in *Terrore nello Spazio* or the plague vampires featured in the two adaptations of Richard Matheson's novel, **I Am Legend**. Some space vampires as in *Queen of Blood* closely re-semble the human type. Others as in *Not of This Earth*, *Spermula*, or *Lifeforce* marginally qualified for inclusion. (3) An occasional "hoax" vampire film also sneaks in. Because they featured the talents of Tod Browning, Lon Chaney, and Bela Lugosi and were important to the early development of the genre, *London After Midnight* and *Mark of the Vampire* must be included. Comic pretenders as in *Transylvania 6-5000* are not.

As before, films are listed by original title (in bold italics) followed by all known alternate titles under which the film may have been released (in normal italics). These alternate names, which are now quite abundant be-cause of frequent retitlings of releases by different video companies, are all cross-indexed. Our release year follows the Academy of Motion Picture Arts and Sciences method, that is, it is based on the initial public showing in the country of origin. This may lead to discrepancies with other sources, particularly those published in Europe. For example, most other sources list the Dan Curtis/Jack Palance *Dracula* as 1973. We list it as 1974 because it first aired on U.S. network television in February of that year. We then list the main technical credits and principal cast with character names *or* as much as is available, which in a few instances may be no more than the year and country of origin. Running times and their reliability vary greatly depending on the source. Wherever possible timings are from the principal U.S. video release. Otherwise or whenever disparities exist, we have used, if available, a consensus or simply gone with what we believe to be the most reliable source.

The half dozen or so books and magazines which include filmographies are noted in the Bibliography, including the two most recent and most un-reliable **Cinematic Vampires** and **Bloodsuckers**. While every attempt has been made to avoid the most egregious errors, such as the flagrant mis-spellings and mis-titlings that plague **Cinematic Vampires**, the profusion of non-English names and the checkered release histories of many low-budget productions makes complete accuracy most unlikely. With a mind towards possible future editions, the Authors invite comments and infor-mation from readers in this regard.

Left, a low point for Béla Lugosi opposite Lou Costello in ABBOTT AND COSTELLO MEET FRANK-ENSTEIN.

Abbott and Costello Meet Frankenstein. (Universal, 1948). USA. Directed by Charles T. Barton. Script by Robert Lees, Frederic Rinaldo, and John Grant. Director of Photography, Charles Van Enger. Production Designers, Bernard Herzbrun, Hilyard Brown. Music, Frank Skinner. Editor, Frank Gross. Starring Bud Abbott, Lou Costello, Lon Chaney, Jr. (Lawrence Talbot), Béla Lugosi (Dracula), Glenn Strange (The Monster), Jane Randolph, Charles Bradstreet, Leonore Aubert, Frank Ferguson. 83 minutes.

Ahkea Kkots (The Bad Flower). (Sunglim, 1961). South Korea. Directed by Yongmin Lee. Script based on **Dracula** by Bram Stoker.

Alucarda (Sisters of Satan, Innocents from Hell). (Films 75/Yuma Films, 1975). Mexico. Produced by Eduardo Moreno and Max Guefen. Script by J.L. Moctezuma, Yolanda I. Moctezuma, and Alexis T. Arroyo. Director of Photography, Xavier Cruz (Color). Starring Tina Romero, Susana Kamini, Claudio Brook, David Silva, Lily Garza, Martin Lasalle. 90 minutes.

L'Amante del Vampiro (The Vampire's Lover, The Vampire and the Ballerina). (ACIF Consorzio, 1961). Italy. Produced by Bruno Bolognesi. Directed by Renato Polselli. Script by Polselli and Ernesto Gastaldi. Director of Photography, Angelo Baistrocchi. Music, Aldo Piga. Starring Walter Brandi (Luca), Maria Luisa Rolando (Contessa), Helene Remy (Louisa), Tina Gloriani (Francesca), Isarco Ravaioli, John Turner. 86 minutes.

Anak Pontianak (Son of the Vampire, Curse of the Vampire). (Shaw, 1958). Malaya. Directed by Ramon Estella.

Andy Warhol's Dracula see *Dracula Cerca Sangue de Vergine e...Mori de Sete*

Angeles y Querubines. (Azteca, 1972). Mexico. Directed by Rafael Corkidi.

Aquellare de Vampiros see *La Llamada del Vampiro*

Assignment Terror see *El Hombre Que Vino de Ummo*

El Ataud del Vampiro (The Vampire's Coffin). (Salazar/Cinematográfica ABSA, 1957). Mexico. Directed by Fernando Mendez. Script by Ramon Obón based on an idea by Raúl Zenteno. Dialogue by Javier Mateos. Director of Photography, Victor Herrera. Music, G. C. Carrion. Starring German Robles (Count Lavud/Du-

val), Ariadna Welter, Abel Salazar, Yeire Beirute, Alicia Montoya, Carlos Ancira.

The Bad Flower see *Ahkea Kkots*

The Bare Breasted Countess see *La Comtesse Noire*

Barry McKenzie Holds His Own. (Satori, 1974). Australia. Produced and Directed by Bruce Beresford. Script by Beresford and Barry Humphries. Director of Photography, Don McAlpine (Color/Scope). Production Designer, John Stoddart. Music, Peter Best. Editor, William Anderson. Starring Barry Crocker (Barry/Kevin McKenzie), Barry Humphries (Edna Everage), Donald Pleasance (Count Plasma), Dick Bentley (Col. Lucas), Roy Kinnear (Bishop of Paris). 93 minutes.

Batman Fights Dracula. (Hemisphere, 1967). Philippines. Starring Jack Smith.

Beast of Morocco see *The Hand of Night*

Beiss Mich, Liebling (Bite Me, Darling). (Cinerama, 1970). West Germany. Written and Directed by Helmut Foernbacher. Director of Photography, Igor Luther (Color). Starring Eva Renzi, Patrick Jordan, Amadeus August. 102 minutes.

La Belle Captive. (Argos, 1983). France. Produced by Bernard Bouix. Directed by Alain Robbe-Grillet. Script by Robbe-Grillet and Frank Verpillat. Director of Photography, Henri Alekan (Color). Production Designer, Anne Deude. Editor, Bob Wade. Starring Daniel Mesguich (Walter), Gabrielle Lazure (Marie-Ange), Cyrielle (Sara), Daniel Emilfork (Inspector), Roland Dubillard (Van de Reeves). 88 minutes.

Beverly Hills Vamp. (Vidmark/Austin, 1988). USA. Produced by Fred Olen Ray and Grant Waldman. Directed by Ray. Script by Ernest D. Farino. Director of Photography, Stephen Blake (Color). Starring Britt Ekland (Madame Cassandra), Eddie Deezen (Kyle), Tim Conway, Jr. (Brock), Dawn Wildsmith (Sherry), Michelle Bauer (Kristina). 89 minutes.

Billy the Kid vs. Dracula. (Avco-Embassy/Circle Films, 1966). USA. Produced by Carroll Case. Directed by William Beaudine. Script by Karl Hittleman. Director of Photography, Lothrop Worth (Color). Production Designer, Paul Sylos. Music, Raoul Kraushaar. Starring John Carradine (Dracula), Bing Russell (Red Thorpe), Chuck Courtney (Billy the Kid), Roy Barcroft (Marshall Griffin), Melinda Plowman

(Betty), Virginia Christine (Eva), Walter Janovitz (Franz Oster), Olive Carey (Dr. Hull), Harry Carey, Jr., Charlita. 72 minutes.

Bite Me, Darling see *Beiss Mich, Liebling*

Black Evil see *Ganja and Hess*

Black Magic Rites–Reincarnations see *Riti Magie Nere e Segrete Orge de Trecento*

The Black Room. (CI/Butler-Crowin, 1984). USA. Produced by Aaron C. Butler. Directed by Elly Kenner and Norman Thaddeus Vane. Script by Vane. Director of Photography, Robert Harmon (Color). Production Designer, Yoram Barzilai. Music, Art Podell. Editor, David Kern. Starring Stephen Knight (Jason), Cassandra Gaviola (Bridget), Jim Stathis (Larry), Clara Perryman (Robin), Charlie Young (Lisa). 87 minutes.

Black Sabbath see *I Tre Volti della Paura*

Black Sunday see *La Maschera del Demonio*

Black Vampire see *Ganja and Hess*

Blacula (American International, 1972). USA. Produced by Joseph T. Naar. Directed by William Crain. Script by Joan Torres and Raymond Koenig. Director of Photography, John Stevens (Color). Production Designer, Walter Herndon. Music, Gene Page. Editor, Allan Jacobs. Starring William Marshall (Mamuwalde/Blacula),

Denise Nicholas (Michelle), Vonetta McGee (Tina), Gordon Pinsent (Lt. Peters), Thalmus Rasulala (Gordon Thomas), Charles McCauley (Dracula), Emily Yancy, Lance Taylor, Ted Harris. Elisha Cook. 92 minutes.

Bloedverwanten (Blood Relations, Les Vampires en Ont Ras le Bol) (Jaap Van Rij Filmproductie, 1977). France/Netherlands. Produced by Jaap Van Rij. Directed by Wim Linder. Script by John Brasom. Director of Photography, Walter Bal (Color). Production Designer, Hans Oosterhuis. Music, J.M. de Scarano. Starring Maxim Hamel, Gregoire Aslan, Sophie Descamps, Robert Dalban, Eddie Constantine, Ralph Arliss. 97 minutes.

Blood. (Bryanston/Kent, 1974). USA. Produced by Walter Kent. Directed by Andy Milligan. (Color). Starring Allen Berendt (Dr. Orlovski), Hope Stansbury, Eve Crosby, Patti Gaul, Pamela Adams. 74 minutes.

Blood and Roses see *Et Mourir de Plaiser*

Blood Ceremony see *Ceremonia Sangrienta*

Blood Couple see *Ganja and Hess*

Blood Cult of Shangri-La see *The Thirsty Dead*

The Blood Demon see *Die Schlangengrube und das Pendel*

The Blood Drinkers (Vampire People). (Hemisphere, 1961). Philippines. Produced by Cirio H. Santiago. Directed by Gerardo de Leon. Script by Cesar Amigo and Rico Omagao. Director of Photography, F. Sacdalan (Color). Production Designer, Ben Otico. Starring Amalia Fuentes, Ronald Remy, Eddie Fernandez. 88 minutes.

Blood Fiend see *Theatre of Blood*

Blood for Dracula see *Dracula Cerca Sangue de Vergine e...Mori de Sete*

Blood Freak. (Royal Video, 1986). USA. Produced, Written, and Directed by Steve Hawkes and Brad Grinter. Music, Gil Ward. Starring Steve Hawkes, Dana Cullivan, Heather Hughes, Bob Currier, Tera Anderson. 86 minutes. [Note: a "non-traditional" film featuring a blood-drinking "turkey-man"]

Blood Hunger see *Vampyres*

Blood Moon see *La Noche de Walpurgis*

Blood of Dracula. (American Int./Carmel, 1957). USA. Produced by Herman Cohen. Directed by Herbert L. Strock. Script by Ralph Thornton. Director of Photography, Monroe

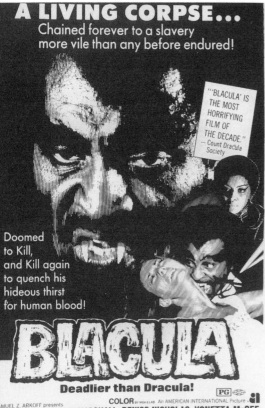

A LIVING CORPSE...
Chained forever to a slavery
more vile than any before endured!

"'BLACULA' IS THE MOST HORRIFYING FILM OF THE DECADE." — Count Dracula Society

Doomed to Kill, and Kill again to quench his hideous thirst for human blood!

BLACULA

Deadlier than Dracula!   PG

COLOR BY MOVIELAB An AMERICAN INTERNATIONAL Picture

SAMUEL Z. ARKOFF presents
"BLACULA" WILLIAM MARSHALL · DENISE NICHOLAS · VONETTA McGEE
GORDON PINSENT THALMUS RASULALA EMILY YANCY LANCE TAYLOR Sr. CHARLES McCAULEY

Askins. Production Designer, Leslie Thomas. Music, Paul Dunlap. Editor, Robert Moore. Starring Sandra Harrison (Nancy Perkins), Louise Lewis (Miss Branding), Gail Ganley (Myra), Jerry Blaine (Tab), Heather Ames (Nola), Malcolm Atterbury (Lt. Dunlap), Mary Adams (Mrs. Thorndyke). 70 minutes.

Blood of Dracula's Castle. (A&E Film Corp./Paragon/Crown International, 1969). USA. Produced by Al Adamson and Rex Carlton. Directed by Adamson and Jean Hewitt. Script by Rex Carlton. Director of Photography, Leslie [Laszlo] Kovacs (Color). Music, Lincoln Mayorage. Editor, Joyce King. Starring John Carradine (George, the Butler), Paula Raymond (Countess Townsend), Alex D'Arcy (Dracula), Robert Dix (Johnny), Gene O'Shane (Glen Cannon), Barbara Bishop (Liz Arden). 82 minutes.

Blood of Frankenstein see *Dracula vs. Frankenstein*

Blood of Nostradamus see *La Sangre de Nostradamus*

Blood of the Vampire. (Universal/Eros, 1958). Great Britain. Directed by Henry Cass. Script by Jimmy Sangster. Director of Photography, Geoffrey Seaholme (Color). Music, Stanley Black. Editor, Douglas Myers. Starring Donald Wolfit (Callistratus), Vincent Ball (Dr. John), Barbara Shelley (Madeleine), Victor Maddern (Carl), John Le Mesurier (Chief Justice), Milton Reid. 85 minutes.

Blood of the Vampire (Philippines) see *Dugo ng Vampira*

Blood Relations see *Bloedverwanten*

The Blood Spattered Bride see *La Novia Ensangrentada*

Blood Thirst. (Chevron, 1971). Philippines. Directed by Newt Arnold. Script by N.I.P. Dennis. Director of Photography, Herme Santos (Color). Starring Robert Winston [Adam Roarke], Katherine Henryk, Yvonne Nelson, Vic Diaz, Eddie Infante.

Bloodthirsty Eyes see *Chi o Suu Me*

Blood Ties. (Fox-TV/Shapiro, 1991). USA. MOW. Produced by Gene Corman. Directed by Jim McBride. Script by Richard Shapiro. Director of Photography, Alfonso Beato (Color). Production Designer, Lisa Fischer. Music, Brad Fiedel. Editor, Stephen Semel. Starring Harley Venton (Harry), Michelle Johnson (Celia), Kim Johnston-Ulrich (Amy), Jason London (Cody),

Below, BLOOD OF THE VAMPIRE

Patrick Bauchau (Eli), Bo Hopkins (Vampire Hunter). 92 minutes.

The Bloodless Vampire. (Journey, 1965). Philippines. Directed by Michael du Pont. Starring Charles Macauley, Helen Thompson.

Bloodlust. (Windhover, 1992). Australia. Produced, Written, Edited, and Directed by Richard Wolstencroft and Jon Hewitt. Director of Photography, Gary Ravenscroft (Color). Production Designer, Nicolas Barclay. Music, Ross Hazeldine. Starring Jane Stuart Wallance (Lear), Kelly Chapman (Frank), Robert J. O'Neill (Tad), Phil Motherwell (Brother Ben), Paul Moder. 87 minutes.

Bloodlust: Subspecies III see *Bloodstone: Subspecies II*

Bloodstone: Subspecies II and *Bloodlust: Subspecies III*. (Full Moon, 1993). USA. Produced by Vlad Paunescu and Oana Paunescu. Written and Directed by Ted Nicolaou. Director of Photography, Vlad Paunescu. Production Designer, Radu Corciova. Music, Aman and Portis Kosinski. Editor, Bert Glatstein. Starring, Anders Hove (Radu), Denice Duff (Michelle), Kevin Blair (Mel), Melanie Shatner (Rebecca), Mi-

BRIDES OF DRACULA: Peter Cushing and Yvonne Monlaur

chael Denish (Porfessor Popescu), Pamela Gordon (Mummy). II: 87 minutes.

Bloodsuckers (Great Britain) see *Incense for the Damned*

Bloodsuckers (Italy) see *La Isla de la Muerte*

The Bloody Vampire see *El Vampiro Sangriento*

The Body Beneath. (Cinemedia/Nova, 1970). Great Britain. Written, Photograhed, and Directed by Andy Milligan (Color). Starring Gavin Read (Father Alexander), Jackie Skarvellis (Susan Ford), Colin Gordon (Graham Ford), Berwick Kaler (Spool), Susan Heard (Alicia Ford). 85 minutes.

Bram Stoker's Dracula. (1974) see *Dracula*

Bram Stoker's Dracula. (Columbia/Zoetrope/ Osiris, 1992). USA. Produced by Francis Ford Coppola, Fred Fuchs, and Charles Mulvehill. Directed by Coppola. Script by James V. Hart, based on the novel by Bram Stoker. Director of Photography, Michael Ballhaus (Color). Production Designer, Thomas Sanders. Music, Wojciech Kilar. Editor, Nicholas C. Smith. Starring Gary Oldman (Dracula), Winona Ryder (Mina/Elisabeta), Anthony Hopkins (Van Helsing), Keanu Reeves (Harker), Richard E. Grant (Dr. Seward), Cary Elwes (Lord Holmwood), Sadie Frost (Lucy), Tom Waits (Renfield), Bill Campbell (Morris). 130 minutes.

Brides of Dracula. (Hammer, 1960). Great Britain. Produced by Anthony Hinds. Directed by Terence Fisher. Script by Jimmy Sangster, Peter Bryan, and Edward Percy. Director of Photogra-

phy, Jack Asher (Color). Production Designer, Bernard Robinson, Thomas Goswell. Music, Malcolm Williamson. Editors, Jim Needs, Alfred Cox. Starring Peter Cushing (Van Helsing), Yvonne Monlaur (Marianne), Freda Jackson (Greta), David Peel (Baron Meinster), Martita Hunt (Baroness Meinster), Andree Melly (Gina), Mona Washbourne (Frau Lang), Henry Oscar (Lang). 85 minutes.

Bring Me the Vampire see *Echenme al Vampiro*

Buffy, the Vampire Slayer. (20th Century-Fox/Sandollar-Kuzui, 1992). USA. Produced by Kaz Kuzui and Howard Rosenman. Directed by Fran Rubel Kuzui. Script by Joss Whedon. Director of Photography, James Hayman (Color). Production Designer, Lawrence Miller. Music, Carter Burwell. Editors, Camilla Toniolo, Jill Savitt. Starring Kristy Swanson (Buffy), Donald Sutherland (Merrick), Paul Reubens (Amilyn), Rutger Hauer (Lothos, the Vampire), Luke Perry (Pike) David Arquette (Benny). 86 minutes.

Caged Virgins see *Vierges et Vampires*

The Cake of Blood see *Pastel de Sangre*

Captain Kronos–Vampire Hunter (Kronos). (Hammer, 1972). Great Britain. Produced by Albert Fennell and Brian Clemens. Written and Directed by Clemens. Director of Photography, Ian Wilson (Color). Production Designer, Robert Jones. Music, Laurie Johnson. Editor, James Needs. Starring Horst Janson (Kronos), Caroline Munro (Carla), Shane Briant (Paul Durward), John Carson (Dr. Marcus), John Carter (Prof. Grost), Lois Daine (Sara). 91 minutes.

Capulina Contra los Vampiros. (Panorama, 1972). Mexico. Directed by Rene Cardona. (Color). Starring Gaspar Henaine.

Caperucita y Pulgarcito contra los Monstruos (Tom Thumb and Little Red Riding Hood vs. the Monsters). (Azteca, 1962). Mexico. Directed by Roberto Rodriquez. Script by Rodriquez, Sergio Magana, Fernando M. Ortiz, and A.T. Portillo. Director of Photography, R. Solano (Color). Music, Raúl Lavista. Starring María Garcia (Little Red Riding Hood), José Moreno, Cesareo Quesades. 90 minutes.

Carmilla. (Showtime/ThinkEntertainment, 1989). USA. Produced by Bridget Terry. Directed by Gabrielle Beaumont. Script by Jonathan Furst based on the novella by J. Sheri-

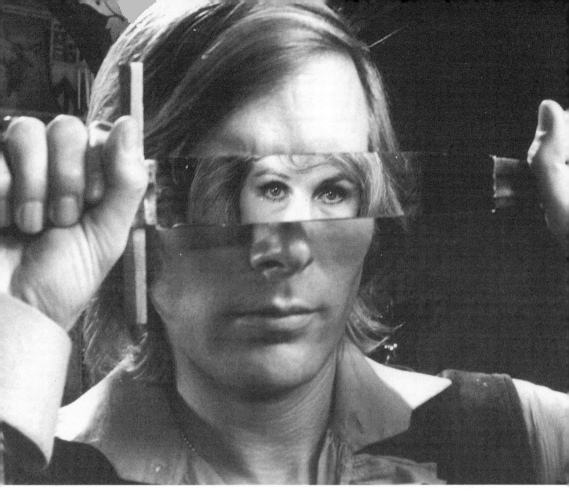

Above, the vampire as Medusa in CAPTAIN KRONOS, VAMPIRE HUNTER

dan Le Fanu. Director of Photography, Ron Vargas (Color). Music, Rick Conrad. Editor, Dick Darling, Chris Cooke. Starring Ione Skye (Marie), Meg Tilly (Carmilla), Roddy McDowall (Inspector), Roy Dotrice (Marie's father). 60 minutes.

Carne de Tu Carne (Flesh of Your Flesh). (Producciones Visuales, 1984). Columbia. Produced by Berta del Carvajál and Fernando Barón. Directed by Carlos Mayolo. Script by Elsa Vasquez, J. Nieto, and Mayolo. Director of Photography, Luís Gabriel Beristain (Color). Production Designer, Miguel Gonzalez. Music, Mario Gomez Vignes. Editors, Luís Ospina, Karen Lamassone. Starring Adriana Herran (Margareth), David Guerrero (Andres Alfonso), Josue Angel (Enrique). 85 minutes.

Carry on Screaming. (SigmaIII/Anglo-Amalgamated/Warner-Pathe, 1966). Great Britain. Produced by Peter Rogers. Directed by Gerald Thomas. Script by Talbot Rothwell. Director of Photography, Peter Rogers (Color). Production Designer, Bert Davey. Music, Eric Rogers. Editor,

Rod Keys. Starring Kenneth Williams, Harry Corbett, Dennis Blake, Joan Sims, Jon Pertwee, Fenella Fielding (Vampire). 87 minutes.

The Case of the Full Moon Murders (The Case of the Smiling Stiffs). (Lobster Enterprises/Dana Films, 1973). USA. Produced by Sean Cunningham and Bud Talbot. Directed by Cunningham. Script by Jerry Hayling. Director of Photography, Gus Graham (Color). Music, Bud Fanton, Jacques Urbont. Editor, Stephen Miner. Starring Harry Reems, Bud Talbot, Fred Lincoln, Ron Browne, Cathy Walker (Vampire), Jean Jennings. 74 minutes.

El Castillo de los Monstruos. (Sotomayor, 1958). Mexico. Directed by Julian Soler. Script by Fernando Galiana and Carlos Orellana. Director of Photography, Victor Herrera. Starring German Robles (Vampire), Clavillazo, Evangelina Elizondo, Carlos Orellana. 85 minutes.

Castle of the Monsters see *El Castillo de los Monstruos*

Casual Relations. (1973). USA. Produced, Written, Directed, and Edited by Mark Rappaport. Directors of Photography, Rappaport and Alan Raymond (Color and Black-and-White). Music, Jim Burton. Starring Mel Austin (Vampire), Sis Smith (Model), Paula Barr, Adrienne Claiborne, Peter Campus, Alan Dahl. 80 minutes. [Note: Contains a film within a film: "A Vampire's Love" and excerpted footage from *Nosferatu* (1922)]

Il Cavaliere Costante Nicosia Demoniaco Ovvero Dracula in Brianza (Dracula in the Provinces). (Coralta Cinematografica, 1975). Italy. Produced by R. Marini. Directed by Lucio Fulci. Script by Fulci, Pupi Avati, Bruno Corbucci, and Mario Amendola. Director of Photography, Sergio Salvati (Color). Production Designer, P. Basile. Music, Franco Bixio. Starring Lando Buzzanca, Moira Orfei, Sylva Koscina, Christa Linder, Rossano Brazzi, Valentina Cortese, Ciccio Ingrassia, John Steiner (Dragulescu). 100 minutes.

Cave of the Living Dead see *Der Fluch der Grünen Augen*

Cemetery Girls see *El Gran Amor del Conde Drácula*

Ceremonia Sangrienta (Blood Ceremony, The Legend of Blood Castle, Ritual of Blood). (X Films/Luís Films, 1973). Spain/Italy. Produced by José María Gonzalez Sinde. Directed by Jorge Grau. Script by Grau, Juan Tebar, and Sandro Continenza. Director of Photography, Fernando Arribas (Color/Scope). Music, Carlo Savina. Editor, Pedro Del Rey. Starring Lucia Bose (Erzebeth Bathory), Karl Ziemmer (Karl), Ewa Aulin (Miriam), Ana Farra, Silvano Tranquilli, Lola Gaos, Franca Grey, Angel Menendez. 102 minutes.

Chanoc contra el Tigre y el Vampiro (Chanoc [or Chano] vs. the Tiger and the Vampire). (Azteca, 1971). Mexico. Directed by Gilberto Mar-

tinez Solares. Script by Raúl Martinez Solares and Rafael Perez Grovas. Starring Tin-Tan [German Valdes], Gregorio Casal, Aurora Cavel.

Chanoc vs. the Tiger and the Vampire see *Chanoc contra el Tigre y el Vampiro*

Chappaqua. (Rooks Prods., 1966). USA. Written and Directed by Conrad Rooks. Director of Photography, Robert Frank (Color). Production Designer, Regis Pagniez. Music, Ravi Shankar. Editor, Kenout Peltier. Starring Jean-Louis Barrault, Conrad Rooks, William S. Burroughs, Allen Ginsberg. 92 minutes.

El Charro de las Calaveras (The Rider of the Skulls). (Azteca, 1967). Mexico. Directed by Alfredo Salazar. Starring Dagoberto Rodriquez, David Silva, Alicia Caro.

Les Chemins de la Violence (Lips of Blood). (Les Films de L'Epée/Gemini, 1972). France. Produced by Michel Grimaud. Directed by Ken Ruder. Director of Photography, Raymond Heil (Color). Starring Michel Flynn, Richard Vitz, Georges Rigaud, Jacques Bernard, Catherine Frank, Sandra Reeves. 71 minutes.

Chi o Suu Bara (The Evil of Dracula). (Toho, 1975). Japan. Produced by Fumio Tanaka. Directed by Michio Yamamoto. Script by Ei Ogawa and Masaru Takasue. Director of Photography, Kazutami Hara (Color/Scope). Production Designer, Kazuo Satsuya. Music, Riichiro Manabe. Editor, Michiko Ikeda. Starring Toshio Kurosawa, Mariko Mochizuki, Shin Kishida, Kunie Tanaka, Katsuhiko Sasaki, Yunosuke Ito. 87 minutes.

Chi o Suu Me (Lake of Dracula, Dracula's Lust for Blood, Bloodthirsty Eyes). (Toho, 1971). Japan. Directed by Michio Yamamoto. Script by Ei Ogawa and Katsu Takeura. Director of Photography, Rokuro Nishigaki (Color/Scope). Starring Mori Kishida, Midori Fujita, Osahide Takahari, Sanae Emi, Kaku Takashima. 82 minutes.

Chi o Suu Ningyo (The Night of the Vampire, Vampire Doll). (Toho, 1970). Japan. Produced by Tomoyuki Tanaka, Fumio Tanaka. Directed by Michio Yamamoto. Script by Ei Ogawa and Hiroshi Nagano. Director of Photography, Kazutami Hara (Color/Scope). Production Designer, Y. Honda. Music, R. Manabe. Starring Kayo Matsuo, Akira Nakao, Yukiko Kobayashi, Yoko Minazaki, Atsuo Nakamura. 71 minutes.

Below, CHI O SUU ME (LAKE OF DRACULA)

Children of the Night. (Fangoria/RCA-Columbia, 1992). USA. Produced by Christopher Webster. Directed by Tony Randel. Script by Webster, Randel, and Nicolas Falacci based on a screenplay by William Hopkins. Director of Photography, Richard Michalak (Color/Scope). Production Designer, Kim Hix. Music, Daniel Licht. Editor, Rick Roberts. Starring Karen Black (Karen Thompson), Peter De Luise (Mark Gardner), Ami Dolenz (Lucy Barrett), Maya McLaughlin (Cindy Thompson), Evan MacKenzie (Frank Aldin), David Sawyer (Czakyr), Garrett Morris (Matty). 90 minutes.

City of the Walking Dead see *Incubo sulla Citta Contaminata*

La Comtesse aux Seins Nus see *La Comtessee Noire*

La Comtesse Noire (The Loves of Irina, La Comtesse aux Seins Nus, The Bare Breasted Countess, The Last Thrill, Erotikill, Jacula). (General Films/Eurocine, 1973). France/Belgium. Produced by Marius Lesouer, Pierre Querut. Directed by J. P. Johnson [Jesus Franco]. Script by P. Belair and David Kuhne [both Franco]. Director of Photography, Joan Vincent [Franco] (Color/Scope). Music, Daniel White. Editor, P. Querut. Starring Lina Romay (Countess), Jack Taylor, Alice Arno [Marie-France Broquet], Monica Swinn, Jess Franck [Franco], Luis Barboo (Servant), Jean-Pierre Bouyxou (Dr. Orloff), Raymond Hardy [Ramon Ardid]. 101 minutes. [Note: also released as *Les Avaleuses*, a hardcore version, with most of the vampirism excised]

El Conde Drácula (Count Dracula, Vampyr). (Towers of London/Fenix Films/Filmar Cinematográfica/Corona Film, 1971). Spain/Italy/West Germany. Produced by Harry Alan Towers. Directed by Jesus Franco. Script by Franco and Augusto Finochi. Adapted by Carlo Fadda, M.G. Cuccia, Peter Welbeck [Harry Alan Towers] based on the novel by Bram Stoker. Director of Photography, Manuel Merino (Color). Production Designer, Karl Schneider. Music, Bruno Nicolai. Starring Christopher Lee (Dracula), Herbert Lom (Van Helsing), Klaus Kinski (Renfield), Frederick Williams (Harker), Maria Rohm (Mina), Soledad Miranda (Lucy), Jack Taylor (Dr. Seward), Paul Muller (Quincy Morris), Teresa Gimpera, Emma Cohen. 98 minutes.

El Conde Frankenhausen see *El Vampiro Sangriento*

Condemned to Live (Cohen Prods./Invincible, 1935). USA. Produced by Maury M. Cohen. Directed by Frank Strayer. Script by Karen De Wolf. Director of Photography, M.A. Anderson. Editor, Roland D. Reed. Starring Ralph Morgan, Maxine Doyle, Russell Gleason, Mischa Auer, Lucy Beaumont, Carl Stockdale. 67 minutes.

Contes Immoraux (Immoral Tales). (Argos, 1974). France. Written, Edited, and Directed by Walerian Borowczyk. Director of Photography, Bernard Daillencourt, Guy Durban, Michel Zolat, Noël Very (Color). Production Designer, Borowczyk. Music, Maurice Le Roux, Borowczyk. Starring Lise Danvers, Paloma Picasso (Countess Bathory), Pascale Christophe, Fabrice Luchini, Charlotta Alexandra. 103 minutes.

Count Down–Son of Dracula (Son of Dracula, Count Downe, Young Dracula). (Apple Films/Cinemation, 1974). Great Britain. Produced by Ringo Starr. Directed by Freddie Francis. Script by Jay Fairbanks. Starring Harry Nilsson (Count Down[e]), Ringo Starr (Merlin), Freddie Jones (Dr. Frankenstein), Dennis Price (Van Helsing), Peter Frampton, Keith Moon,

Christopher Lee in EL CONDE DRÁCULA , below

John Bonham (Count's band). 90 minutes. (Color).

Count Dracula see *El Conde Drácula*

Count Dracula and His Vampire Bride see *Satanic Rites of Dracula*

Count Dracula. (BBC, 1978). Great Britain. Produced by Morris Barry. Directed by Phillip Saville. Script by Gerald Savory based on the novel by Bram Stoker. Director of Photography, Peter Hall (Color). Production Designer, Michael Young. Music, Kenyon Emrys-Roberts. Editors, Richard Bedford, Ron Waldron. Starring Louis Jourdan (Dracula), Frank Finlay (Van Helsing), Jack Shepard (Renfield), Bosco Hogan (Harker), Susan Penhaligon (Lucy), Judi Bowker (Mina), Mark Burns (Seward). 151 minutes.

Count Dracula, the True Story. (Documentary, 1979). Canada. Directed by Yurek Filjalkowski.

Count Erotica, Vampire. (Lobo, 1971). USA. Directed by Tony Teresi. Script by Antonio Teritoni and Hans Klepper. Director of Photography, Ron Pitts (Color). Starring John Peters, Mary Simon.

Count Yorga, Vampire. (American International, 1970). USA. Produced by Michael Macready. Written and Directed by Bob Kelljan. Director of Photography, Arch Archambault (Color). Music, William Marx. Editor, Tony De Zarraga. Starring Robert Quarry (Count Yorga), Roger Perry (Dr. Hayes), Michael Murphy (Paul), Michael Macready (Michael), Donna Anders (Donna), Judith Lang (Erica), Edward Walsh (Brudah), Marsha Jordan, George Macready (Narrator). 90 minutes.

Countess Dracula. (Hammer, 1971). Great Britain. Produced by Alexander Paul. Directed by Peter Sasdy. Script by Jeremy Paul from a story by Sasdy, Paul, and Gabriel Ronay. Director of Photography, Ken Talbot (Color). Production Designer, Philip Harrison. Music, Harry Robinson. Editor, Henry Richardson. Starring Ingrid

Pitt (Countess Elisabeth Nadasdy), Nigel Green (Captain Dobi), Sandor Eles (Imre Toth), Maurice Denham (Master Fabio), Patience Collier (Julia), Peter Jeffrey (Captain Balogh), Lesley-Anne Down (Ilona), Leon Lissek (Sergeant), Jessie Evans (Rosa), Nike Arrighi (Gypsy). 93 minutes.

Countess Dracula (Italy) see *Il Plenilunio delle Vergini*

Creatures of Evil see *Dugo ng Vampira*

Creatures of the Prehistoric Planet (Horror of the Blood Monsters, Vampire Men of the Lost Planet). (Independent International, 1969). USA. Produced and Directed by Al Adamson. Script by Sue McNair. Director of Photography, Leslie (Laszlo) Kovacs (Color). Music, M. Valarde. Starring John Carradine, Robert Dix, Vicki Volante. [Released in 1971 with added footage and re-editing as *Horror of the Blood Monsters* or *Vampire Men of the Lost Planet.]*

Crime Doctor's Courage. (Columbia, 1944). USA. Produced by Rudolph C. Flothow. Directed by George Sherman. Script by Eric Taylor, based on the radio program. Director of Photography, L. W. O'Connell. Production Designer, John Datu. Editor, Dwight Caldwell. Starring Warner Baxter (Dr. Robert Ordway), Hillary Brooke (Kathleen), Jerome Cowan (Jeffers Jerome), Robert Scott (Bob), Lloyd Corrigan (John Massey). 70 minutes.

La Cripta e l'Incubo (La Maldición de los Karnstein, The Crypt of Horror, Terror in the Crypt, The Curse of the Karnsteins). (Hispamer/Mec, 1963). Italy/Spain. Produced by William Mulligan. Directed by Thomas Miller [Camillo Mastocinque]. Script by Julian Berry {Ernesto Gastaldi], Robert Bohr [Bruno Valeri], José L. Monter, and María del Carmen Martinez Roman based on **Carmilla** by J. Sheridan Le Fanu. Directors of Photography, Giuseppe Aquari, Julio Ortas. Music, Carlo Savina. Starring Christopher Lee (Count Karnstein), Audr[e]y Amber [Adriana Ambesi] (Laura), Ursula Davis (Lyuba), José Campos, Vera Valmont, Nela Conjiu, José Villasante, Angela Minervini. 84 minutes.

The Crypt of Horror see *La Cripta e l'Incubo*

Crypt of the Living Dead see *La Tumba de la Isla Maldita*

Curse of Dracula see *The Return of Dracula*

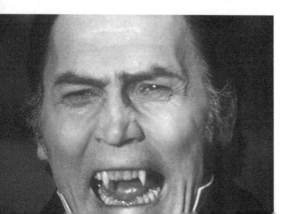

Left, Jack Palance as the tortured Count in the original Curtis/Matheson *Bram Stoker's Dracula.*

The Curse of Dracula. (NBC, 1979, episodes in the *Cliffhangers* television series). USA. Starring Michael Nouri, Stephen Johnson, Carol Baxter.

Curse of Nostradamus see *La Maldición de Nostradamus*

Curse of the Blood Ghouls see *La Strage dei Vampiri*

Curse of the Devil see *El Retorno de Walpurgis*

The Curse of the Karnsteins see *La Cripta e l'Incubo*

Curse of the Undead. (Universal, 1959). USA. Produced by Joseph Gershenson. Directed by Edward Dein. Script by Edward Dein and Mildred Dein. Director of Photography, Ellis Carter. Production Designer, Alexander Golitzen, Robert Clatworthy. Music, Irving Gertz, Milton Rosen. Editor, George Gittens. Starring Eric Fleming (Preacher Dan Young), Kathleen Crowley (Dolores Carter), Michael Pate (Drake Robey), John Hoyt (Dr. John Carter), Bruce Gordon (Buffer), Jimmy Murphy (Tim Carter), Helen Kleeb (Dora). 79 minutes.

Curse of the Vampire see *Anak Pontianak*

Curse of the Vampire (Spain) see *La Llamada del Vampiro*

Curse of the Vampires see *Dugo ng Vampira*

Curse of the Walking Dead see *Die Schlangengrube und das Pendel*

Dance of the Damned. (Concorde/New Classics, 1989). USA. Produced by Andy Ruben. Directed by Katt Shea Ruben. Script by Andy Ruben and Katt Shea Ruben. Director of Photography, Phedon Papamichael (Color). Production Designer, Stephen Greenberg. Music, Gary Stockdale. Editor, Carole Kravetz. Starring Starr Andreeff (Jodi), Cyril O'Reilly (Vampire), Deborah Ann Nassar (Stripper), Maria Ford (Stripper). 83 minutes.

Dance of the Vampires (The Fearless Vampire Killers or Pardon Me, but Your Teeth Are in My Neck). (Ransohoff/Polanski Productions/Cadre Films/Filmways, 1967). Great Britain. Produced by Gene Gutowski. Directed by Roman Polanski. Script by Polanski and Gerard Brach. Director of Photography, Douglas Slocombe (Color). Production Designer, Fred Carter. Music, Krzystof Komeda. Editor, Alistair McIntyre. Starring Jack MacGowran (Prof. Abronsius), Sharon Tate (Sarah), Alfie Bass (Yoine Shagal), Ferdy Mayne (Count Krolock), Terry Downes (Koukol), Roman Polanski (Alfred), Jessie Robbins (Rebecca), Fiona Lewis (Magda), Iain Quarrier (Herbert). 98 minutes [Original British version was 118 minutes. Martin Ransohoff recut, redubbed, and altered sound effects and music on the 98-minute version. He also added a cartoon at the beginning.]

Dark Shadows. (ABC, 1968-1971). USA. Television series. Produced by Dan Curtis.

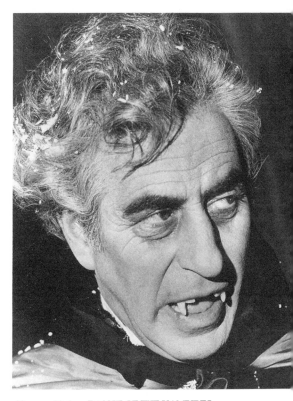

Above and below, DANCE OF THE VAMPIRES with Ferdy Mayne

Above, Barbara Steele and Ben Cross in the 1991 television series, DARK SHADOWS

Dark Shadows. (NBC/Dan Curtis/MGM-UA, 1991). USA. Two-part MOW and series. Produced by Dan Curtis. Starring Ben Cross, Barbara Steele.

Daughter of Darkness. (MOW, CBS/King Phoenix Ent., 1990). USA. Produced by Andras Hamori. Directed by Stuart Gordon. Script by Andrew Laskos. Director of Photography, Mark Ivan (Color). Production Designer, Tamas Hornyanszky. Starring Mia Sara, Anthony Perkins (Vampire), Jack Coleman, Robert Reynolds, Mari Kiss. 120 minutes.

Daughter of Dracula see ***A Filha de Dracula***

Daughters of Darkness (France) see ***Le Rouge aux Lèvres***

Daughters of Darkness (Great Britian) see ***Vampyres***

Daughters of Dracula see ***Vampyres***

Dead Men Walk. (PRC/Pathe, 1942). USA. Produced by Sigmund Neufeld. Directed by Sam Newfield. Script by Fred Myton. Director of Photography, Jack Greenhalgh. Editor, Holbrook N. Todd. Starring George Zucco, Mary Carlisle, Ned Young, Dwight Frye, Fern Emmett, Robert Strange. 64 minutes.

Deafula. (Signscope, 1975). USA. Produced by Gary R. Holmstrum. Directed by Peter Wechsberg. Script by Wechsberg. Starring Peter Wechsberg, James Randall, Dudley Hemstreet, Lee Darrel, Gary R. Holmstrum (Dracula). 90 minutes.

Death on a Barge. (Episode of the *Night Gallery* television series, NBC, 1973). USA. Directed by Leonard Nimoy. Script by Hallstead Wells. Starring Robert Pratt, Lesley Warren, Lou Antonio, Brooke Bundy, Jim Boles.

The Deathmaster. (American International, 1972). USA. Produced by Fred Sadoff. Directed by Ray Danton. Script by R.L. Grove. Director of Photography, Wilmer C. Butler (Color). Music, Bill Marx. Editor, Harold Lime. Starring Robert Quarry (Khorda), Bill Ewing (Pico), Brenda Dickson (Rona), John Fiedler (Pop), Betty Anne Rees (Esslin), William Jordan (Monk), Le Sesne Hilton (Barbado), John Lasell (Detective). 88 minutes.

Def by Temptation. (Orpheus/Bonded Filmworks/Troma, 1990). USA. Written, Produced, and Directed by James Bond III. Director of Photography, Ernest Dickerson (Color). Production Designer, David Carrington. Music, Paul Lawrence. Editor, Li-Shin Yu. Starring James Bond III (Joel), Kadeem Hardison ("K"), Cynthia Bond (Temptation), Bill Nunn (Dougy), Minnie Gentry (Grandma), Melba Moore (Mme. Sonya). 101 minutes.

The Demon Planet see ***Terrore nello Spazio***

Dendam Pontianak (Revenge of the Vampire). (Keris, 1957). Malaya. Directed by B.N. Rao. Starring Maria Menado (Vampire), M. Maarof.

Devil's Commandment see *I Vampiri*

Devil's Mistress. (Holiday/WGW, 1966). USA. Written and Directed by Orville Wanzer. Director of Photography, Teddy Gregory (Color). Starring Joan Stapleton (Leah), Arthur Resley.

Devil's Plaything see *Veil of Blood*

Devil's Wedding Night see *Il Plenilunio delle Vergini*

Devils of Darkness. (Planet/20th Century-Fox, 1965). Great Britain. Produced by Tom Blakeley. Directed by Lance Comfort. Script by Lyn Fairhust. Director of Photography, Reg Wyer. Music, Bernie Fenton. Editor, John Trumper. Starring William Sylvester, Hubert Noel (Count Sinistre), Tracy Reed, Carole Gray, Diana Decker, Rona Anderson, Victor Brooks. 90 minutes.

Dinner with a Vampire. (Dania/Devon/ReiItalia, 1988). Italy. Directed by Lamberto Bava. Script by Dardano Sachetti and Bava from a story by Luciano Martino. Director of Photography, Gianfranco Trasunto. Production Designer, Antonello Geleng. Music, Simon Boswell and Mario Tagliaferri. Editor, Daniele Alabiso. Starring George Hilton, Patrizia Pellegrino, Riccardo Rossi, Valeria Milillo, Yvonne Scio, Daniele Aldrovondi.

Disciple of Death. (Heritage/Chromage, 1972). Great Britain. Produced by Tom Parkinson and Chuston Fairman. Directed by Parkinson. Script by Parkinson and Fairman. Director of Photography, William Brayne (Color). Starring Mike Raven, Marguerite Hardiman, Ronald Lacey, Virginia Wetherell, Stephen Bradley, Nicholas Amer, George Belbin. 84 minutes.

Disciples of Dracula. (First-West, 1975). USA. Starring Ervin Cartwright.

Doctor in the Nude, see *Traitement de Choc*

Dr. Terror's Gallery of Horrors (Return from the Past, The Blood Drinkers, The Blood Suckers). (American General, 1967). USA. Directed by David L. Hewitt. Script by Gary Heacock, David Prentiss, and Russ Jones. Director of Photography, Austin McKinney (Color). Starring Lon Chaney, Jr., John Carradine, Rochelle Hudson, Roger Gentry, Mitch Evans, Russ Jones. 82 minutes.

Dr. Terror's House of Horrors. (Gallery of Horrors) (Amicus, 1964). Great Britain. Produced by Milton Subotsky and Max J. Rosenberg. Directed by Freddie Francis. Script by Subotsky. Director of Photography, Alan Hume (Color/Scope). Music, Tubby Hayes. Editor, Thelma Connell. Starring Peter Cushing (Dr. Shreck). 1. "Werewolf": Neil McCallum, Ursula Howells, Peter Madden. 2. "Creeping Vine": Alan Freeman, Ann Bell, Bernard Lee. 3. "Voodoo": Roy Castle, Kenny Lynch, Harold Lang. 4. "Crawling Hand": Christopher Lee, Michael Gough, Isla Blair, Judy Cornwell. 5. "Vampire": Donald Sutherland, Max Adrian, Jennifer Jayne, Irene Richmond. 98 minutes.

Does Dracula Really Suck? see *Dracula and the Boys*

Double Possession see *Ganja and Hess*

Dracula. (Russia, 1920). [Purported early, unlicensed adaptation]

Dracula. (Universal, 1931). USA. Produced by Carl Laemmle, Jr. Directed by Tod Browning. Script by Garrett Fort with additional dialogue by Dudley Murphy based the play by John Balderston and Hamilton Deane and the treatment by Louis Bromfield, adapted from the novel by Bram Stoker. Director of Photography, Karl Freund. Production Designers, Charles D. Hall; (associates) Herman Rosse, John Hoffman. Music, Tchaikovsky *(Swan Lake)*, Wagner *(Die Meistersinger)*, Schubert *(Unfinished Symphony)*. Editor, Milton Carruth. Starring Béla Lugosi (Dracula), David Manners (John Harker), Helen Chandler (Mina Seward), Dwight Frye (Renfield), Edward Van Sloan (Van Helsing), Herbert Bunston (Dr. Seward), Charles Gerrard (Martin), Frances Dade (Lucy), Joan Standing (Briggs). 78 minutes.

Drácula. (Universal, 1931). USA. Produced by Carl Laemmle, Jr. and Paul Kohner (associate). Directed by George Melford. Spanish version of the script adapted by B[altazar] Fernandez Cue. Director of Photography, George Robinson. Production Designer, Charles D. Hall. Editor, Arturo Tavares. Starring Carlos Villar[ias] (Dracula), Lupita Tovar (Eva [Mina]), Pablo Alvarez Rubio (Renfield), Eduardo Arozemena (Van Helsing), Barry Norton (Juan Harker). 103 minutes. [Spanish language version of the Browning/Lugosi film]

Dracula. (NBC, Matinee Theater, 1957). USA. Starring John Carradine.

THE BLOOD IN HIS VEINS ONCE
FLOWED THROUGH HERS

now she's one of
the dead-alive
brides of
DRACULA!

ALL NEW!
TECHNICOLOR

Hammer Film Productions, Ltd. Presents

HORROR OF DRACULA

DON'T DARE SEE IT... ALONE! THE TERRIFYING LOVER WHO DIED...YET **LIVED!**

starring
PETER CUSHING · MICHAEL GOUGH and MELISSA STRIBLING with CHRISTOPHER LEE as DRACULA

also starring

..... by JIMMY SANGSTER. From the novel by BRAM STOKER. Directed by TERENCE FISHER. Executive Producer MICHAEL CARRERAS Associate producer ANTHONY NELSON-KEYS. Produced by ANTHONY HINDS
A UNIVERSAL-INTERNATIONAL RELEASE

Dracula (Horror of Dracula). (Hammer, 1958). Great Britain. Produced by Anthony Hinds. Directed by Terence Fisher. Script by Jimmy Sangster based on the novel by Bram Stoker. Director of Photography, Jack Asher (Color). Production Designer, Bernard Robinson. Music, James Bernard. Editor, James Needs, Bill Lenny. Starring Peter Cushing (Dr. Van Helsing), Christopher Lee (Dracula), Michael Gough (Arthur), Melissa Stribling (Mina), Carol Marsh (Lucy), Olga Dickie (Gerda), John Van Essen (Jonathan), Valerie Gaunt (Vampire Bride). 82 minutes.

Dracula. (Episode of the *Mystery and Imagination* series). (Thames, 1965). Great Britain. Produced by Raymond Collier. Directed by Patrick Dromgoole. Script by Charles Graham based on the novel by Bram Stoker. Production Designer, David Marshall. Music, Paul Lewis. Starring Corin Redgrave (Jonathan Harker), Denholm Elliott (Dracula), Suzanne Neve (Mina), Susan George (Lucy Weston), Bernard Archard (Van Helsing), James Maxwell (Dr. Seward), Joan Hickson (Mrs. Weston). 90 minutes.

Dracula. (CBC, 1973). Canada. MOW. Directed by Jack Nixon Browne. Script by Rod

Coneybeare. Starring Norman Walsh, Blair Brown, Nehemiah Persoff.

Dracula (Bram Stoker's Dracula). (Curtis Prods., 1974). USA. Produced and Directed by Dan Curtis. Script by Richard Matheson, based on the novel by Bram Stoker. Director of Photography, Oswald Morris (Color). Production Designer, Trevor Williams. Music, Robert Cobert. Editor, Richard A. Harris. Starring Jack Palance (Dracula), Nigel Davenport (Van Helsing), Simon Ward (Arthur Holmwood), Fiona Lewis (Lucy Westenra), Penelope Horner (Mina Murray), Murray Brown (Jonathan Harker), Pamela Brown (Mrs. Westenra). 100 minutes.

Dracula. (Mirisch/UA, 1979). USA. Produced by Walter Mirisch. Directed by John Badham. Script by W. D. Richter based on the novel by Bram Stoker and the play by John Balderston and Hamilton Deane. Director of Photography, Gilbert Taylor (Color/Scope). Production Designer, Peter Murton. Music, John Williams. Editor, John Bloom. Starring Frank Langella (Dracula), Laurence Olivier (Van Helsing), Donald Pleasance (Seward), Kate Nelligan (Lucy), Trevor Eve (Harker), Jan Francis (Mina Van Helsing), Tony Haygarth (Renfield). 109 minutes.

Dracula and the Boys (Does Dracula Really Suck?, Dracula, Does He...?). (Laurence Merrick Prods., 1969). USA. Directed by Laurence Merrick.

Dracula and Son see *Dracula, Père et Fils*

Dracula A.D. 1972. (Hammer/Warner Bros., 1972). Great Britain. Produced by Josephine Douglas. Directed by Alan Gibson. Script by Don Houghton. Director of Photography, Richard Bush (Color). Production Designer, Don Mingaye. Music, Michael Vickers. Editor, James Needs. Starring Christopher Lee (Dracula), Peter Cushing (Van Helsing), Stephanie Beacham (Jessica Van Helsing), Michael Coles (Inspector Murray), Christopher Neame (Johnny Alucard), William Elis (Joe Mitchum), Marsha Hunt (Gaynor), Caroline Munro (Laura), Philip Miller (Bob). 95 minutes.

Dracula Blows His Cool see *Graf Dracula Beisst Jetzt in Oberbayern*

The Dracula Business. (BBC, 1974). Great Britain. Television documentary. Directed by Anthony de Latbiniere.

Dracula Cerca Sangue de Vergine e...Mori de Sete (Dracula Vuole Vivere: Cerca Sangue de Vergine, Blood for Dracula, Andy Warhol's Dracula). (CC Champion/Jean Yanne–Jean Pierre Rassam/Warhol Prods., 1973). Italy/France. Produced by Andrew Braunsberg. Directed by Paul Morrissey and (uncredited) Anthony Dawson [Antonio Margheriti]. Script by Morrissey. Director of Photography, Luigi Kueveillier (Color). Production Designer, Enrico Job. Music, Claudio Gizzi. Editor, Ted Johnson. Starring Udo Kier (Dracula), Joe Dallesandro (Mario), Vittorio de Sica (Marquis), Maxime McKendry (Marquisa), Arno Juerging (Anton), Milena Vukotic (Esmeralda). 90 minutes.

Above, Peter Cushing and Christopher Lee square off in DRACULA A.D. 1972; below, Lee cringes before the cross in HORROR OF DRACULA

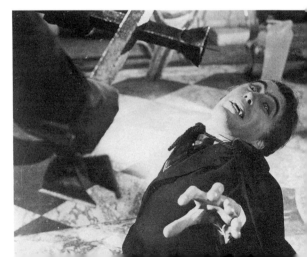

Dracula Contra Frankenstein (The Screaming Dead, Dracula, Prisonnier de Frankenstein). (Ferrix/Comptoir Francais du Film, 1972). Spain/France. Produced by Robert de Nesle and Arturo Marcos. Written and Directed by Jesus Franco. Director of Photography, José Climent (Color/Scope). Music, Daniel White and Bruno Nicolai. Starring Howard Vernon (Dracula), Dennis Price (Dr. Frankenstein), Alberto Dalbes, Britt Nichols, Anne Libert [Josiane Gibert], Mary Francis. 87 minutes.

Dracula, Does He...? see *Dracula and the Boys*

Dracula Exotica. (VCA, 1981). Written and Produced by K. Schwartz. Directed by Warren Evans. Starring Jamie Gillis (Dracula), Vanessa del Rio, Samantha Fox.

Dracula, Father and Son see *Dracula, Pere et Fils*

Dracula Has Risen from the Grave. (Hammer/Warner Bros., 1968). Great Britain. Produced by Aida Young. Directed by Freddie Francis. Script by John Elder [Anthony Hinds]. Director of Photography, Arthur Grant (Color). Production Designer, Bernard Robinson. Music, James Bernard. Editor, Spencer Reeve. Starring Christopher Lee (Dracula), Rupert Davies (Monsignor), Veronica Carlson (Maria), Barbara Ewing (Zena), Barry Andrews (Paul), Ewan Hooper (Priest), Marion Mathie (Anna), Michael Ripper (Max). 92 minutes.

Dracula Hunts Frankenstein see *El Hombre Que Vino de Ummo*

Dracula in Istanbul see *Drakula Istanbulda*

Dracula in the Provinces see *Il Cavaliere Costante Nicosia Demoniaco Ovvero Dracula in Brianza*

A scene from Stoker's novel staged by Terence Fisher in DRACULA, PRINCE OF DARKNESS

Dracula 90 (Dracula, the Series) (RHI/Cinexus/Blair, 1990-91). USA. Syndicated television series. Produced by Robert Halmi, Jr. and David Patterson. Directed by Alan Eastman, Allan King, René Bonniere, Randy Bradshaw, Jeff Woolnough. Scripts by William Laurin, Glenn Davis, Phil Bedard, Larry Lalonde, Peter Meech, Stu Wooley. Starring Geordie Johnson (Dracula/Alexander Alucard}, Joe Roncetti (Chris Townsend), Jacob Tierney (Max Townsend), Bernard Behrens (Uncle Gustav Helsing), Mia Kirshner (Sophie Metternich).

Dracula, Père et Fils (Dracula, Father and Son, Dracula and Son). (Gaumont/Production 2000, 1976). France. Written and Directed by Eduardo Molinaro. Director of Photography, Alain Levent (Color). Production Designer, Jacques Bufnoir. Music, Vladimir Cosma. Editor, Robert Isnardon. Starring Christopher Lee (Dracula), Bernard Menez (Son), Marie-Hélène Breillat (Nicole), Catherine Breillat (Wife), Anna Gael (Woman). 105 minutes.

Dracula, Prince of Darkness. (Hammer/Warner Bros., 1965). Great Britain. Produced by Anthony Nelson Keys. Directed by Terence Fisher. Script by John Sansom from an idea by John Elder [Anthony Hinds]. Director of Photography, Michael Reed (Color/Scope). Production Designers, Don Mingaye, Bernard Robinson. Music, James Bernard. Editor, Chris Barnes. Starring Christopher Lee (Dracula), Barbara Shelley (Helen), Andrew Keir (Father Sandor), Francis Matthews (Charles), Suzan Farmer (Diana), Charles Tingwell (Alan), Thorley Walters (Ludwig), Philip Latham (Klove), Walter Brown (Brother Mark). 90 minutes.

Dracula, Prisonnier de Frankenstein see *Dracula contra Frankenstein*

Dracula Rises from the Coffin. (Tai Chang, Inc., 1982). South Korea. Produced by Lim Won Sik. Directed by Lee Hyoung Pyo. Script by Lee Hee Woo. Director of Photography, Lee Sung Sub (Color). Starring Kang Yong Suk, Park Yang Rae. 92 minutes.

Dracula Rising. (Concorde/New Horizons, 1993). USA. Produced by Roger Corman. Directed by Fred Gallo. Script by Rodman Flender and Daniella Purcell. Director of Photography, Ivan Varimazov (Color). Music, Ed Tomney. Editor, Glenn Garland. Starring Christopher Atkins (Vlad), Stacey Travis (Theresa), Doug Wert (Alec). 80 minutes

Dracula Sucks (Dracula's Bride). (Backstreet Prods./Kodiak Films, 1979). USA. Produced by Darryl A. Marshak. Directed by Philip Morris [Marshak]. Script by Marshak, David J. Kern, William Margold, and Mitch Morrill. Director of Photography, Bruce Edwards [Hanania Baer] (Color/Scope). Production Designer, Richard Kingsley. Music, Lionel Thomas. Editor, Nettie Peña. Starring Jamie Gillis (Dracula), Annette Haven (Mina), Serena (Lucy Webster), John Leslie (Seward), Paul Thomas (Harker), Kay Parker (Dr. Seward), Detlef van Berg (Van Helsing). 82 minutes.

Dracula Tan Exarchia. (Allagi Films, 1983). Color. Greece. Directed by Nikos Zervos. Script by Zervos, Yannis Panousis, and Vangelis Cotronis. Starring Kostas Soumas, Yannis Panousis, Vangelis Cotronis. 84 minutes.

Dracula: The Bloodline Coninues see *La Saga de Los Drácula*

Dracula, the Dirty Old Man. (Boyd Prods., 1969). USA. Produced by Whit Boyd. Written and Directed by William Edwards. Director of Photography, William Troiam (Color). Starring Vince Kelly (Count Dracula/Alucard), Ann Hollis.

Dracula vs. Frankenstein (Blood of Frankenstein, Revenge of Dracula). (Independent International, 1971). USA. Produced by Al Adamson and Samuel M. Sherman. Directed by Adamson. Script by William Pugsley and Sam M. Sherman. Directors of Photography, Gary Graver, Paul Glickman (Color). Starring J. Carrol Naish (Dr. Frankenstein), Lon Chaney, Jr. (Groton, the Zombie), Zandor Vorkov [Roger Engel] (Dracula), Russ Tamblyn, Jim Davis, Anthony Eisley, Regina Carrol. 90 minutes.

Dracula vs. Frankenstein (Spain/West Germany/Italy) see *El Hombre Que Vino de Ummo*

Dracula Vuole Vivere: Cerca Sangue de Vergine see *Dracula Cerca Sangue de Vergine e...Mori de Sete*

Dracula's Blood Bride see *Fracchia contro Dracula*

Dracula's Bride see *Dracula Sucks*

Dracula's Daughter. (Universal, 1936). USA. Produced by E.M. Asher. Directed by Lambert Hillyer. Script by Garrett Fort and John Balderston suggested by Oliver Jeffries based on the story, "Dracula's Guest," by Bram Stoker. Director of Photography, George Robinson. Production Designer, Albert D'Agostino. Music, Heinz Roemheld. Editor, Milton Carruth. Starring Otto Kruger (Dr. Jeffrey Garth), Gloria Holden (Countess Maria Zaleska/Countess Dracula), Edward Van Sloan (Van or Von Helsing), Marguerite Churchill (Janet Blake), Irving Pichel (Sandor), Gilbert Emery (Sir Basil), Hedda Hopper (Lady Hammond), Nan Grey (The Model). 69 minutes.

Dracula's Dog (Zoltan–Hound of Dracula). (Vic/Crown, 1977). USA. Produced by Albert Band and Frank Ray Perilli. Directed by Band. Script by Perilli. Director of Photography, Bruce Logan (Color). Music, Andrew Belling. Editor, Harry Keramidas. Starring Michael Pataki (Michael Drake), José Ferrer (Inspector Branco), Reggie Nalder (Veidt-Smit), Jan Shutan (Maria Drake), Libbie Chase (Linda Drake), John Levin (Steve Drake). 90 minutes. [Note: a film featuring the non-traditional creature, the vampiric dog of the title]

Dracula's Great Love see *El Gran Amor del Conde Drácula*

Dracula's Last Rites see *Last Rites*

Dracula's Lust for Blood see *Chi o Suu Me*

Dracula's Lusterne Vampire (Dracula's Vampire Lust). (Monarex, 1970). Switzerland. Directed by Mario D'Alcala. Starring Des Roberts.

Dracula's Saga see *La Saga de los Drácula*

Dracula's Vampire Lust see *Dracula's Lusterne Vampire*

Dracula's Virgin Lovers see *El Gran Amor del Conde Drácula*

Dracula's Widow. (DeLaurentiis, 1989). USA. Produced by Stephen Traxler. Directed by Chris Coppola. Script by Coppola and Kathryn Ann Thomas. Director of Photography, Giuseppi Macari (Color). Production Designer, Alexandra Kicenik. Music, James Campbell. Editor, Tom Siiter. Starring Sylvia Kristel (Vanessa, Dracula's Widow), Josef Sommer (Lt. Lannon), Lenny Van Dohlen (Raymond Everett), Marc Coppola (Brad), Stefan Schnabel (Van Helsing). 86 minutes.

Dragula (Moss Prods., 1973). USA. Directed by James Moss. Starring W. Casey Donovan, Walter Kent.

Drakula. (Hungary, 1921). Directed by Károly Lajthay. [Early, unlicensed adaptation of which no known prints survive]

Drakula Istanbulda (Dracula in Istanbul) (1952). Turkey. Directed by Mehmet Muhtar. Script by Umit Deniz from **The Impaling Voivode** by Ali Riza Seyfi and the novel by Bram Stoker. Starring Atif Kaptan (Drakula).

Drakulita. (Hemisphere, 1969). Philippines. Directed by Consuelo Osorio. Starring Lito Legaspi, Gina Laforteza, Joseph Gallego, Rosanna Ortiz.

A Dream of Vampires see *Um Sonho de Vampiros*

Dugo ng Vampira (Curse of the Vampires, Creatures of Evil). (Hemisphere/Scepter, 1970). Philippines. Produced by Amalia Muhlach. Directed by Gerardo de Leon. Script by Ben Feleo and Pierre L. Salas from a story by Feleo. Director of Photography, Mike Accion (Color). Music, Tito Arevalo. Starring Amalia Fuentes, Eddie Garcia, Romeo Vasquez, Johnny Monteiro, Rosario del Pilar. 90 minutes.

Echenme al Vampiro (Throw me to the Vampire, Bring Me the Vampire). (Clasa-Mohme, 1964). Mexico. Produced by Mario Garcia Camberos. Directed by A. E. Crevenna. Script by Alfredo Ruanova from a story by Camberos. Director of Photography, F. Colin. Starring Carlos Riquelme, Hector Godoy, Mantequilla, Borolas.

The Empire of Dracula see *El Imperio de Drácula*

L'Empreinte de Dracula see *El Retorno de Walpurgis*

Die Erbin des Dracula see *Vampyros Lesbos*

Ercole al Centro della Terra (Hercules in the Center of the Earth, Hercules in the Haunted World). (SPA Cinematografica, 1961). Italy. Produced by Achille Piazzi. Directed by Mario Bava. Script by Alessandro Continenza, Bava, Giorgio Prosperi, and Duccio Tessari. Directors of Photography, Bava, Ubaldo Terzano (Color/Scope). Production Designer, Franco Lolli. Music, Armando Trovajoli. Editor, Mario Serandrei. Starring Reg Park (Hercules), Leonora Ruffo (Deianira), Christopher Lee (Lichas/Lico), Giorgio Ardisson (Theseus), Ida Galli, Ely Draco, Marisa Belli. 90 minutes; 77 minutes (U.S.).

Erotikill see *La Comtesse Noire*

Every Home Should Have One (Think Dirty). (Example, 1970). Great Britain. Directed by Jim Clark. Script by Marty Feldman, Barry Took, Denis Norden. Director of Photography, Ken Hodges (Color). Starring Marty Feldman, Barry Took, Julie Ege. 94 minutes. (Very short vampire sequence).

The Evil of Dracula see *Chi o Suu Bara*

Evils of the Night. (Shapiro/Mars, 1985). USA. Produced and Directed by Marti Rustam. Script by Rustam and Phillip Dennis Connors. Director of Photography, Don Stern (Color). Music, Robert O. Ragland. Editor, Henri Chapro. Starring Neville Brand (Kurt), Aldo Ray (Fred), John Carradine (Leader), Tina Louise (Cora), Julie Newmar. 85 minutes.

El Extraño Amor de los Vampiros (The Strange Love of the Vampires, Night of the Walking Dead). (Richard Films, 1975). Spain. Directed by Leon Klimovsky. Script by Juan José Daza, Carlos Pumares, and Juan José Porto. Director of Photography, Miguel Mila (Color/Scope). Starring Emma Cohen, Carlos Ballesteros, Vicky Lusson, Rafael Hernandez, Barta Barry, Mari Paz Pondal, Roberto Camardiel. 91 minutes.

Face of Marble. (Monogram, 1946). USA. Produced by Jeffrey Bernard. Directed by William Beaudine. Script by Michael Jacoby based on a story by William Thiele and Edmund Hartman. Director of Photography, Harry Neumann. Production Designer, David Milton. Music, Edward Kay. Editor, William Austin. Starring John Carradine (Prof. Randolph), Claudia Drake (Elaine Randolph), Robert Shayne (David Conklin), Maris Wrixon (Linda), Thomas E. Jackson (Inspector Norton), Rosa Rey (Maria). 70 minutes. [Note: another non-traditional film featuring a vampiric dog]

Fangs of the Vampire see *La Nipote del Vampiro*

Fascination. (Les Films ABC/COMEX, 1979). France. Produced by Joe de Lara. Directed by Jean Rollin. Directors of Photography, Georges Fromentin, D. Lacambe (Color). Music, Philippe D'Aram. Editor, Dominique Saint-Cyr. Starring Brigitte Lahaie (Eva), Franca Mai (Elisabeth), Jean-Marie Lemaire (Marc), Fanny Magier, Miriam Watteau, Alain Plumey, Muriel Montosse. 80 minutes.

The Fearless Vampire Killers, or Pardon Me, but Your Teeth Are in My Neck see *Dance of the Vampires*

The Female Vampire see *Onna Kyuketsuki*

Les Femmes Vampires see *Le Viol du Vampire*

Ferat Vampire. (Barrandov, 1982). Czechoslovakia. Directed by Juraj Herz. Script by Herz and Jan Fleischer based on a story by Josef Nesvadba. Director of Photography, R. Valenta (Color). Production Designer, V. Labsky. Music, Petr Hapka. 90 minutes.

Fiend. (Cinema Ent., 1980). USA. Written, Edited, and Directed by Don Dohler. Directors of Photography, Dohler, R. Geiwitz (Color). Production Designer, Mark Supensky. Music, Paul Woznicki. Starring Don Leiffert. 93 minutes.

A Filha de Dracula (La Fille de Dracula, Daughter of Dracula, La Hija de Drácula). (Interfilme/Comptoir Francais du Film, 1972). France/Portugal. Produced by Victor de Costa. Directed by Jesus Franco. Script by Franco based on **Carmilla** by J. Sheridan Le Fanu. Director of Photography, José Climent. Music, Rene Silviano. Starring Howard Vernon (Count Karnstein), Britt Nichols (Maria Karnstein), Soledad Miranda, Alberto Dalbes, Luis Barboo, Jesus Franco, Daniel White. 87 minutes.

La Fille de Dracula see *A Filha de Dracula*

First Man into Space. (MGM/Amalgamated, 1959). Great Britain. Produced by John Croydon. Directed by Robert Day. Script by John C. Cooper and Lance Z. Hargreaves. Director of Photography, Geoffrey Faithfull. Music, Buxton Orr. Editor, Peter Mayhew. Starring Marshall Thompson (Commander Prescott), Marla Landi (Tia), Bill Edwards (Lt. Prescott), Robert Ayres (Capt. Richards), Bill Nagy (Wilson). 78 minutes. [Note: another non-traditional film featuring a vampiric alien creature aboard a space craft]

Flesh of Your Flesh see *Carne de Tu Carne*

Der Fluch der Grünen Augen (The Curse of the Green Eyes, Night of the Vampires, Cave of the Living Dead). (Objectiv/Triglav, 1963). West Germany/Yugoslavia. Directed by Akos von Rathony. Script by C.V. Rock from an idea by Rathony. Director of Photography, Saric Hrvoj. Production Designer, Ivan Pengov. Editor, Klaus Dudenhofer. Starring Adrian Hoven (Inspector Doren), Erika Remberg (Maria), Carl Mohner (Der Arzt), Wolfgang Preiss (Prof. Adelsberg), Karin Field (Karin), Emmerich Schrenk, John Kitzmiller. 85 minutes.

Forbidden Femininity see *Sexy Proibitissimo*

Forever Knight. (Paragon/Tri-Star/CBS, 1992-93). USA/Canada. Televison series. Produced by Richard Borchiver. Created by James Parriott and Barney Cohen. Starring Geraint Wyn Davies, Gary Farmer, Catherine Disher, Nigel Bennett.

Fracchia Contro Dracula (Dracula's Blood Brides). (1985). Italy. Directed by Neri Parenti. Starring Paolo Villaggio, Gigi Reder, Edmund Purdom.

Frankenstein, El Vampiro, y Cia (Frankenstein, the Vampire and Co.). (Calderon, 1961). Mexico. Directed by Benito Alazraki. Script by Alfredo Salazar. Starring Manuel "Loco" Valdes, José Jasso, Nora Vetran, Arturo Castro. Director of Photography, Enrique Wallace. 80 minutes.

Frankenstein's Bloody Terror see *La Marca del Hombre Lobo*

Fright Night. (Columbia, 1985). USA. Produced by Herb Jaffe. Written and Directed by Tom Holland. Director of Photography, Jan Kiesser (Color). Production Designer, John De Cuir, Jr. Music, Brad Fiedel. Editor, Kent Beyda. Starring Chris Sarandon (Jerry Dandridge), William Ragsdale ((Charley Brewster), Amanda Bearse (Amy), Roddy McDowall (Peter Vincent), Stephen Geoffreys (Evil Ed), Jonathan Stark (Billy Cole). 105 minutes.

Fright Night Part 2. (Tri-Star/Vista, 1988). USA. Produced by Herb Jaffe and Mort Engelberg. Directed by Tommy Lee Wallace. Script by Tim Metcalfe, Miguel Tejada-Flores, and Wallace. Director of Photography, Mark Irwin (Color/Scope). Production Designer, Dean Tschetter. Music, Brad Fiedel, Don Great, Alan Ett. Editors, Jay Lash Cassidy, Jonathan P. Shaw, Duwayne Dunham. Starring Julie Carmen (Regine, Vampiress), Roddy McDowall (Peter Vincent), William Ragsdale (Charley

Below, FRIGHT NIGHT PART 2

Brewster), Traci Lin (Alex), Jonathan Gries (Louie), Russell Clark (Belle). 104 minutes.

Frightmare. (Saturn, 1982). USA. Produced by Patrick Wright, Tallie Wright. Written and Directed by Norman Thaddeus Vane. Director of Photography, Joel King (Color). Music, Jerry Moseley. Editor, Douglas Jackson. Starring Luca Bercovici (Saint), Ferdinand Mayne (Conrad Ragzoff, Vampire), Nita Talbot, Jennifer Starret, Barbara Pilavin, Carlene Olson. 88 minutes.

Le Frisson des Vampires (Vampire Thrills, Shudder of the Vampire). (Les Films Modernes, 1970). France. Written and Directed by Jean Rollin. Director of Photography, Jean-Jacques Rénon (Color). Production Designer, Michel Delesalle. Music, Groupe Acanthus. Starring Sandra Jul[l]ien, Jean-Marie Durand, Michel Délahaye, Jacques Robiolles, Marie-Pierre, Kuelan Herca, Dominique. 95 minutes.

Full Moon of the Virgins see *Il Plenilunio delle Vergini*

Gallery of Horrors see *Dr. Terror's House of Horrors*

Ganja and Hess (Double Possession, Blood Couple, Black Evil, Black Vampire). (Kelly-Jordan Enterprises/Heritage, 1973). USA. Produced by Chiz Schultz. Written and Directed by Bill Gunn. Director of Photography, James E. Hinton (Color). Production Designer, Tom John. Music, Sam Waymon. Editor, Victor Kanefsky. Starring Duane Jones (Dr. Hess), Marlene Clark (Ganja), Bill Gunn (George Meda), Leonard Jackson (Archie), Mabel King (Queen Helga), Sam Waymon (Rev. Williams). 112 minutes. [Note: *Blood Couple* and other alternate titles are releases of a re-edited version by Fima Noveck [F.H. Novikov] which incorporates several scenes cut from the original but is severely abridged to 80 total minutes. Noveck is credited as Director on all alternate versions]

Garu, the Mad Monk. (Maipix, 1970). Great Britain. Photographed and Directed by Andy Milligan (Color). Script by Milligan based on a story by M.A. Isaacs. Production Designer, Lillian Greneker. Starring Neil Flanagan (Father Garu), Jacqueline Webb (Olga), Judith Isral (Nadja), Julia Willis. 57 minutes.

Gebissen Wird nur Nachts (Happening der Vampire, The Vampire Happening). (Aquila, 1970). West Germany. Produced by Pier A. Caminnecci. Directed by Freddie Francis. Script by August Rieger and Karl Heinz Hummel. Director of Photography, Gerard Vandenburg (Color). Music, Jerry Van Rooyen. Starring Ferdy Mayne (Dracula), Pia Degermark, Yvor Murillo. 102 minutes.

Geek Maggot Bingo. (Weirdo Prods., 1983). USA. Produced, Written, Photographed (Color), Designed, Edited, and Directed by Nick Zedd. Starring Robert Andrews, Brenda Bergman, Richard Hell, Donna Death (Vampire). 73 minutes.

Genie of Darkness see *Nostradamus y el Genio de las Tinieblas*

The Ghastly Orgies of Count Dracula see *Riti Magie Nere e Segrete Orge de Trecento*

Goke: Body Snatcher from Hell see *Kyuketsuki Gokemidoro*

Goliath and the Vampires see *Maciste contro il Vampiro*

Graf Dracula Beisst Jetzt in Oberbayern *(Dracula Blows His Cool).* (Lisa/Barthonia Films, 1979). West Germany. Produced by Martin Friedman. Directed by Carlo Ombra. Script by Gruenbach and Rosenthal. Director of Photography, Heinz Hoelscher (Color). Music, Gerhard Heinz. Starring Gianni Garko (Dracula), Betty Verges (Countess Olivia), Giacomo Rizzo, Linda Grondier, Bea Fielder, Ralf Walter, Ellen Umlauf (Ellen Van Helsing). 97 minutes.

El Gran Amor del Conde Drácula (Dracula's Great Love, Cemetery Girls, Dracula's Virgin Lovers). (Janus Films/Eva Films, 1972). Spain. Produced by Francisco Lara Polop. Directed by Javier Aguirre. Script by Aquirre, Jacinto Molina, and A. Insua. Director of Photography, R.P. Cubero (Color). Production Designer, Cubero-Galicia. Music, Carmelo Belona. Editor, Petra Denieva. Starring Paul Naschy [Jacinto Molina] (Dracula), Haydee Politoff, Rossana Yanni, Vic Winner [Victor Alcazar], Mista Miller, Ingrid Garbo. 91 minutes.

Grave of the Vampire. (Entertainment Pyramid/Millenium, 1974). USA. Produced by Daniel Cady. Directed by John Hayes. Script by David Chase. Director of Photography, Paul Hipp (Color). Production Designer, Earl Marshall. Editor, Ron Johnson. Starring William Smith (James Eastman), Mike Pataki (Caleb Croft/Prof. Lockwood), Lynn Peters (Anne), Dianne Holden (Anita), Jay Adler (Zack), Kitty Vallacher (Leslie), Jay Scott, Lieux Dressler, Inga Neilsen. 95 minutes.

Graveyard Shift. (Cinema Ventures/Lightshow Communications, 1987). USA. Produced by Michael Bockner. Written and Directed by Gerard Ciccoriti. Director of Photography, Robert Bergman (Color). Music, Nicholas Pike. Editors, Robert Bergman, Norman Smith. Starring Silvio Oliviero (Stephen Tepes), Helen Papas (Michelle), Cliff Stoker (Eric Hayden), Dorin Ferber (Gilda), Dan Rose (Robert Kopple). 89 minutes.

Graveyard Shift II:The Understudy. (Cinema Ventures, 1989). USA. Produced by Stephen R. Flaks, Arnold H. Bruck. Written and Directed by Gerard Ciccoriti. Director of Photography, Barry Stone (Color). Production Designer, Ciccoriti. Music, Philip Stern. Editor, Neil Grieve. Starring Wendy Gazelle (Camilla), Mark Soper (Matthew), Silvio Oliviero (Vampire Baissez), Ilse Von Glatz (Ash). 88 minutes.

Guess What Happened to Count Dracula? (Merrick Int., 1971). USA. Produced by Leo Rivers. Written and Directed by Laurence Merrick. Director of Photography, Bob Caramico (Color). Production Designer, Mike Minor. Music, Des Roberts. Editor, George Watters. Starring Des Roberts (Count), Claudia Barron, John Landon. 80 minutes.

The Halloween That Almost Wasn't. (The Night Dracula Saved the World) (ABC, 1979). USA. MOW. Produced by Coleman Jacoby. Directed by Bruce Bilson. Script by Gaby Monet. Starring Judd Hirsch (Dracula). 90 minutes. Color.

The Hand of Night (Beast of Morocco). (Schoenfield/Associated British Pathe, 1965). Great Britain. Produced by Harry Field. Directed by Frederick Goode. Script by Bruce Stewart. Director of Photography, William Jordan (Color). Production Designer, Peter Moll. Music, John Shakespeare. Editor, Fred Ives. Starring William Sylvester (Paul Carver), Diane Clare (Chantal), Edward Underdown (Gunther), Terence de Marney (Omar), Alizia Gur (Marisa). 72 minutes.

Hannah, Queen of the Vampires see *La Tumba de la Isla Maldita*

Happening der Vampire see *Gebissen Wird nur Nachts*

Hard Times for Vampires see *Tempi Duri per i Vampiri*

The Hardy Boys and Nancy Drew Meet Dracula. (ABC/Universal, 1977, Two one-hour episodes of the television series). USA. Starring Parker Stevenson, Shaun Cassidy, Pamela Sue Martin, Lorne Greene, Paul Williams.

Haunted Castle see *Le Manoir du Diable*

Hercules in the Center of the Earth see *Ercole al Centro della Terra*

Hercules in the Haunted World see *Ercole al Centro della Terra*

Heritage of Dracula see *Vampyros Lesbos*

La Hija de Drácula see *A Filha de Dracula*

The Historical Dracula: Facts Behind the Fiction. (Documentary, 1976). USA/Romania. Directed by Ian Boston.

El Hombre Que Vino de Ummo (Dracula vs. Frankenstein, Dracula Hunts Frankenstein, Assignment Terror). (Producciones Jaime Prades/Eichberg Film/International Jaguar, 1969). Spain/Italy/West Germany. Produced by

Jonathan Frid as Barnabas Collins in HOUSE OF DARK SHADOWS

Jaime Prades. Directed by Tulio Demichelli and (uncredited) Hugo Fregonese. Script by Jacinto Molina. Director of Photography, Godofredo Pacheco (Color/Scope). Starring Michael Rennie, Karin Dor, Craig Hill, Paul Naschy [Jacinto Molina], Patty Shepard. 89 minutes.

The Horrible Orgies of Count Dracula see *Riti Magie Nere e Segrete Orge de Trecento*

The Horrible Sexy Vampire see *El Vampiro de la Autopista*

Horror of the Blood Monsters see *Creatures of the Prehistoric Planet*

Horror of Dracula see *Dracula (1958)*

House of Dark Shadows. (Curtis Prods./MGM, 1970). USA. Produced and Directed by Dan Curtis. Script by Sam Hall and Gordon Russell. Director of Photography, Arthur Ornitz (Color). Production Designer, Trevor Williams, Ken Fitzpatrick. Music, Robert Cobert. Editor, Arline Garson. Starring Jonathan Frid (Barnabas Collins), Grayson Hall (Dr. Julia Hoffman), Kathryn Leigh Scott (Maggie Evans), Roger Davis (Jeff Clark), Nancy Barrett (Carolyn Stoddard), John Karlen (Willie), Thayer David (Prof. Stokes), Joan Bennett (Elizabeth Stoddard). 97 minutes.

House of Dracula. (Universal, 1945). USA. Produced by Paul Malvern. Directed by Erle C. Kenton. Script by Edward T. Lowe. Director of Photography, George Robinson. Production Designer, John B. Goodman, Martin Obzina. Music, Edgar Fairchild. Editor, Russell Schoengarth. Starring John Carradine (Dracula/Baron Latoes), Lon Chaney, Jr. (Lawrence Talbot), Onslow Stevens (Dr. Edelman), Martha O'Driscoll (Miliza), Lionel Atwill (Inspector), Glenn Strange (The Monster), Jane Adams (Nina). 67 minutes.

House of Frankenstein. (Universal, 1944). USA. Produced by Paul Malvern. Directed by Erle C. Kenton. Script by Edward T. Lowe from a story by Curt Siodmak. Director of Photography, George Robinson. Production Designer, John B. Goodman, Martin Obzina. Music, H.J. Salter. Editor, Philip Cahn. Starring Boris Karloff (Dr. Niemann), J. Carrol Naish (Daniel), Lon Chaney, Jr. (Lawrence Talbot), John Carradine (Dracula), Anne Gwynne (Rita), Peter Coe (Carl), Lionel Atwill (Arnz), George Zucco (Lampini), Elena Verdugo (Ilonka). 70 minutes.

The House That Dripped Blood. (Amicus/Cinerama, 1970). Great Britain. Produced by Max J. Rosenberg and Milton Subotsky. Directed by Peter Duffell. Script by Robert Bloch. Director of Photography, Ray Parslow (Color). Production Designer, Tony Curtis. Music, Michael Dress. Editor, Peter Tanner. Starring 1. "Method for Murder": Denholm Elliott, Joanna Dunham, Tom Adams. 2. "Waxworks": Peter Cushing, Joss Ackland, Wolfe Morris. 3. "Sweets to the Sweet": Christopher Lee, Nyree Dawn Porter. 4. "The Cloak" (Vampire Story): Ingrid Pitt (Carla), Jon Pertwee (Paul Henderson). 101 minutes.

Howling VI: The Freaks. (Allied Lane, 1993). USA. Produced by Robert Pringle. Directed by Hope Perello. Script by Kevin Rock based on the **Howling** novels by Gary Branover. Director of Photography, Edward Pei (Color). Music, Patrick Gleeson. Editor, Adam Wolfe. Starring Brendan Hughes (Ian), Michelle Matheson (Elizabeth), Sean Gregory Sullivan (Winston), Antonio Fargas (Bellamy), Bruce Martin Payne (Harker), Carlos Cervantes (Sheriff). 102 minutes.

La Huella Macabra (The Macabre Mark). (Azteca, 1963). Mexico. Directed by Alfredo B. Crevenna. Starring Guillermo Murray, Rosa Carmina, Carmen Molina, Jaime Fernandez.

The Hunger. (MGM/UA, 1983). USA. Produced by Richard Shepherd. Directed by Tony Scott. Script by Ivan Davis and Michael Thomas based on the novel by Whitley Strieber. Director of Photography, Stephen Goldblatt (Color). Production Designer, Brian Morris. Music, Michael Rubini, Denny Jaeger. Editor, Pamela Bower. Starring David Bowie (John), Catherine Deneuve (Miriam), Susan Sarandon (Sarah), Cliff de Young (Tom Haver), Beth Ehlers (Alice Cavender). 97 minutes.

I, Desire. (ABC/Green/Epstein/Columbia, 1982). USA. MOW. Produced by Audrey Blasdel-Goddard. Directed by John L. Moxey. Script by Robert Foster. Director of Photography, Robert L. Morrison (Color). Production Designers, Fredric P. Hope, Ross Bellah. Music, Don Peake. Editor, Donald R. Rode. Starring David Naughton (David Balsiger), Dorian Harewood (Det. Van Ness), Marilyn Jones (Cheryl Gillen), Barbara Stock (Mona), Arthur Rosenberg (Milton King), James Victor (Dr. Herrera). 97 minutes.

Above, THE HOUSE THAT DRIPPED BLOOD

John Carradine as an urbane Count Dracula with Onslow Stevens, above, in HOUSE OF DRACULA, and Boris Karloff, below, in HOUSE OF FRANKENSTEIN

I Married a Vampire. (Troma/Full Moon, 1983). USA. Produced by Jay Raskin and Vicky Prodromidou. Written and Directed by Jay Raskin. Director of Photography, Oren Rudavsky (Color). Music, Steve Monahan. Starring Rachel Golden, Brendan Hickey.

Immoral Tales see *Contes Immoraux*

El Imperio de Drácula (The Empire of Dracula, Las Mujeres de Drácula). (Vergara, 1967). Mexico. Produced by Luís Enrique Vergara. Directed by Federico Curiel. Script by Ramon Obón. Director of Photography, Alfredo Uribe (Color/Scope). Starring Ethel Carrillo, Eric del Castillo, Cesar del Campo, Lucha Villa. 90 minutes.

In Search of Dracula. (Documentary, 1971). Sweden. Directed by Calvin Floyd, Tony Forsberg. Narrated by Christopher Lee.

In the Midnight Hour see *Midnight Kiss*

Incense for the Damned (Bloodsuckers, Vampire Sacrifice). (Chevron/Paragon/Titan/Lucinda, 1970). Great Britain. Produced by Graham Harris. Directed by Michael Burrowes [Robert Hartford-Davis]. Script by Julian More from *Doctors Wear Scarlet* by Simon Raven. Director of Photography, Desmond Dickinson (Color/Scope). Music, Bobby Richards. Starring Peter Cushing (Dr. Walter Goodrich), Patrick Macnee (Major Derek Longbow), Patrick Mower (Richard), Alex Davion (Tony), Johnny Sekka (Robert), Madeline Hinde (Penelope). 87 minutes.

Incubo sulla Citta Contaminata (Nightmare City, City of the Walking Dead, Invasion of the Atomic Zombies). (Dialchi Film/Lotus Film, 1980). Italy/Spain. Produced by Diego Alchimede, Luís Mendez. Directed by Umberto Lenzi. Script by Antonio Corti, Piero Regnoli, and Luís María Delgado. Director of Photography, Hans Burman (Color). Starring Hans Stiglitz, Laura Trotter, Mel Ferrer, Francisco Rabal, Maria Rosaria Omaggio, Sonia Viviani. 92 minutes.

The In-Laws of Dracula see *Mga Manuggang ni Dracula*

The Inn of the Flying Dragon (The Sleep of the Dead, Ondskans Vardshus). (National Films Studios of Ireland/Dragon/Aspekt, 1981). Ireland/Sweden. Produced by Rudolf Hertzog. Directed by Calvin Floyd. Script by Yvonne and Calvin Floyd based on a story by J. Sheridan Le Fanu, "The Room in the Dragon Volant." Directors of Photography, Jiri Tirl and Tony Forsberg (Color/Scope). Starring Per Oscarsson, Patrick Magee, Marilu Tolo, Brendan Price, Curt Jurgens. 93 minutes.

Innocent Blood. (Warner Bros., 1992). USA. Produced by Lee Rich, Leslie Belzberg. Directed by John Landis. Script by Michael Wolk. Director of Photography, Mac Ahlberg (Color). Production Designer, Richard Sawyer. Music, Ira Newborn. Editor, Dale Bedwin. Starring Anne Parillaud (Marie, Vampire), David Proval (Lenny), Rocco Sisto (Gilly), Chazz Palminteri (Tony), Anthony La Paglia (Joe), Robert Loggia (Sal), Don Rickles (Emmanuel). 115 minutes.

Innocents from Hell see *Alucarda*

La Invasión de los Muertos (The Invasion of the Dead). (Azteca, 1972). Mexico. Directed by Rene Cardona. Starring The Blue Demon, Jorge Mistral, Cesar Silva, C. Linder.

La Invasión de los Vampiros (Invasion of the Vampires). (Tele-Talia/Sono, 1962). Mexico. Produced by Rafael Perez Grovas. Written and Directed by Miguel Morayta. Director of Photography, Raúl M. Solares. Starring Carlos Agosti (The Vampire, Count Frankenhausen), Bertha Moss, Rafael Etienne, Tito Junco, David Reynoso, Fernando "Mantequilla" Soto. 78 minutes.

Invasion of the Atomic Zombies see *Incubo sulla Citta Contaminata*

The Invasion of the Dead see *La Invasión de los Muertos*

Invasion of the Vampires see *La Invasión de los Vampiros*

La Isla de la Muerte (Bloodsuckers, Isle of the Damned). (Orbita/Tefi, 1966). Spain/West Germany. Produced by Geroge Ferrer. Directed by Ernest Von Theumer [Mel Welles]. Script by Welles, Ira Meltcher, Stephen Schmidt. Director of Photography, Cecilio Paniagua (Color/Scope). Starring Cameron Mitchell, Elisa Montes, George Martin, Kay Fisher, Matilde Sampredro. 88 minutes. [Note: A non-traditional film featuring vampire trees]

Island of the Damned see *Traitement de Choc*

Isle of the Damned see *La Isla de la Muerte*

Jacula see *La Comtesse Noire*

The Jitters. (Skouras, 1989). USA. Produced and Directed by John M. Fasano. Script by Jeff

McKay and Sonoko Kondo. Director of Photography, Paul Mitchnick (Color). Starring Sal Viviano, Marilyn Tokuda, James Hong, Frank Dietz.

Jonathan. (Iduna Films, 1970). West Germany. Produced by Ullrich Steffen. Written and Directed by Hans W. Geissendorfer. Director of Photography, Robby Muller (Color). Production Designer, Hans Gailling. Music, Roland Kovac. Editor, Wolfgang Hedinger. Starring Jurgen Jung (Jonathan), Hans Dieter Jendreyko (Josef), Paul Albert Krumm (The Count), Thomas Astan (Thomas), Ilse Kunkele (Lena's Mother), Oskar von Schaab (Professor). 103 minutes.

El Jovencito Drácula (Young Dracula). (Los Films del Mediterraneo, 1975). Spain. Produced by Carlos Benito Parra. Directed by Carlos Benpar [Carlos Benito Parra] and Jorge Gigo. Script by Benpar, José Domenech, and Patricio Raoran. Director of Photography, Tomas Pladevall (Color/Scope). Starring Carlos Benpar, Susanna Estrada, Victor Israel, Marina Ferri, Veronica Miriel, Norma Kerr. 95 minutes.

Kiss Me Quick. (Fantasy Films, 1964). USA. Directed by Russ Meyer. Starring Jackie DeWitt, Althea Currier, Frank Coe.

Kiss of the Vampire. (Hammer, 1963). Great Britain. Produced by Anthony Hinds. Directed by Don Sharp. Script by John Elder [Anthony Hinds]. Director of Photography, Alan Hume (Color). Production Designer, Don Mingaye, Bernard Robinson. Music, James Bernard. Editor, James Needs. Starring Clifford Evans (Prof. Zimmer), Noel Willman (Ravna), Edward de Souza (Gerald Harcourt), Jennifer Daniel (Marianne), Barry Warren (Carl), Jaquie Wallis (Sabena), Isobel Black (Tania), Peter Madden (Bruno), Vera Cook (Anna). 87 minutes.

Kronos see *Captain Kronos–Vampire Hunter*

Kung Fu Vampire Buster see *Mr. Vampire*

Kyuketsu Dukorosen (Living Skeleton). (Shochiku, 1968). Japan. Produced by Shiro Kido. Directed by Hiroshi Matsuno. Script by Kikuma Shimoizaka and Kyuzo Kobayashi. Director of Photography, Masayuki Kato (Scope). Production Designer, K. Morita. Music, N. Nishiyama. Starring Kikko Matsuoka, Kyuzo Kobayashi, Akira Nishimura, Masumi Okada, Nobuo Kaneko. 81 minutes.

Kyuketsu Ga (Vampire Moth). (Toho, 1956). Japan. Directed by Nobuo Nakagawa. Script based on the novel by Seishi Yokomizo. Starring Ryo Ikebe, Akio Kobori, Asami Kuji, Kyoko Anzai, Kinuto Ito. 88 minutes. [Note: another in the menagerie of non-traditional vampires, as indicated by the English-language title]

Kyuketsuki Dorakyura Kobe Ni Arawaru: Akuma Wa Onna Utsukushiku Suru (The Vampire Dracula Comes to Kobe: Evil Makes Beautiful Women). (1979). Japan. MOW. Directed by Hajime Sato. Starring Masumi Okada (Dracula), Kei Taguichi.

Kyuketsuki Gokemidoro (Goke: Body Snatcher from Hell). (Shochiku, 1968). Japan. Directed by Hajime Satô. Script by Susumu Takaku and Kyûzô Kobayashi. Director of Photography, Shizuo Hirase (Color/Scope). Production Designer, Tadataka Yoshino. Music, Shinsuke Kikuchi. Starring Hideo Ko, Terio Yoshida, Tomomi Sato, E. Kitamura. 84 minutes.

Lady Dracula. (TV 13/IFV Prods., 1977). West Germany. MOW. Produced by Guenther Sturm and Kurt Kodal. Directed by Franz-Joseph Gottlieb. Script by Redis Read. Director of Photography, Ernst W. Kalinke (Color). Starring Evelyne Kraft, Christine Buchegger, Brad Harris, Theo Lingen, Eddi Arent, Walter Giller. 86 minutes.

Lake of Dracula see *Chi o Suu Me*

Below, a familiar pose from JONATHAN

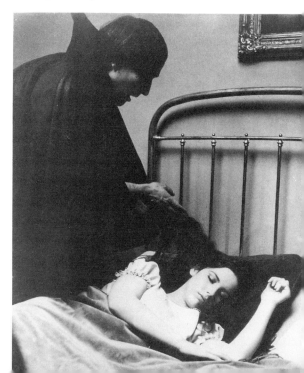

The Last Man on Earth. (Associated Producers, Inc./Produzioni La Regina/American International, 1964). Italy/USA. Produced by Robert L. Lippert. Directed by Sidney Salkow. Script by Logan Swanson and William P. Leicester from the novel *I Am Legend* by Richard Matheson. Director of Photography, Franco Delli Colli. Production Designer, Giorgio Giovannini. Music, Paul Sawtell, Bert Shefter. Editor, Gene Ruggiero. Starring Vincent Price (Robert Morgan), Franca Bettoia (Ruth), Emma Danieli (Virginia), Giacomo Rossi Stuart (Ben Cortman), Umberto Rau. 86 minutes. [Another non-traditional concept from Matheson's novel which treats vampirism as a plague-like disease]

Last Rites (Dracula's Last Rites). (New Empire/Cannon, 1980). USA. Produced by Domonic Paris and Kelly Van Horn. Directed by Domonic Paris. Script by Paris and Ben Donnelly. Director of Photography, Paris (Color). Music, Paul Jost, George Small. Editor, Elizabeth Lombardo. Starring Patricia Lee Hammond, Gerald Fielding, Victor Jorge, Michael Lally, Mimi Weddell. 88 minutes.

The Last Thrill see *La Comtesse Noire*

Legacy of Satan. (Damiano Prods., 1973). USA. Written and Directed by Gerard Damiano. (Color). Starring Lisa Christian. 68 minutes.

The Legend of Blood Castle see *Ceremonia Sangrienta*

The Legend of the Seven Golden Vampires (The Seven Brothers meet Dracula). (Hammer/Shaw Bros., 1974). Great Britain/Hong Kong. Produced by Don Houghton. Directed by Roy Ward Baker. Script by Houghton. Directors of Photography, John Wilcox, Roy Ford (Color/Scope). Production Designer, Johnson Tsau. Music, James Bernard. Starring Peter Cushing (Van Helsing), Julie Ege (Vanessa), David Chiang (Hsi Ching), Shih Szu (Mai Kwei), Robin Stewart (Leyland), Robert Hanna 110 minutes.

The Legendary Curse of Lemora (Lemora–Lady Dracula, Lemora–A Child's Tale of the Supernatural). (Blackfern, 1973). USA. Produced by Robert Fern. Directed by Richard Blackburn. Script by Blackburn and Fern. Director of Photography, Robert Caramico (Color). Production Designer, Sterling Franck. Music, Daniel Neufeld. Starring Lesley Gibb (Lemora), Cheryl [Rainbeaux] Smith (Lila), William Whirton, Hy Pyke, Maxine Ballantyne, Richard Blackburn (Reverend). 90 minutes.

The Lemon Grove Kids Meet the Green Grasshoppper and the Vampire Lady from Outer Space. (Steckler, 1963). USA. Directed by Ted Rotter. Starring R.D. Steckler, Carolyn Brandt.

The Lemon Grove Kids Meet the Monsters. (Morgan-Steckler, 1966). USA. Directed by Ray Steckler. Script by Jim Harmon, Ron Haydock. (Color).

Lemora–Lady Dracula see *The Legendary Curse of Lemora*

Lemora–A Child's Tale of the Supernatural see *The Legendary Curse of Lemora*

Leonor. (Arcadie Productions/Films 66/Uranus/Goya/TransEuropa, 1975). Spain/France/Italy. Directed by Juan Buñuel. Script by Buñuel, Philippe Nuridzany, Pierre Maintigneux, Jean Claude Carriere and C.B. Wood. Director of Photography, Luciano Tovoli (Color). Starring Michel Piccoli, Liv Ullmann, Ornella Muti, Antonio Ferrandis. 100 minutes.

Lesbian Vampires see *Vampyros Lesbos*

Lèvres de Sang. (Off Productions/Scorpion 5/Nordia, 1975). France. Produced by Jean-Marc Ghanassia. Directed by Jean Rollin. Script by Jean Rollin and Jean-Loup Philippe. Director of Photography, J.F. Robin (Color). Music, D.W. Lepauw. Starring Jean-Loup Philippe, Anne Briand, Nathalie Perrey, Willy Braque, Paul Biscaglia, Cathy Castel, Pony Castel, Martine Grimaud, Anita Berglund. 90 minutes.

Lifeforce. (Tri-Star/Golan-Globus, 1985). USA. Produced by Menahem Golam and Yoram Globus. Directed by Tobe Hooper. Script by Dan O'Bannon and Don Jakoby based on the novel, **The Space Vampires**, by Colin Wilson. Director of Photography, Alan Hume (Color). Production Designer, John Graysmark. Music, Henry Mancini. Editor, John Grover. Starring Mathilda May (Space Vampire), Steve Railsback (Carlsen), Peter Firth (Caine), Frank Finlay (Fallada), Patrick Stewart (Dr. Armstrong), Michael Gothard (Bukovsky). 101 minutes. [Note: a non-traditional film featuring "space vampires"]

Lips of Blood see *Les Chemins de la Violence*

The Living Dead Girl see *La Morte Vivante*

Living Skeleton see *Kyuketsu Dukorosen*

La Llamada del Vampiro (Aquellare de Vampiros, Curse of the Vampyr). (Lacy/Sesena/Arco,

1971). Spain. Produced by Ricardo Vazquez. Directed by Joseph de Lacy [José María Elorietta]. Script by Enrique Gonzalez Macho, de Lacy. Director of Photography, Juan Ruíz Romero (Color). Starring Beatríz Lacy, Nicholas Ney, Diana Sorel, Inés Skorpio. 102 minutes.

London After Midnight. (MGM, 1927). USA. Produced and Directed by Tod Browning. Script by Waldemar Young from a story by Browning. Director of Photography, Merritt B. Gerstad. Production Designers, Cedric Gibbons, Arnold Gillespie. Editor, Harry Reynolds. Starring Lon Chaney (Inspector Burke/"Vampire"), Henry B. Walthall (Sir James Hamlin), Marceline Day (Lucille), Conrad Nagel, Polly Moran. 75 minutes.

The Lost Boys. (Warner Bros., 1987). USA. Produced by Harvey Bernhard. Directed by Joel Schumacher. Script by Janice Fischer, James Jeremias, and Jeffrey Boam from a story by Fischer and Jeremias. Director of Photography, Michael Chapman (Color/Panavision). Production Designer, Bo Welch. Music, Thomas Newman. Editor, Robert Brown. Starring Jason Patric (Michael Emerson), Corey Haim (Sam Emerson), Dianne Wiest (Lucy Emerson), Barnard Hughes (Grandpa), Edward Herrmann (Max), Kiefer Sutherland (David), Jami Gertz (Star), Corey Feldman (Edgar), Jamison Newlander (Alex). 97 minutes.

Love at First Bite. (Simon Prods./AIP, 1979). USA. Produced by Joel Freeman. Directed by Stan Dragoti. Script by Robert Kaufman. Director of Photography, Edward Rosson (Color). Production Designer, Serge Krizman. Music, Charles Bernstein. Editors, Mort Fallick, Allan Jacobs. Starring George Hamilton (Dracula), Susan Saint James (Cindy), Richard Benjamin (Dr. Jeff Rosenberg), Dick Shawn (Lt. Ferguson), Arte Johnson (Renfield), Sherman Hemsley (Rev. Mike). 96 minutes.

Love Bites (The Reluctant Vampire). (Waymar/Moviestore, 1993). USA. Produced by Wayne Marmorstein. Written and Directed by Malcolm Marmorstein based on his play. Director of Photography, Stephen Lighthill. Production Designer, Mayne Schuyler Berke. Music, Mark Koval. Editor, Robert Gordon. Starring Adam Ant (Zachary Simms), Kimberly Foster (Kendall Gordon), Roger Rose (Dwight Putnam), Michelle Forbes (Nerissa), Philip

Bruns (Vinnie Helsting), Judy Tenuta (Sgt. Farfalloni). 94 minutes.

The Loves of Irina see *La Comtesse Noire*

The Lurking Vampire see *El Vampiro Aecheca*

Lust for a Vampire. (Hammer/MGM/EMI, 1971). Great Britain. Produced by Harry Fine. Directed by Jimmy Sangster. Script by Tudor Gates based on **Carmilla** by J. Sheridan Le Fanu. Director of Photography, David Muir (Color). Production Designer, Don Mingaye. Music, Harry Robinson, Frank Godwin. Editor, Spencer Reeve. Starring Ralph Bates (Giles Barton), Barbara Jefford (Countess), Suzanna Leigh (Janet), Michael Johnson (Richard Lestrange), Yutte Stensgaard (Mircalla), Mike Raven (Count Karnstein), Helen Christie (Miss Simpson), David Healy (Pelley), Pippa Steele (Susan), Luan Peters (Trudi). 95 minutes.

The Macabre Mark see *La Huella Macabra*

O Macabro Dr. Scivano. (Natus, 1971). Brazil. Produced by Faustino Correia Campos, Raúl Calhado, and Laercio Silva. Directed by Calhado and Rosalvo Cacador. Script by Calhado. Directora of Photography, W. Silva and Calhado (Color). Production Designer, Napoleao Resendo. Starring Raúl Calhado, Luiz Lime, Oswaldo de Souza, Henricao, Lauro Sawaya. 72 minutes.

Maciste contro il Vampiro (Maciste vs. the Vampire, Goliath and the Vampires). (Ambrosiana Cinematografica, 1961). Italy. Produced by Dino De Laurentiis and Paolo Moffa. Directed by Giacomo Gentilomo and Sergio Corbucci. Script by Sergio Corbucci, Duccio Tessari. Director of Photography, Alvaro Maniori (Color/Scope). Editor, Eraldo Da Roma. Starring Gordon Scott (Maciste [Goalith in English-language Version]), Gianna Maria Canale (Astra), Leonora Ruffo (Giulia), Annabella Incontrera (Magda), Rocco Vitolazzi, Jacques Sernas. 92 minutes.

Maciste vs. the Vampire see *Maciste contro il Vampiro*

The Mad Love of a Hot Vampire. (Martex, 1971). USA. Starring Jim Parker, Jane Bond, Kim Kim.

Mad Monster Party. (English Videocraft International/Embassy, 1967). Great Britain. Directed by Jules Bass. Script by Len Korobkin and Harvey Kurtzman (Color). Starring Puppets with the voices of Boris Karloff, Phyllis Diller. 94 minutes.

Mágia (Magic). (Corvin, 1917). Hungary. Directed by Alexander Korda. Script by K. Sztrokay, F. Karinthy. Starring Mihály Várkonyi.

The Magic Christian. (Grand, 1969). Directed by Joseph McGrath. Script by Terry Southern, Peter Sellers, Joseph McGrath from the book by Southern. Director of Photography, Geoffrey Unsworth (Color). Production Designer, A. Gorton. Music, Ken Thorne. Editor, Kevin Connor. Starring Christopher Lee (Ship's Vampire), Peter Sellers, Ringo Starr, Raquel Welch. 93 minutes.

La Maldición de los Karnsteins see **La Cripta e L'Incubo**

La Maldición de Nostradamus (The Curse of Mostradamus). (Bosas Priego, 1960). Mexico. Directed by Federico Curiel. Script by Carlos Taboada, Alfredo Ruanova. Director of Photography, Fernando Colin. Editor, Joseph Munguia. Starring German Robles (Nostradamus), Domingo Soler, Julio Aleman. 78 minutes.

The Male Vampire see *Onna Kyuketsuki*

Malenka the Vampire see *La Nipote del Vampiro*

Mama Dracula. (Valisa Films/Radio Television Belge Francaise/SND, 1979). Belgium. Produced by Boris Szulzinger. Directed by Boris Szulzinger. Script by Szulzinger and Marc-Henri Wajnberg. Director of Photography, Willy Kurant (Color). Music, Roy Budd. Starring Maria Schneider, Louise Fletcher (Countess), Marc-Henri Wajnberg, Alex Wajnberg, Jimmy Shuman, Jess Hahn, Michel Israel. 90 minutes.

Le Manoir du Diable (The Haunted Castle, The Manor of the Devil). (Star, 1896). France. Directed by George Mélèes.

La Marca del Hombre Lobo (Mark of the Wolfman, Frankenstein's Bloody Terror). (Maxper, 1969). Spain. Directed by Enrique L. Eguiluz. Script by Jacinto Molina. Director of Photography, Emilio Foriscot (Color, 3-D, 70mm). Production Designer, José Luís R. Ferrer. Music, Angel Arteaga. Starring Paul Naschy [Jacinto Molina], Dianik Zurakowska, Manuel Manzaneque, Rosanna Yanni, Julian Ugarte. 133 minutes.

Below, the legendary Carroll Borland as Luna with her mentor, Béla Lugosi (right), in MARK OF THE VAMPIRE.

Mark of the Vampire. (MGM, 1935). USA. Produced by E.J. Mannix. Directed by Tod Browning. Script by Guy Endore and Bernard Schubert, from the story by Browning. Director of Photography, James Wong Howe. Production Designer, Cedric Gibbons. Editor, Ben Lewis. Starring Béla Lugosi (Count Mora), Lionel Barrymore, Carroll Borland (Luna), Elizabeth Allan, Lionel Atwill, Jean Hersholt, Henry Wadsworth, Donald Meek, Jessie Ralph, . 62 minutes. [A remake of *London after Midnight.*]

Mark of the Wolfman see *La Marca del Hombre Lobo*

Martin. (Braddock Associates/Libra/Laurel Group, 1976). USA. Produced by Richard Rubinstein. Written, Edited, and Directed by George Romero. Director of Photography, Michael Gornick (Color). Music, Donald Rubinstein. Starring John Amplas (Martin), Lincoln Maazel (Cuda), Christine Forrest (Christina), Elayne Nadeau (Mrs. Santim), Tom Savini (Arthur), Sarah Venable (Housewife). 95 minutes.

Mary, Mary, Bloody Mary. (Translor Films/Proa, 1974). USA/Mexico. Produced by Henri Bollinger and Robert Yamin. Directed by Juan L. Moctezuma. Script by Malcolm Marmorstein based on a story by Don Rico and Don Henderson. Director of Photography, Miguel Garzon (Color). Music, Tom Bahler. Editor, Federico Landeros. Starring Christina Ferrare, John Carradine, David Young, Helena Rojo, Arturo Hansel, Enrique Lucero. 101 minutes.

La Maschera del Demonio (Black Sunday, Mask of the Demon, Revenge of the Vampire). (Galatea/Jolly/American International, 1960). Italy. Produced by Massimo de Rita. Directed by Mario Bava. Script by Bava, Ennio de Concini, Marcello Coscia, and Mario Serandrei from the story "The Vij" [or "Viy"] by Nikolai Gogol. Director of Photography, Mario Bava, Ubaldo Terzano. Production Designer, Giorgio Giovannini. Music, Roberto Nicolosi (Italian version); Les Baxter (US version). Editor, Mario Serandrei. Starring Barbara Steele (The Witch Princess, Asa/Katia), John Richardson (Dr. Gorobec), Ivo Garrani (Katia's Father), Andrea Checchi (Dr. Choma), Arturo Dominici (Javutich), Enrico Olivieri (Katia's Brother), Clara Bindi (Innkeeper), Germana Dominici (Innkeeper's Daughter). 84 minutes.

Mask of the Demon see *La Maschera del Demonio*

Men of Action Meet the Women of Dracula. (Villanueva, 1969). Philippines. Directed by Artemio Marquez. Starring Dante Varona, Eddie Torrente, Ruben Obligacion.

Mga Manuggang ni Dracula (The Secrets of Dracula, The In-Laws of Dracula). (Hemisphere, 1964). Philippines.

The Midnight Hour. (ABC, 1985). USA. MOW Produced by Ervin Zavada. Directed by Jack Bender. Script by Bill Bleich. Director of Photography, Rexford Metz (Color). Music, Brad Fiedel. Starring Shari Belafonte, LeVar Burton, Peter De Luise, Kevin McCarthy, Lee Montgomery. 96 minutes.

Midnight Kiss (In The Midnight Hour). (Overseas, 1993). USA. Produced by Manette Rosen and Marion Zola. Directed by Joel Bender. Script by John Weidner and Ken Lamplugh. Director of Photography, Alan Caso (Color). Production Designer, Don Day. Music, Emilio Kauderer. Editors, Mark Helfrich, Joel Bender. Starring Michelle Owens (Carrie Blass), Michael McMillen (Dennis Blass), Gregory A. Greer (the Vampire), Robert Miano (Capt. Nicoletti), B.J. Gates (Willis), Michael Shawn (Ross), Darla Grant (Carol). 89 minutes.

Mr. and Mrs. Dracula. (ABC, 1980). USA. Televison series. Written and Produced by Robert Klane. Directed by Doug Rogers. Starring Dick Shawn (Dracula), Carol Lawrence, Barry Gordon.

Below, Barbara Steele in BLACK SUNDAY.

Mr. Vampire. (II, III, IV, New Mr Vampire I and II, Kung Fu Vampire Buster). (Six part "hopping vampire" series, Golden Harvest, 1985 (I), 1986 (II), 1987 (III), 1988 (IV). Hong Kong. Directed by Liu Kun-Wai (I), Sung Kan Shing (II), Wang Kee Hung (III), Xen Lung Ting (New I), Mason Ching (New II). Starring Ricky Hui (I, IV and New I), Richard Ng (III), Chin Sui-ho, Lam Ching-ying.

The Monster Club. (Chips Prods./ITC/Sword and Sorcery, 1980). Great Britain. Produced by Milton Subotsky. Directed by Roy Ward Baker. Script by Edward and Valerie Abraham from stories by Ronald Chetwynd-Hayes. Director of Photography, Peter Jessop (Color). Production Designer, Tony Curtis. Music, Douglas Gamley, John Giorgiadis, Alan Hankshaw. Editor, Peter Tanner. Starring Vincent Price, Donald Pleasance, John Carradine, Stuart Whitman, Britt Ekland, Simon Ward. 97 minutes.

The Monster Squad. (Tri-Star/Taft/Barish, 1987). USA. Produced by Jonathan A. Zimbert. Directed by Fred Dekker. Script by Shane Black and Dekker. Director of Photography, Bradford May (Color/Scope). Production Designer, Albert Brenner. Music, Bruce Broughton. Editor, James Mitchell. Starring Andre Gower (Sean Crenshaw), Robby Kiger (Patrick), Stephen Macht (Del Crenshaw), Duncan Regehr (Count Dracula), Tom Noon (Frankenstein's Monster). 82 minutes.

The Monsters Demolisher see *Nostradamus y el Destructor de Monstruos*

La Morte Vivante (The Living Dead Girl). (Les Films ABC/Films Aleriaz/Films du Yaka, 1982). France. Produced by Sam Selsky. Written and Directed by Jean Rollin. Director of Photography, Max Monteillet (Color). Music, Philippe d'Aram. Starring Marina Pierro, Françoise Blanchard, Mike Marshall, Carina Barone, Fanny Magier, Jean-Pierre Bouyxou. 98 minutes.

Il Mostro dell'Opera see *Il Vampiro dell'Opera*

Et Mourir de Plaisir (Blood and Roses). (E.G.E. Films/Documento Films/Paramount, 1960). France/Italy. Produced by Raymond Eger. Directed by Roger Vadim. Script by

Below, John Carradine and Vincent Price in THE MONSTER CLUB.

Vadim and Roger Vailand, adapted by Claude Brule and C. Martin from **Carmilla** by J. Sheridan Le Fanu. Martin. Director of Photography, Claude Renoir (Color/Scope). Production Designer, Jean Andre. Music, Podromines. Editor, Victoria Mericanton. Starring Mel Ferrer (Leopoldo De Karnstein), Elsa Martinelli (Georgia Monteverdi), Annette Vadim (Carmilla Von Karnstein), Jacques-René Chauffard (Dr. Verari), Marc Allégret (Judge Monteverdi), Alberto Bonucci (Carlo), Serge Marquand (Giuseppe). 87 minutes (later cut to 74 minutes).

Las Mujeres de Drácula see *El Imperio de Drácula*

El Mundo de los Vampiros (The World of the Vampires). (Cinematográfica ABSA, 1960). Mexico. Produced by Abel Salazar. Directed by Alfonso Corona Blake. Script by Javier Torya and Ramon Obon from a story by Raúl Zenteno. Director of Photography, Jack Draper. Starring Mauricio Garces, Silvia Fournier, Erna Martha Bauman, José Baviera. 85 minutes.

Munster, Go Home. (Universal, 1966). USA. Produced by Joe Connelly, Bob Mosher. Directed by Earl Bellamy. Script by G. Tibbles, Connelly, and osher. Director of Photography, Benjamin Kline (Color). Starring John Carradine, Yvonne De Carlo, Al Lewis, Fred Gwynne, Butch Patrick, Debbie Watson, Hermione Gingold. 96 minutes.

The Munsters. (CBS, 1964-1966). USA. Televison Series. Produced by Joe Connelly and Bob Mosher. Starring Fred Gwynne (Herman), Yvonne De Carlo (Lily), Al Lewis (Grandpa).

The Munsters' Revenge. (NBC/Universal, 1980). USA. Produced by Don Nelson and Arthur Alsberg. Directed by Don Weis. Script by Nelson and Alsberg. Director of Photography, Harry L. Wolf (Color). Production Designer, James Martin Bachman. Music, Vic Mizzy. Editor, Frederic Baratta. Starring Fred Gwynne, Al Lewis, Yvonne DeCarlo, Jo McDonnell, K.C. Martel. 120 minutes.

The Munsters Today. (MCA Television, 1988-1990). Syndicated television series. USA. Produced by Bryan Joseph. Starring John Schuck (Herman), Lee Meriwether (Lily), James Marsden, Hilary Van Dyke, Howard Morton.

My Best Friend Is a Vampire. (Kings Road, 1988). Produced by Dennis Murphy. Directed by Jimmy Huston. Script by Tab Murphy. Director of Photography, James Bartle (Color).

Production Designer, Michael Molly. Music, Steve Dorff. Editor, Janice Hampton. Starring Rene Auberjonois (Modoo), Robert Sean Leonard (Jeremy Capello), Evan Mirand (Ralph), Cheryl Pollak (Darla Blake), Fannie Flagg (Mrs. Capello). 90 minutes.

My Grandpa Is a Vampire. (Republic, 1993). USA/New Zealand. Directed by David Blyth. Starring Al Lewis. Color.

The Naked Vampire see *La Vampire Nue*

National Lampoon's Class Reunion. (20th Century-Fox/ABC, 1982). USA. Produced by Matty Simmons. Directed by Michael Miller. Script by John Hughes. Director of Photography, Phil Lathrop (Color). Production Designer, Dean Edward Mitzner. Music, Peter Bernstein, Mark Goldenberg. Editor, Richard C. Meyer, Ann Mills. Starring Gerrit Graham, Michael Lerner, Fred McCarren, Miriam Flynn, Stephen Furst, Marya Small. 84 minutes.

Near Dark. (De Laurentiis/Feldman-Meeker, 1987).USA. Produced by Steven-Charles Joffe. Directed by Kathryn Bigelow. Script by Eric Red and Bigelow. Director of Photography, Adam Greenberg (Color). Production Designer, Stephen Altman. Music, Tangerine Dream. Editor, Howard Smith. Starring Jenny Wright (Mae), Adrian Pasdar (Caleb Colton), Lance Henriksen (Jesse), Bill Paxton (Severen), Jenette Goldstein (Diamondback), Joshua Miller (Homer), Tim Thomerson (Loy Colton). 94 minutes.

New Mr. Vampire see *Mr. Vampire*

Nick Knight. (CBS Pilot/Universal, 1989). USA. Directed by Farhad Mann. Script by James D. Parriott from a story by Parriott and Barney Cohen. Producers, Parriott, Barry Weitz, and Roberta Becker Siegel. Starring Rick Springfield, Robert Harper, John Kapelos, Laura Johnson, Michael Nader.

The Night Dracula Saved the World see *The Halloween That Almost Wasn't*

Night Gallery. (NBC, 1970-1972). USA. Produced by William Sackheim. Creator-Host: Rod Serling. Television series with several vampire episodes including "How To Cure the Common Vampire," "The Devil Is Not Mocked," and "The Funeral." See also *Death on a Barge*

Night of the Devils see *La Notte dei Diavoli*

The Night of the Vampire see *Chi o Suu Ningyo*

Night of the Vampire see *Der Fluch der Grünen Augen*

Night of the Walking Dead see *El Extraño Amor de los Vampiros*

The Night Stalker. (Curtis Films/ABC, 1972). USA. MOW. Produced by Dan Curtis. Directed by John L. Moxey. Script by Richard Matheson. Director of Photography, Michael Hugo (Color). Music, Robert Colbert. Editor, Desmond Marquette. Starring Darren McGavin (Carl Kolchak), Carol Lynley (Gail Foster), Simon Oakland (Vincenzo), Ralph Meeker (Bernie), Claude Akins (Sheriff Butcher), Charles McGraw (Chief Masterson), Barry Atwater (Janos Skorzeny), Kent Smith (D.A.). 75 minutes.

Nightlife. (Universal, 1989). USA. Produced by Robert T. Skodis. Directed by Daniel Taplitz. Script by Taplitz and Anne Beatts from a story by Beatts. Director of Photography, Peter Fernberger. Music, Dana Kaproff. Editor, Edward Abroms. Starring Maryam D'Abo (Angelique), Ben Cross (Vlad), Keith Szarabajka (Dr. Zuckerman), Camilla Saviola (Rosa), Jesse Corti, Glenn Shadix, Oliver Clark. 91 minutes.

Nightmare City see *Incubo sulla Citta Contaminata*

Nightmare in Blood. (PFE/Xeromega, 1975). USA. Produced by John Stanley and Kenn Davis. Directed by John Stanley. Script by Stanley and Davis. Director of Photography, Charles Rudnick (Color).Editor, Alfred Katzman. Starring Jenny Walton, Barrie Youngfellow, Kerwin Matthews (Prince Zaroff), Jerry Walter, Dan Caldwell. 90 minutes.

La Nipote del Vampiro (The Niece of the Vampire, Malenka the Vampire, La Sobrina del Vampiro, Fangs of the Vampire). (Triton/Victory, 1968). Spain/Italian. Written and Directed by Amando de Ossorio. Director of Photography, Fulvio Testi. Music, Carlo Savina. Starring Anita Ekberg (Silvia/Malenka), John Hamilton, Diane Lorys, Julian Ugarte, Audrey Ambert [Adriana Ambesi]. 94 minutes.

No Such Thing As A Vampire. (Episode of the *Dead of Night* television series also aired as *Trilogy of Terror*, NBC, 1977). USA. Produced and Directed by Dan Curtis. Script by Richard Matheson. (Color). Production Designer, Trevor Williams. Music, Robert Cobert. Starring Horst Bucholz, Ed Begley, Jr., Joan Hackett, Patrick Macnee, Lee Montgomery, An-

janette Comer, Elisha Cook, Jr., Ann Doran. 74 minutes.

La Noche de los Diablos see *La Notte dei Diavoli*

La Noche de Hombre Lobo see *El Retorno del Hombre Lobo*

La Noche de las Orgias de los Vampiros (Vampire's Night Orgy, Orgy of the Vampires). (International Amusements/Atlantida/Frade, 1973). Spain. Directed by Leon Klimovsky. Script by Gabriel Antonio. Director of Photography, Antonio Ballesteros (Color/Scope). Editors, Antonio Ramirez de Loaysa, Federico Vich. Starring Helga Line, Jack Taylor, John Richard, Charo Soriano, David Aller, Dianik Zurakowska. 85 minutes.

La Noche de Walpurgis (The Night of Walpurgis, The Werewolf vs. the Vampire Woman, Blood Moon). (Plata Films/Western International/Ellma Enterprises, 1970). Spain/West Germany. Produced by Salvadore Romero. Directed by Leon Klimovsky. Script by James Molin [Jacinto Molina] and Robert Oliver [Hans Munkell]. Director of Photography, Leo Williams [Leopoldo Villaseñor] (Color/Scope). Production Designer, Ludwig Orny. Music, Anton Abril. Editor, Tony Gimm. Starring Paul Naschy [Jacinto Molina] (Waldemar), Gaby Fuchs, Patty Shepard (Countess), Barbara Capell, Yelena Samarina, Andres Resino. 88 minutes.

Nocturna. (Compass/Bonet, 1979). USA. Directed by Harry Tampa. Script by Tampa and Nai Bonet. Director of Photography, Mac Ahlberg (Color). Production Designers, Jack Krueger, Steve De Vita. Music, Reid Whitelaw, Norman Bergen. Starring Nai Bonet, John Carradine (Dracula), Yvonne De Carlo (Jugulia), Brother Theodore, Adam Keefe, John Blyth Barrymore. 83 minutes.

Le Nosferat ou les Eaux Glacées du Calcul Egoiste. (Les Films du Groupe de Chambre, 1974). Belgium. Written and Directed by Maurice Rabinowicz. Director of Photography, Jean-Jacques Mathy (Color). Starring Veronique Peynet, Maite Nahyr, Martine Bertrand, Guy Pion, Quentin Milo. 100 minutes.

Nosferatu, Eine Symphonie des Grauens (A Symphony of Horrors). (Prana Film, 1922). Germany. Directed by F. W. Murnau. Script by Henrik Galeen from **Dracula** by Bram Stoker. Director of Photography, Fritz Arno Wagner.

Production Designer, Albin Grau. Starring Max Schreck (Graf Orlof/Nosferatu), Alexander Granach (Knock, an estate agent), Gustav von Wangenheim (Hutter, his assistant), Greta Schroeder (Ellen, Hutter's wife), G.H. Schnell (Harding), Ruth Landshoff (Annie), John Gottowt (Professor Bulwer). 65 minutes.

Nosferatu: Phantom der Nacht. (Herzog/Gaumont, 1979). West Germany/France. Produced and Directed by Werner Herzog. Script by Herzong based on the motion picture by Murnau and Galeen and **Dracula** by Bram Stoker. Director of Photography, Jorg Schmidt-Reitwein (Color). Production Designer, Henning Von Gierke. Music, Popol Voh. Editor, Beate Mainka-Jellinghaus. Starring Klaus Kinski (Nosferatu), Isabelle Adjani (Lucy Harker), Bruno Ganz (Jonathan Harker), Jacques Dufilho (Captain), Roland Topor (Renfield), Walter Laderigast (Van Helsing). 106 minutes.

Nosferatu in Venice. (Medusa, 1981). Italy. Produced, Written, and Directed by Augusto Caminito. Starring Klaus Kinski (Nosferatu), Donald Pleasance, Barbara De Rossi, Yorgo Voyagis, Anne Knecht, Christopher Plummer.

Nostradamus and the Destroyer of Monsters see *Nostradamus y el Destructor de Monstruos*

Nostradamus and the Genie of Darkness see *Nostradamus y el Genio de las Tinieblas*

Nostradamus y el Destructor de Monstruos (Nostradamus and the Destroyer of Monsters, The Monsters Demolisher). (Bosas Priego, 1962). Mexico. Produced by Victor Parra. Directed by Federico Curiel. Script by Alfredo Ruanova and Carlos Taboada. Director of Photography, Fernando Colin. Editor, Joseph J. Munguia. Starring Germán Robles (Nostradamus), Julio Alemán, Domingo Soler, Aurora Alvarado. 77 minutes.

Nostradamus y el Genio de Tinieblas (Nostradamus and the Genie of Darkness, Genie of Darkness). (Bosas Priego, 1960). Mexico. Directed by Federico Curiel. Script by Carlos Taboada and Alfredo Ruanova. Director of Photography, Fernando Colin. Editor, Joseph J. Munguia. Starring German Robles (Nostradamus), Domingo Soler. 77 minutes.

Not of This Earth. (Allied Artists, 1956). USA. Produced and Directed by Roger Corman. Script by Charles Griffith and Mark Hanna. Director of Photography, John Mescall. Music, Ronald Stein. Editor, Charles Gross. Starring

Paul Birch (Paul Johnson), Beverly Garland (Nadine), Morgan Jones (Harry Sherbourne), William Roerick (Dr. Rochelle), Jonathan Haze (Jeremy), Dick Miller (Joe Piper). 67 minutes. [Note: a non-traditional film featuring extra-terrestrial blood drinkers]

Not of This Earth. (Concorde, 1988). USA. Produced and Directed by Jim Wynorski. Script by P.J. Robertson and Wynorski based on the script by Charles Griffith and Mark Hanna. Director of Photography, Zoran Hockstatter (Color). Production Designer, Hayden Yates. Editor, Kevin Tent. Starring Traci Lords (Nadine), Arthur Roberts (Alien), Lenny Juliano (Jeremy) Ace Mask (Dr. Rochelle). 80 minutes. [A remake]

La Notte dei Diavoli (Night of the Devils, La Noche de los Diablos). (Filmes Cinematográfica/Due Cinematografica/Copernices, 1972). Italy/Spain. Produced by Luigi Mariani. Directed by Giorgio Ferroni. Script by Romano Migliorini, Gianbattista Mussetto, and Eduardo Brochero based on Alexis Tolstoy's "The Wurdalak." Director of Photography, Manuel Berenguer (Color/Scope). Production Designer, Galicia Liverani. Music, Giorgio Gaslini. Starring Agostina Belli, Mark Roberts, Cinzia de

Above, the phantom coach; below, the ominous shadow of the vampire from Murnau's NOSFERATU

Carlos, Teresa Gimpera, Umberto Raho, William Vanders. 91 minutes.

La Novia Ensangrentada (The Blood-Spattered Bride, 'Til Death Us Do Part). (Morgan Films, 1972). Spain. Produced by José Lopez Moreno. Directed by Vicente Aranda. Script by Aranda based on **Carmilla** by J. Sheridan Le Fanu. Director of Photography, Fernando Arribas (Color). Production Designer, J. A. Solér. Music, A.P. Olea. Editor, Pablo G. Del Amo. Starring Simon Andreu (He/Husband), Maribel Martin (Susan), Alexandra Bastedo (Carmilla/Mircalla), Dean Selmier (Doctor), Monserrat Julio (Maid), Angel Lombarte (Servant), María Rosa Rodriquez (Carol). 102 minutes.

The Nude Vampire see *La Vampire Nue*

Old Dracula see *Vampira*

The Omega Man. (Warner Bros./Seltzer Prods., 1970). USA. Produced by Walter Seltzer. Directed by Boris Sagal. Script by John William Corrington and Joyce H. Corrington from the novel *I Am Legend* by Richard Matheson. Director of Photography, Russell Metty (Color/Scope). Production Designers, Arthur Loel, Walter M. Simmonds. Music, Ron Grainer. Editor, William Ziegler. Starring Charlton Heston (Neville), Anthony Zerbe (Mathias), Rosalind Cash (Lisa), Paul Koslo, Lincoln Kilpatrick. 98 minutes. [Non-traditional plague-vampires from the Matheson novel]

Once Bitten. (Goldwyn, 1985). USA. Produced by Dimitri Villard, Robby Wald, and Frank E. Hilderbrand. Directed by Howard Storm. Script by David Hines, Jeffrey Hause, and Jonathan Roberts. Director of Photography, Adam Greenberg (Color). Production Designer, Gene Rudolf. Music, John Du Prez. Editor, Marc Grossman. Starring Lauren Hutton (Countess), Jim Carrey (Mark Kendall), Karen Kopins (Robin), Cleavon Little (Sebastian), Thomas Ballatore (Jamie). 93 minutes.

Ondskans Vardshus see *The Inn of the Flying Dragon*

Onna Kyuketsuki (The Female Vampire, Vampire Woman, The Male Vampire). (Shin Toho, 1959). Japan. Produced by Mitsuga Okura. Directed by Nobuo Nakagawa. Script by Shin Nakazawa and Katsuyoshi Nakatsu, from a novel by Yoichiro Tachibana. Director of Photography, Yoshimi Hirano (Scope). Starring Shigeru Amachi, Yoko Mihara, Keinosuke Wada, Junko Ikeuchi. 81 minutes.

Orgy of the Vampires see *La Noche de las Orgias de Vampiros*

Pale Blood. (Noble Entertainment Group, 1992). USA. Produced by Omar Kaczmarczyk and Michael W. Leighton. Directed by V.V. Dachin Hsu. Script by Takashi Matsuoka and Hsu. Director of Photography, Gerry Lively (Color). Production Designer, Shane Nelsen. Music, Jan A.P. Kaczmarek. Editor, Michael Kewley and Stewart Schill. Starring George Chakiris (Michael Fury), Wings Hauser (Van Vandemeer), Pamela Ludwig (Lori), Diana Frank (Jenny), Darcy DeMoss (Cherry). 93 minutes.

Pastel de Sangre (Cake of Blood). (P.C. Tiede, 1972). Spain. Written and Directed by José María Valles, Emilio Martinez Lazaro, Francisco Bellmunt, and Jaime Chavarrí. Director of Photography, Luís Cuadrado (Color/Scope). Starring Marta May, Charo Lopez, Marisa Paredes, Romy, Julian Ugarte, Carlos Otero, Luís Ciges, Jaime Chavarrí. (4 episodes). 89 minutes.

Planet of Blood see *Queen of Blood*

Planet of the Vampires (Italy) see *Terrore nello Spazio*

Planet of Vampires (USA) see *Queen of Blood*

Playgirls and the Vampire see *L'Ultima Preda del Vampiro*

Il Plenilunio delle Vergini (Full Moon of the Virgins, Devil's Wedding Night, Countess Dracula). (Virginia Cinematografica, 1973). Italy. Produced by Ralph Zucker. Directed by Paul Solvay [Luigi Batzella]. Script by Zucker and Alan Harris [Walter Bigari]. Director of Photography, Aristide Massaccesi (Color/Scope). Starring Sara Bay [Rosalba Neri] (Countess), Mark Damon, Frances Davis [Francesca Romana Davila], Miriam Barrios [Esmeralda Barros], Stan Papps [Xiro Papas]. 85 minutes.

El Pobrecito Drácula. (Mezquiriz, 1976). Spain. Directed by Juan Fortuny. Starring Joe Rigoli.

A Polish Vampire in Burbank. (Pirro Prods., 1986). USA. Produced, Directed, Written and Edited by Mark Pirro. Director of Photography, Craig Bassuk. Music, George Gross, Sergio Bandera. Starring Mark Pirro (Dupa), Eddie Deezen (Sphincter), Lori Sutton (Dolores Lane), Bobbi Dorsch (Misty), Hugh O. Fields (Papa), Marya Gant (Yvonne). 83 minutes.

Pontianak (The Vampire). (Keris, 1957). Malaya. Starring Maria Menado.

Pontianak Gua Musang (The Vampire of the Cave). (Keris, 1964). Malaya. Directed by B.N. Rao. Starring Suraya Haron.

Pontianak Kembali (The Vampire Returns). (Keris, 1963). Malaya. Directed by R. Estellia. Starring Maria Menado.

Prehistoric Planet see *Queen of Blood*

The Promise of Red Lips see *Le Rouge aux Lèvres*

Pura Sangre (Pure Blood). (Luís Ospina Films, 1983). Columbia. Edited and Directed by Luís Ospina. Script by Ospina and Alberto Quiroga. Director of Photography, Ramon Suarez (Color). Production Designer, Karen Lamassone. Music, Gabriel and Bernardo Ossa. Starring Florina Lemaitre (Florencia), Carlos Mayolo (Perfecto), Humberto Arango (Ramon), Luís Alberto Garcia (Adolfo), Gilberto Forero (El Monstruo). 98 minutes.

Pure Blood see *Pura Sangre*

Queen of Blood (Planet of Blood, Planet of Vampires, Prehistoric Planet). (American International, 1966). USA. Produced by George Edwards. Directed by Curtis Harrington. Script by Harrington from the story "The Veiled Woman." Director of Photography, Vilis Lapenieks (Color). Production Designer, Albert Locatelli. Music, Leonard Morand. Editor, Leo Shreve. Starring Basil Rathbone (Dr. Farraday), Florence Marly (Queen Velana), Judi Meredith (Laura James), John Saxon (Allan Brenner), Dennis Hopper (Paul Grant), Forrest J. Ackerman (Dr. Forrester), Terry Lee. 79 minutes. [Note: a non-traditional film featuring "space vampires"]

Queen of the Vampires see *Le Viol du Vampire*

Rape of the Vampires see *Le Viol du Vampire*

Red Blooded American Girl. (SC Entertainment/Prism, 1990). Canada. Produced by Paco Alvarez and Nicolas Stiliadis. Directed by David Blyth. Script by Alan Moyle. Director of Photography, Ludek Bogner (Color). Production Designer, Ian Brock. Music, Jim Manzie. Editor, Nick Rotundo. Starring Heather Thomas (Paula), Andrew Stevens (Owen Augustus), Lydie Denier (Rebecca), Christopher Plummer (Dr. Alcore), Kim Coates (Dennis). 95 minutes.

La Reine des Vampires see *Le Viol du Vampire*

The Reluctant Vampire see *Love Bites*

Requiem pour un Vampire see *Vierges et Vampires*

El Retorno de Walpurgis. (Curse of the Devil, L'Empreinte de Dracula) (Dalmata, 1973). Spain. Directed by Carlos Aured. Script by Jack Moll [Jacinto Molina]. Director of Photography, Francisco Sanchez (Color). Starring Paul Naschy [Jacinto Molina] (Waldemar), Maritza Olivares, Fabiola Falcón, Vidal Molina, María Silva, Patty Shepard (Countess). 87 minutes.

El Retorno del Hombre Lobo (The Return of the Wolfman, La Noche de Hombrelobo). (Dalmata Films, 1980). Spain. Produced by Modesto Perez Redondo. Written and Directed by Jacinto Molina. Director of Photography, Alejandro Ulloa (Color). Starring Paul Naschy [Jacinto Molina], Silvia Aguilar, Azucena Hernandez, Julia Saly, Beatríz Elorietta, Pilar Alcón, Pepe Ruíz. 97 minutes.

Return of Count Yorga. (American International, 1971). USA. Produced by Michael Macready. Directed by Bob Kelljan. Script by Kelljan and Yvonne Wilder. Director of Photography, Bill Butler (Color). Production Designer, Vince Cresceman. Music, Bill Marx. Editor, Fabien Todjmann. Starring Robert Quarry (Count Yorga), Mariette Hartley (Cynthia), Roger Perry (David), Yvonne Wilder (Jennifer), Tom Toner (Rev. Thomas), Craig Nelson (Policeman), Philip Frame (Tommy), George Macready (Professor). 96 minutes.

Return of Dracula (Curse of Dracula). (Levy-Gardner Prods./UA, 1958). USA. Produced by Jules V. Levy, Arthur Gardner. Directed by Paul Landres. Script by Pat Fielder. Director of Photography, Jack MacKenzie. Production Designer, James Vance. Music, Gerald Fried. Editor, Sherman Rose. Starring Francis Lederer (Dracula/Bellac), Norma Eberhardt (Rachel), Ray Stricklyn (Tim), Jimmie Baird (Mickey Mayberry), Greta Granstedt (Cora Mayberry). 77 minutes.

The Return of the Vampire. (Columbia, 1943). USA. Produced by Sam White. Directed by Lew Landers. Script by Griffin Jay from an idea by Kurt Neumann, with additional dialogue by by Randall Faye. Directors of Photography, John Stumar, L.W. O'Connell. Music, Mario Castelnuovo-Tedesco. Editor, Paul Borofsky. Starring Béla Lugosi (Armand Tesla), Frieda Inescort (Lady Jane Ainsley), Nina Foch (Nicki Saunders), Roland Varno (John Ainsley), Miles

Mander (Sir Frederick), Matt Willis (Andreas Obry). 69 minutes.

A Return to Salem's Lot. (WB/Larco, 1987). USA. Produced by Paul Kurta. Directed by Larry Cohen. Script by Cohen and James Dixon based on the Stephen King novel 'Salem's Lot. Director of Photography, Daniel Pearl (Color). Production Designer, Richard Frisch. Music, Michael Minard. Editor, Armond Leibowitz. Starring Michael Moriarity (Dad), Samuel Fuller (Van Meer), Andrew Duggan (Judge), Evelyn Keyes, Ronee Blakley, June Havoc. 95 minutes.

Revenge of Dracula see *Dracula vs. Frankenstein*

Revenge of the Vampire (Italy) see *La Maschera del Demonio*

Revenge of the Vampire (Malaya) see *Dendam Pontianak*

Revival of Dracula see *Il Risveglio di Dracula*

The Rider of the Skulls see *El Charro de las Calaveras*

Il Risveglio di Dracula (Revival of Dracula). (1968). Italy. Directed by U. Paolessi. Script by L. Mauri. Starring Gabby Paul, Gill Chadwick.

Riti Magie Nere e Segrete Orge de Trecento (The Reincarnation of Isabel, The Ghastly Orgies of Count Dracula, The Horrible Orgies of Count Dracula, Black Magic Rites–Reincarnations). (GRP, 1973). Italy. Written and Directed by Ralph Brown [Renato Polselli]. Director of Photography, Ugo Brunelli (Color/Scope). Music, Gianfranco Reverberi, Romolo Forlai. Starring Mickey Hargitay, Rita Calderon, Max Dorian, Consolata Moschera, Marcello Bonini, W. Darni. 100 minutes.

Ritual of Blood see *Ceremonia Sangrienta*

Rockula. (Cannon, 1990). USA. Produced by Jeffery Levy. Directed by Luca Bercovici. Script by Levy and Christopher Verwiel. Director of Photography, John Schwartzman (Color). Production Designer, Jane Ann Stewart. Music, Hilary Bercovici. Editor, Maureen O'Connell. Starring Dean Cameron (Ralph), Toni Basil (Phoebe), Tawny Fere (Mona), Thomas Dolby (Stanley), Susan Tyrrell (Chuck). 91 minutes.

Le Rouge aux Lèvres (The Promise of Red Lips, Daughters of Darkness). (Showking/Cine Vog.Maya/Roxy Films/Mediterranea Films/Gemini/Marion Films, 1970). Belgium/France/West Germany/Spain. Produced by Paul Collet and Alain C. Guilleaume. Directed by Harry Kumel. Script by Pierre Drouot, Harry Kumel, and J.J. Amiell. Director of Photography, Edward van der Enden (Color). Production Designer, Françoise Hardy. Music, François de Roubaix. Editors, Gust Verschueren, Denis Bonan. Starring Delphine Seyrig (Countess Elizabeth Bathory), Daniele Ouimet (Valerie), John Karlen (Stefan), Andrea Rau (Ilona), Paul Esser (Porter), George Jamin (The Man), Fons Rademakers (The Mother). 96 minutes.

Le Sadique aux Dents Rouges. (Cinevision, 1971). Belgium. Directed by Jean-Louis Van Belle. Director of Photography, J. Crévin (Color). Music, Raymond Legrand. Starring Jane Clayton, Albert Simono, Daniel Moosman. 80 minutes.

La Saga de los Drácula (The Saga of the Draculas, Dracula's Saga, Dracula: The Bloodline Continues). (Profilmes/Brandon, 1972). Spain. Produced by José Antonio Perez Giner. Directed by Leon Klimovsky. Script by Erika Zsell and Lazarus Kaplan. Director of Photography, Francisco Sanchez (Color/Scope). Production Designer, G. Andres. Editor, Antonio Ramirez. Music, Bach. Starring Helga Line, Tina Saenz, Tony Isbert, Narciso Ibanez-Menta (Dracula), Cristiana Suriana, María Kost, J.J. Paladino. 102 minutes.

Salem's Lot. (Miniseries in Two Parts, CBS/WB, 1980). USA. Produced by Richard Kobritz. Directed by Tobe Hooper. Script by Paul Monash from the novel by Stephen King. Director of Photography, Jules Brenner (Color). Production Designer, Mort Rabinowitz. Music, Harry Sukman. Editors, Carroll Sax, Tom Pryor. Starring David Soul (Ben Mears), James Mason (Richard Straker), Lance Kerwin (Mark Petrie), Bonnie Bedelia (Susan Norton), Lew Ayres (Jason Burke), Ed Flanders (Dr. Norton), Kenneth McMillan (Constable Gillespie), Geoffrey Lewis (Mike), Reggie Nalder (Mr. Barlow). 190 minutes [released in a 110 minute version for Cable television and Videocassette].

Samson vs. the Vampire Women see *Santo contra las Mujeres Vampiras*

La Sangre de Nostradamus (Blood of Nostradamus). (Bosas Priego, 1960). Mexico. Produced by Victor Parra. Directed by Federico Curiel. Script by Carlos Taboada and Alfredo Ruanova. Director of Photography, Fernando Colin.

Editor, Joseph J. Munguia. Starring German Robles (Nostradamus), Julio Aleman, Domingo Soler. 98 minutes.

Sangre de Virgenes (Blood of the Virgins). (Azteca, 1968). Mexico. Produced by Orestes Trucco. Directed by Emilio Vieyra. Starring Gloria Prat, Ricardo Bauleo, Rolo Puente, Susana Beltran.

Santo and Dracula's Treasure see *El Vampiro y el Sexo*

El Santo contra el Baron Brakola (Santo against Baron Brakola). (Vergara, 1965). Mexico. Directed by José Diaz Morales. Starring Santo [Rodolfo Guzmán Huerta], Fernando Oses, Susana Robles.

Santo contra las Mujeres Vampiras (Santo vs. the Vampire Women, Samson vs. the Vampire Women). (Tele-Cine-Radio, 1962). Mexico. Directed by Alfonso Corona Blake. Script by Blake from a story by A. Orellana, F. Oses, and R.G. Travesí. Director of Photography, Manuel Gonzalez. Production Designer, Roberto Silva. Music, Raúl Lavista. Starring Santo [Rodolfo Guzman Huerta], Lorena Velazquez, María Duval, Jaime Fernandez, Augusto Benedico, Ofelia Montesco.

Santo en la Venganza de las Mujeres Vampiro (Santo in the Revenge of the Vampire Women, La Venganza de las Mujeres Vampiro). (Cinemat Flama, 1968). Mexico. Produced by Garcia Besne. Directed by Federico Curiel. Script by Besne and Fernando Oses. Director of Photography, José Ortiz Ramos (Color). Production Designer, Alberto Lopez. Music, Gustavo Carreon. Editor, María Salazar. Starring Santo [Rodolfo Guzmán Huerta], Gina Roman, Norma Lazareno, Aldo Monti, Victor Junce, Patricia Ferrer. 90 minutes.

Santo y Blue Demon contra Dracula y el Hombre Lobo (Santo and the Blue Demon vs. Dracula and the Wolf Man). (Cinematográfica Calderon, 1973). Mexico. (Color). Starring Santo [Rodolfo Guzmán Huerta], Aldo Monti, Agustin Martinez Solares.

El Santo y Blue Demon contra los Monstruos (Santo and the Blue Demon vs. the Monsters). (Sotomayor, 1969). Mexico. Directed by Gilberto Martinez Solares. (Color). Starring Santo [Rodolfo Guzmán Huerta], Resortes, Heydi Blue.

Satan's Black Wedding. (World Video, 1975). USA. Produced by Tamara Brown. Written and Directed by Philip Miller. Director of Photography, Paul Rogers (Color). Production Designer, Carl Le Master. Music, Roger Stein. Editor, Jack Fletcher. Starring Lisa Milano, Ray Miles, Greg Braddock.

Satan's Sisters see *Vampyres*

Satanic Rites of Dracula. (Count Dracula and his Vampire Bride) (Columbia/Warner, 1974). Great Britain. Produced by Roy Skeggs. Directed by Alan Gibson. Script by Don Houghton. Director of Photography, Brian Probyn (Color). Production Designer, Lionel Conch. Music, John Cacavas. Editor, Chris Barnes. Starring Christopher Lee (Dracula), Peter Cushing (Van Helsing), Michael Coles (Inspector Murray), Freddie Jones (Prof. Keeley), Joanna Lumley (Jessica Van Helsing), Richard Vernon (Colonel Matthews), William Franklyn. 87 minutes.

Above and below, wrestlers, bloodsuckers, and wolfmen in a bizarre tag team match from the SANTO series

Scars of Dracula. (Hammer/EMI/MGM, 1970). Great Britain. Produced by Aida Young. Directed by Roy Ward Baker. Script by John Elder [Anthony Hinds]. Director of Photography, Moray Grant (Color). Production Designer, Scott MacGregor. Music, James Bernard. Editor, James Needs. Starring Christopher Lee (Dracula), Dennis Waterman (Simon), Jenny Hanley (Sarah), Christopher Matthews (Paul), Patrick Troughton (Klove), Michael Gwynn (Priest), Wendy Hamilton (Julie), Anoushka Hempel (Tania). 96 minutes.

Die Schlangengrube und das Pendel (The Snake Pit and the Pendulum, The Blood Demon, The Curse of the Walking Dead, The Torture Chamber of Dr. Sadism, Le Vampire et Le Sang des Vierges). (Constantin, 1967). West Germany. Produced by Wolfgang Kuehnlenz. Directed by Harald Reinl. Script by Manfred R. Kohler. Directors of Photography, Ernst W. Kalinke, Dieter Liphardt (Color/Scope). Production Designers, Gabriel Pellon, W. M. Achtmann. Music, Peter Thomas. Editor, Hermann Heller. Starring Christopher Lee, Lex Barker, Karin Dor, Carl Lange. 85 minutes.

Scream and Scream Again. (American International, 1970). Great Britain. Produced by Max J. Rosenberg and Milton Subotsky. Directed by Gordon Hessler. Script by Christopher Wicking from the novel by Paul Saxon. Director of Photography, John Coquillon (Color). Production Designer, Bill Constable. Music, Dave Whittaker. Editor, Peter Elliot. Starring Vincent Price (Dr. Browning), Christopher Lee (Freemont), Peter Cushing (Benedek), Judy Huxtable (Sylvia), Alfred Marks (Supt. Bellaver), Michael Gothard (Keith). 94 minutes.

Scream, Blacula, Scream. (American International, 1973). USA. Produced by Joseph T. Naar. Directed by Bob Kelljan. Script by Joan Torres, Raymond Koenig, and Maurice Jules from a story by Torres. Director of Photography, Isidore Mankofsky (Color). Production Designer, Alfeo Boccicchio. Music, Bill Marx. Editor, Fabien Tordjmann. Starring William Marshall (Mamuwalde/Blacula), Don Mitchell (Justin), Pam Grier (Lisa), Michael Conrad (Sheriff Dunlop), Richard Lawson (Willis), Lynn Moody (Denny), Janee Michelle (Gloria), Barbara Rhoades (Elaine). 95 minutes.

The Screaming Dead see *Dracula contra Frankenstein*

The Secrets of Dracula see *Mga Manuggang ni Dracula*

The Seven Brothers meet Dracula see *The Legend of the Seven Golden Vampires*

Sex and the Vampire see *Le Viol du Vampire*

Sex Express. (Blackwater, 1975). Great Britain. Written and Directed by Derek Ford. Director of Photography, G. Glover (Color). Production Designer, E. Konkel. Music, De Wolfe. Starring Heather Deeley, James Lister (Vampire). 50 minutes.

Sexy Interdit see *Sexy Proibitissimo*

Sexy Proibitissimo (Forbidden Femininity, Sexy-Super Interdit, Sexy Interdit). (Gino Nordini Produzioni, 1963). Italy. Written and Directed by Marcello Martinelli. Director of Photography, Adalberto Albertini (Color). 87 minutes.

Sexy-Super Interdit see *Sexy Proibitissimo*

Shock Treatment see *Traitement de Choc*

Shudder of the Vampire see *Le Frisson des Vampires*

El Signo del Vampiro see *Vampyros Lesbos*

Sisters of Satan see *Alucarda*

Slaughter of the Vampires see *La Strage dei Vampiri*

The Sleep of the Dead see *The Inn of the Flying Dragon*

The Snake Pit and the Pendulum see *Die Schlangengrube und das Pendel*

La Sobrina del Vampiro see *La Nipote del Vampiro*

Son of Darkness: To Die For II. (Trimark/Arrowhead/Lee Caplin/Greg H. Sims, 1991). USA. Produced by Richard Weinman. Directed by David F. Price. Script by Leslie King. Director of Photography, Gerry Lively (Color). Music, Mark McKenzie. Editor, Barry Zetlin. Starring Rosalind Allen (Nina), Steve Bond (Tom), Scott Jacoby (Martin), Michael Praed (Max Schreck/Vlad Tepish), Amanda Wyss (Celia). 96 minutes.

Son of Dracula. (Universal, 1943). USA. Produced by Ford Beebe. Directed by Robert Siodmak. Script by Eric Taylor from a story by Curt Siodmak. Director of Photography, George Robinson. Production Designer, John B. Goodman, Martin Obzina. Music, Hans J. Salter. Editor, Saul Goodkind. Starring Lon Chaney, Jr. (Count Alucard/Dracula), Louise Albritton

(Katherine Caldwell), George Irving (Colonel Caldwell), Robert Paige (Frank Stanley), Frank Craven (Dr. Brewster), J. Edward Bromberg (Prof. Lazlo), Evelyn Ankers (Claire Caldwell), Samuel S. Hinds (Judge Simmons). 78 minutes.

Son of the Vampire see *Anak Pontianak*

Um Sonho de Vampiros *(A Dream of Vampires, The Vampire's Dream).* (Servicine-Servicos Cinematograficos/U.C.B.-Uniao/R.P.I. Filmes Brasileiros, 1968). Brazil. Written, Produced, and Directed by Ibere Cavalcanti. Director of Photography, Renato Neumann (Color). Production Designer, Maria Augusta. Music, Joao Silverio Trevisan. Editor, Nello Melli. Starring Ankito (Dr. Pan), Irma Alvarez (The Vampire), Janet Chermont (Rosinha), Sonelio Costa (Camillo), Augusto Maia Filho (Death), Janira Santiago. 80 minutes.

Spermula. (Film and Co., 1976). France. Written and Directed by Charles Matton. Director of Photography, Jean-Jacques Flori (Color/Scope). Music, José Bartel. Starring Udo Kier, Dayle Haddon (Spermula), Georges Geret, Ginette Leclerc, Isabelle Mercanton. 88 minutes. [Space vampires]

La Strage dei Vampiri *(Slaughter of the Vampires, Vampire, Homme ou Femme?, Curse of the Blood Ghouls).* (Dino Sant'Ambrogio/Mercury/Pacemaker, 1962). Italy. Written and Directed by Roberto Mauri. Director of Photography, Ugo Brunelli. Production Designer, Giuseppe Ranieri. Music, Aldo Piga. Editor, Jenner Menghi. Starring Walter Brandt (Count), Graziella Granata (Louise), Dieter Eppler, Alfredo Rizzo, Paolo Solvay. 84 minutes.

The Strange Love of the Vampires see *El Extraño Amor de los Vampiros*

Subspecies. (Full Moon, 1991). USA/Romania. Produced by Charles Band. Directed by Ted Nicolaou. Script by Jackson Barr and David Pabian based on an idea by Band. Director of Photography, Vlad Paunescu (Color). Production Designer, Lucian Nicolau. Editors, Bert Glatstein, William Young. Starring Michael Watson (Stefan), Laura Tate (Michelle), Anders Hove (Radu), Michelle McBride (Lillian), Irina Movila (Maria), Ivan Rado (Karl). 90 minutes.

Below, Lon Chaney, Jr. as the original SON OF DRACULA

Above, Christopher Lee keeps running into the same-sized iron cross in TASTE THE BLOOD OF DRACULA

Subspecies II and *III* see *Bloodstone*

Sumpah Pontianak (The Vampire's Curse). (Keris, 1958). Malaya.

Sundown: The Vampire in Retreat. (Vestron, 1990). USA. Produced by Jeff Richard. Directed by Anthony Hickox. Script by Hickox and John Burgess. Director of Photography, Levie Isaacs (Color/Scope). Production Designer, David Brian Miller. Music, Richard Stone. Editor, Chris Cibelli. Starring David Carradine (Count Mardulak), Jim Metzler (David Harrison), Morgan Brittany (Sarah), Maxwell Caulfield (Shane), M. Emmet Walsh (Milt), Deborah Foreman (Sandy), Bruce Campbell (Van Helsing), John Ireland (Jefferson), Maxwell Caulfield (Shane). 104 minutes.

Tale of a Vampire. (Tsuburaya Eizo/State Screen, 1992). Great Britain/Japan. Produced by Simon Johnson. Directed by Shimako Sato. Script by Sato and Jane Corbett from a story by Sato. Director of Photography, Zubin Mistry (Color). Production Designer, Alice Normington. Music, Julian Joseph. Editor, Chris Wright. Starring Julian Sands (Alexander d'-Hiver), Suzanne Hamilton (Anne/Virginia Clemm), Kenneth Cranham (Edgar), Marion Diamond (Denise), Michael Kentor (Newspaper Man). 103 minutes.

Tales from the Crypt. (HBO, 1990-1991). USA. Cable television series with several vampire episodes including "The Reluctant Vampire." Produced by Gilbert Adler. Directed by Elliot Silverstein. Script by Terry Black based on a story by William Gaines. Starring Malcolm McDowell (Vampire), Sandra Searles Dickinson, George Wendt, Michael Berryman (Van Helsing). 23 minutes.

A Taste of Blood. (Creative Film Enterprises, 1967). USA. Produced by Herschell Gordon Lewis. Directed by Herschell Gordon Lewis. Script by Donald Stanford. Director of Photography, Andy Romanoff (Color). Starring Bill Rogers, Elizabeth Wilkinson, Thomas Wood, Otto Schlesinger. 120 minutes.

Taste the Blood of Dracula. (Hammer/Warner Bros., 1969). Great Britain. Produced by Aida Young. Directed by Peter Sasdy. Script by John Elder [Anthony Hinds]. Director of Photography, Arthur Grant (Color). Production Designer, Scott MacGregor. Music, James Bernard. Editor, Chris Barnes. Starring Christopher Lee (Dracula), Geoffrey Keen (William Hargood), Gwen Watford (Martha Hargood), Linda Hayden (Alice Hargood), Peter Sallis (Samuel Paxton), Anthony Corlan (Paul Paxton), Isla Blair (Lucy Paxton), John Carson (Jonathan). 95 minutes.

Teen Vamp. (New World, 1988). Produced by Jim McCullough. Written and Directed by Samuel Bradford. Director of Photography, Richard Mann (Color). Music, Robert Sprayberry. Starring Clu Gulager (Reverend), Karen Carlson (Mom), Angie Brown (Connie), Beau Bishop (Murphy), Mike Lane, Edd Anderson. 90 minutes.

Tempi Duri per i Vampiri (Hard Times for Vampires, Uncle Was a Vampire). (Maxima/Cei Incom/Montflour Films, 1959). Italy. Produced by Mario Cecchi Gori. Directed by Steno [Stefano Vanzina]. Script by Edoardo Anton, Dino Verde, and Alessandro Continenza. Director of Photography, Marco Scarpelli (Color/Scope). Production Designer, Andrea Tomassi. Starring Renato Rascel (Osvaldo Lambertenghi), Sylva Koscina (Carla), Christopher Lee (Vampire), Lia Zoppelli (Letizia), Kay Fisher, Susanna Loret, Carl Wery. 95 minutes.

The Tenderness of the Wolves see *Die Zärtlichkeit der Wölfe*

Tendre Dracula (Tender Dracula, Vampire). (Malle Prods., 1973). France. Directed by Pierre Grunstein. Script by Justin Lenoir, Harold Brav, and Grunstein. Director of Photography, Jean-Jacques Tarbes. Production Designer, Jean

Gourmelin. Music, Karl Heinz Schafer. Editor, Anne-Marie Deshayes. Starring Peter Cushing (MacGregor), Miou Miou (Marie), Alida Valli (Heloise), Bernard Menez, Nathalie Courval, Stephane Shandour. 86 minutes.

Terror in Outer Space see *Terrore nello Spazio*

Terror in the Crypt see *La Cripta e l'Incubo*

Terrore nello Spazio (Terror in Outer Space, Planet of the Vampires, The Demon Planet). (Italian International Film/Castilla Cooperativa, 1965). Italy/Spain. Produced by Fulvio Lucisano. Directed by Mario Bava. Script by Bava, Alberto Bevilacqua, Rafael J. Salvia, Antonio Roman, and Callisto Cosulich from a story by Renato Pestriniero; Ib Melchior and Louis Heyward (U.S. version). Director of Photography, Antonio Rinaldi (Color/Scope). Production Designer, Giorgio Giovannini. Music, Gino Marinuzzi, Jr., Antonio Perez Olca. Editor, Antonio Gimeno. Starring Barry Sullivan (Markary), Norma Bengeli (Sonya), Angel Aranda (Wess), Evi Marandi (Tiona). 87 minutes. [Non-traditional space vampires]

Theatre of Death (Blood Fiend). (Hemisphere/Pennea, 1966). Great Britain. Produced by Michael Smedley-Aston. Directed by Samuel Gallu. Script by Ellis Kadison and Roger Marshall. Director of Photography, Gilbert Taylor (Color/Scope). Production Designer, Peter Proud. Music, Elizabeth Lutyens. Editor, Barrie Vince. Starring Christopher Lee (Philippe Darvas), Lelia Goldoni (Daria), Jenny Till (Nicole), Ivor Dean (Inspector), Julian Glover. 91 minutes.

Think Dirty see *Every Home Should Have One*

Thirst. (FG Films/New South Wales Film Corp/Greater Union Org., 1979). Australia. Produced by Anthony I. Ginnane. Directed by Rod Hardy. Script by John Pinkney. Director of Photography, Vincent Monton (Color). Production Designers, Jon Dowding, Jill Eden. Music, Brian May. Editor, Phil Reid. Starring Chantal Contouri (Kate Davis), David Hemmings (Dr. Fraser), Henry Silva (Dr. Gauss), Max Phipps (Hodge), Shirley Cameron (Mrs. Barker), Rod Mullinar (Derek). 96 minutes.

The Thirsty Dead (Blood Cult of Shangri-La). (World/Rochelle/International Amusements, 1974). USA/Philippines. Directed by Terry Becker. Director of Photography, Nonong Rasca (Color). Starring John Considine, Jennifer Billingsley, Tani Guthrie, Judith McConnell. 96 minutes.

The Three Faces of Fear see *I Tre Volti della Paura*

Thriller. (NBC, 1960). USA. Host: Boris Karloff. Produced by Hubbell Robinson. Television series with a vampire episode entitled "Masquerade" starring Tom Poston and John Carradine.

Throw Me to the Vampire see *Echenme al Vampiro*

'Til Death Us Do Part see *La Novia Ensangrentada*

To Die For. (Entertainment/Lee Caplin/Skouras/Arrowhead/Sims 1989). USA. Produced by Barin Kumar. Directed by Deren Sarafian. Script by Leslie King. Director of Photography, David Boyd (Color). Production Designer, Greg Oehler. Music, Cliff Eidelman. Starring Brendan Hughes (Vlad Tepish), Sydney Walsh (Kat Wooten), Amanda Wyss (Celia Katt), Scott Jacoby (Martin). 90 minutes.

To Sleep with a Vampire. (Concorde/New Horizons, 1993). USA. Produced by Mike Elliott. Directed by Adam Friedman. Script by Patricia Harrington ([Carolyn Gail] from the uncredited screenplay by Katt Shea and Andy Ruben). Director of Photography, Michael Crain (Color). Production Designer, Stuart Blatt. Music, Nigel Holton. Editor, Lorne Morris. Starring Scott Valentine (Jacob, the Vampire), Charlie Spradling (Nina), Richard Zobel (Cabbie), Ingrid Vold (Stripper #1), Stephanie Hardy (Stripper #2). [A remake of *Dance of the Damned*]

Tom Thumb and Little Red Riding Hood vs. the Monsters see *Caperucita y Pulgarcito contra los Monstruos*

Tore Ng Diyablo (Tower of the Devil). (Santiago, 1969). Philippines. Directed by Lauro Pacheco. Script by José Flores Sibal from the comic book by Nela Morales. (Color). Music, Pablo Vergara. Starring Jimmy Morato, Pilar Pilapil, Rodolfo Garcia, Lucita Soriano. 90 minutes.

The Torture Chamber of Dr. Sadism see *Die Schlangengrube und das Pendel*

Tower of the Devil see *Tore Ng Diyablo*

Track of the Vampire (Filmgroup, 1966). USA/Yugoslavia. Produced by Jack Hill. Written and Directed by Hill, Stephanie Rothman and {unredited} Rados Novakovic. Executive Producer, Roger Corman. Director of Photogra-

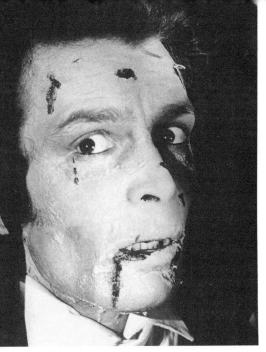

Two victims of local superstion in TWINS OF EVIL: above Judy Mathesc as the Woodman's Daughter; left, Damien Thomas as Count Karnstein.

phy, Alfred Taylor. Music, Ronald Stein (supervisor) and (uncredited) Mark Lowry. Editors, Candace Kane and (uncredited) Mort Tubor. Starring William Campbell (Sordi), Marrisa Mathes (Daisy), Linda Saunders (Melizza), Sandra Knight (Donna), Jonathan Haze (Beatnik), Patrick Magee (body). 75 minutes. [Re-edited version of *Blood Bath*, itself a re-edited version of *Portrait of Terror*, with a few vampire scenes added]

Traitement de Choc (Shock Treatment, Doctor in the Nude, Island of the Damned). (New Line, 1973). France/Italy. Produced by Raymond Danon. Written and Directed by Alain Jessua. Director of Photography, Jacques Robin (Color). Production Designer, Yannis Kokos. Music, René Koering and Jessua. Editor, Hélène Piemmianikov. Starring Alain Delon (Dr. Devilers), Annie Girardot (Hélène Masson), Michel Duchaussoy (Dr. Bernard), Robert Hirsch (Jérôme). 90 minutes. [Note: a "Bathory"-type film in which blood is used to retain youth]

Transylvania Twist. (Concorde, 1990). USA. Produced by Alida Camp. Directed by Jim Wynorski. Script by R.J. Robertson. Director of Photography, Zoran Hochstatter (Color). Production Designer, Gary Randall. Music, Chuck Cirino. Editor, Nina Gilberti. Starring Robert Vaughn (Lord Byron Orlock, Vampire), Teri Copley (Marisa Orlock), Steve Altman (Dexter Ward), Ace Mask (Van Helsing), Becky LeBeau (Rita), Angus Scrimm (Stefan), Monique Gabrielle (Patricia). 82 minutes.

I Tre Volti della Paura (The Three Faces of Fear, Black Sabbath). (Galatea/Emmepi Cinematografica/Lyre/American International, 1963). Italy. Produced by Paolo Mercuri. Directed by Mario Bava. Script by Marcello Fondato, Bava, Alberto Bevilacqua, and Ugo Guerra based on stories by F.G. Snyder ("The Telephone"), Ivan [Alexis] Tolstoy ("The Wurdalak"), and Anton Chekhov [Bava] ("The Drop of Water"). Director of Photography, Ubaldo Terzano (Color). Production Designer, Giorgio Giovannini. Music, Roberto Nicolosi (Italian version): Les Baxter (US version). Editor, Mario Serandrei. Starring 1. "The Telephone": Michele Mercier (Rosy), Lidia Alfonsi (Mary). 2. "The Wurdalak": Boris Karloff (Gorca), Susy Andersen (Sdenka), Mark Damon (Vladimir), Glauco Onorato (Giorgio), Rika Dialina (Wife), Massimo Righi (Pietro). 3. "The Drop of Water": Jacqueline Pierreux (Helen), Miny Monti (The Maid). Boris Karloff introduces the episodes. 99 minutes. [The U.S. version altered the order of the stories by beginning with "The Drop of Water" and changed the dialogue in dubbing]

Trilogy of Terror see *No Such Thing as a Vampire*

La Tumba de la Isla Maldita (Hannah, Queen of the Vampires, Crypt of the Living Dead, Vampire Women, Young Hannah). (Orbita Films/Atlas/Coast 1973). Spain. Directed by Julio Salvador [English language prints credit Ray Danton]. Script by Julio Salvador [English language prints credit Wolf Schmidt, Lou Shaw, and Lois Gibson]. Director of Photography, Juan Gelpi (Color/Scope). Production Designer, Juan Alberto. Music, Phillip Lambro. Starring Andrew Prine, Teresa Gimpera, Mark Damon, Patty Shepard, Jack La Rue, Jr. 99 minutes.

Twins of Evil. (Hammer/Universal, 1971). Great Britain. Produced by Harry Fine and Michael Style. Directed by John Hough. Script by Tudor Gates based on the characters in **Carmilla** by J. Sheridan Le Fanu. Director of Photography, Dick Bush (Color). Production Designer, Roy Stannard. Music, Harry Robinson. Editor, Spencer Reeve. Starring Madeleine Collinson (Frieda Gelhorn), Mary Collinson (Maria Gelhorn), Peter Cushing (Gustav Weil), Kathleen Byron (Katy Weil), Dennis Price (Dietrich), Harvey Hall (Franz), Isobel Black (Ingrid), Damien Thomas (Count Karnstein), Katya Keith (Countess Mircalla). 87 minutes.

L'Ultima Preda del Vampiro (The Playgirls and the Vampire). (Tiziano Longo, 1960). Italy. Written and Directed by Piero Regnoli. Director of Photography, Ugo Brunelli, Aldo Greci. Music, Aldo Piga. Editor, Mario Arditti. Starring Lyla Rocco (Vera), Walter Brandi (Count Gabor Kernassy), Alfredo Rizzo (Lukas), Maria Giovannini (Katia). 85 minutes.

Uncle Was a Vampire see *Tempi Duri per i Vampiri*

Undying Love. (Slaughtered Lamb Prods., 1991). USA. Produced by Ed Walloga. Written and Directed by Greg Lamberson. Director of Photography, John Rosnell (Color). Music, Danny Sciarra, Mauro J. De Trizio. Editor, Lamberson. Starring Tommy Sweeney (Scott Kelly), Julie Lynch (Carmilla), Andrew Lee Barrett (Evan), Lee Kayman (Det. Wint), Mary Huner (Leslie). 76 minutes.

L'Urlo del Vampiro. (Pao Films, 1962). Italy. Directed by T. Fec. Starring F. Fioucci.

Vaarwel. (Cinema Films, 1973). Holland. Produced by Joseph Vliegen. Directed by Guido Pieters. Script by Pieters and Tom Ruys. Director of Photography, Theo van de Sande (Color). Music, Ennio Morricone. Editor, Ruys. Starring Pieke Dassen, Nettie Blanken (Vampire), Rik Bravenboer. 85 minutes.

Valerie a Tyden Divu (Valerie and the Week of Wonders). (Barrandov, 1969). Czechoslovakia. Directed by Jaromil Jires. Script by Ester Krumbachova. Director of Photography, Jan Curik (Color). Production Designer, Krumbachova.

Music, Lubos Fiser. Starring Jaroslava Musil, Helena Anyzkova. 85 minutes.

Valley of the Zombies. (Republic, 1946). USA. Directed by Philip Ford. Script by D. McGowan and Stuart McGowan based on a story by Royal K. Cole and Sherman T. Lowe. Director of Photography, Reggie Lanning. Production Designer, Hilyard Brown. Music, Richard Cherwin. Editor, William P. Thompson. Starring Robert Livingston (Dr. Terry Evans), Adrian Booth (Susan Drake), Ian Keith (Ormand Murks), Thomas Jackson (Blair), Charles Trowbridge (Dr. Maynard). 56 minutes.

Vamp. (New World/Balcor, 1986). USA. Produced by Donald P. Borchers. Directed by Richard Wenk. Script by Wenk from a story by Borchers. Director of Photography, Elliot Davis (Color). Production Designer, Alan Roderick-Jones. Music, Jonathan Elias. Editor, Marc Grossman. Starring Grace Jones (Katrina, Vamp), Chris Makepeace (Keith), Sandy Baron (Vic), Robert Rusler (A.J.), Dedee Pfeiffer (Amaretto), Gedde Watanabe (Duncan). 94 minutes.

Vampir (1969). Spain. Written, Produced and Directed by Pedro Portabella. 66 minutes. [Documentary on the making of *El Conde Drácula*]

Vampira (Old Dracula, Vampirella). (World Film Services, 1974). Great Britain. Produced by Jack H. Wiener. Directed by Clive Donner. Script by Jeremy Lloyd. Director of Photography, Tony Richmond (Color). Production Designer, Philip Harrison. Music, David Whitaker. Editor, Bill Butler. Starring Teresa Graves (Countess Vampira), David Niven (Dracula), Peter Bayliss (Maltravers), Nicky Henson (Marc), Jennie Linden (Angela), Bernard Bresslaw (Pottinger), Linda Hayden (Helga), Veronica Carlson, Freddie Jones. 88 minutes.

Las Vampiras see *Vampyros Lesbos*

Las Vampiras (The Vampire Girls). (Vergara, 1968). Mexico. Produced by Luís Enrique Vergara. Directed by Federico Curiel. Script by Adolfo Torres Portillo, Curiel. Director of Photography, Alfredo Uribe (Color). Production Designers, Octavia Ocampo, José Mendez. Music, Gustavo César Carreón. Editor, Juan José Munquia. Starring John Carradine, Mel Mascaras, María Dubal, Martha Romero, Maura Monti. 90 minutes.

Vampire (France) see *Tendre Dracula*

Vampire. (ABC/MTM, 1979). USA. MOW. Produced by Gregory Hoblit. Directed by E.W. Swackhammer. Script by Steve Bochco and Michael Kozoll. Director of Photography, Dennis Dalzell (Color). Production Designer, James G. Hulsey. Music, Fred Karlin. Editor, Chris Nelson. Starring Richard Lynch (Anton Voytek, Vampire), Kathryn Harrold (Leslie), Jason Miller (John Rawlins), Barrie Youngfellow (Andrea Parker), Michael Tucker (Chris Bell), Jessica Walter (Nicole de Camp). 120 minutes.

The Vampire (Malaya) see *Pontianak*

The Vampire (Mexico) see *El Vampiro*

The Vampire. (UA/Gardner-Levy, 1957). USA. Produced by Jules Levy and Arthur Gardner. Directed by Paul Landres. Script by Pat Fielder. Director of Photography, Jack McKenzie. Production Designer, James Vance. Music, Gerald Fried. Editor, Johnny Faure. Starring John Beal (Dr. Paul Beecher), Kenneth Tobey (Buck), Lydia Reed (Betsy Beecher), Dabbs Greer (Dr. William Beaumont), Herb Vigran (George Ryan), Ann Staunton (Marion Wilkins). 75 minutes.

The Vampire (Episode of *The Night Stalker* television series, Universal, 1974). Produced by Cy Chermak. Directed by Don Weis. Script by David Chase from a story by Bill Stratton. Director of Photography, Ronald W. Browne. Music, Gil Melle. Production Designer, David Beal. Editors, John Elias, J. Howard Terrell. Starring, Darren McGavin (Carl Kolchak), Simon Oakland (Vincenzo), William Daniels (Lt. Matteo), Suzanne Charny (Katherine Rawlins), John Doucette (Sheriff Sample), Jan Murray

(Ichabod Grace), Larry Storch (Swede), Kathleen Nolan (Fay Kruger). 51 minutes.

The Vampire and Sex see *El Vampiro y el Sexo*

The Vampire and the Ballerina see *L'Amante del Vampiro*

Vampire at Midnight. (Skouras, 1988). USA. Produced by Jason Williams and Tom Friedman. Directed by Gregory McClatchy. Script by Dulany Ross Clements based on a story by Williams and Friedman. Director of Photography, Daniel Yarussi (Color). Music, Robert Etoll. Editor, Kaye Davis. Starring Jason Williams (Roger Sutter), Gustav Vintas (Victor Radkoff), Leslie Milne (Jenny), Esther Alise (Lucia), Jeanie Moore (Amalia). 95 minutes.

Vampire Circus. (Hammer, 1971). Great Britain. Produced by Wilbur Stark. Directed by Robert Young. Script by Judson Kinberg from a story by George Baxt and Wilbur Stark. Director of Photography, Moray Grant (Color). Production Designer, Scott MacGregor. Music, David Whittaker. Editor, Peter Musgrave. Starring Adrienne Cori (Gypsy Woman), Laurence Payne (Mueller), Thorley Walters (Burgomaster), John Moulder Brown (Anton Kersh), Lynne Frederick (Dora Mueller), Elizabeth Seal (Gerta), Anthony Corlan (Emil), Richard Owens (Dr. Kersh), Domini Blythe (Anna Mueller), Robert Tayman (Count Mitterhouse), Mary Wimbush (Elvira). 87 minutes.

Vampire Cop (Panorama Entertainment, 1990). USA. Produced by Max Chesney and Faye Chesney. Written and Directed by Donald Farmer. Starring Melissa Moore, Ed Cannon, Terence Jenkins, Michelle Berman.

Le Vampire de Dusseldorf. (Rome-Paris Films/B. Perojo/Manoletti, 1964). France/Spain/Italy. Directed by Robert Hossein. Script by Hossein, Claude Desailly, and George and André Tabet. Director of Photography, Alain Levent. Starring Robert Hossein (Peter Kurten), Marie-France Pisier, Roger Dutoit, Annie Andersson, Paloma Valdes, Danick Patisson, Michel Dacquin. 86 minutes.

Vampire Doll see *Chi o Suu Ningyo*

Vampire Dracula Comes to Kobe see *Kyuketsuki Dorakyura*

Le Vampire et Le Sang des Vierges see *Die Schlangengrube und das Pendel*

A Vampire for Two see *Un Vampiro para Dos*

The Vampire Girls see *Las Vampiras*

The Vampire Happening see *Gebissen Wird nur Nachts*

Vampire, Homme ou Femme? see *La Strage dei Vampiri*

Vampire Hookers. (Caprican 3/Cosa Nueva, 1979). USA/Philippines. Directed by Cirio Santiago. Script by Howard Cohen. (Color). Starring John Carradine, Bruce Fairbairn, Trey Wilson, Karen Stride. 78 minutes.

The Vampire Lovers. (Hammer/AIP, 1970). Great Britain. Produced by Harry Fine and Michael Style. Directed by Roy Ward Baker. Script by Tudor Gates based on **Carmilla** by J. Sheridan Le Fanu. Director of Photography, Moray Grant (Color). Production Designer, Scott MacGregor. Music, Harry Robinson. Editor, James Needs. Starring Ingrid Pitt (Carmilla Karnstein), Madeline Smith (Emma Morton), Peter Cushing (The General), Pippa Steele (Laura), George Cole (Mr. Morton), Dawn Addams (The Countess), Kate O'Mara (The Governess), Douglas Wilmer (Baron), Jon Finch (Carl), Ferdy Mayne (The Doctor). 90 minutes.

Vampire Men of the Lost Planet see *Creatures of the Prehistoric Planet*

Vampire Moth see *Kyuketsu Ga*

La Vampire Nue *(The Naked Vampire, The Nude Vampire).* (ABC Films, 1969). France. Produced and Directed by Jean Rollin. Script by Rollin and S.H. Mosti. Director of Photography, Jean-Jacques Renon (Color). Production Designer, Jio Berk. Music, Yvon Geraud, François Tusques. Starring Christine François, Olivier Martin, Maurice Lemaitre, Ly Letrong, Bernard Musson, Jean Aron, Ursule Pauly. 90 minutes.

The Vampire of Castle Frankenstein see *El Vampiro de la Autopista*

The Vampire of the Cave see *Pontianak Gua Musang*

The Vampire of the Highway see *El Vampiro de la Autopista*

The Vampire of the Opera see *Il Vampiro dell'Opera*

Vampire People see *The Blood Drinkers*

The Vampire Returns see *Pontianak Kembali*

Vampire Sacrifice see *Incense for the Damned*

Vampire Thrills see *Le Frisson des Vampires*

Vampire Woman see *Onna Kyuketsuki*

Vampire Women see *La Tumba de la Isla Maldita*

Vampirella see *Vampira*

The Vampire's Coffin see *El Ataud del Vampiro*

The Vampire's Curse see *Sumpah Pontianak*

A Vampire's Dream see *Um Sonho de Vampiros*

The Vampire's Ghost. (Republic, 1945). USA. Produced by Rudy Abel. Directed by Lesley Selander. Script by Leigh Brackett and John K. Butler. Director of Photography, Robert Pittack, Ellis Thackeray. Production Designer, Russell Kimball. Music, Richard Cherwin. Editor, Tony Martinelli. Starring John Abbott (Webb Fallon), Peggy Stewart (Julie Vance), Grant Withers (Father Gilchrist), Charles Gordon (Roy Hendrick), Adela Mara (Lisa), Emmet Vogan (Thomas Vance), Roy Barcroft (Jim). 59 minutes.

Vampire's Kiss. (Hemdale, 1989). USA. Produced by Barbara Zitwer and Barry Shils. Directed by Robert Bierman. Script by Joseph Minion. Director of Photography, Stefan Czapsky (Color). Production Designer, Chris Nowak. Music, Colin Towns. Editor, Angus Newton. Starring Nicolas Cage (Peter Loew), Maria Conchita Alonso (Alva), Jennifer Beals (Rachel), Elizabeth Ashley (Dr. Glaser), Kasi Lemmons (Jackie), Bob Lujan (Emilio).105 minutes.

The Vampire's Lover see *L'Amante del Vampiro*

Vampire's Night Orgy see *La Noche de las Orgias de los Vampiros*

Vampires see *Vij*

Les Vampires en Ont Ras le Bol see *Bloedverwanten*

I Vampiri *(The Devil's Commandment).* (Titanus/Athena, 1956). Italy. Directed by Riccardo Freda and (uncredited) Mario Bava. Script by Piero Regnoli and Rik Sjöström [Riccardo Freda]. Director of Photography, Bava (Scope). Production Designer, Beni Montresor. Music, Roman Vlad and Franco Mannino. Editor, Roberto Cinquini. Starring Gianna Maria Canale (Marguerite/Duchess Gisele), Antonine Balpêtré (Dr. Du Grand), Paul Müller (Joseph), Carlo D'Angelo (Santel), Wandisa Guida (Laurette), Dario Michaelis (Valentin), Renato Tontini (Du Grand's assistant). 90 minutes. [Note: another "Bathory"-type film in which blood gives eternal youth]

Above, Gianna Maria Canale needs blood to maintain her youth in I VAMPIRI, photographed and co-directed by Mario Bava

El Vampiro Aececha *The Lurking Vampire.* (1962). Argentina. Script based on a story by William Irish [Cornell Woolrich]. Starring German Robles, Abel Salazar.

El Vampiro *(The Vampire).* (Salazar/Cinematográfica ABSA, 1956). Mexico. Produced by Abel Salazar. Directed by Fernando Mendez. Script by H. Rodriquez and Ramon Obón. Director of Photography, Rosario Solano. Production Designer, Gunther Gerzo. Music, Gustavo C. Carrión. Starring German Robles (Count Lavud/Duval), Ariadna Welter, Abel Salazar, July Danery, Joseph Chavez, Amado Zumaya. Mercedes Soler. 95 minutes.

El Vampiro de la Autopista *(The Vampire of the Highway, The Vampire of Castle Frankenstein, The Horrible Sexy Vampire).* (Cinefilms, 1969). Spain. Produced by Al Peppard. Written and Directed by Delavena [José Luís Madrid]. Director of Photography, Francisco Madurga (Color/Scope). Starring Valdemar Wohlfahrt, Patricia Loran, Luís Induni, Barta Barry, Adele Tauler, Anastasio Campoy. 91 minutes.

Il Vampiro dell'Opera *(Il Mostro dell'Opera, The Vampire of the Opera).* (NIF, 1964). Italy. Written and Directed by Renato Polselli. Star-

ring John McDouglas [Giuseppe Addobati], Vittoria Prada, Marc Marian [Marco Mariani], Barbara Howard, Catla Cavelli. 80 minutes.

Un Vampiro para Dos *(A Vampire for Two).* (Belmar P.C./Bravo Murillo, 1965). Spain. Directed by Pedro Lazanga Sabater. Script by Lazanga Sabater and José María Palacio. Director of Photography, Eloy Molla (Scope). Starring Gracita Morales, José Luís Lopez Vazquez, Fernando Fernan Gomez, Trini Alonso, Goyo Lebreros. 85 minutes.

El Vampiro Sangriento *(The Bloody Vampire, El Conde Frankenhausen).* (Tele-Talia, 1962). Mexico. Produced by Rafael Perez Grovas. Written and Directed by Miguel Morayta. Director of Photography, Raúl M. Solares. Music, Luís Hernandez Breton. Editor, Gloria Schoemann. Starring Carlos Agosti (Count Frankenhausen), Begona Palacios (Inés), Raúl Farell (Richard), Antonio Raxell, E. Martha Bauman (Countess Frankenhausen). 110 minutes.

Vampiro 2000. (1972). Italy. Directed by Riccardo Ghione. Starring Nino Castelnuovo, Dominique Boschero.

El Vampiro y el Sexo *(The Vampire and Sex, Santo and Dracula's Treasure).* (Cinematográfica Calderón, 1969). Mexico. Produced by Guillermo Calderon. Directed by Rene Cardona. Script by Alfredo Salazar. Director of Photography, Raúl Martinez Solares (Color). Music, Sergio Guerrera. Starring Santo [Rodolfo Guzmán Huerta], Noelia Noel, Aldo Monti, Carlos Agosti, Alberto Rojas, Roberto Rivera, Jorge Mondragón, Gina Moret. 81 minutes.

Los Vampiros de Coyoacan. (Agrasanchez, 1973). Mexico. Directed by Arturo Martinez.

Vampyr. (Tobis-Klangfilm, 1932). Germany/France. Produced by Carl Dreyer and Nicholas de Gunzburg. Directed by Dreyer. Script by Dreyer and Christen Jul based on **Carmilla** and other stories in the anthology **In A Glass Darkly** by J. Sheridan Le Fanu. Directors of Photography, Rudolph Maté, Louis Née. Production Designers, Hermann Warm, Hans Bittmann, Cesare Silvani. Music, Wolfgang Zeller. Starring Julian West [Baron Nicolas de Gunzburg] (David Gray), Maurice Schutz (Lord of the Manor), Sybille Schmitz (Leone), Rena Mandel (Gisele), Henriette Gerard (Marguerite), Jan Hieronimko (The Doctor), Albert Bras (The Servant), A. Babanini (His Wife). 65 minutes.

Vampyr (Spain) see *El Conde Drácula*

Vampyre. (Panorama Entertainment/Pagan, 1990). USA. Produced by Bruce G. Hallenbeck and Antonio Panetta. Written and Directed by Hallenbeck. Director of Photography, Panetta. Starring Randy Scott Rozler, Cathy Seyler, John Brent, Marilyn Semerad.

The Vampyre Orgy see *Vampyres*

Vampyres (Daughters of Darkness, The Vampyre Orgy, Blood Hunger, Satan's Daughters, Daughters of Dracula). (Essay Films, 1974). Great Britain. Produced by Brian Smedley-Aston. Directed by Joseph (Jose) Larraz. Script by Diana Daubeney. Director of Photography, Harry Waxman (Color/Scope). Production Designer, Ken Bridgeman. Music, James Clark. Editor, Geoff Brown. Starring Marianne Morris (Fran), Anulka (Miriam), Murray Brown (Ted), Brian Deacon (John), Sally Faulkner (Harriet), Bessie Love, Michael Byrne, Elliott Sullivan. 87 minutes.

Vampyros Lesbos (Die Erbin des Dracula, Las Vampiras, Lesbian Vampires, El Signo del Vampiro, Heritage of Dracula). (CCC Telecine/Fenix Films, 1970). Spain/West Germany. Produced by Arturo Marcos. Directed by Franco

Manera [Jesus Franco]. Script by Franco and Jaime Chavarri. Director of Photography, Manuel Merino (Color). Music, Mannfred

Above and below: images from Carl Dreyer's Expressionistic *tour de force* VAMPYR.

Above, Marguerite (Cathy Seyler) has a cup of blood in *Vampyre.*

Hubler, Siegfried Schwab. Editor, Clarissa Anbach. Starring Susan Korda [Soledad Miranda], Dennis Price, Ewa Stroemberg, Paul Mueller, Hiedrin Kassim, Victor Feldman, Jesus Franco, Michael Berling. 92 minutes.

Vault of Horror. (Metromedia/Amicus, 1973). Great Britain. Produced by Max J. Rosenberg and Milton Subotsky. Directed by Roy Ward Baker. Script by Subotsky based on tales in William Gaines' comic books. Director of Photography, Denys Coop (Color). Production Designer, Tony Curtis. Editor, Oswlad Hafenrichter. Starring Daniel Massey, Anna Massey, Michael Craig, Curt Jurgens, Dawn Addams, TerryThomas, Glynis Johns, Tom Baker, Denholm Elliott. 93 minutes. (The first of the five tales is a vampire story).

Veil of Blood (Devil's Plaything). (Leisure Time/Monarex, 1973). Switzerland. Produced by Chris D. Nebe. Written and Directed by Joe Sarno. Director of Photography, S. Silverman (Color). Production Designers, Cleo Nora, Armin Ryf. Music, RalfSans Mueller. Editors, R.S. Fugunt, D. Preuss. Starring Nadia Senk-

owa, Untel Syring, Ulrike Butz, Nico Wolf. 88 minutes.

La Venganza de Las Mujeres Vampiro see *Santo en la Venganza de las Mujeres Vampiro*

Vierges et Vampires (Virgins and Vampires, Requiem pour un Vampire, Caged Virgins). (ABC Films, 1972). France. Produced by Sam Selsky. Written and Directed by Jean Rollin. Director of Photography, Renan Polles (Color). Starring Marie Pierre Castel, Mireille D'Argent, Philippe Gaste, Dominique, Michel De la Salle, Olivier François, Louise Dhour. 95 minutes.

Vij (Vampires). (Mosfilm, 1967). USSR. Directed by Constantin Erchov and Guerorgiu Kropatchov. Script by A. Ptouchko, Erchov, and Kropatchov based on the story by Gogol. (Color). Starring Natalia Varlei, Leonid Kouraviliev.

Le Viol du Vampire (The Rape of the Vampire, Les Femmes Vampires, Sex and the Vampire, La Reine des Vampires, Queen of the Vampires). (ABC Films, 1967). France. Produced by Sam Selsky. Written and Directed by Jean Rollin. Director of Photography, Guy Leblond, Antoine Harispe. Music, Yvon Geraud, François Tusques. Editor, Jean-Denis Bonan. Starring Bernard Letrou (Thomas), Solange Pradel (Solange), Ursule Pauly (Ursulle), Nicole Romain (Blind Vampire), Jacqueline Sieger. 100 minutes.

Virgins and Vampires see *Vierges et Vampires*

Voodoo Heartbeat. (Molina Prods., 1972). USA Directed by Charles Nizet. (Color). Starring R. Molina, Philip Ahn, Ern Dugo. 88 minutes.

Walpurgis Night see *La Noche de Walpurgis*

Waxwork. (Vestron/Filmrullen/Palla/Mario Sotela, 1988). USA. Produced by Staffan Ahrenberg. Written and Directed by Anthony Hickox. Director of Photography, Gerry Lively (Color). Production Designer, Gianni Quaranta. Music, Roger Bellon. Editor, Christopher Cibelli. Starring Deborah Foreman (Sarah), Zach Galligan (Mark), Michelle Johnson (China), Dana Ashbrook (Tony), Miles O'Keefe (Dracula). 97 minutes.

The Werewolf vs. the Vampire Woman see *La Noche de Walpurgis*

The World of the Vampires see *El Mundo de los Vampiros*

Young Dracula (Great Britain) see *Count Down-Son of Dracula*

Young Dracula (Spain) see *El Jovencito Drácula*

Young Hannah see *La Tumba de la Isla Maldita*

Die Zärtlichkeit der Wölfe (The Tenderness of the Wolves). (Tango Film, 1973). West Germany. Produced by Rainer Werner Fassbinder. Directed by Ulli Lommel. Script by Kurt Raab. Director of Photography, Jurgen Jorges (Color). Starring Kurt Raab (Fritz Haarmann), Jeff Roden, Margit Carstensen, Wolfgang Schreck, R. W. Fassbinder. 87 minutes.

Zoltan, Hound of Dracula see *Dracula's Dog*

A Zsarnok Szíve avagy Boccacio Magyarországon (The Tyrant's Heart or Boccacio in Hungary). (Magfilm/Italiana-Leone, 1981). Hungary/Italy. Directed by Miklós Jancsó). Script by Jancsó and Giovarina Gagliardo from stories by Boccaccio. Director of Photography, Janós Kende (Color). Starring Ninetto Davoli, László Gálffy, Theresa-Ann Savoy. 88 minutes.

ADDITIONAL FILMOGRAPHY:

Abadon see *Vampires*

Addicted to Murder. (Brimstone Productions, 1995). USA. Produced, Directed and Edited by Kevin J. Lindenmuth. Written by Lindenmuth and Tom Piccirilli. Director of Photography, Lindenmuth. Music, Steve Maruzzelli, Hector Milia. Starring Mick McCleery (Joel Winter), Laura McLauchlin (Rachel), Sasha Graham (Angie), Bernadette Pauley (Kathy), Candice Meade (Sabrina), Jolee Becker (Allison), Gordon Linzner (Dr. Noland). 90 minutes.

The Addiction. (Fast Films, 1995). USA. Produced by Dennis Hann, Fernando Sulichin. Directed by Abel Ferrara. Written by Nicholas St. John [Abel Ferrara]. Director of Photography, Ken Kelsch (Black and White). Production Designer, Charles M. Lagola. Music, Joe Delia. Editor, Mayin Lo. Starring Lili Taylor (Kathleen), Christopher Walken (Peina), Annabella Sciorra (Casanova), Edie Falco (Jean), Paul Calderon (Professor), Kathryn Erbe (Student). 82 minutes.

Alabama's Ghost. (Ellman/Bremson, 1972). USA. Starring Lani Freeman, Pierre LePage, Turk Murphy.

Alfred Hitchcock Presents: Night Creatures. (A.H.F./Paragon/Michael Sloan, 1988). USA Television Episode. Directed by Richard J. Lewis. Starring Brett Cullen, Louise Vallance, Michael Rhoades, Jason Blicker, Ray James.

Anemia. (RAI-TV/Channel 3, 1986). Italy. Directed and Written by Alberto Abbruzzese and Achille Pisanit. Director of Photography, Angelo Sciarra. Production Designer, Nicola Rubertelli. Editor, Mirella Mencio. Starring Hanns Zischler (Umberto), Gioia Maria Scola (Marcella), Gerard Landry (Grandfather).

Bandh Darwaza. (Ramsay Films Combine, 1990). India. Produced and Directed by Tulsi Ramsay, Shyam Ramsay. Written by Dev Kisan, Shyam Ramsay. Director of Photography, Gangu Ramsay. Starring Hasmat Khan, Manjeet Kular, Kunika, Satish Kaul. 145 minutes.

Blade the Vampire Slayer. (New Line Cinema/Amen Ra Films, 1997). USA. Produced by Peter Frankfurt, Wesley Snipes, Bob Engelman. Directed by Steve Norrington. Written by

Below, Angie (Sasha Graham), the younger vampiress in *Addicted to Murder.*

David Goyer based on the Marvel Comic Book series. Director of Photography, Theo Van De Sante. Production Designer, Kirk Petruccelli. Editor, Paul Rubell. Starring Wesley Snipes (Blade), Stephen Dorff (Frost), Kris Kristofferson, Kevin Patrick Walls (Scream).

Blonde Heaven. (Torchlight, 1995). USA. Produced by Karen L. Spencer. Directed by Ellen Cabot [David DeCoteau]. Written by Kenneth J.Hall, Mark Millenko, Matthew Jason Walsh. Director of Photography, James Lawrence Spencer. Production Designer, John Zachary. Music, Reg Powell. Editor, Paul Petschek. Starring Julie Strain (Illyana), Raelyn Saalman (Angie), Michelle Bauer (Amanda), Joe Estevez (Carl), Alton Butler (Kyle), Jason Clow (Pluto), Mary Tudor (Natasha), Monique Parent (Viva). 80 minutes.

Blood & Donuts. (Live Entertainment, 1995). Canada. Produced Steven Hoban. Directed by Holly Dale. Written by Andrew Rai Berzins. Director of Photography, Paul Sarossy. Production Designer, David Moe. Music, Nash the Slash. Editors, Stephan Fanfara, Brett C. Sullivan. Starring Gordon Currie (Boya), Justin

Below, what can happen if you're out after *Darkness* falls in Kansas.

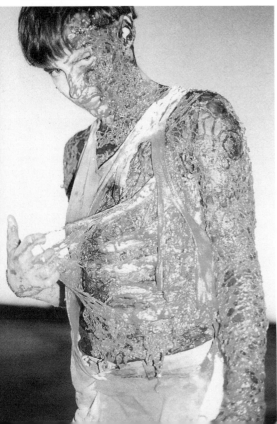

Louis (Earl), Helene Clarkson (Molly), Fiona Reid (Rita), Frank Moore (Pierce), Hadley Kay (Axel), David Cronenberg (Stephen). 88 minutes.

Blood-Suckers see *Pyushchye Krovy*

Buffy the Vampire Slayer. (WB-TV/20th Century Fox/Mutant Enemy/Kuzu/Sandollar, 1997). USA Television Series. Created by Joss Whedon. Starring Sarah Michelle Gellar (Buffy), Anthony S. Head, Nicholas Brendon, Alyson Hannigan, Charisma Carpenter.

Caress of the Vampire. (Brain Escape, 1996). USA. Produced by Frank Iffranove, Bob Gonzo. Directed and Written by The Beckerman Brothers. Director of Photography, Abad R. Rosa. Starring, Paulina Monet, Jessica English, Darien Price. 75 minutes.

Carmilla. (1987). Spain Television. Directed by Jaime Picas. Starring Marisa Paredes (Carmilla), Maria Enriquetta Caballeira. Based on the story by J. Sheridan Le Fanu.

Children of the Night see *Hijos de la Noche*

Chillers. (1988). USA. Directed by Daniel Boyd. Starring Jesse Emery, Marjorie Fitzsimmons, Laurie Pennington, Tom McGee.

City of the Vampires. (Salt City, 1994).USA. Produced, Directed, and Written by Ron Bonk. Director of Photography, Roger Spigette. Production Designer, Bo Carlisle. Music, Matthew Jason Walsh. Starring Walsh (Sam Helling), Ann-Marie O'Keefe, Pam Simmons, Noel Bonk (Legion). 83 minutes.

Close Encounter of the Vampire see *Vampire Jiangshi Papa*

Le Couer Petrifie: Carmilla. (FR3 Alsace, 1987). France Television. Directed by Paul Planchon. Based on the story by J. Sheridan Le Fanu. Starring Aurelle Doazan, Emmanuelle Meysignac (Carmilla), Marc Michel, Yvette Stahl.

Crazy Safari. (Win's Movies/Samico/ Golden Harvest, 1990). Hong Kong. Produced by J. and C. Heung. Directed by Chan Fu Lee. Starring Lam Ching Ying, Sam Christopher Chan, NiXau.

Cronos. (Universidad de Guadalajara/Fondo de Fomento a la Calidad Cinematografica/Iguana/Ventana/IMCINE, 1993). Mexico. Produced by Arthur Gorson, Bertha Navarro. Directed and Written by Guillermo Del Toro. Director of Photography, Guillermo

Navarro. Production Designer, Tolita Figuero. Music, Javier Alvarez. Editors, Raul Davalos, Paul O'Bryan. Starring Federico Luppi (Jesus Gris), Ron Perlman (Angel), Claudio Brook (Dieter de la Guardia), Margarita Isabel (Mercedes Gris), Tamara Shanath (Aurora Gris), Daniel Gimenez Cacho (Tito), Mario Ivan Martinez (Fulcanelli the Alchemist), Farnesio De Bernal (Manuelito), Juan Carlos Colombo (Funeral Director). 95 minutes.

Dark Waters see ***Karanik Sufa***

Darkness. (Norsemen/Film Threat, 1993). Produced, Directed and Written by Leif Jonker. Di-

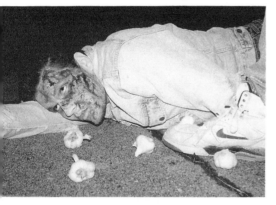

rector of Photography, Franklin Hardesty [Jonker]. Music, Michael Curtis, Billy Davis. Editor, John T. Chance [Jonker]. Starring Gary Miller (Tobe), Michael Gisick (Greg), Randall Aviks (Liven), Cena Donham (Kelly), Steve Brown (Jodie), Lisa Franz (Dianne), Bill Hooper (Glenn), Christopher Owen Michael (Steve), Brian Cardwell (Vampire). 90 minutes.

Dawn. (Shooting Gallery, 1991). UK. Produced, Directed and Written by Niall Johnson. Director of Photography, Nic Coleclough. Starring Elizabeth Rees, Geoff Sloan, Craig Johnson, Kate Jones Davies, Meg Whelan. 78 minutes.

Deadly Love. (Lifetime/ABC, 1995). USA. Starring Susan Dey (Rebecca Barnes), Stephen McHattie (Detective), Eric Peterson (Elliott).

Demonsoul. (Vista Street, 1995). UK. Produced by Daniel Figueroa, E. C. Kennedy [Elisar Cabrera]. Directed and Written by Kennedy [Cabrera], based on a story by Kennedy and Gerald Feifer. Directory of Photography, Alvin Leong. Music, Thomas Docherty. Editors, D. Kenrick, Stuart Lansdowne. Starring, Kerry Norton (Erica), Eileen Daly (Selena), Daniel Jordan (Dr Bucher), Janine Ulfane (Rosemary),

High and low garlic budgets: above, apparently a few cloves can go a long way on the anonymous night crawlers in *City of the Vampires*. Below, a consultation under a canopy of garlic between Van Helsing (Mel Brooks, center) and Seward (Harvey Korman) over the condition of Lucy (Lysette Anthony) in *Dracula Dead and Loving It*.

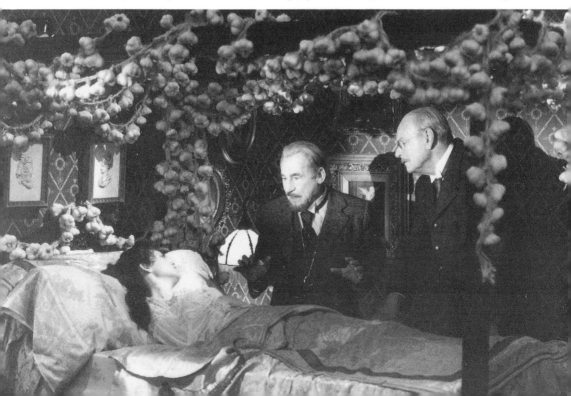

High and low budget eroticism. Above, a little blood-sucking, a little bondage: anonymous tramp vamps bend over a fresh kill in *Demonsoul*. Below, Salma Hayek as the snake-dancing vampiress Santanica Pandemonium in *From Dusk Till Dawn*.

Drew Rhys-Williams (Alex), Sue Scadding (Marilyn), Erich Redman (Richard Kurtz), Pixie Roscoe (Young Erica). 81 minutes.

Les Deux Orphelines Vampires. (1995). France. Directed by Jean Rollin.

Dr. Vampire. (Golden Harvest, 1990). Hong Kong. Produced by Anthony Chow. Directed by Jamie Luk. Starring Lam Bo Yi, Ellen Chan, Chan Shuk Lan, Crystal Kwok.

Dracula: Dead and Loving It. (Brooksfilms/Columbia/Castle Rock, 1995). USA. Produced and Directed by Mel Brooks. Written by Brooks, Rudy De Luca, Steve Haberman based a story by De Luca and Haberman and characters created by Bram Stoker. Director of Photography, Michael D. O'Shea. Production Designer, Roy Forge Smith. Music, Hummie Mann. Editor, Adam Weiss. Starring Leslie Nielsen (Dracula), Peter MacNicol (Renfield), Steven Weber (Jonathan Harker), Amy Yasbeck (Mina), Lysette Anthony (Lucy), Harvey Korman (Dr. Seward), Mel Brooks (Dr. Van Helsing), Mark Blankfield (Martin), Megan Cavanaugh (Essie), Clive Revill (Sykes). 90 minutes.

Dracula: Flesh and Blood see ***Mark of Dracula***

Dracula: Nocturnal Appetite (DNA) see ***Mark of Dracula***

Dracula's Hair. (Arto Studio/Rosfilmexport, 1992). Commonwealth of Independent States. Directed by Vadim Prodan. Written by Elga Lyndina.

Dragon against Vampire. (Golden Harvest, 1985). Hong Kong. Directed by Lionel Leung.

Elusive Song of the Vampire (1987). Taiwan. Directed by Takako Shira.

Embrace of the Vampire. (General Media/New Line/The Ministry of Film, 1994). USA. Produced by Matthew Ferro, Ladd Vance, Marilyn Vance-Straker. Directed by Anne Goursaud. Written by Rick Bitzelberger, Nicole Coady, Halle Eaton. Director of Photography, Suki Medencevic. Production Designer, Peter Stolz. Music, Joseph Williams. Editor, Teri Shropshire. Starring Alyssa Milano (Charlotte), Martin Kemp (Vampire), Harrison Pruett (Chris), Rachel True (Nicole), Jordan Ladd (Eliza), Rebecca Ferratti (Princess), Jennifer Tilly (Marika). 93 minutes.

Encounters of the Spooky Kind II. (Long Bojon Pictures, 1990). Hong Kong. Produced by Samo Hung. Directed by Lau Kwon Wai. Starring Samo Hung.

First Vampire in China. (Golden Harvest, 1990). Hong Kong. Directed by Yam Chun-Lu.

Friday the Thirteenth the Series: The Baron's Bride (Paramount/Variety Artists, 1987). USA Television Series Episode. Directed by Bradford May. Starring John D. LeMay (Ryan), Robey (Micki), Chris Wiggins, Tom McCamus (Vampire), Kevin Bundy, Susannah Hoffman.

From Dusk Till Dawn. (Dimension/Los Hooligans/Miramax/Band Apart, 1996). USA. Produced by Gianni Nunnari, Meir Teper. Directed by Robert Rodriguez. Written by Quentin Tarantino based on a story by Kurtzman. Director of Photography, Guillermo Navarro. Production Designer, Cecilia Montiel. Music, Graeme Revell. Editor, Rodriguez. Starring Harvey Keitel (Jacob Fuller), George Clooney (Seth Gecko), Quentin Tarantino (Richard Gecko), Juliette Lewis (Kate Fuller), Cheech Marin (Border Guard/Chet Pussy/Carlos), Fred Williamson (Frost), Ernest Liu (Scott Fuller), Salma Hayek (Santanica Pandemonium). Tom Savini (Sex

Below, posed against the neon flames of a vampire hell hole, Jacob Fuller (Harvey Keitel, left) and Seth Gecko (George Clooney) prepare to make a stand in *From Dusk Till Dawn*.

Machine), Michael Parks (Ranger). 108 minutes.

The Ghost Brigade (*The Killing Box, Grey Knight*). (MPCA, 1993). USA. Produced by Steve Stabler, Brad Krevoy. Directed by George Hickenlooper. Written by Matt Greenberg. Director of Photography, Kent Wakeford. Production Designer, Mick Strawn. Music, Bill Boll. Editor, Monte Hellman. Starring Adrian Pasdar (Capt. Harling), Corbin Bernsen (Col. Strayn), Cynda Williams (Rebecca), Ray Wise (Col. Thalman), Roger Wilson (Maj. Elkins), Billy Bob Thornton (Langston). 92 minutes.

Ghostly Vixen. (Golden Flare/Golden Harvest, 1990). Hong Kong. Directed by Wellson Chin. Starring Sandra Ng, Chan Pak Cheung, Amy Yip.

The Girl with the Hungry Eyes. (Kastenbaum/Smoking Gun, 1995). USA. Produced by Cassian Elwes, David Niven, Jr., Merton Shapiro, Michael and Seth Kastenbaum. Directed and Written by Jon Jacobs. Director of Photography, Gary Tieche. Production Designer, Clare Brown. Music, Paul Linder, Oscar O'Lochlainn. Editor, Ethan Holzman. Starring Christina Fulton (Louise), Isaac Turner (Carlos), Leon Herbert (Johnny), Bret Carr (Bud), Susan Rhodes (Mandy), Jon Jacobs (Henry), Leroy Jones, Omar Martinez. 85 minutes.

Grey Knight see ***The Ghost Brigade***

Haunted Cop Shot I and II. (Golden Harvest, 1984 and 1986). Hong Kong.

Hello, Dracula. (Golden Harvest, 1985). Hong Kong. Directed by Wong Chi-Chung. Starring Choi Yeung-Ming, Chan Chun-Leung.

Heartstopper. (Surbuban Tempe, 1989). USA. Produced by Charles A. Gelini. Directed and Written by John Russo, based on the novel ***The Awakening*** by Russo. Director of Photography, John Rice. Music and Editor, Paul McCollough. Starring Kevin Kindlin (Dr. Latham), Moon Zappa (Leonora Clayton), Tom Savini (Lt. Vargo) , John Hall, Tommy LaFitte, Michael J. Pollard. 96 minutes.

Hijos de la Noche (*Children of the Night*). (Tikal, 1997). México. Executive Producer, Iván

Below, Confederate officers instead of Eastern European noblemen: Major Elkins (Roger Wilson) gives the vampire's kiss to the mute descendant of African vampire hunters, Rebecca (Cynda Williams) in *Grey Knight* aka *The Ghost Brigade*.

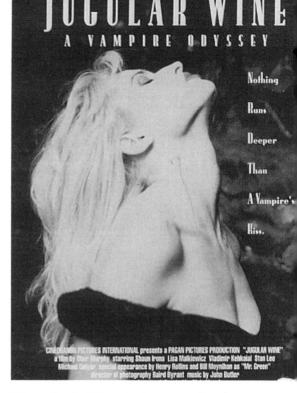

Suárez. Written and Directed by Marcos Villaseñor. Directors of Photography, Alfredo Zuñiga, Iván Suárez. Editors, Sebastian Pérez, Marcos Villaseñor, Iván Suárez, Alfredo Zúñiga. Music, Hades. Starring Lucio Gutiérrez (Mario), Bárbara Ruiz (Vanessa), Marcos Villaseñor (Martin), Iván Suárez (Claudio), Kathia Ibarrola (Mariana), Fabián Rivera (vampire), David Bello (Gael), David Arroyo, Daniel Rodríguez (officers)

The Hunger: Necros (Showtime/Telescene, 1997). USA/Canada Television Series Episode. Executive Producers, Tony Scott, Ridley Scott, Jeff Fazio, Robin Spry. Produced by Wendy Grean. Directed by Russel Mulcahy. Written by Steven and Audrey Salzburg, based on a story by Brian Lumley. Director of Photography, François Protat. Production Designer, Michel Proulx. Music, Mike Hewer, Michelle Currant. Editor, Patrick Moore. Starring Philip Casnoff (William Cobb), Celine Bonnier (Helma), Leonardo Cimino (Nero Lucchesi).

Huphyokwi Yanyo (*Vengeful Vampire Girl*). (Han Jin Enterprises, 1981). South Korea. Directed by Kim In Soo. Starring Choi Bong, Chong Hi Jung.

I Like Bats see *Lubie Nietoperze*

Interview with the Vampire, The Vampire Chronicles. (Geffen/Warner Bros., 1994). USA. Produced by David Geffen and Stephen Woolley. Directed by Neil Jordan. Written by Anne Rice based on her novel. Director of Photography, Phillippe Rousselot. Production Designer, Dante Ferretti. Music, Elliot Goldenthal. Editor, Mick Audsley, Joke Van Wijk. Starring Brad Pitt (Louis), Tom Cruise (Lestat), Christian Slater (Malloy), Stephen Rea (Santiago), Antonio Banderas (Armand), Kirsten Dunst (Claudia), Thandie Newton (Yvette), Indra Ove (New Orleans prostitute), Domiziana Giordano (Madeleine). 120 minutes.

Jiangshi Papa (*Close Encounter of the Vampire*). (Feiteng Film, 1986). Taiwan. Produced by Yuen Family. Directed by Yuen Woo-Ping. Written by Yuen Family. Director of Photography, Lam Chi-Wing. Starring Leung Ka-Yan, Yuen Cheung-Yan, Yuen Sun-Yi, Yuen Yat-Choch, Jan Chi-Jing. 96 minutes.

Jugular Wine. (Skywood, 1994). USA. Produced and Directed by Blair Murphy. Director of Photography, Baird Bryant. Music, John Butler.Starring Shaun Irons (James), Stan Lee (Pro-

Below, a fur-clad Alexandra (anonymous for union reasons) and her human lover Jason (Shaun Irons) in *Jugular Wine*.

fessor Baker), Frank Miller (Frank), Alexandra ("Alexandra"), Rachelle Packer (Monica), Meghan Bashaw (Meghan), Legion ("?"). 95 minutes.

Karmina. (Cinepix/Lux/SODEC, 1996). Canada. Produced by Ann Burke, Nicole Robert, Luc Vandal. Directed by Gabriel Pelletier. Written by Burke, Andree Pelletier, Gabriel Pelletier, Yves Pelletier. Music, Patrick Bourgeois, Gildor Roy. Editor, Gaetan Huot. Starring Isabelle Cyr (Karmina), Robert Brouillette (Phillipe), Yves Pelletier (Vlad), France Castel (Esmeralda), Gildor Roy (Ghislain). 104 minutes.

Karanik Sufar (*Dark Waters, Serpent's Tale*). (1995). Turkey. Directed and Written by Kutlug Ataman. Starring Gonen Bozbey, Daniel Chace, Metin Uygun.

Kathavai Thatteya Mohni Paye. (1975). India. Directed and Written by M.A. Rajaraman. Starring C.R. Patiban, Sanjivirajan, Desikan, Liza.

The Killing Box see *The Ghost Brigade*

Kindred: The Embraced. (Aaron Spelling Prods./Fox-TV, 1996). USA. Television Series. Produced by John Leekley. Starring Brian Thompson, Ed O'Ross, Stacy Haiduk, Blair Valk.

Kingdom of the Vampire. (Suburban Tempe,1992).USA. Executive Producer, David DeCoteau. Produced by Scott Plummer, J.R. Bookwalter. Directed by J.R. Bookwalter. Script by Matthew Jason Walsh based on a story by Walsh and Bookwalter. Director of Photography, Lance Randas. Production Designer, Anthony Ferrari. Music. Walsh. Editor, Darryl Squatmpump. Starring Matthew Jason Walsh (Jeff), Cherie Patry (Mom), Shannon Doyle (Nina), Tom Stephan (Sheriff), Joe Norcia. 90 minutes.

The Little Vampire. (Norflicks Prods., 1985). UK/Germany Television. Directed by Rene Bonniere. Starring Joel Dacks (Rudiger), Christopher Stanton (Anton), Marsha Moreau, Gert Frobe, Michael Gough.

The Lost Platoon. (AIP, 1989). USA. Directed by David A. Prior. Starring David Parry, William Knight, Sean Heyman, David Parry, Lew Pipes, Kimberly Casey. 92 minutes.

Love Me, Vampire. (Golden Harvest, 1987). Hong Kong. Directed by Irene Wang.

Lubie Nietoperze (*I Like Bats*). (Polish Film Corporation for Film Production, 1983). Po-land. Directed by Grzegorz Warchol. Starring Katarzyna Walter (Vampire), Marek Barbasiewicz, Malgorzata Lorentowicz, Jonasz Kofta, Edwin Petrykat.

My Lovely Monster. (Xenon/WDR/SFB, 1990). Germany. Produced, Directed and Written by Michael Bergmann. Additional Dialogue by Forrest J. Ackerman. Directory of Photography, Fernando Arguelles. Production Designer, Christian Bussmann. Music, Jurgen Walter. Editor, Ursula Hoff. Starring Silvio Francesco (Maximilian), Forrest J. Ackerman (The Master), Nicole Fischer (Nina), Matthias Fuchs (Father), Peter Voss (Duke). 84 minutes.

Mark of Dracula (*Dracula: Flesh and Blood, Dracula: Noctural Appetite [DNA]*). (Wildcat Entertainment, 1997). USA. Produced by Mark J. Gordon. Written and Directed by Ron Ford. Director of Photography, Clarke Jordan. Music, Ian Zapczynski. Starring Mark Allen (Dracula), Tonja McCoy (Suzanne Gayle), William Terry (Matt Gayle), Tim Sullivan (Dr. Warren), Ron Ford (Sheriff Cobb), Roxanne Coyne (Lucy Westenra), Randal Malone (Poe), Valerie Belardinelli (Kendal Lucas), Mark Sawyer (Hank Lucas).

Mom. (Elwes Prods./RCA-Columbia, 1989). USA. Produced by Leon Dudevoir. Directed and Written by Patrick Rand. Directory of Photography, David Sperling. Production Designer, Steven Michael Casey. Editor, Rand. Starring Mark Thomas Miller (Clay), Jeanne Bates (Emily), Brion James (Nestor), Stella Stevens (Beverly Hills), Claudia Christian (Virginia). 95 minutes.

Moon Legend. (Golden Harvest, 1991). Hong Kong. Directed by Joey Wang.

Mrs. Amworth. (BBC/CBC, 1975). UK/Canada. Directed by Alvin Rakoff. Starring Glynis Johns.

My Soul Is Slashed. (1992). Japan. Directed by Saka Kawamura, Shusuke Kaneko. Starring Ken Ogaka, Narumi Yaseda, Hikari Ishida.

Nadja. (Kino Link, 1994). USA. Produced by David Lynch, May Sweeney. Directed and Written by Michael Almereyda.Director of Photography, Jim Denault (Black and White). Production Designer, Kurt Ossenfort. Music, Simon Fisher-Turner. Editor, David Leonard. Starring Elina Löwensohn (Nadja), Suzy Amis (Cassandra), Galaxy Craze (Lucy), Martin Donovan (Jim), Peter Fonda (Dr. Van Helsing),

Jared Harris (Edgar), Karl Geary (Renfield). 100 minutes.

The Night Flier (New Amsterdam Entertainment, 1997). USA. Produced by Mitchell Galin and Richard P. Rubinstein. Directed by Mark Pavia. Written by Jack O'Donnell and Pavis, from the story by Stephen King. Production Designer, Burton Rencher. Music, Brian Keane. Editor, Elizabeth Schwartz. Starring Julie Entwisle (Katherine Blair), Miguel Ferrer (Richard Dees), Dan Monahan (Merton Morrison). Michael H. Moss (The Night Flier).

Night Hunter. (Amritraj Premiere Entertainment, 1995). USA. Produced by Don Wilson, James Holt. Directed by Rick Jacobson. Written by William A. Martell. Director of Photography, John B. Aronson. Music, Terry Plumeri. Editor, John Gilbert. Starring Don "the Dragon" Wilson (Jack Cutter), Melanie Smith (Raimy), Nicholas Guest (Bruno Fischer), Sid Sham (Sid O'Mack), Maria Ford (Tournier), Cash Casey (Detective). 86 minutes.

Night Owl. (Franco Prods., 1993). USA. Produced, Directed and Written by Jeffrey Arsenault. Directors of Photography, Pierre Clavel, Howard Krupa, Neil Shapiro (Black and White). Music, Rubio Hernandez, Mark Styles. Starring John Leguizamo (Angel, Caroline Munro (herself) Lisa Napoli (Frances),James Raferty (Jake), Karen Wexler (Zorha), Ali Thomas (Anne), David Roya (Dario), Holly Woodlawn (Barfly).

Night Shade. (SC Prods./Playboy, 1996). USA. Produced by Roger Collins. Directed by Nicholas Medina. Script by Sean O'Bannon. Director of Photography, James Spencer. Production Designer, Helen Harwell. Music, Revo. Editor, James Barwood. Starring Tim Abell (Scott), Teresa Langley (Jennifer/Electra), Tane McClure (Charmagne), Ross Hagen (Detective Crank), Don Scribner (Jack). 92 minutes.

Not of This Earth. (Showtime/Corman, 1996). USA Television. Executive Producer, Roger Corman. Produced by Mike Elliot. Directed by Terence H. Winkless. Written by Charles B. Griffith, Mark Hanna, and Charles Philip Moore. Starring Michael York, Elizabeth Barondes, Richard Belzer, Parker Stevenson. 92 minutes.

Outback Vampires (*The Wicked*). (Guild/Select, 1987). Australia. Directed by Colin Eggleston. Starring Brett Climo, Richard Morgan, Angela Kennedy.

Pao Dan Fei Che (*The Trail*). (Golden Harvest, 1983). Hong Kong. Produced by Xu Guanwen (Michael Hui). Directed by Ronny Yu. Written by Ronny Yu and Xu Guanwen. Director of Photography: Chen Xiaoming (James Chan). Starring Xu Guanying (Ricky Hui), Zhang Zeshi, Cheung Fat, Miao Tian, Tin Liang. 100 minutes.

Project Vampire. (NBV Prods., 1992). USA. Directed by Peter Flynn. Starring Myron Natwick (Dr. Frederick Klaus), Brian Knudson,

Below, more vampire cheesecake: Caroline (Ghetty Chasun) poses provocatively in *Red Lips*.

Mary-Louis Gemmill, Paula Randoi-Smith, Christopher Wof.

Pyushchye Krovy (*Blood-Suckers, Those Feed on Blood*). (Lenfilm, 1991). Directed by Eugeny Tatarsky. Written by Artur Makarov. Director of Photography,Konstantin Ryzhov. Starring Marina Vlady, Andrey Sokolov, Marina Maiko. Based on Alexei Tolstoy's "The Wurdalak." 110 minutes.

Red and Black. (1986). China. Directed by Andrew Kam Yuen.

Red Lips. (Video Void, 1995). USA. Produced by Christopher M. Harris. Directed and Written by Donald Farmer. Directors of Photography, Donald Farmer, Christopher Harris, Larry Mitchell, Mike Manikowski. Music, Murray. Editor, Chuck Barker. Starring Ghetty Chasun (Caroline), Michelle Bauer (Lisa), Danny Fendley (Tony), Francesca Natividad (Amy), Jasmine Pona (Gina), Mandy Leigh (Doctor), Matthew Adams (Nick).

Red Lips II. (Video Void, 1996).USA. Produced, Directed, and Written by Donald Farmer. Starring Debbie Rochon (Holly), J.J. North, Manon Kelley, George Stover.

El Retorno de los Vampiros. (1971). Spain. Directed by José María Zabalza. Starring Simón Andreu, M. Monterrey.

The Romance of the Vampires see *Xi Wo Yi Ge Wen*

The Secret. (HBO, 1990). USA Televison. Directed by Michael Riva. Starring Larry Drake, Grace Zabriskie, Mike Simmrin, Georgann Johnson, Stella Hall.

Serpent's Tale see *Karanik Sufar*

The Seven Vampires see *As Sete Vampiros*

Sherlock Holmes in Caracas. (Big Ben/Tiuna/Foncine, 1992). Venezuela. Directed by Juan E. Fresan. Starring Jean Manuel Montesinos (Sherlock Holmes), Gilbert Dacournan (Watson), Carolina Luzardo, Maria Eugenia Cruz.

Sleepover Massacre. (W.A.V.E., 1989). USA. Directed and Written by Gary Whitson. Starring, Launa Kane [Terri Lewandowski] (Vampiress), Clancey McCauley, Carol Livingston, Chris Stonage. 95 minutes.

Sorority House Vampires. (Digital Vision Ent., 1992). USA. Directed by Geoffrey de Valois. Starring Natalia Bondurant, Eugenie Bondurant, Rachel Wolkow, Shay More, Kenny Gibbs, Robert Bucholz (Vlad).

As Sete Vampiros (*The Seven Vampires*). (Embrafilme/Superoito Productions, 1986). Brazil. Produced by Ivan Cardoso, Mauro Taubman, Claudio Klabin, Antonio Avilez, Flavio Holanda. Directed by Cardoso. Written by R.F. Lucchetti. Director of Photographay, Carlos Egbert Silveira. Starring Alvamar Tadei, Andrea Beltrao, Ariel Coehlo, Bene Nunes, Cole Carlo Mossi, Danielle Daumerri. 100 minutes.

Below, famous last names: Rafe Guttman (Dennis Miller) and his client Katherine Verdoux (Erika Eleniak) in the parody *Bordello of Blood*.

Spooky Family. (Golden Harvest, 1989). Hong Kong. Produced by Ng Ken Hoi, Chan Wui Yuen. Directed by Chin Yue Sang. Starring Kent Cheng, Nina Li Chi, Pauline Wong.

State of Decay. (BBC, 1980). UK Television. Directed by Peter Moffatt. Starring Tom Baker, Lalla Ward, Matthew Waterhouse, William Lindsay, Rachel Davies.

Strange Love. (Laurel Entertainment, 1986). USA Television. Directed by Ted Gershuny. Starring Harsh Nayyar, Patrick Kilpatrick, Marcia Cross.

Superboy: Run, Dracula, Run. (Cantharus Prods./Salkind, 1990). USA Television Series Episode. Directed by Richard Lewis. Starring Gerard Christopher (Superboy), Stacy Haiduk (Lana), Kevin Bernhardt, Louise Seeger Crune.

Supernatural: Dorabella (BBC, 1977). UK Televison Series Episode. Directed by Simon Langton. Starring Jeremy Clyde, David Robb, Ania Marson, Jonathan Hyde.

Tales from the Crypt Presents: Bordello of Blood. (Universal, 1996). USA. Produced by Gilbert Adler, Alexander Collett, A.L. Katz. Directed by Gilbert Adler. Written by Adler, Bob Gale, A.L. Katz, Robert Zemeckis. Director of Photography, Tom Priestley, Jr. Production Designer, Gregory Melton. Music, Chris Boardman. Editor, Stephen Lovejoy. Starring Angie Everhart (Lillith), Dennis Miller (Rafe), Erika Eleniak (Katherine), Chris Sarandon (Reverend), Corey Feldman (Caleb), Aubrey Morris (McCutcheon). 87 minutes.

Those Feed on Blood see *Pyushchye Krovy*

Tiempos Duros para Drácula. (Aitor/Espacio Prods.,1976). Spain/Argentina. Directed by Jorge M. Darnell. Starring José Luiz Lifante, Miguel Ligero, María Noel.

Toothless Vampires. (1987). Hong Kong. Directed by Lee Hun Yu.

The Twilight Zone: Monsters. (CBS/Persistence of Vision, 1986) USA Television Series Episode. Directed by B.W.L. Norton. Starring Ralph Bellamy (Emile), Oliver Robins (Toby), Kathleen Lloyd, Bruce Solomon.

Twisted Tales: Hungry Like A... Bat? (Brimstone/One on One, 1991). USA. Directed, Written, Photographed, and Edited by Kevin Lindenmuth. Music, Mike O'Brien. Starring, Mick McCleery (Charlie), Laura McLauchlin (Allison), Theresa Oliva (Dr. Goodman), Arija Bareikis (Tracey).

The Trail see *Pao Dan Fei Che*

The Ultimate Vampire. (Eagle Films/Newport Entertainment, 1991). Hong Kong. Produced by

Above, role reversal from *Addicted to Murder*, Laura McLauchlin as Allison and Mick McCleery as Charlie the vampire in *Twisted Tales*. Below, more bondage, bloodletting, and big fangs, the video box from the ultra-low budget *Vampire Brides*.

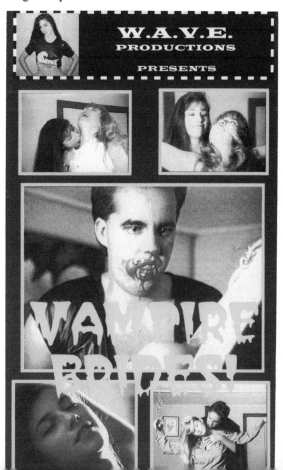

Above, Maximilian's (Eddie Murphy) mind is on loftier endeavors as his ghoul Julius (Kadeem Hardison) drags his coffin upstairs in *Vampire in Brooklyn*.

Wong Ying, Leung Wai Fun, Mak Tak. Directed by Lau Wai Keung. Starring Lam Ching Ying, Chin Siu Ho, Carrie Ng, Lui Xun.

Valerie. (1991). USA. Directed by Jay Lind. Starring Debbie Rochon, Austin Pendleton, Maria Pechukas. Based on "Carmilla" by J. Sheridan Le Fanu.

Vampire Brides (W.A.V.E., 1993) USA. Directed and Written by Gary Whitson. Starring Terri Lewandowski (mother), Christine Cavalier (daughter), Dave Castiglione (master vampire), Michelle Caporaletti, Cristie Clark (brides), Aven Warren (the Zombie).

Vampire Centerfolds. (1996). USA. Produced by Geoffrey de Valois. Starring Jasmine Jean, Tonya Qualls, Joan A. Teeter, Kim Blair, Barbara Savage, Liddy Roley, Heather LeMire, Kathy Presgrave, Missy Browning, Carrie Janisse, Eugene Bondurant, Doria Rone, Julie Covarrubias, and Beth Ann Rible.

The Vampire Conspiracy. (Sierra Sky Entertainment/Digital Entertainment, 1995). USA. Executive Producers, Gary B. Horton, Geoffrey de Valois. Co-Producer, John La Monte. Directed by de Valois. Written by de Valois and La Monte. Director of Photography, Michael Goi. Music, William Ashford. Editor, Chris R.

Leong. Starring Heather Le Mire (Lisa), Jasmine Jean (Vampire Centerfold), Floyd Irons (Dr. Keaton), Megan Crawford (Susan), Michaella Stoicova (Katja), Joan A. Teeter (Jana), Liddy Roley (Melissa), Barbara Savage (Allison). 95 minutes.

Vampire in Brooklyn. (Paramount, 1995). USA. Produced by Mark Lipsky. Directed by Wes Craven. Written by Michael Lucker, Charlie Murphy, Chris Parker. Director of Photography, Mark Irwin. Production Designer, Gary Diamond. Music, J. Peter Robinson. Editor, Patrick Lussier. Starring Eddie Murphy (Maximilian/Preacher/Guido), Angela Bassett (Rita), Allen Payne (Justice), Kadeem Hardison (Julius), John Witherspoon (Silas), William Blount (Deacon Brown), W. Earl Brown (Thrasher), Joanna Cassidy (Dewey), Ray Combs (Game Show Host), Zakes Mokae (Dr. Zeko), Simbi Khali (Nikki), Nick Corri (Anthony). 100 minutes.

Vampire Journals. (Full Moon Studios, 1997). USA. Executive Producer, Charles Band. Produced by Vlad Paunescu. Directed and Written by Ted Nicolaou. Director of Photography, Adolfo Bartoli. Production Designer, Valentin Calinescu. Music, Richard Kosinski. Editor, Gregory Sanders. Starring Jonathon Morris

(Ash), Kirsten Cerre (Sofia), David Gunn (Zachary), Ilinka Goya (Cassandra), Dan Condurache (Anton), Starr Andreeff (Iris). 92 minutes.

Vampire Kids. (Chung Sing Film Co./High Grow Films/D&B, 1991). Hong Kong. Produced by Cheung Shik Kui. Directed by Lee Pak Ling. Starring Billy Lau, Sandra Ng, Amy Ip, Shing Fu On.

Vampire Knights. (Peterson-Dodson, 1987). USA. Produced by Daniel Peterson and James Dodson. Directed by Daniel Peterson. Written by Peterson. Director of Photography, Thomas Callaway. Starring. Ken Abraham, Billy Frank, Daniel Peterson, Robin Rochelle, Thomas Kingsley. 90 minutes.

Vampire on Bikini Beach. (Maldonado/Bartlett, 1988). USA. Produced by Richard A Jones. Directed by Jerry Brady. Written by Max Headley. Production Designer, Daniel Cahmi, David Holland. Starring Jennifer Badham (Judy), Todd Kaufmann (Harold), Stephen Matthews (Bob), Nancy Rogers (Kim), Amanda Hughes (Clarke).

The Vampire Trailer Park. (Cinemondo, 1991). USA. Directed by Steve Latshaw. Starring Robert Shurtz, Patrick Moran, Blake Pickett, Bentley Little, Michael Street.

Vampire vs. Vampire. (Golden Harvest/Diagonal Pics, 1989). Hong Kong. Produced by Leonard Ho. Directed by Lam Jing Ying. Starring Lam Jing Ying, Chin Siu Ho, Liu Fong, Sandra Ng.

Vampire Vixens from Venus. (Filmline/Austin Film Group, 1995). USA. Produced Directed and Written by Ted A. Bohus.Director of Photography, Curtis Mattikow. Music, Ariel Shallit. Editor, Katia Milani. Starring Leon Head (Detective), Michelle Bauer (Shampay), Theresa Lynn (Shirley), J.J. North (Arylai), Leslie Glass (Omay), Charlie Callas (Bartender), John Knox (Jack), Joseph Pallister (Arnold). 90 minutes.

Vampirella. (Concorde-New Horizon/Showtime/Sunset Films, 1996). USA Television. Produced by Roger Corman, Paul Hertzberg, Jim Wynorski. Directed by Wynorski. Written by Gary Gerani based on the comic book character. Director of Photography, Andrea V. Rossotto. Music, Joel Goldsmith. Editor, Richard Gentner. Starring Talisa Soto (Vampirella), Roger Daltrey (Vlad/Jamie Blood), Richard

Joseph Paul (Adam Van Helsing), Brian Bloom (Demos), Corinna Harney (Sallah), Rusty Meyers (Quinn), David B. Katz (Forrest J. Ackerman), Angus Scrimm (High Elder). 82 minutes.

Vampire's Breakfast. (1986). Hong Kong. Directed by Wong Chun.

The Vampire's Embrace. (1991). USA. Directed by Glen Andreiev.

The Vampire's Rope (Vinovata Li Ya). (Nord Co., 1992). Commonwealth of Independent States. Directed by Nikolai Gibu. Written by Klara Luchko and Zinaida Chirkova. Director of Photography, Yuri Mikhailishin. Production Designer, Ilya Jovu and Irina Ostanovko. Music, Yevgeni Doga. Starring Korina Druk, Dmitri Kryuchkov, Svetlana Kryuchkova, Klara Luchko, Andrei Myagkov, Vyacheslav Shalevich, Mikhai Volontir.

Vampires (Abadon). (Scala, 1988). USA. Produced and Directed by Len Anthony. Written by James Harrington, Len Anthony. Directors of Photography, Ernest Dickerson, Larry Revene. Production Designer, Cosmo Vinyl. Music, Chris Burke. Starring Duane Jones (Dr. Charles Harmon), Orly Benyair (Ione), Kit Jones (Young Abadon), Jackie Harmon (Madeline), John Bly (Mike).

Vampires. (Largo Entertainment, 1998). USA. Produced by Bill Todman, Joel Simon, Gerry Laffy, David Michaels, Directed by John Carpenter. Written by Don Jacoby and Carpenter, based on the novel by John Steakley. Starring James Woods (Jack Crow), Sheryl Lee, Daniel Baldwin, Maximillian Schell, Tim Guinee.

Vampires and Other Stereotypes. (Brimstone, 1992). USA. Produced, Directed, Written, and Edited by Kevin J. Lindemuth. Director of Photography, Tullio Tedeschi. Music, The Krypt. Starring Bill White (Ivan), Wendy Bednarz (Kirsten), Ed Hubbard (Harry), Rick Poli (Albert), Anna DiPace (Linda), Suzanne Scott (Jennifer), Mick McCleery (Erik), Laura McLauchlin (Rosa). 87 minutes.

Vampires from Outer Space. (1990). USA. Produced and Written by Gail Postal and Steve Postal. Directed by Steve Postal. Director of Photography, Steve Postal. Starring Alan Ramey, Angela Shepard, Jennifer Tuck. 114 minutes.

Vampires Settle on Police Camp. (World Power/Top Sun, 1991). Hong Kong. Directed

Above, newly created vampire Heather (Jennifer Huss) after being initiated by Tasha (Jenny Wallace, below) in *Vamps Deadly Dreamgirls*.

by Chan Chi Wah. Starring Sandra Ng, Kong Yan Yin, Billy Lau.

Vamps Deadly Dreamgirls. (B+ Productions, 1995). USA. Produced, Directed and Written by Mark Burchett and Michael D. Fox. Director of Photography, Jeff Barklage. Music, Steve Gatch, J. Storm, Aaron Mahoney. Editor, Fox. Starring Jennifer Huss (Heather), Paul Morris (Seamus), Jenny Wallace (Tasha), Amber Newman (Randi), Stacey Sparks (Tabitha), Charles Cooper (Max). 87 minutes.

The Vampyr: A Soap Opera. (BBC, 1992). UK Television. Producerd by Janet Street-Porter. Directed by Nigel Finch. Libretto by Charles Hart, from a story by Street-Porter and Finch and the text by W.A. Wohlbrück, based on "The Vampyre" by John Polidori. Music, Heinrich Marschner. Starring Omar Ebrahim (Ripley, the Vampire), Philip Salmon (Alex), Winston (High Priestess of Satan), Willemijn Van Gent (Ginny), Roberto Salvatori (Berkeley), Colenton Freeman (George), Roy Gregory (Police Inspector).

The Vampyre War. (Rosebud Entertainment 1997). USA. Producer by Gene Kirkwood. Directed by Hugh Parks. Written by William D. Malone and Jeffrey Ward. Director of Photography, Gregg Pattterson. Production Designer, William Perretti. Starring Chris Sarandon, Amanda Plummer, Robert Englund, Maximilian Schell.

Vengeful Vampire Girl see *Huphyokwi Yanyo*

Vinovata Li Ya see *The Vampire's Rope*

The Waiting Game. (Laurel Ent./ABC, 1990). USA Television. Directed by John Fox. Starring Doug McKeon, Stephen Burleigh, Anthony Battaglia, Gail Mayron.

The Wicked see *Outback Vampires*

Witchcraft VII: Judgment Hour. (Vista Street, 1996). USA. Produced by Michael Feifer. Directed by Michael Paul Girard. Written by Peter Fleming. Director of Photography, Denis Maloney. Production Designer, Helmut Dusek. Music, Miriam Cutler. Editor, Tony Miller. Starring David Byrnes (Will), April Breneman (Keli), Alisa Christensen (Lutz), John Cragen (Garner), Loren Schmalle (Martin), Ashlie Rhey (Rachel), Mai-Lis Holmes (Sally). 90 minutes.

Xena: Warrior Princess: Bacchae. (Universal/Renaissance, 1997). USA Television Series Episode. Executive Producer, Robert Tapert. Starring Lucy Lawless (Xena), Renee O'Connor, Anthony Ray Parker.

Xi Wo Yi Ge Wen (*The Romance of the Vampires*). (Tai Seng/Bravo, 1994). Hong Kong. Directed by Ricky Lau Koon-Wai. Starring Louie Unyuen Siu-Cheung, Ben Lam Kwok-Pun.

Young Dracula. (Cantharus Prods./Salkind, 1989). USA Television. Directed by David Nutter. Starring Gerard Christopher, Stacy Haiduk, Kevin Bernhardt, Lloyd Bochner.

Vampire Redux:
Other Studies of the Vampire Film

Having now studied the vampire film for more than two decades—which is also the span of time between the first and third editions of this book—we no longer feel compelled to justify our efforts by the assertion that all these films are serious business. Obviously we are being a bit waggish with that remark; but from the early days of the silent era, horror has been as much a part of mainstream filmmaking as of independent and schlock production. As for vampire films, as the sub-title of the newest edition of our own study indicates, "from *Nosferatu* to *Interview with the Vampire*," major directors have worked in the genre. Unfortunately like much of the ad art that accompanies the release of the films themselves, many of the books on the subject have taken a sensationalistic approach. The dripping red letters on the dust jacket of the first edition of our book seem merely tacky by comparison to some recent publications, such as **The Vampire Interview Book**, which features a yellow-eyed, fangs-bared (and eyebrows-arched) Ben Cross, or Robert Marrero's **Vampire Movies** which displays a reticulated and anamorphosized set of fangs on its cover. Images from the 70s, like the bats over a full moon rising behind a castle in **The Dracula Scrapbook** or the line screen rendering of a sneering Christopher Lee on Donald Glut's **The Dracula Book** (1975), seem staid by comparison.

The point is that vampires and their bloodsucking activities may be amusing and/or titillating to many movie-goers, but, as we have noted, the tradition of vampires in myth and serious literature goes back for centuries. The wide range of other poets, dramatists, philosophers, and artists from Byron, Keats, and Baudelaire to Goethe, Dumas, and Gautier has irrevocably legitimized the vampire as a figure in "serious" fiction and made this preternatural monster into something of a Romantic archetype.

Since our earliest writing on the subject, our perspective has been of film critics writing about a sub-genre that happens to feature strange and frightening
supernatural beings. The vampire is not always a Romantic protagonist, not
necessarily a protagonist of any sort, as that designation often falls to those who
oppose him or her. But all of the characters in vampire fiction, supernatural or
human, have a dramatic, mythical, and literary validity.

The earliest discussions of vampire films, in the 60s, were as chapters or sub-
sections of works surveying the horror film in general; and, as such, they were
necessarily sketchy. Ron Borst's series of articles for *Photon* magazine and the
first edition of Walt Lee's **Reference Guide to Fantastic Films** in 1972 helped to
established a rough consensus of the what titles constituted the basic vampire filmography. The first book-length study, **The Vampire on Screen** (1965), was
from the president of the Count Dracula society, Donald A. Reed. Even as "fan"
book, this hapless volume is amateurish, unenlightening, and, like its subject,
best left interred. The first quasi-scholarly book-length studies appeared in the
70s. Whatever the cover illustrations may have connoted, our book and several
others took a straight approach in that decade.

Donald Glut's **The Dracula Book** is a comprehensive and scholarly discourse
that opens with a history of Vlad the Impaler and features a picture of his
"authentic remains" housed, as luck would have it, in the Weird Museum in
Hollywood. We have not personally visited this institution and cannot speak
about the legitimacy of these bones; but the first chapter sets the tone for Glut's
book. He continues his survey–derived from an earlier book on vampires in history–in the next chapter, discussing legendary traits and actual figures such as
Elizabeth Bathory. All non-Dracula vampire films are lumped together in a
third chapter, "The Ancestors of Dracula," which concentrates on Polidori's
Lord Ruthven and Le Fanu's Carmilla. The remaining chapters are a chronology from *Nosferatu* onward–with occasional disgressions such as a few words
about *Black Sunday*. Glut mixes film history with plot summaries and personal
opinions in a discursive manner. The biggest problem with his book is that it is
now woefully out of date.

Unfortunately, the same problem holds true for both Barrie Pattison's **The
Seal of Dracula** (1975) and David Pirie's **The Vampire Cinema** (1977). Both are
profusely illustrated general surveys, although the designers seem intent on featuring dripping fangs and blood spurting from staked hearts, occasionally in
color. Both open with surveys of the silent era then group films geographically
and by sub-genres. Both have chapters on the "Sex Vampire[s]"; but Pattison's
tongue is a bit more obviously in his cheek with essays on "Cowboys, Spacemen,
and Nazi Beasts" or "Lust, Blood, and God." Despite the sometimes garish illustrations with monochrome washes and reticulated effects, both authors treat
their subject seriously; and Pirie goes deeper into selected areas, even beyond it
in praising directors certain directors such as Mario Bava and Willard Huyck.

While **The Celluloid Vampires: A History and Filmography, 1897-1979** by Michael J. Murphy is a notch above some more recent disgraces, it offers very little in the way of serious thought or analysis on the vampire sub-genre. It is mainly notable for its filmography which is fairly complete at over 140 pages, although one could wish for more credits on each film. If Murphy has a failing which is fatal to many researchers it is putting too much stock in publicity releases. This lead him to list two projects—one by Ken Russell entitled *Bram Stoker's Original Dracula* and one by Roger Vadim, *Vadim's Dracula*—as bona fide, completed feature films. Unfortunately neither was made; but for the most part Murphy's facts are reliable.

His text however is another matter. He begins the book discussing the early history of photography and film technology but, mysteriously, never relates it to vampire films. Why is it there then? He calls one of his chapters "A Return to Tradition" but never explains how the period under discussion—the 1960s and 70s—were in any way retrograde or traditional. If anything, vampire films from that period were groundbreaking and revisionist with increased emphasis on Freudian psychology, sexual explicitness, and self-reflexive satire. Most of the text consists of lengthy plot summaries of the films that Murphy considers important; and when he does venture into criticism/analysis he depends on others for opinions. Strangely enough the "authorities" he quotes are not critics or film historians but stars like Christopher Lee and Robert Quarry. Most readers would probably prefer Murphy's assessment of Tod Browning's *Dracula* than Lee's or Quarry's respective put-downs of the film. Murphy's bibliography is very sketchy.

Martin V. Riccardo's 1983 book, **Vampires Unearthed: the Complete Multimedia Vampire and Dracula Bibliography**, is an obscure little book that we've never encountered outside of a specialty library. Riccardo is a professional hypnotist and vampire amateur; and this modest volume bespeaks the latter status. Still, however scant its filmographic information, it is soundly researched.

One can always hope that a university publication will at least have a critical position and some seriousness of intent; and in that respect Gregory Waller's **The Living and the Undead from Stoker's Dracula to Romero's Dawn of the Dead** (1986) does not disappoint. What it lacks in filmography (it has none), it makes up for in insightful and thought-provoking discussion. Waller's thesis is that movies and literature about the "undead"–he includes vampires within the larger "genre" of films dealing with the undead–are at their core explorations of the issue of survival. He sees these works delineating a battle between the human desire for continuity and immortality and an equally strong desire for death and closure. The ambivalence humans feel towards these opposing issues inform most undead films, some falling on the side of closure and what Waller calls the "butcher work" (for instance, Tod Browning's *Dracula*) and some on immortality (John Badham's *Dracula*).

In developing his thesis Waller relies heavily on Freud, particularly **Totem and Taboo,** as well as structuralist critic Tzvetan Todorov and semiologist Christian Metz. All his chapters are meticulously organized, his research annotated, and his analysis carefully delineated. Waller is also remarkable in that he does not confine himself to the traditional canon of "great" vampire films. In one chapter he analyzes *Horror of Dracula* and attendant Hammer films alongside Jesus Franco's *El Conde Drácula*. He is perspicacious enough to discern the "thought" and "control" Franco demonstrates in his film rather than just dismissing him as a quirky minor director working with a minuscule budget. He also discusses the film as an alternate reworking of the Dracula legend.

In another portion of the book Waller devotes an entire chapter to a comparison of Dan Curtis' TV *Dracula* and the BBC production starring Louis Jourdan. Both films were watershed works in their own way, revising old concepts of the Dracula myth as well as experimenting with new ones. The Curtis *Dracula* of course created the whole Romantic back story for the main character from which other filmmakers have drawn, most notably Coppola in *Bram Stoker's Dracula*.

Waller's analysis of George Romero's zombie films, *Night of the Living Dead, Dawn of the Dead*, etc., near the end of the book further reinforces his critical position. He quotes film critic Robin Wood's observation that most horror films feature "normality threatened by the monster" and then demonstrates how Romero's films express an ambiguity towards the "butcher work" of destroying the "immortal monsters." In these films individual destruction has turned into mass extermination in an attempt to bring closure and stamp out the "threat" of immortality. Waller's book is not easy reading. He is an academic and his analysis sometimes is fairly dense. But in a field filled with sensationalist frou frou and misinformation, this book is an oasis.

John Flynn's **Cinematic Vampires: The Living Dead on Film and Television, from The Devil's Castle to Bram Stoker's Dracula** (which must certainly be one of the most long-winded titles of 1992) is simply stated a "must-avoid." The text is riddled with errors and misinformation, so many that the entire space of this Appendix could be devoted to its shortcomings. The kind of errors Flynn wallows in are not the honest ones. As we've said, most film historians and critics make mistakes while delving into the morass of contradictory information about motion pictures. We certainly include ourselves, as for example when we previously included the non-film *Culte du Vampire*. Vampire films, in particular, are hard to research. But Flynn's work is purely (or should we say, "impurely") shoddy; and this is particularly unacceptable from a book that retails for over forty dollars.

Early in the text the reader is treated to a discussion of Louis Feuillade's (called by Flynn "Fevillade") serial *Les Vampires* about which Flynn blithely claims that the thieves are actual vampires, when the only vampiric element in the films are the costumes and the name of the gang. It is obvious that he has never seen the series as he goes off on a tangent ending with a discussion of August Strindberg. Louis Feuillade is a pioneer of filmmaking who should be known to any self-respecting film scholar. An equally egregious and less obvious blunder is his inclusion and discussion of Luis Buñuel's classic *Tristana*. Not only does he not know the country of origin for this film but he claims that Fernando Rey's character in the film is a vampire. Buñuel may be one of the fathers of surrealistic cinema and given to non-linear, dreamlike references, but no one except Flynn has discovered any vampiric allusions. Is this an example of surrealist criticism on the part of Flynn? Glaring errors such as these aside, the book has laughably mangled plot summaries, faulty credits, and marginal analysis.

Almost as bad as Flynn is Scott Nance's **Bloodsuckers, Vampires at the Movies** (1992). The back cover of **Bloodsuckers** screams out "caveat emptor" to anyone thinking of purchasing this oversized paperback. From behind a barrier the evil, leering face of Anthony Hopkins from *The Silence of the Lambs* emerges, only to be identified in the caption as Anthony Perkins portraying Van Helsing in Francis Ford Coppola's *Bram Stoker's Dracula*. How mixed up can one caption be? The reader who still insists on taking this book home is rewarded with pages filled with oversized fonts and plenty of blank space (for taking notes, possibly?). Some pages have has few as fifteen lines. Admittedly the book is only $14.95; but one still can expect a little more meat on the corpse for fifteen dollars. But what is most appalling is the duplication of some pages, so that you get the same superficial analysis of a film twice. Even his bibliography is skimpy, with only eight entries. Yet the book features no less than eleven pages of advertisement for other books by the same publisher (with such promising titles as **Rocky and the Films of Stallone** and **The Gunsmoke Years**). The filmography is even more remarkably inept. Foreign titles are alphabetized according to their articles ("*Il*", "*La*", etc.) This makes the process of finding films quite a challenge if you don't know the language. In addition Nance has fairly well-known vampire films like *Terror in the Crypt (La Cripta e L'Incubo)* as "starring Christopher Lee" with no additional credits while he spends almost a page describing the plot of the eminently forgettable *Teen Vamp* with Clu Gulager (and then reprinting the page for those who didn't get it the first time). Sadly, it is books like this which only give further justification to those who heap opprobrium on the field of horror film research and criticism in general.

Some bibliographies indicate that Robert Marrero published a book entitled **Vampires, Hammer Style** in 1974. We have never seen this volume; but if Marrero's other books are any indication, aside from the punning possibilities of the title, there is probably no reason to look for it. Marrero's other books, **Dracula-the Vampire Legend on Film** (1992) and **Vampire Movies** (1994), have scant value. The more recent book, which purports to be "encyclopedic" in scope, is just a list of titles with producer, director, and writer credits only (except for the occasional cinematographer credit thrown in at odd intervals). There are bits of plot summary and opinion and little else. The films are grouped not alphabetically, but by decade (the basic chapters) and then by year; and there is no index of any sort. This seems a rather poor organizational scheme for encyclopedic information. On its face, this would make finding a particular picture rather difficult. To further aggravate the problem the years used for sequencing are variously that of production, original release, and U.S. release. Of course, many of these years, as well as the plots, and other information are inaccurately given. So unless you're amused by Marrero's opinions, why would you want to look up a film in this book anyway? Marrero's entry on the Japanese *Chi o Suu Me*, which he discusses not under that title or its U.S. title, *Lake of Dracula*, but as *Bloodthirsty Eyes* is typical. Three-fourths is plot summary with allusions to Hammer influence and then the lament that "many vampire fans will never get to see" this picture. Marrero ends by asserting that "very little is known about" *The Evil of Dracula* [*Chi o Suu Bara*] from the same director. Perhaps Marrero knows very little about it; but, as other commentators have seen it, what other basis is there for his generalization? It seems to be only for the sake of tossing out *bon mots* that Marrero includes a couple of hundred words on a picture like *She was a Hippy Vampire* before concluding "you can't see the picture and it's not about vampires." So why is it here? By comparison the "very obscure, rarely-seen" but available on videotape *Pale Blood* features 45 words and two plot points, both of which are wrong. Marrero apparently has an extensive still collection, and, although some of the color stills have experienced a chroma shift, the photo reproduction is good quality, which is the only reason to own this book.

A digression: **Vampires: An Uneasy Essay on the Undead in Film** (1994). What is the point of this book? Jalal Toufic talks about the brakes on his car being down to 5% and driving to Pittsburgh between meandering musings on *The Passenger* and *Vincent and Theo* as Vietnam allegory. Occasionally his free-form ramblings stumble over a vampire trait or a vampire film. This is not much to show for 79 chapter headings and 248 footnotes. Perhaps Toufic believes that European style quotes indicate «artfullness» or, at least, an advanced word processor. Perhaps he believes that vampires can only be approached through "a commodious vicus of recirculation"; and what if Joyce had written a portrait of an artist as a young vampire? Perhaps Toufic should have spoken to George Romero or, at least, John Russo when he was in Pittsburgh.

This brings us to **The Vampire Encyclopedia** (1993) by Matthew Bunson and **The Vampire Book** (1994) by J. Gordon Melton, which is also a self-proclaimed "encyclopedia of the undead." The approach for both is quite similar but Bunson's survey is a slender 300 pages and Meltons, while essentially the same price, is thick (in terms of pages, that is, weighing in with 851 of them, some double column). Both have a *de riguer* red and black cover; but Melton's comes with a clove of garlic (not really, but it should). Bunson used a bat graphic as a *leitmotif*, but Melton has an added bonus: silhouettes of bats appear in every right margin, so that if you riffle the pages, their wings seem to go up and down.

Actually, neither is a bad book; but Melton's could have been so much better. Bunson's **The Vampire Encyclopedia** makes no claims to be more than an overview. The entries are all succinct but include all the major and many minor subjects. Still the vampire film is a limited sub-topic; and for a book published in 1993 not to mention *Interview with a Vampire* is a significant omission. The photographs are few, being confined to two signatures, but high quality. The list of films, as well as the bibliographies is highly selective; and there is no index.

The Vampire Book plumbs exactly the same waters but to much greater depth. It has scores of sources including obscure data culled from Martin Riccardo. Unlike Marrero's pitiful efforts, **The Vampire Book** is truly encyclopedic, at least for its 707 pages, where it dutifully details legends, real figures, books, play, writers, actors, and even fan clubs. After perfunctory introductions and a vampire chronology cribbed from Christopher Frayling's excellent book, **Vampyres**, the encyclopedia opens with.an entry on Forrest James Ackerman (!?). There is even a very poor photo of Ackerman holding what is either a crucifix or crossed breadsticks to fend off Nai Bonet in *Nocturna*. As if one low contrast snapshot was not enough a few pages later Donald A. Reed is captured presiding over his fabled Count Dracula Society while *Famous Monsters'* Ackerman guest lectures. Unfortunately, also unlike Marrero, most of the illustrations in this volume are bizarrely chosen and poorly reproduced. A very common shot of Lugosi posed with claw-like hands in the 1931 *Dracula* on page 178 is so blown out that his bow tie blends into his collar; and, despite some of the heaviest eye make-up in the history of vampire movies, the white of one eye almost leaks onto his cheek. In contrast (pun intended), the picture of Langella from the 1979 *Dracula* on page 183 makes him look more tan than George Hamilton in *Love at First Bite*.

The Vampire Book filmography is organized using a variant of the Marrero/Flynn method, by decade. While this organizing principal has some merit and precedent—most notably in Phil Hardy's comprehensive genre studies— we must ask, "What is wrong with a good, old-fashioned A-to-Z filmography?" Alphabetical structure works for Melton's main text, why not here? What is much worse is that the editor seems to have taken every entry from every previous vampire filmography and thrown it in, which means the egregious errors of Murphy, Flynn et al. are repeated: so, of course, poor old Louis Feuillade is spelled "Fevillade." Since his vampire serial is as far removed from bloodsuckers as a Burne-Jones' painting, it may be time either to spell his name correctly or just drop him. Not only filmmakers get short shrift, Burne-Jones is mentioned, with the wrong first name, as the painter who inspired Kipling's poem. Of course, entirely omitted is Edvard Munch, whose better-known (one would have thought) "Vampire" is a painting of a creature that might have inspired Carl Dreyer.

One has to expect certain errors and omissions in any book that tries to be comprehensive, but some of the errors in both text and filmography are just sloppy. The titles are accessible through the Master Index (which is less convenient but workable) but why are there duplicate listings for *Dracula* (1973) and *Dracula* (1974). This is the same film, Dan Curtis' version, which some entries date correctly by release year (1974) and others by production year (1973). The entry on "Television Movies" identifies it as a 1973 film "released in 1974"!? The same entry remarks that the BBC/Louis Jourdan *Count Dracula* is based on Gerald Savory's novel. Of course, it's the other way around: Savory's book is a novelization of his TV-script adaptation of Stoker. Mysteriously, neither of these versions is even in the filmography. The real 1973 *Dracula*, a Canadian MOW, is in the filmography. It is not in the "Television Movies" essay, and it is in the index. Confused yet? We certainly were.

Of course, included are plenty of non-vampire movies, porno vampires, and even some non-movies. Technically, *Black Vampire* is a real movie, i.e., it has a physical existence; but wouldn't it make more sense to identify it as a re-cut version of *Ganja and Hess* with altered credits and title? Speaking of *Altered States*, again we catch a fleeting glimpse of that lost film, Ken Russell's *Bram Stoker's Original Dracula*, which here is even given the annotation "This was a remake of *Dracula*," as if the reader could not deduce this from the title. Any commentator at this point might feel like *Monty Python*'s John Cleese looking for a refund on his dead parrot. *Bram Stoker's Original Dracula* is not a remake of anything. This is a non-existent movie. If *Lair of the White Worm* is any indication, it would probably have been a twisted, off-the-wall Russell romp; but it was never made. How hard is it to figure this out? Russell is not an obscure filmmaker. He's no Louis Fevillade. There are entire books on his work. Speaking of entire books, since most entries have bibliographic information at the end, what is really missing from **The Vampire Book**, despite page after page of vampire novels, plays, operas, and even ballets, is a Master Bibliography. The spawn of **The Vampire Book** is Melton's **VideoHound's Vampires on Video** (1997), which by definition is supposed to consider only vampire films available on videotape. This means that the Ken Russell version of *Dracula* is finally dropped because, after all, if a film does not exist, it cannot be on video. But somehow Russell's *Lair of the White Worm* is included. Too bad it's not a vampire film. Of course, further inspection of technical information which is in very small print reveals that many of the titles lack a video distributor. Does this mean that they are not on video or just that the video hound could not sniff out the details? You'd think with this many hands—there are over 40 names in the "Credits"—they could be a little more thorough. Some of the misinformation may be simple errors of judgment: is

The Thing a vampire film? (We don't think so.) Was it directed by Howard Hawks? (This is short shrift for Christian Nyby. Okay, Hawks was there on the set. Does this mean Steven Spielberg directed *Poltergeist?* We don't think so.) There are several appendices of marginal value, no bibliography, and the usual errors in which the Video Hound manages to turn executive producers into directors, actresses into production companies, cassette size into running time, and color into black-and-white (do dogs see in color?). For us, though, the ultimate indignity is listing the wrong URL for our website and commenting, most inaccurately, that our filmography only includes cast, running time, and production company. Does this mean they really didn't look at the videos either? At least the illustrations, replete with the Video Hound's attempt at zany captions, are decent quality.

At first glance, there does not seem to be much to recommend the 1993 British book, Stephen Jones' **The Illustrated Vampire Movie Guide.** It is almost all filmography but the credits are scant: year, director, stars (no character names) company, and a 25-words-or-less-style synopsis. Like so many others the organization is by decade, permitting Jones to throw in a few introductory comments at the beginning of each section. In striving for completeness, Jones also throws just about every film imaginable from *Wanda Does Transylvania* (annotation: "hardcore vampires") to Jerry Lewis' *The Ladies Man.* There are so many non-vampire titles that on some pages of this book, those titles actually outnumber the genuine articles. To complete the sense of superficiality, Jones rates the pictures in mock *Cahiers du Cinéma*-style from one to five bats. Ironically these admittedly "biased opinions" are given a fine tuning—many one-winged, half-bat increments—that the rest of the book could sorely use. Foreign titles are alphabetized in Italian, Tagalog, etc., except for pictures such as *Black Sunday* or *Blood and Roses* where the English title is used. Somehow Franco's *El Conde Drácula* becomes *Bram Stoker's Count Dracula* (British video title?).

At second glance, there may be a couple of reasons to acquire Jones' book. It is, indeed, an illustrated guide, full of high-quality stills and four-color poster reproductions in the pulp British tradition going back to Pattison's **Seal of Dracula.** And then there is his Appendix 1 (Appendix 2 is the Index?), a "selected" but extensive list of the vampire on the small screen. This list is purely alphabetical. Of course, Jones does muck that up by using the promotional titles first, so that, for instance, two television *Carmillas* are listed under *Mystery and Imagination* and *Nightmare Classics.* And, of course, do not look for the Dan Curtis/Richard Matheson *Dracula* in this section, as it is in with the feature films. The Index is by film titles only and the Bibliography (not Appendix 3) is the final insult. Not because neither edition of **The Vampire Film** is included. We are not British and we understand that someone confined to that tight little island could have rigorously researched the vampire film and not come across a book with that very title. But no mention of David Pirie's **Vampire Cinema**—

how can this be?.

As if two vampire encyclopedias were not enough, David Skal, the author of **Hollywood Gothic**, weighs in with **V is for Vampire** (1996). Given his background as a film commentator, it is understandable that Skal allots a greater proportion of words to motion pictures than either Bunson or lton. One wonders why he did not focus entirely on film and not bother going over the same "other" material with less depth than either predecessor. For example all three have a list of vampire novels in their appendices. Bunson cites about 150 novels in standard bibliographic format. Melton includes over 500, before and after 1970, with both original and reprint information. Skal's survey is by year with Title and Author only. Aside from serving as pure filler (with large font and plenty of space between entries, Skal fills 18 pages to Melton's 22 with less than half as many titles and no publisher data), there seems little point to Skal's redundant entries and appendices. Where Skal does excel is in the brief analyses of the films. The illustrations are good quality and not confined to signatures.

While Skal knows how to spell Feuillade, his filmography is heavily drawn from Jones' and replicates many of those errors plus a couple of his own (e.g. listing both *Midnight Kiss* and its alternate title *In the Midnight Hour* as if it were a different film released a year earlier). Again the organization is chronological and begins with a lot of unseen and/or lost silent films, many of which are not about supernatural beings. If this simple criterion were brought to bear, commentators on the vampire film would not have to concern themselves with how to spell Feuillade.

In the end, of course, we are prejudiced: not against competing volumes, but in favor of common sense and pertinent facts. There is hope yet that the 90s will yield a new book on vampire films as well-constructed as Pirie's or as thoughtful as Waller's. In the meantime, one might be well advised to stick with the classics.

Below, Christopher Lee drives home a point in *Taste the Blood of Dracula.*

Bibliography

BOOKS

Ackerman, Forrest J. **Mr. Monster's Movie Gold.** Virginia Beach/Norfolk: Donning, 1981.

Adkinson, Robert, Eyles, Allen and Fry, Nicholas. **The House of Horror.** London: Lorrimer, 1973.

Auerbach, Nina. **Our Vampires, Ourselves.** Chicago: University of Chicago Press, 1995.

Aylesworth, Thomas G. **Monsters from the Movies.** New York: J.B. Lippincott, 1972.

Baraket, Mark. **Scream Gems.** New York: Drake, 1977.

Barber, Dulan. **Monsters' Who's Who.** New York: Crescent, 1974.

Barber, Paul. **Vampires, Burial and Death: Folklore and Reality.** New Haven and London: Yale University Press, 1988.

Baxter, John. **Hollywood in the Thirties.** London: Tantivy, 1968.

Beck, Calvin. **Heroes of the Horrors.** New York: Macmillan, 1975.

_____. **Scream Queens.** New York: Macmillan, 1978.

Bedford, Michael and Dettman, Bruce. **The Horror Factory: The Horror Films of Universal, 1931-1955.** New York: Gordon, 1976.

Belmans, Jacques. **Roman Polanski.** Paris: Seghers, 1971.

Bojarski, Richard. **The Films of Bela Lugosi.** Secaucus, New Jersey: Citadel, 1980.

Bourgoin, Stephane. **Terence Fisher.** Paris: Edilig, 1986.

Brokaw, Kurt. **A Night in Transylvania: The Dracula Scrapbook.** New York: Grosset and Dunlap, 1976.

Brosnan, John. **The Horror People.** New York: St. Martin's, 1976.

Brunas, Michael, Brunas, John and Weaver, Tom. **Universal Horrors: The Studio's Classic Films.** Jefferson, North Carolina/London: McFarland, 1990.

Buckley, J.H. **The Victorian Temper.** New York: Vintage, 1964.

Bunson, Matthew, **The Vampire Encyclopedia.** New York: Crown, 1993.

Butler, Ivan. **Horror in the Cinema.** London: Tantivy, 1967.

_____. **The Cinema of Roman Polanski.** London: Tantivy, 1970.

Byrne, Richard B. **Films of Tyranny.** Madison, Wisconsin: College, 1966.

Carter, Margaret L. **Vampirism in Literature: Shadow of a Shade.** New York: Gordon, 1975.

Clarens, Carlos. **An Illustrated History of the Horror Film.** New York: G.P. Putnam, 1967.

Cohen, Daniel. **Horror in the Movies.** New York: Clarion, 1982.

_____. **Horror Movies.** New York: Gallery, 1984.

Copper, Basil. **The Vampire in Legend, Fact and Art.** London: Robert Hale, 1972.

Coppola, Francis Ford and Hart, James V. **Bram Stoker's Dracula: The Film and the Legend.** New York: Newmarket, 1992.

Coppola, Francis Ford and Isioika, Eiko. **Coppola and Eiko on Bram Stoker's Dracula.** San Francisco: Collins, 1992.

Coulteary, George De. **Sadism in the Movies.** New York: Medical, 1965. Translator: Steve Hult.

Cremer, Robert. **Lugosi: The Man Behind the Cape.** New York: Roy, 1951.

Daniels, Les. **Living in Fear: A History of Horror in Mass Media.** New York: Charles Scribner's, 1975.

Del Vecchio, Deborah and Johnson Tom. **Peter Cushing.** Jefferson, North Carolina/London: McFarland, 1992.

Derry, Charles. **Dark Dreams: A Psychological History of the Modern Horror Film.** Cranbury, New Jersey: A.S. Barnes and Co., 1977.

Dilliard, R.H.W. **Man and the Movies.** Louisiana: Louisiana State Univesity, 1967.

_____. **Horror Films.** New York: Simon and Schuster, 1976.

Dixon, Wheeler Winston. **The Charm of Evil: The Life and Times of Terence Fisher.** Metuchen, New Jersey: Scarecrow, 1991.

Dorn, Margit. **Vampirfilme und ihre sozialen Funktionen: ein Beitrag zur Genregeschichte.** Frankfurt: P. Lang, 1994.

Douglas, Drake. **Horror.** Toronto: Collier-Macmillan Co., 1969.

Dresser, Norine. **American Vampires: Fans, Victims, Practitioners.** New York: Random House, 1989.

Durgnat, Raymond. **Films and Feelings.** Massachusetts: MIT, 1967.

_____. **A Mirror for England.** New York: Praeger, 1971.

Edelson, Ed. **Great Monsters of the Movies.** New York: Doubleday and Co., 1973.

Eisner, Lotte. **The Haunted Screen.** Berkeley: University of California, 1969. Translator: Roger Greaves.

_____. **Murnau.** Berkeley: University of California, 1973.

Everson, William K. **Classics of the Horror Film.** Secaucus, New Jersey: Citadel, 1974.

Eyles, Allen (ed.). **The House of Horror, the Story of Hammer Films.** London: Lorrimer, 1973.

Faivre, Tony. **Les Vampires.** Paris: Le Terrain Vague, 1971.

Farson, Daniel. **Vampires, Zombies, and Monster Men.** London: Aldus, 1970.

_____. **The Who Wrote Dracula: A Biography of Bram Stoker.** London: Michael Joseph, 1975.

Fischer, Dennis. **Horror Film Directors, 1931-1990.** Jefferson, North Carolina/London: McFarland, 1991.

Florescu, Radu. **Dracula, Prince of Many Faces.** New York: Little Brown, 1990.

Flynn, John L. **Cinematic Vampires.** Jefferson, North Carolina/London: McFarland, 1992. [unreliable Filmography]

Frank, Alan G. **Horror Movies, Tales of Terror in the Cinema.** London: Octopus, 1974.

_____. **Monsters and Vampires.** London: Octopus, 1976.

_____. **The Horror Film Handbook.** New Jersey: Barnes and Noble,, 1982.

Frayling, Christopher. **Vampyres.** London: Faber and Faber, 1991.

Frid, Jonathan.**The Barnabas Collins Personal Picture Album.** New York: Paperback, 1974.

Friedman, Favius. **Great Horror Movies.** New York: Scholastic Book Services, 1974.

Garden, Nancy. **Vampires.** New York: J.B. Lippincott, 1973.

Gifford, Denis. **Movie Monsters.** London: Studio Vista, 1969.

_____. **A Pictorial History of Horror Movies.** New York: Hamlyn, 1973.

Glut, Donald. **True Vampires of History.** New York: HC, 1971.

_____. **The Dracula Book.** Metuchen, New Jersey: Scarecrow, 1975.

_____. **Classic Movie Monsters.** Metuchen, New Jersey: Scarecrow, 1978.

Golden, Christopher (ed.). **CUT! Horror Writers on Horror Film.** New York: Berkeley, 1992.

Grant, Barry Keith (ed.). **Planks of Reason: Essays on the Horror Film.** Metuchen, New Jersey: Scarecrow, 1984.

Gross, Edward and Shapiro, Marc. **The Vampire Interview Book.** New York: Image, 1991.

Guilley, Rosemary Ellen. **Vampires Among Us.** New York: Pocket Books, 1991.

_____. **The Complete Vampire Companion.** New York: MacMillan, 1994.

Haining, Peter (ed.). **The Ghouls.** New York: Stein and Day, 1971.

_____. **The Dracula Scrapbook.** New York: Crown/Brahhall House, 1976.

_____. **Midnight People.** New York: Popular Library, 1968.

Halliwell, Leslie. **The Dead That Walk.** New York: Continuum, 1988.

Hanke, Ken. **A Critical Guide to Horror Film Series.** New York: Garland, 1991.

Hardy, Phil. **The Encyclopedia of Horror Movies.** New York: Harper and Row, 1986. [General Filmography]

Hart, Douglas C. and Pohle, Robert W., Jr. **The Films of Christopher Lee.** Metuchen, New Jersey: Scarecrow, 1983.

Haworth-Maden, Clare. **The Essential Dracula.** New York: Crescent, 1992.

Hays, H.R. **The Dangerous Sex.** New York: Pocket, 1972.

Hill, Douglas. **Return from the Dead.** London: McDonald, 1970.

Hogan, David J. **Dark Romance: Sexuality in the Horror Film.** Jefferson, North Carolina/London: McFarland, 1986.

_____. **Who's Who of the Horrors and Other Fantasy Films.** Cranbury, New Jersey: A.S. Barnes, 1980.

Hoyt, Olga. **Lust for Blood: The Consuming Story of Vampires.** New York: Scarborough House, 1984.

Hurwood, Bernhardt J. **Monsters Galore.** New York: Fawcett, 1965.

_____. **Monsters and Nightmares.** New York: Belmont, 1967.

_____. **Vampires, Werewolves, and Ghouls.** New York: Ace, 1968.

_____. **Vampires.** New York: Quick Fox, 1981. [Filmography]

Huss, Roy and Ross, T.J. (Eds.) **Focus on the Horror Film.** New Jersey: Prentice-Hall, 1972.

Hutchinson, Tom. **Horror and Fanstasy in the Movies.** New York: Crescent, 1974.

Jones, Ernest. **On the Nightmare.** New York: Liveright, 1971.

Jones, Stephen. **The Illustrated Vampire Movie Guide.** London: Titan, 1993. [Filmography].

Kaplan, Stephen. **In Pursuit of Premature Gods and Contemporary Vampires.** New York: Vampire Research Center, 1976.

Kendrick, Walter. **The Thrill of Fear: 250 Years of Scary Entertainment.** New York: Grove Weidenfeld, 1991.

King, Stephen. **Danse Macabre.** New York: Everest House, 1981.

Konstantinos. **Vampires, The Occult Truth.** St. Paul, Minnesota: Llewellyn Publications, 1996.

Kracauer, Siegfried. **From Caligari to Hitler.** London: Princeton University, 1947.

Krafft-Ebing, Richard Von. **Psychopathia Sexualis.** New York: G.P. Putnam's Sons, 1965.

Kyrou, Ado. **Le Surrealisme au Cinéma.** Paris: Le Terrain Vague, 1963.

Laing, R.D. **Self and Others.** Middlesex: Penguin, 1971.

Leatherdale, Clive. **Dracula: The Novel and the Legend.** Wellingborough: Aquarian, 1987.

_____. **The Origins of Dracula.** London: William Kimber, 1987.

Lee, Christopher. **Tall, Dark, and Gruesome: An Autobiography.** London: W.H. Allen, 1977.

Lee, Walt. **Reference Guide to Fantastic Films.** California: Walt Lee, 1972 (three volumes). [General Filmography]

Lenne, Gerard. **Le Cinéma Fantastique et Ses Mythologies.** Paris: Éditions du Cert, 1970.

Lennig, Arthur. **Classics of the Film.** Wisconsin: Wisconsin Film Society, 1965.

_____. **The Count: The Life and Films of Bela Lugosi.** New York: G.P. Putnam, 1974.

Lentz, Harris M. **Science Fiction, Horror and Fantasy Film and Television Credits.** Jefferson, North Carolina/London: McFarland, Volume I: 1983, Volume II: 1989, Supplement: 1989.

London, Rose. **Zombie, the Living Dead.** New York: Bounty, 1976.

Lovecraft, H.P. **Supernatural Horror in Literature.** in **Dagon.** New York: Panther, 1969.

Lucas, Tim. **The Video Watchdog Book.** Cincinnati, Ohio: Video Watchdog, 1992.

Lucchetti, R. F and Cardoso, Ivan. **I Vampirismo: o Cinema em Panico.** Brasileiro: Editora Brasil-America (Fundacao do Cinema), 1990.

Ludlam, Harry. **A Biography of Dracula.** London: W. Foulsham, 1962.

McNally, Raymond T. and Florescu, Radu. **In Search of Dracula.** New York: New York Graphic Society, 1972.

_____. **Dracula: A Historical Biography of the Impaler.** New York: Hawthorn, 1973

McNally, Raymond T. **A Clutch of Vampires.** New York: Warner, 1975.

_____. **Dracula was A Woman.** New York: McGraw-Hill, 1983.

Manchel, Frank. **Terrors of the Screen.** New York: Prentice-Hall, 1970.

Manck, Gregory William. **Karloff and Lugosi.** Jefferson, North Carolina/London: McFarland, 1990.

Marrero, Robert. **Dracula: The Vampire Legend on Film.** Florida: Fantama, 1992.

Martinet, Pascal. **Mario Bava.** Paris: Edilig, 1985.

Mascetti, Manuela Dunn. **Vampire. The Complete Guide to the World of the Undead.** New York: Viking, 1992.

Masters, Anthony. **The Natural History of the Vampire.** New York: G.P. Putnam's Sons, 1972.

Masters, R.E.L. and Lea, Eduard. **Sex Crimes in History.** New York: Julian, 1963.

Maxford, Howard. **The A-Z of Horror Films.** Bloomington, Indiana: Indiana University Press, 1997.

Mayo, H. **On the Truths Contained in Popular Superstition.** London: William Blackwood and Sons, 1851.

Melton, J. Gordon. **The Vampire Book.** Detroit: Visible Ink, 1994. [Filmography]

_____. **Videohound's Vampires on Video,** Detroit: Visible Ink Press, 1997.

Mercer, Mick. **Hex Files: Goth, Vampire, Fetish, Pagan.** New York: Overlook, 1997.

Milne, Tom. **The Cinema of Carl Dreyer.** London: Tantivy, 1971.

Milne, Tom and Willemen, Paul. **The Encyclopedia of Horror Movies.** New York: Harper and Row, 1986.

Moore, Darrell. **The Best, Worst, and Most Unusual: Horror Films.** New York: Beekman House, 1983.

Moss, Robert F. **Karloff and Company, the Horror Film.** New York: Pyramid Publications, 1974.

Murphy, Michael J. **The Celluloid Vampires: A History and Filmography, 1897-1979.** Ann Arbor, Michigan: Pieran, 1979. [Filmography. Some late listings were never produced.]

Naha, Ed. **Horrors from Screen to Scream, an Encyclopedic Guide to the Greatest Horror and Fantasy Films of All Time.** New York: Avon, 1975.

Nance, Scott. **Bloodsuckers: Vampires and the Movies.** Las Vegas: Pioneer, 1992. [unreliable Filmography]

Newman, Kim. **Nightmare Movies: A Critical History of the Horror Film Since 1968.** New York: Proteus, 1984.

_____ (ed.). **The BFI Companion to Horror.** London: Cassell, 1997.

Noll, Richard. **Vampires, Werewolves, and Demons: 20th Century Reports in the Psychiatric Literature.** New York: Brunner/Mazel, 1992.

Page, Carol. **Bloodlust.** New York: Harper, Collins, 1991.

Pattison, Barrie. **The Seal of Dracula.** New York: Bounty, 1975. [Filmography with abridged credits]

Pearsall, Ronald. **The Worm in the Bud:The World of Victorian Sexuality.** London: Penguin, 1983.

Perrin, Claude. **Carl Dreyer.** Paris: Seghers, 1969.

Pirie, David. **A Heritage of Horror.** London: Gordon Fraser, 1973.

_____. **The Vampire Cinema.** New York: Crescent, 1977.

Pitts, Michael R. **Horror Film Stars.** Jefferson, North Carolina/London: McFarland, 1991.

Prawer, S.S. **Caligari's Children: The Film as Tale of Terror.** Oxford: Oxford University, 1980.

Praz, Mario. **The Romantic Agony.** London and New York: Oxford University, 1970.

Predal, Rene. **Le Cinéma Fantastique.** Paris: Seghers, 1970.

Prussmann, Karsten. **Die Dracula-Filme von Friedrich Wilhelm Murnau bis Francis Ford Coppola.** Munchen: W. Heyne, c1993.

Price, Vincent and Price, V.B. **Monsters.** New York: Grosset and Dunlap, 1981.

Reed, Donald. **The Vampire on the Screen.** Inglewood: Wagon and Star, 1965.

Riccardo, Martin V. **Vampires Unearthed.** New York: Garland, 1983. [Filmography with abridged credits]

Riva, Valerio and Volta, Ornella (Editors). **Histoire des Vampires.** Paris: Robert Laffont, 1961.

Rockett, Will H. **Devouring Whirlwind: Terror and Transcendence in the Cinema of Cruelty.** New York: Greenwood, 1988.

Ronay, Gabriel. **The Truth about Dracula.** London: Stein and Day, 1973.

Rudorff, Raymond. **The Dracula Archives.** New York: Arbor House, 1971.

Ruitenbeck, Hendrik M. (Editor) **Death:Interpretations.** New York: Dell, 1969.

Rycaut, Paul. **The Present State of the Greek and Armenian Churches.** London: John Starkey, 1678.

Searles, Harold F. **The Nonhuman Environment.** New York: International Universities, 1960.

Senf, Carol. **The Vampire in Nineteenth Century English Literature.** Bowling Green: Bowling Green State University Press, 1988.

Senn, Bryan and Johnson, John. **Fantastic Cinema Subject Guide.** Jefferson, North Carolina/London: McFarland, 1992.

Skal, David J. **Hollywood Gothic.** New York: W.W. Norton and Co., 1990.

_____. **V is for Vampire.** New York: Plume, 1996. [Filmography]

Soren, David. **The Rise and Fall of the Horror Film: An Art Historical Approach to Fantasy Cinema.** Columbia, Missouri: Lucas Bros., 1977.

Stacy, Jan and Syvertsen, Ryder. **The Great Book of Movie Monsters.** Chicago: Contemporary, 1983.

Stanley, John. **Revenge of the Creature Features Movie Guide.** Pacifica, California: Creatures at Large, 1988.

Stedman, Raymond W. **The Serials.** Oklahoma: University of Oklahoma, 1971.

Steiger, Brad. **Monsters, Maidens and Mayhem.** New York: Camera Arts, 1965.

Stoker, Bram. **The Illustrated Dracula.** New York: Drake, 1975.

Summers, Montague. **The Vampire: His Kith and Kin.** London: Routledge, Kegan Paul, 1928.

_____. **The Vampire in Europe.** London: Kegan Paul, Trench, Trubner, and Co., 1929.

Thorne, Ian. **Dracula.** Minnesota: Crestwood, 1977.

Twitchell, James B. **Dreadful Pleasures: An Anatomy of Modern Horror.** New York/Oxford: Oxford University, 1985.

_____. **The Living Dead: A Study of the Vampire in Romantic Literature.** Durham, North Carolina: University, 1981.

Varna, Devendra (Ed.). **Voices from the Vaults: Authentic Tales of Vampires and Ghosts.** Toronto: Key Porter, 1987

Volta, Ornella. **Frankenstein and Company.** Milan: Sugar, 1966.

_____. **Le Vampire.** Paris: Jean-Jacques Pauvert, 1962.

Walker, Alexander. **The Celluloid Sacrifice.** New York: Hawthorn, 1967.

Waller, Gregory A. **The Living and the Undead from Stoker's Dracula to Romero's Dawn of the Dead.** Urbana/Chicago: University of Illinois, 1986.

_____. **American Horrors: Essays on the Modern Horror Film.** Urbana/Chicago: University of Chicago, 1987.

Wathen, Stephen C. **The Great Universal Horror Films.** San Jose, California: Collector's Corner, 1975.

Weaver, Tom. **Interviews with B Science Fiction and Horror Movie Makers.** Jefferson, North Carolina/London: McFarland, 1988.

_____. **Science Fiction Stars and Horror Heroes.** Jefferson, North Carolina/London: McFarland, 1991.

Weldon, Michael. **The Psychotronic Encyclopedia of Film.** New York: Ballantine, 1983.

Wiater, Stanley. **Dark Visions: Conversations with the Masters of the Horror Film.** New York: Avon, 1992.

Willis, Donald C. **Horror and Science Fiction Films: A Checklist.** Metuchen, New Jersey: Scarecrow, 1972. [First volume with General Filmography]

_____. **Horror and Science Fiction Films II.** Metuchen, New Jersey: Scarecrow, 1982. [General Filmography]

_____. **Horror and Science Fiction Films III.** Metuchen, New Jersey: Scarecrow, 1984. [General Filmography]

Wolf, Leonard. **A Dream of Dracula.** New York: Little Brown, 1972.

_____. **The Annotated Dracula.** New York: Clarkson N. Potter, Inc., 1975.

_____. **Horror: A Connoisseur's Guide to Literature and Film.** New York: Facts on File, 1989.

_____. **The Essential Dracula.** New York:Knopf, 1993 [includes Filmography]

Wright, Dudley. **Vampires and Vampirism.** London: William Rider and Son, 1924.

Wright, Gene. **Horrorshows.** New York: Facts on Film, 1986.

PERIODICALS

Alpert, Hollis and Beaumont, Charles. "The Horror of It All." *Playboy.* March, 1959, page 68.

Amis, Kingsley. "Son of Horror Film." *Los Angeles Times Magazine.* October 26, 1969.

Arecco, S. "La Piega barocca del vampiro." *Filmcritica.* May, 1993, pages 227-231.

Armstrong, Michael. "Some Like It Chilled–Part 3:Theme–The Undead." *Films and Filming.* April, 1971, page 37.

Avant-Scene. "Special Issue–Vampires." No. 228, May 15, 1979.

Balbo, Lucas. "Unbearable Films and Terrible Headaches: A Conversation with Jess Franco." *Video Watchdog.* No. 1, pages 39-41.

Bean, Robin. "Dracula and the Mad Monk." *Films and Filming.* August, 1965, page 55.

Biodrowski, Steve. "Coppola's *Dracula*: The Untold Story." *Cinefantastique.* October, 1992, pages 12-13.

Biodrowski, Steve. "Coppola's *Dracula.*" *Cinefantastique.* December, 1992, pages 24-26.

Bizarre. "Cinema Fantastique–L'Epouvante." Nos. 24-5. [Articles and Filmographies on Tod Browning and Bela Lugosi.]

Boisset, Yves and Romer, Jean-Claude. "Entretien avec Don Sharp." *Midi-Minuit Fantastique.* No. 9, page 77.

Borst, Ron. "The Vampire in the Cinema." *Photon.* Nos. 18, 19, and 21. [Filmography in Nos. 19 and 21]

Broeske, Pat. "Hollywood Goes Batty for Vampires." *New York Times.* April 26, 1992, page 22.

Brower, Brock. "The Vulgarization of American Demonology." *Esquire.* June, 1964, page 94.

Caën, Michel. "Entretien avec Barbara Steele." *Midi-Minuit Fantastique.* No. 12, page 29.

_____. "Entretien avec Christopher Lee." *Midi-Minuit Fantastique.* No. 14, page 5.

_____. "Entretien avec Terence Fisher." *Midi-Minuit Fantastique.* No. 10-11, page 1.

Caron-Lowins, E. "Sang et Encens (à propos de Terence Fisher)." *Positif* 165. January, 1975, pages 32-35.

Carroll, N. "Nightmare and the Horror Film: The Symbolic Biology of Fantastic Beings." *Film Quarterly.* Spring, 1981, pages 16-25.

Chauffard, R.J. "Qui Est Jean Rollin?" *Midi-Minuit Fantastique.* No. 24, page 50.

Cinefantastique. "Interview with Jean Rollin." Volume 3, No. 1.

Cinefantastique. "Issue on Terence Fisher." Volume 4, No. 3.

Cinéma (Paris). "En Tant Que Créateur Je Dois Suivre Mon Instinct." (Interview with Peter Sasdy). September-October, 1972, page 93.

Connor, Edward. "The Return of the Dead." *Films in Review.* March, 1964, pages 146-160.

Craft, Chris. "Kiss Me with Those Red Lips: Gender and Inversion in Dracula." *Representations* 8 (Fall, 1984).

Cutts, John. "Vampyr." *Films and Filming.* December, 1960, page 17.

Dahoun, R. "Le Fétichisme dans le Film d'Horreur." *Cahiers de la Cinémathèque.* Summer, 1972, pages 64-77.

Dargis, Manohla. "His Bloody Valentine." *The Village Voice.* November 24, 1992, page 66.

Dawidziak, Mark. "The Return of Dark Shadows." *Cinefantastique.* December, 1990, pages 24-33.

Degaudenzi, J.L. "Mythe et Réalité: Le Véritable Dracula." *Midi-Minuit Fantastique.* No. 24, page 74.

Dietrich, Christopher and Beckman, Peter. "Karma, Catsup, and Caskets: The Barbara Steele Interview." *Video Watchdog.* No. 7, September/October, 1991, pages 48-62.

Durgnat, Raymond. "The Subconscious: From Pleasure Castle to Libido Motel." *Films and Filming.* January, 1962, pages 13-15, 41, 46.

Dyer, Peter John. "Some Nights of Horror." *Films and Filming.* July, 1958, page 13.

Dyer, R. "Dracula and Desire." *Sight and Sound.* January 12, 1993.

Evans, Walter. "Monster Movies: A Sexual Theory." *The Journal of Popular Film.* Volume II, No. 4.

_____. "Monster Movies and Rites of Initiation." *Journal of Popular Film.* Volume IV, No. 2 (1975), pages 124-142.

Everson, William K. "Horror Films." *Films in Review.* January, 1954, page 111.

_____. "A Family Tree of Monsters." *Film Culture.* January, 1955, page 24.

_____. "Karloff and Lugosi." *Screen Facts.* No. 7, page 40.

Figenshu, T. "Screams of a Summer Night." *Film Comment.* September/October, 1979, pages 49-53.

Film Journal. "The Art of the Horror Film" (Special Issue). January-March, 1973, pages 6-8.

Films in Review. "Tod Browning." October, 1953, page 410.

Fisher, Terence. "Horror is My Business." *Films and Filming.* July, 1964, page 7.

Florescu, Jean. "A Night in Dracula's Castle." *Seventeen.* January, 1974, page 36.

Fox, J. "The Golden Age of Terror: 1930-1936." (In Five Parts). *Films and Filming.* June, July, August, September, October, 1976.

Garsault, A. "Comme le phoenix--Dracula." *Positif.* No. 383, January 1993, pages 30-32.

Gehman, Richard. "The Hollywood Horrors." *Cosmopolitan.* November, 1958, page 38.

Glazebrook, Philip. "The Anti-Heroes of Horror." *Films and Filming.* October, 1966, page 36.

Glover, D.J. "Travels in Romania:myths or origins, myths of blood." *Discourse.* Fall, 1993, pages 126-144.

Gomez, Jewell. "Vamps and Victims." *Village Voice.* December 15, 1992, page 72.

Grotjahn, Martin. "Horror–Yes, It Can Do You Good." *Films and Filming.* October, 1958, page 9.

Hall, Derek. "The Face of Horror." *Sight and Sound.* Winter, 1958-59, page 6.

Halliwell, Leslie. "The Baron, the Count, and Their Ghoul Friends." *Films and Filming.* June-July, 1969, page 12.

Harrington, Curtis. "Ghoulies and Ghosties." *Sight and Sound.* April-June, 1952, page 157.

Heard, Colin. "Hammering the Box Office." *Films and Filming.* June, 1969, pages 17-19.

Houck, Catherine. "The Cosmo Girl Meets Dracula." *Cosmopolitan.* September, 1979, pages 261, 336-340.

Jacobowitz, F. "The American Nightmare." *Cinema Canada.* October-November, 1979, pages 49-53.

Jenks, Carol. "Daughters of Darkness: A Lesbian Vampire Art Film," in Black, Andy (ed.). **Necronomicon: Book One.** London: Creation Books, 1996 pages 22-34

Kahan, Saul. "Transylvania–Polanski Style." *Cinema* (USA). Volume 3, No. 4, page 7.

Kane, J. "Beauties, Beasts, and Male Chauvinist Monsters." *Take One.* July, 1974, pages 8-10.

Kennedy, H. "Things That Go Howl in the Id." *Film Comment.* March-April, 1982, pages 37-39.

Knight, Chris and Nicholson, Peter. "A Chat with Peter Cushing about Dracula Today." *Cinefantastique.* Volume 2, No. 2.

Lopez, Aranda. "El Vampiro en el Cine." *Cine.* June-July, 1980, pages 21-26.

Losano, Wayne. "The Vampire Rises Again in the Films of the 70's." *The Film Journal.* Volume 2, No. 2, page 60.

Lowry, E. "Genre and Enunciation: The Case of Horror." *Journal of Film and Video.* Spring, 1984, pages 13-20.

Lucas, Tim. "How To Read a Franco Film." *Video Watchdog.* No. 1, 1990, pages 18-38.

_____. "*Black Sabbath*, the Unmaking of Mario Bava's *Three Faces of Fear.*" *Video Watchdog,* No. 5, May-June, 1991, pages 32-59.

Mangracite, Andrew. "Once Upon A Time in the Crypt". *Film Comment.* January-February, 1993, p. 50-52.

Marshall, L. "Vampire Films of the Seventies." *Midnight Marquee.* Summer, 1993, pages 6-19.

Martani, M. "Sex, vampires, and videotape." *Cineforum.* September, 1993, pages 86-90.

Martini, E. "Il ballo dei vampiri." *Cineforum.* Jan/Feb, 1993, pages 16-18+.

Meeker, Oden and Olivia. "The Screamy-Weamies." *Collier's*. January 12, 1946, page 42.

Michel, Jean-Claude. "Les Vampires a L'Écran." *L'Écran Fantastique*. No. 2, 1971.

Midi-Minuit Fantastique. "Dracula Issue.". No. 4-5. [Articles on Dracula in literature and films, including filmographies and biliographies]

Midi-Minuit Fantastique. "Érotisme et Épouvante dans le Cinéma Anglais." No. 8. [Articles, interviews, and filmographies on the English horror film]

Midi-Minuit Fantastique. "Terence Fisher Issue." No. 1. [Articles, interviews, and filmographies on Fisher, Peter Cushing, and Christopher Lee]

Midi-Minuit Fantastique. "Vamps Fantastiques Issue." No. 2.

Midnight Marquee (Vampire Issue). No. 49, Summer 1995.

Morlot, Jean-Claude. "Impossible Is Not French." *Cinefantastique*. Volume 3, No. 1, page 38.

Moss, Morton. "The Devil's Advocate." *Los Angeles Herald Examiner*. November 28, 1972.

Newman, Kim. "Blood Lines." *Sight and Sound*. January, 1993, pages 12-13.

Oms, M. "Les Éternels Voleurs d'Énergie." *Cahiers de la Cinématheque*. Summer, 1972, pages 24-33.

Parish, James Robert and Pitts, Michael R. "Christopher Lee–A career Article." *Cinefantastique*. Volume 3, No. 1, page 4.

Pendo, Steven. "Universal's Golden Age of Horror: 1931-1941." *Films In Review*. March, 1975, pages 155-161.

Perez, Turrent. "The House of Horror." *Cine*. June-July, 1980, pages 10-20.

Perrot, Michel. *Midi-Minuit Fantastique*. "Entretien avec Roman Polanski." No. 20, page 26.

Pirie, David. "New Blood." *Sight and Sound*. Spring, 1971, page 73.

Piton, Jean-Pierre. "Nouvelle Vague des Vampires." *L'Ecran Fantastique*. November, 1988, pages 58-67.

Polanski, Roman. "Satisfaction–A Most Unpleasant Feeling." *Films and Filming*. April, 1969, page 15.

Rickels, L.A. "Missing Marx:or, how to take better aim." *Strategies*. No. 6, 1991

Ringel, Harry. "The Horrible Hammer Films of Terence Fisher." *Take One*. January-February, 1972, page 8.

_____. "A Hank of Hair and a Piece of Bone." *Film Journal* II/4, 1975, pages 14-18.

Rivenburg, Roy. "Up to Our Necks." *Los Angeles Times*. October 28, 1992.

Rockett, Will H. "The Door Ajar: Structure and Convention in Horror Films." *Journal of Popular Film*. Fall, 1982, pages 130-136.

Ross, Art. "The Vampire Legend Lives On...and On...and On." *Backstage*. November 15, 1985, page 42.

Screen. "Body Horror." January-February, 1986 (Special Issue).

Segui, J-L. "El Vampiro y Su Doble." *Cinema 2000*. November, 1979, pages 54+.

Silver, Alain and Ursini, James. "Mario Bava:The Illusion of Reality." *Photon*. No. 26, page 42.

Sinclair, Iain; Dyer, Richard; Newman, Kim; and Sheehan, Harry. "Dracula and Desire". *Sight and Sound*. January, 1993, pp. 8-15.

Starlog Movie Magazines Presents. "Dracula, the Complete Vampire" (Issue on Vampire Films). No. 6.

Steranko, James. *"Bram Stoker's Dracula." Prevue*, November/February, 1993. pages 18-39, 53-59.

Stewart-Gordon, J. "Durable Dracula: Beloved Fiend of the Horror Circuit." *Reader's Digest*. Novermber, 1975, pages 49-52.

Tavernier, Bertrand. "Entretien avec Terence Fisher." *Midi-Minuit Fantastique*. No. 7, page 9.

Upchurch, Alan. "The Dark Queen." *Film Comment*. January-February, 1993, p. 53.

Volta, Ornella. "Entretien avec Mario Bava." *Positif*. No. 138, page 44.

Walker, Alexander. "Films." *Man, Myth, and Magic*. No. 34.

Walker, David and Lucas, Tim. "Ganja and Hess". *Video Watchdog*, No. 3, Jan.-Feb., 1991, pages 38-57.

Wallace, Bruce. "Vampires Revamped." *Omni*. June, 1979, page 146.

Weinberg, Herman and Gretchen. "Vampyr–An Interview with Baron de Gunzburg." *Film Culture*. Spring, 1965, page 57.

White, Dennis. "The Poetics of Horror: More Than Meets the Eye." *Cinema Journal*. Spring, 1971, page 1.

Williams, T. "Horror in the Family." *Focus on Film*. October, 1980, pages 14-20.

Wood, Robin. "Neglected Nightmares." *Film Comment*. March-April, 1980, pages 25-32.

Bonnie Zimmerman, "Daughters of Darkness:Lesbian Vampires." *Jump Cut*. Issue 24 (1981), pages 23-4

Below, Carroll Borland as Luna poses with her co-stars from *Mark of the Vampire*. In 1994, shortly before her death, she published a novel called **Countess Dracula**.

Index

Because the Filmographies are organized alphabetically and contain their own cross-references to alternate titles, this is an Index of the main text only. However, all the illustrations in the main text, Filmography, and elsewhere are included in this Index. All illustrations are indicated by page numbers in italics; and those appearing in the Filmography or other after matter are separated by a semi-colon.

As in the main text, italics are used to indicate film titles, including shorts and television episodes, and boldface for books, novels, and other long form fiction. Plays, short stories, etc. are enclosed within quotation marks. Parenthetical annotations provide additional information; in the case of persons who have several occupations, the most relevant one is given. Films with the same title are distinguished by year of release.

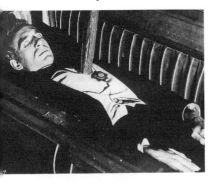

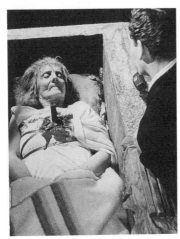

How vampires meet their end.
Or do they?